MW01053495

Synopsis *of a* Purer Theology

Volume II | *Disputations 32–52*

EDITED BY WILLIAM DEN BOER & RIEMER A. FABER

TRANSLATED BY RIEMER A. FABER

DAVENANT PRESS

ISBN: 978-1-949716-23-8

ISBN-10: 1-949716-23-6

Cover design by Orange Peal Design

Typeset and proofread by Mikael Good

Indexed by Brian Marr

Praise for *Synopsis of a Purer Theology*

"In the Christian faith, we cannot do without each other, but we need the insights of each. In the *Synopsis of a Purer Theology*, Reformed theology from the best theologians of the time comes together, resulting in a finely crafted rendition of the Christian faith. For the study of Christian faith and Reformed theology, this handbook is indispensable today."

—**Willem van Vlastuin**, Professor of the Theology and the Spirituality of Reformed Protestantism, Vrije Universiteit Amsterdam, Dean of the Hersteld Hervormd Seminary, and Director of the Jonathan Edwards Centre Benelux

"Having taught theology at Leiden University myself for several years, I can only rejoice over this republication and translation of one its most outstanding and influential theological products ever: the so-called *Leiden Synopsis*. It is a great benefit to so many pastors, scholars, and interested lay people alike that this complete survey of solid Reformed Scholastic theology is now becoming widely available and accessible."

—**Gijsbert van den Brink**, Professor of Theology and Science, Vrije Universiteit Amsterdam

"Finally in English in two volumes, the *Leiden Synopsis* can now take its well-deserved place as a standard reference work for a wide readership. Its clear organization, careful distinction-making, transparency to scriptural sources, respectful engagement with the full Christian tradition, and organic coherence as a system make it a tool to be used regularly. The four authors' steady awareness of their location in a particular confessional tradition makes their work eminently useful not only for those who share their full confessional position, but also for those who listen in to overhear Reformed Protestant theology at its best."

—**Fred Sanders**, Torrey Honors College, Biola University

"Through the publication of the. *Leiden Synopsis* in English, the essence of Reformed theology is no longer exclusively available to traditional, Western historiography and church history. Its original Latin format limited its impact to professional theologians and specialized philologists focusing on theology, while its religious core remained inaccessible not only to the general public but also to geographical venues beyond the West. Now, however, this treasure of theological insights is no longer the appanage of expert scholars; from lay people to academics with vested interests in religion, the *Synopsis* will become accessible to every person who wishes to know more about Reformed theology regardless of whether one lives in the West, the East, or the Global South. This is an achievement with unprecedented possibilities for Reformed theology and its rich ecclesiastical tradition."

—**Corneliu C. Simuţ**, Aurel Vlaicu University (Romania)

"The Leiden theology faculty was the 'Sorbonne' of Reformed orthodoxy. And the *Leiden Synopsis* represented the consensus after the Synod of Dort. Weaving into its exegetical arguments support from patristic and medieval sources, the authors display the catholic and evangelical spirit of Reformed theology. Avoiding internecine disputes, the *Synopsis* focuses on the doctrines that all Reformed Christians confess. Given its spirit, scope, and learned arguments, it deserves to inform the tradition today as it did so persuasively in the past."

—**Michael Horton**, J. Gresham Machen Professor of Systematic Theology and Apologetics, Westminster Seminary California

"The *Synopsis of a Purer Theology* is a codification of Reformed orthodoxy, concise and precise in its presentation of early modern Reformed theology. The translator, editors, and publisher are commended for making this monumental work available in English. Indispensable for any serious scholar and student in Post-reformation Reformed theology."

—**Adriaan C. Neele**, Vice President, Professor of Historical Theology and Homiletics, Puritan Reformed Theological Seminary

"The *Leiden Synopsis* is among the most important and comprehensive systematic accounts of Reformed theology of the seventeenth century. Its appearance in this English-only edition will doubtless invite a fresh outpouring of scholarly and lay reflection."

—**S. Mark Hamilton**, Senior Managing Editor, Davenant Institute and Research Associate, JESociety.org

"Doctrinal controversy brings strife but it also brings clarity and precision to doctrinal formulation, which is a blessing. This benefit of debate is no less true of the *Leiden Synopsis*, written in the wake of the Arminian controversy. This collection of theological disputations is grounded in Scripture, razor sharp in its distinctions, and conversant with the history of doctrine. No serious student of theology can afford to ignore this theological work."

—**J. V. Fesko**, Harriet Barbour Professor of Systematic and Historical Theology, Reformed Theological Seminary, Jackson, Mississippi

"The *Leiden Synopsis* distills the principles of Reformed theology with clarity and economy. It needs no endorsement, but if it did: Herman Bavinck ranked it alongside giants like Zanchius, Junius, and Voetius. Thanks to the translator and Davenant Press, this indispensable resource is now also accessible and affordable."

—**Tyler R. Wittman**, Assistant Professor of Theology, New Orleans Baptist Theological Seminary

"The *Synopsis of a Purer Theology* is one of the most significant translation projects in recent memory. This set of disputations is already considered essential for work in Reformed theology, and so I am delighted that Davenant is making it available for a wider audience. For Reformed pastors and theologians, the *Leiden Synopsis* proves to be a profoundly useful companion, and I have no doubt that it will be a significant aid in the work to retrieve Reformed Scholastic theology."

—**Kyle Strobel**, Associate Professor of Classical Theology, Talbot School of Theology, Biola University

"The *Leiden Synopsis* has long been a theological treasure. The publication of this edition will bring its rich theological wisdom to pastors, theologians, and theology lovers."

—**Gayle Doornbos**, Associate Professor of Theology Dordt University

"Davenant does theology and church a great service with offering this selection of the *Leiden Synopsis*. That deep and highly relevant source of Reformation theology becomes now available to even a much wider community, what the *Synopsis* deserves and the community needs. I'm also very happy that the great efforts of Riemer A. Faber and William den Boer can be made fruitful for all interested in clear, biblical theology. There is no doubt that this publication will find many readers."

—**Herman Selderhuis**, Theological University Apeldoorn / REFORC

"Set forth in the wake of Dort, the *Leiden Synopsis* has enjoyed critical influence on Reformed thought since the early seventeenth century. This accessible, two-volume edition of Riemer Faber's hailed English translation—with fresh editorial guidance by William den Boer and Faber— is a ready resource for learning today from the Leiden faculty's attempt to read Scripture in conversation with those who came before."

—**Christina Larsen**, Associate Professor of Theology, Grand Canyon Theological Seminary & College of Theology

"The *Leiden Synopsis* is one of the crown jewels of Reformed theology. Profoundly collegial in its origins, it presents a compact yet compelling account of post-Reformation dogmatics that is deeply rooted in Scripture yet acutely aware of tradition. It serves not only as a historical landmark in the development of the Reformed tradition, but also as a contemporary provocation to engage deeply with the wisdom and insight it offers. This elegant translation of the *Synopsis* will thus reward careful reading and re-reading, and comes warmly recommended."

—**Paul T. Nimmo**, King's Chair of Systematic Theology, University of Aberdeen

"Can the past inform the present? Absolutely! Here the seventeenth-century theology, piety, and practice of the *Leiden Synopsis* informs the Reformed church in the twenty-first century. The Davenant Institute is to be commended for publishing this time-honored resource. Scholars, professors, ministers, and even laypersons of Reformed theology will benefit from these excellent volumes."

—**Tyler Taber**, Minister of Word and Sacrament, Redeemer Presbyterian Church, Amarillo, Texas

"Both polemical and pastoral, the *Synopsis* deserves wide and careful attention in the church today. Deeply rooted in careful exegesis of Scripture, this doctrinal and moral theology from the early modern period remains a treasure house for subsequent generations. Contemporary readers will quickly note that the *Synopsis* is a work appropriately shaped by the Spirit's work in the fathers of the church from every generation, because the work of theologians should be done in obedience to the fifth commandment."

—**Rev. Michael McClenahan**, Union Theological College, Belfast, Northern Ireland

Table of Contents

Acknowledgements

Gratitude is expressed to the following former or current members of the research group 'Classic Reformed Theology' (in Dutch: 'Werkgezelschap Oude Gereformeerde Theologie'), as this edition would not have been made possible without their prior unstinting efforts. This group was founded in 1982 for the purpose of studying early modern scholastic theology. Throughout the years it has conducted research and organized conferences leading to publications in Dutch and English. Please see the Introduction for a brief account of the project that culminated in the publication of the three-volume academic edition, *Synopsis Purioris Theologiae / Synopsis of a Purer Theology* (Leiden: Brill, 2014–20). We are grateful to Brill Academic Publishers for permission to use the English translation of that edition here.

Andreas J. Beck
Simon Burton
Kees de Niet
Rein Ferwerda
Philip J. Fisk
Albert Gootjes
Harm Goris
Jeannette Kreijkes-van Esch
Matthias Mangold
Pieter Rouwendal

Siebold Schipper
Dolf te Velde
Willem J. van Asselt †
Henk van den Belt
Gert van den Brink
Elco van Burg
Jan van Helden
Kees Jan van Linden
Wilco Veltkamp
Antonie Vos

In 2020 the research group commenced a new project: 'Early Modern Reformed Disputations on Divine Providence.' For further details, please see the website: www.classic-reformed-theology.org.

VOLUME II

VOLUME 0

ON REPENTANCE

President: Antonius Walaeus
Respondent: Adrianus Jansonius

Regarding repentance, the Synopsis distinguishes between repentance in a general or broad sense that includes regeneration (as a disposition the Holy Spirit works in one's heart) and repentance in a restricted sense (or penitence) that comes from the disposition and consists in grieving for sin. Regeneration (4–26) is a renewal of the whole human soul 'with all its faculties, including intellect, will and affections' (18). Special attention is paid to the question of whether 'the grace of regeneration' also affects the will (19–23), and it is emphasized that all actions produced by regeneration are effects of grace, not of the human will (24–26). Penitence, or active repentance, is treated in thesis 27–53. Persons who are genuinely penitent turn from evil towards the good, and change their minds for the better (31). So true repentance consists of a 'life-saving transformation' (32) from evil to good, from sin and Satan to Christ and righteousness (33). True repentance is characterized by contrition of the heart and hope for forgiveness (34–35, 39, 42); it is accompanied by a hatred of sin itself and a delight in observing God's Law (38–39, 42). In order to possess all this 'it is altogether necessary that in faith we first apply Christ to ourselves, and in him to regard God as a kindly father' (42). In a more general sense repentance includes faith insofar as it may denote the conversion from all sin and a turning towards God; in a stricter sense faith may be described as the cause while repentance is an effect of it (40–41). The disputation goes on to caution against the wrong Romanist perception of repentance as acts of penitence (43–47), and against Anabaptist ecclesiastical discipline whereby sinners in the process of repentance are withheld from the communion of saints (52).

1. Since the main point in the preaching of the Gospel consists of faith and repentance, and as we have dealt with faith in the previous disputation, it follows now that we should treat the second element, namely, repentance.

2. It is customary to consider this repentance in two ways: either as a spiritual disposition poured into our hearts by the Holy Spirit, or as an action from us that proceeds from that disposition. In the first way, it is properly speaking and in its strict sense called regeneration; in the second way, it is called repentance, taken in a more restricted sense, or penitence. And when the two are taken together it is called the circumcision of the heart, the conversion to God, the renewal of the Spirit, the sanctification of man, the new creation, and the first resurrection.

3. First we shall offer some explanations of the two [regeneration and repentance] considered jointly, and then we shall deal in particular with penitence (in the strict sense) and its properties.

4. The principal, effective cause is God through his Spirit, for "unless one is born again of the water and the Spirit he cannot enter into the kingdom of God" (John 3:5), and just as God raised "the author and preserver of life" to his right hand "in order to give repentance to Israel" (Acts 5:31), so too did the Israelite church glorify God "because God has given also to the gentiles repentance unto life" (Acts 11:18).

5. The meritorious cause of this gift is not any prior disposition of our own, or preparation we have done, or some superior exercise of our natural ability to judge (as some people wrongly think); for "when the kindness of God our Savior and his love for mankind appeared, he saved us, not because of works done by us in righteousness, but according to his own mercy, by the washing of regeneration and renewal of the Holy Spirit, whom he poured out upon us richly through Jesus Christ our Savior," as the apostle says in Titus 3:4–6.

6. We do not deny, however, that before He makes people partakers of this benefit, God himself ordinarily uses various ways to prepare them for it, a little at a time, whether through proofs evident in the natural world (Rom 2:4) or through the word of the Law and the Gospel, as we shall explain below. But we do deny that God is bound to behave in this ordinary way; this is clear from the case of the robber who was crucified with Christ [Luke 23:40–43], and of Paul when he was persecuting the Church [Acts 9:1–19]. And we also deny that there is some sort of preparation or disposition that earns this kind of gift on the basis of congruity, for that is shown in Titus 3:5, a passage we have cited earlier. And lastly, we deny that any sort of disposition or preparation that precedes faith is a precursor to which God has attached a sure promise for this gift, for "whatever is not from faith is sin" (Rom

14:23) and "without faith it is impossible to please God," that is, to please him to one's own salvation (Heb 11:6).

7. And we even state that this grace is undeserved for any man, regardless of the extent he has been predisposed; because whatever his disposition, man is guilty of condemnation. For no-one is released from this condemnation "except only those who are in Christ, and who do not walk according to the flesh but according to the Spirit" (Rom 8:1, 4).

8. At the same time we state also that those who refuse to accept the proofs evident in the natural world or in the Law and the Gospel that call them to repentance, or who suppress them by their wickedness, by so doing bring yet another guilt upon themselves and a new degree of condemnation, and so they are more and more without excuse in the judgment of God, as the same apostle teaches us (Rom 1:20, 2:1; John 15:22).

9. The initiating cause of the double benefit of regeneration and repentance is the death and resurrection of Christ, as the apostle teaches clearly in Rom 6:3, Heb 9:14, 1 Pet 1:18–19, etc. For since through his death Christ has saved us from our sins that we might be servants not of sin but of Christ, it was necessary also that his death and resurrection could effectively put the old man to death and cause the new one to live. And the main point of the apostle's prayers (and, following his example, the main point of all believers' prayers) is not merely that "they may be found in Christ, not having a righteousness of their own that comes from the law, but one that is through faith in Christ, the righteousness which comes from God by faith." But above and beyond that the prayer is "that they might know Christ and the power of his resurrection and the fellowship of his sufferings, and be conformed to his death" (Phil 3:9–10).

10. The instrumental cause of this benefit is the Word of God, both that of the Law and that of the Gospel.

11. For it is by the Law, as recorded in nature (Rom 1) and as renewed on the stone tablets (2 Cor 3) that man is led to truly realize his own condemnation and wretched state, as was explained elsewhere [Disputation 23.5–7]. If he does not realize this, man cannot possibly grasp the regeneration and repentance that bring salvation, since Christ himself bears witness "that he has not come to call the righteous, but sinners to repentance" (Matt 9:13 [KJV]).

12. But it is through the Gospel and its promises that man conceives a godly sorrow, lifts up his downcast conscience to hope for forgiveness, and then makes Christ his own. He does so not only for the forgiveness of prior sins, but also for doing away with the old man and bringing to life the new one. For this reason, the Gospel is called "the ministry of the Spirit and of life" (2 Cor 3[:8–10]) and "the immortal seed of God that remains forever, through which we are born again" (1 Pet 1:23; Jas 1:18).

13. The form of regeneration and repentance consists of the dying of the old man, or the abolition of his innate corrupt nature; it also consists of the restoration of the new man who is created in true righteousness and holiness after God (Eph 4[:22–24], Col 3[:8–12]). And this form not only keeps the nature of the old man in check (as some wrongly think), but it even does away with it entirely, and puts in its place true holiness and righteousness which also shines forth in the very fruits of repentance.

14. If one considers this form from the perspective of its ultimate, completed state, it is not brought about all at once, but rather by degrees, and for this reason some who have been born again are likened to children, while others are likened to fully grown adults (Heb 5[:13–14]; Eph 4[:13–16]).

15. But just as children do possess the whole form of a human being and all the parts that comprise it, and although they display it in a somewhat imperfect way, so too do we consider no-one to be truly repentant or born again unless he has the whole form of regeneration, in the perfection of parts (as the expression has it), although he must make daily progress in the perfection of degrees.

16. This essential perfection consists firstly in the renewal of all the faculties of the human soul, the intellect, the will, and the affections, according to all of God's precepts. Secondly it consists in their renewal to the point that "sin no longer reigns in them" (Rom 6[:12]) and that they "do not walk according to the flesh but according to the Spirit" (Rom 8:1).

17. For even though the rule of the Spirit is weaker and less visible in some people while more established and evident in others, we deny that any regenerate person has reached the point in this life where no remnants of the old man still live in him any longer. For this reason those who are born again must pray every day "forgive us our sins," and daily they must produce new deeds of repentance by their true faith in Christ.

18. The subject of this regeneration is the entire man who has been (or is to be) planted in Christ through faith, for "it is by faith that our hearts are cleansed" (Acts 15:9). And just as the principal subject of sin is the soul of man, fitted out with all its natural faculties (while the body is a less principal subject, as the seat or instrument of the soul), so too that same soul, with all its faculties, including intellect, will and affections, is the proper seat and principal subject of regeneration. And in the true regeneration and repentance that lead to salvation all these faculties are more and more affected by the supernatural and inherent grace that comes from God through the Spirit, an action that is direct and immediate.

19. As far as the intellect is concerned, this process is obvious, because by this benefit [of regeneration and repentance] it is enlightened unto the knowledge of God and our Savior Jesus Christ [Eph 1:17–18]. And concerning the affections, no further proof is required, because everyone acknowledges that the same gift stirs the affections to hate sin and Satan, to love God and righteousness, and to hope for eternal life and the inheritance. Regarding the will, however, since there are some who dare to say that the inherent grace of regeneration does not affect the will, we shall have to establish the proof of it briefly with a few arguments.

20. I show this first from the prior corruption of the will, for this spiritual generation renews and corrects everything that has been corrupted on the spiritual level. And Scripture states in many places that the natural man's will was corrupted entirely in and of itself; see Eph 2:3, and 1 Pet 4:3. For this reason also the apostle says "that he does not do the good that he wants, but the evil that he does not want to do" (Rom 7:19), and "I find this law, that when I want to do good evil lies close at hand" (Rom 7:21). He shows that it is by his will, insofar as it was regenerated, that he even seeks after the spiritual good, but that on account of the remnants of the flesh that still cling to him he does not will it so effectively and fully that he always achieves the result that he wishes and wills.

21. In the second place it is demonstrated by the very spiritual quality that is brought on by regeneration. For not only do love and trust in God have their proper place in the will, but so too the holiness and righteousness of the new man (Eph 4:24) is a proper affection of the will, as all the ethical philosophers admit. It is for this reason that the lawyers define righteousness as "the constant willingness to grant to everyone his due."

22. Thirdly, it is proved effectively by the ways in which the Scriptures everywhere speak about this matter. For when it says that God places a new Spirit within us [Ezek 36:26], or that He circumcises the heart [Deut 30:6; Rom 2:29], creates in us a new heart [Ps 51:10], turns our hard hearts of stone into hearts of flesh [Ezek 36:26], removes the foreskin of our hearts [Deut 10:16], and many similar things, no-one has ever explained them as concerning only the baser appetites that we have in common with animals. Nor can these be taken directly to mean the intellect, since no place will be found in Scripture where it is the intellect that is called hard or stony, or where it says that it is the intellect that is circumcised, or that its foreskin is removed, or that it is being created anew in us. To the contrary, when the intellect is treated in Scripture, it is usually called blind or darkened; and the renewal of the intellect is called the enlightening of the eyes of the mind, the writing of the Law upon the hearts, the removal of the veil from our hearts, and the gift of a new mind.

23. And finally, it is proved by the vows and prayers of the saints. For "since it is God who works in us both to will and to act according to his own good will" (Phil 2:13), who would dare to think that apart from the illumination of the mind and the amendment of our affections it is not necessary to ask for the renewal of the will and an inclination towards the spiritual good? Take David, for example, in Ps 119:36. Especially because it is not possible that the will, equipped with only natural powers, of its own accord follows the intellect that has already been affected by the supernatural gift, or that the intellect impresses the will with some inherent supernatural quality. For Scripture everywhere states clearly that this comes only from the Spirit of God, and that the intellect is no more capable of impressing such power upon the will than it can produce the will itself on its own. But just as it is God who has created in man the faculty of the intellect and the faculty of the will, so also is it upon the one as well as the other faculty that he grants the additional supernatural gifts through that new creation.

24. And in order to produce spiritual actions from this spiritual condition it is not sufficient to have only the initial conferment or habitual possession of this gift. But just as preceding and operating grace first produces this gift in our hearts, so too is it necessary that the accompanying, co-operating grace similarly stir up that gift for actions that are worthy of repentance and make the will more and more perfect every day. For "He who goes before the

unwilling so that he wills, follows him when he is willing, so that he does not will in vain." (Augustine, *Enchiridion* 32).

25. For this reason Christ says to his disciples that "they can do nothing without him, and that he prunes every branch in him that bears fruit that it may bear even more fruit" (John 15:2). And hence it says also that "the Spirit helps our infirmities, so that we know what we should pray for as we ought" (Rom 8:26). And the apostle prays in Heb 13:21 and elsewhere that "God equip them with every good thing, working in them what is pleasing in his sight through Jesus Christ."

26. We should not make curious enquiries about the way in which God performs this action in us; but at the same time we should be careful to avoid the errors of the Pelagians, semi-Pelagians, and certain Sophists. They stated that this grace is given on the grounds of our merits, or the good movements of our will, or, in their words, through moral counsels alone and not real works—in short, that the efficacy of the working of God depends on the natural choice of man. All these and similar errors of the Pelagians and semi-Pelagians were condemned long ago, and we, too, condemn them, because they do injustice to the grace of God, and for the man who distinguishes himself they leave some opportunity for boasting. But we, following Augustine, state that "grace would not be grace at all if it were not entirely freely given." And the certain effect of grace that is operating and co-operating in us comes not by the choice of our will but by what the merciful God has purposed [Rom 9:16].

27. Now that we have, in our view, explained the doctrine of regeneration sufficiently, it remains for us to append a few things about penitence, or rather and especially the so-called active repentance.

28. It is obvious that the word 'penitence' derives from 'penalty,' for as A[ulus] Gellius rightly observes, "whatever is cause for trouble and shame has the force of punishment." Therefore, whoever is really driven by penitence over some deed or other within his own heart exacts from himself what amounts to punishment, to the point that the affection of his heart bears the name 'penitence.' For this reason, also the apostle himself, in 2 Cor 7:11, lists among the true properties of repentance "indignation and vengeance" which the sinner demands of himself for that inner feeling of regret which usually comes on the heels of wrongdoings.

29. And in this regard we may allow the word 'penitence' (even though it does not entail the entire form of true repentance) to be kept in usage in Christ's Church as an expression of the part for the whole, provided that we do not think that grief of this sort is able to make satisfaction for sins, as happens among the papal teachers.

30. The word *metameleia*, which properly means the anxious worry of the heart after some punishable deed, corresponds fairly well to the word 'penitence' and is used frequently for the kind of trouble and grief that are not followed by a change in lifestyle; yet it is employed sometimes in order to mean true repentance, as in Matt 21:29 and elsewhere.

31. The Hebrew word *teshuva*, 'return,' or conversion, and also the Greek word *metanoia*, that is, the change of heart for the better after a deed, or 'repentance' as Lactantius translates the Hebrew word (in book 6, chapter 24), are better suited to denote the sense of what we are treating. For someone who is genuinely penitent turns himself from evil towards the good, and he changes his mind for the better, although one finds the word *metanoia* used for a merely legal conversion, for instance Wis 5:3.

32. From what we have said already about the terms one can gather easily what true penitence, or rather repentance, is. For since every change has both a point from which it starts and a point where it ends, so for the life-saving transformation of one's heart we should pay attention to both points.

33. The point from which conversion starts is the evil, or the reign of sin and Satan; the point where it ends is its opposite: the good, or the reign of Christ and righteousness. Regarding the former point, conversion is called "a turning away from sins and evil ways" (1 Kgs 8:35, Isa 59:20). Regarding the latter point, it is called the "turning toward the God of Israel" (Jer 16:19). The two points occur together in Acts 26:18, as people "turn from darkness to light, and from the power of Satan to God." These two aspects of repentance are what is sometimes understood in the New Testament by 'the putting to death of the old man' and 'the coming to life of the new.'

34. And although the whole nature of conversion is expressed in these two aspects or points, certain properties are associated with each of them, and without these it is no repentance.

35. Connected to this turning away from evil is a grief within the soul that is called by some 'contrition' or 'attrition.' And connected to turning towards

the good is a hope for forgiveness and a delight of the soul, because when the wrong way is left behind a shift has been made towards the right way. For "the truly penitent man grieves over his sins, and he is pleased with his grieving."

36. In 2 Cor 7:10 the apostle Paul states that this grief is twofold: it is "a worldly grief that brings death and a godly grief that leads to repentance unto salvation."

37. Worldly grief comes about when the sinner does indeed grieve over a sin he has committed, but then he does so for the same reasons as the people of this world are accustomed to doing. Such grief arises from a verdict of disgrace in the eyes of the Law, either in punishment or in the conscience, a verdict that proceeds from the threats of the Law and from taking them seriously (Rom 2:5, 4:15). If the sinner does not proceed to go beyond this grief, or if he is obsessed by it, then he also falls headlong into despair, as we see in the case of Judas who betrayed Christ. Or, if the sinner does succeed in overcoming his grief, then he reverts to his characteristic ways, as is evidenced in the case of Ahab.

38. But godly grief is distinguished from worldly grief not just in its effect (as the apostle points out in the previously mentioned place) but also in its own nature, because it not only arises from self-love and fear of punishment, but also is accompanied by a hatred and displeasure of sin itself (Rom 7:15, etc.) and a shame for having offended God, whom he now, in faith, begins to regard as a kindly father, as is clear from Rom 6:21, and from the examples of David, Peter, and the parable of the prodigal son.

39. Linked to the turning to God is an approval of God's Law (Rom 7:16) and a delight in observing it (Ps 1[:1] and 119[:18]), a hope for forgiveness drawn from the Gospel promises that have been received in faith (Ps 130:4), and even a sense of comfort and spiritual joy because "God's love is poured into our hearts through the Holy Spirit whom He gave to us" (Rom 5:2, 5; similarly verse 13 and 17).

40. From what we have said thus far there is an obvious answer to the fairly difficult question whether faith is part of repentance, a question over which some of the foremost authors of the Reformed Church seem to disagree. For if we take the word repentance in the wider sense of the whole work of our conversion, as it is used in some places in Scripture (Acts 3:19 and 11:18),

then indeed faith also is included in it, in the same way as the apostle understands faithlessness—the opposite of faith—to reside in the heart that is unrepentant (Rom 2:5).

41. But if we take the word repentance in the stricter sense as we defined it earlier, then it is usually kept distinct from faith, as a cause and the proper effect and result of that cause; it is in this way that Scripture itself in various places distinguishes repentance (Mark 1:15, Acts 20:21, etc.).

42. In order for us to have a true hatred of our sins, genuinely grieve for the offenses we have committed against God as against our kindly father, to cherish righteousness, and in our souls to begin fostering the hope for forgiveness and spiritual joy from him, it is altogether necessary that in faith we first apply Christ to ourselves, and in him to regard God as a kindly father. But we also grant freely that the inner sense of saving faith is strengthened and displayed more and more in us through the corresponding sense of true repentance.

43. From the explanations given thus far we see what we ought to think about that doctrine of the papal teachers who create three parts for penitence (and who also wrongly make it into a sacrament), namely: the contrition of the heart, the confession of the mouth, and the satisfaction in works.

44. As far as contrition is concerned, we deem that it is an element necessary for true penitence in the sense we explained above, provided that we understand the grief for our sins to be a godly grief and also not count it as sufficient satisfaction for our sins. For we must ascribe the forgiveness of sins to the grace of God and not to our own contrition, as it is rightly explained in the note *On Penitence*, distinction 2, chapter 1 (contrary to the definition of the Council of Trent, session 14, chapter 4).

45. And we also approve two kinds of confession as something that belongs to true penitence. Hereby the sinner acknowledges his own sins before God, privately (Ps 32) or publicly as part of the entire church (Neh 9), or in the presence of the church in the case of public scandals (2 Cor 2). Or the confession is made before individual people, the brothers who have been offended, in order to reconcile with them (Luke 17:9).

46. We do not deny that when there is serious mental anguish it is prudent for the sinner, in order to obtain consolation, sometimes to confess his own sins before other, upright men, especially ministers of the Word (for which

one could refer also to Jas 5:16). And yet it does not follow from this that the papist practice of auricular confession should be introduced into the Church, since that is a most cruel torture of the soul, something contrived apart from God's Word, and also impossible for the Christian. "For who discerns his own sins?" (Ps 19:12).

47. And lastly, for the satisfaction of sins in the presence of God we recognize nothing other than the precious blood of Jesus Christ our Savior, "which alone cleanses us from all our sins" (1 John 1:7); and "by his one offering he has for ever made perfect those who are sanctified" (Heb 10:14). And there is no instrument whereby we make the satisfaction by Christ our own except by faith in him, "because God has presented him as the atoning sacrifice for us, through faith in his blood" (Rom 3:25). The fruit and inseparable companion of that faith is the true repentance that we have thus far described.

48. True Gospel-based repentance consists of two types. Universal repentance occurs whenever someone crosses over from a state of sin to a state of righteousness and is converted to God for the first time. And particular repentance occurs when someone who has already been converted and believes is overtaken by sin and then grieves over it and repents from it.

49. And this particular repentance, in turn, is twofold, either ordinary or extraordinary. Ordinary repentance is the one which true believers and saints throughout the course of their entire lives are bound to exercise out of awareness of their weaknesses and daily shortcomings (Rom 7:24). Extraordinary repentance occurs when the faithful fall into some serious sin that hurts their conscience deeply, such as we see in the case of David or Peter after they fell.

50. Then again, this [extraordinary] repentance may be that of a single believer or of the entire congregation and church; and in Scripture one comes across many examples of this type of penitence intended to assuage God's anger or to forestall what he intends to do. And, whether public or private, this penitence is always accompanied by extraordinary signs of grief and humility, such as fasting, weeping, wearing a shirt of goat's hair, tearing one's clothes, etc.

51. For this reason the Novatians make a serious mistake when they think that it is useless to do penitence for back-sliding after one has been baptized,

and when they state that those who have fallen back into sin should not be admitted into the communion of the Church. For, to use the words of Tertullian, "if someone needs to repent a second time, his soul should not immediately be plunged into or be overwhelmed by despair. Let him be ashamed for having put himself at risk a second time, but not for being delivered again. No-one should be ashamed when it is necessary to repeat a cure for a recurring illness."

52. On this point some of the Anabaptists are equally mistaken when they think that sinners should be removed from the communion of the Church and handed over to Satan [1 Cor 5:5] so that they can do penance outside rather than within the Church—even though the sinners have repented. For while we admit that those who have fallen into serious sins can be withheld from the signs of grace for a period of time so that meanwhile the scandal can be removed from the Church and the genuineness of the repentance may be tested by its fruits, yet it is contrary to the clearly-spoken words of Christ (in Matt 18:17) and the practice of the whole apostolic church that the very same church before which a sinner has publicly declared his repentance should treat him as a heathen and a tax-collector.

53. It is this life that we currently lead which forms the goal, or end, of repentance, and for that reason we should not put off repentance any longer but we should attend to it today, while it is yet called 'today' (Heb 3:13). For, as Augustine puts it, it is only here and now that repentance bears fruit; repentance that is to be done in the future is of no benefit, as Christ taught in the parable of the wise and foolish maidens (Matt 25:11 ff.).

ON THE JUSTIFICATION OF MAN IN THE SIGHT OF GOD

President: Antonius Thysius
Respondent: Jacobus Dissius

Justification is 'the foremost locus in theology, and for us the most salutary'; without a sound doctrine of justification, other doctrines cannot be sound either, nor will it be possible to maintain a true Church (1). Justification is defined as 'the judgment of God whereby He pronounces righteous the person who is unholy and of himself a sinner subject to God's wrath' (7). The two parts of justification are distinguished as God's pardon of the sinner and his imputation of Christ's righteousness (8); thereupon the Synopsis treats the different causes of justification (9–32). God is identified as the efficient cause of justification (9), while the proclamation of the Gospel is the attendant, assisting cause (10), and God's peculiar grace is the internally impelling cause (11). Christ the Mediator is the meritorious, or externally initiating cause (13), while righteousness freely bestowed upon us is the material cause (18). Justification takes form in its application and declaration (21, 24), and the goal of it is the glorification of God and salvation of mortals (32). Christ's righteousness plays a crucial role in our justification, since it is because *of his righteousness, by* his righteousness, *and* through *his righteousness that we are justified (23). For man's part, we are made righteous by an appropriating faith in Christ, including trust, as the instrument by which we are made partakers of Christ and his righteousness (25–28). While our justification comes by a faith that is not apart from works, yet it is apart from works that we are justified (29). The justification that arises from these causes produces various fruits, like peace with God, perseverance and hope (33), and sanctification or 'works of righteousness' (35). Thesis 37 sums up: we are justified by the Father as judge seated on a throne of grace, and in Christ who has made satisfaction and acts as our advocate; and we are justified through the Holy Spirit who grants faith and seals grace in our hearts by the preaching of the Gospel. The disputation also includes several antitheses aimed especially at those Roman Catholic teachers who understand justification as referring to the in-pouring of the quality of righteousness, rather than a forensic act of God. Unlike the Romanist perception of justification as a 'habit' of love that is instilled in human beings, the Synopsis views it as the imputation of Christ's satisfaction and his merits which cause the believer to partake of Christ's righteousness in faith.*

1. Now that we have treated the calling [of man] and the obedience—both of faith and of repentance—that answers to it, it follows that we deal with man's justification and sanctification (or sacred works) by faith. And we shall deal first with the justification of the sinner in the sight of God, as this is easily the foremost locus in theology, and for us the one most salutary. And if this locus is suppressed, falsified, or overturned, it would not be possible to keep the purity of the teaching in other loci or to maintain a true Church. Now the main point and basis of this locus is the fact that a merciful and just God pardons the sins of believers through the righteousness of his Son and causes them to be saved.

2. The word 'to justify,' and thence 'justification,' which renders the Hebrew word *hitzdiq* according to its proper usage in the Hebrew language, is strictly speaking nearly always a forensic term denoting a forensic act of judgment by a judge, that is, of setting a guilty party free instead of condemning him (Deut 25:1; Prov 17:15). But it may also denote the actions that precede, accompany, or follow it (even actions undertaken privately), whereby someone is declared, confirmed, commended, or deemed to be righteous.

3. But the word is used with that specialized meaning when it concerns the judgment of God as He absolves the sinner who stands before his judgment seat (Ps 143:2; Rom 5:16 and 8:33–34). And so this entire act of justification is depicted as a forensic process. Yet we still grant that justification sometimes appears also to include sanctification as its consequence because of the very strong, close connection between the two (Rom 8:30; Titus 3:7, etc.).

4. Synonyms and similar words are "to be righteous before God" (Rom 2:13), "to make righteous" (Rom 5:19), "to impute righteousness" (Rom 4:3), "to bless" and "blessedness" (Rom 4:6).

5. And as for justification, insofar as it is "righteousness regarding the person" (whereby a person is justified generally—not with respect to a particular cause, usually called "the righteousness regarding the cause"—and

which is nothing other than the conformity of the entire man and his actions to God's Law), it is twofold: legal justification and Gospel-justification; the former justification is out of the Law and its works, while the latter is out of faith (Acts 13:38–39; Rom 3:20–21, 28; Gal 3:11–12). The former is inherent, the latter is by the imputation of alien righteousness (Rom 4:4–6, and 10:3–5, 6). After the fall no-one is justified by the former, but by the latter everyone is justified who has been granted true faith in Christ (Rom 3:20, 26, 30).

6. This latter one also goes by the name of "reconciliation," "blessing," and "salvation" (Rom 5:10–11; Gal 3:8, 14; Titus 3:4,5), although reconciliation is more a consequence and effect of justification, while salvation often has a broader range of meaning.

7. In the law-court of God, then, the justification of man as sinner is the judgment of God whereby, He pronounces righteous the person who is unholy and of himself a sinner subject to God's wrath. He does so out of his own mere grace and mercy, for the sake of the perfect obedience and righteousness of Christ that was offered on our behalf and that is received by faith. That is, He pardons the sinner from sin and the curse, and imputes to him the righteousness of his Son and so awards to him life eternal, for the salvation of the believing person and the glory of the merciful and just God. Nearly every part of this definition is included by the apostle in Rom 3:24–26.

8. There are two parts to justification: the imputation of passive righteousness (or the absolution of sins), and the imputation of active righteousness. By the former we are set free from guilt and condemnation and delivered from eternal death; by the latter we are deemed worthy even of a reward, and we receive the right to life eternal, which is awarded to us (Rom 5:17–18, 8:3–4). And because of the very close relationship between them, the one entails the other, as a part entails the whole (Rom 4:22), although justification taken in its most specific sense is often considered to consist in the remission of sins (Ps 32:1; Rom 4:7).

9. The efficient cause for justification, i.e., the one by whom we are justified, is God (Rom 3:26, 30 and 8:33; Gal 3:8). For He is the only one, as God and Lord, and so also as the lawgiver and judge, against whom sins are committed and by whom they therefore can be forgiven (Isa 43:25; Luke 5:21; Jas 4:12). It is even by the Trinity as a whole: the Father (Rom 8:33), the Son (Isa 53:11 and Matt 9:2,6), who himself will be the judge of the living and the dead, and

the Holy Spirit (1 Cor 6:11; John 16:8,11), while an order and distinction in persons is retained, so that it is the Father who justifies in the Son through the Spirit. As for the principle of acting and the certain, specific economy, the act of justification belongs to the Father, just as the merit for it is attributed to the Son and the application of that merit is attributed to the Spirit.

10. The assisting cause is the preaching of the word of promise or the Gospel. In this sense the Gospel itself is "the power of God unto salvation" and in it "the righteousness of God is revealed" (Rom 1:17); and it is "the word of reconciliation" (2 Cor 5:19). And it says that the preachers themselves "justify" (Dan 12:3), "bind and loosen" (Matt 18:18), "save" (1 Tim 4:16; Jas 5:20).

11. The internal impelling cause whereby God the Father was moved by himself to justify us is the peculiar grace of God, his mercy, philanthropy, love, and affection, whereby He not only granted a Redeemer (John 3:16; Rom 5:8–9; Titus 2:11 and 3:4) and handed him over to death for our righteousness and justification (Rom 4:25), but also deemed valid and pleasing the obedience that his own Son presented apart from us but on our behalf (Eph 5:2). With respect to both of them together, 2 Cor 5:18 states that He has reconciled us to himself in Christ. And finally, hereby He destined it according to his eternal decree and applied it to his elect by faith through the Spirit (Rom 8:30).

12. And so Rom 3:24 states that we are justified "freely, by his grace," and Isa 43:25 that "he for his own sake blots out our iniquities." It says in Ps 130:4 that "with him there is forgiveness," that our justification itself is "grace" of God, his "freely given favor," a "gift and donation," and it is given "by grace" or by his liberality (Rom 5:15–16). And as far as it concerns us, justification is clearly the opposite of what our works merit (2 Tim 1:9; Rom 4:4 and 11).

13. The initiating external cause, which is also the meritorious cause, is Christ the Mediator and Redeemer, the God-and-man; that is, the Son of God who in one person is true God and true Man (John 6:51; Acts 20:28; Gal 4:4; 1 John 1:7). And he is the cause insofar as he is the Mediator and Redeemer, or, it is his obedience, righteousness, and satisfaction (Isaiah 53). And this satisfaction is expressed synecdochically by the word 'blood' or 'death'

wherein the 'ransom' lies and 'the ransom-price' or 'redemption,' the 'atonement and propitiation' (Matt 20:28; Rom 3:24 and 25; 1 Tim 2:6).

14. And as far as God's part is concerned, this verdict of God did not at all come for free, but only upon the payment of a most costly price (1 Pet 1[:19]). And this had to take place because while God is merciful, He is also just (Rom 3:25), and also because that warning of his truly remains forever and cannot be altered: "On the day that you eat of the forbidden tree, you shall surely die" (Gen 2:17 and 3:3). For this reason, "there could be no remission of sins without the shedding of blood" (Heb 9:22). Hence it says that we are justified "through" and "for the sake of Christ" (Rom 3:24). And this satisfaction is put directly opposite our works and their merits.

15. Regarding the material cause of justification we deny (to put it negatively) that it consists of our works. For we are not justified "by the law, in the law, out of the law, or through the law" (Gal 3:11 and 2:21); and we are justified "not by the law of Moses" (Acts 13:39), "not by works" (Rom 4:2; Eph 2:9), "not by works of the law" (Rom 3:20 and 9:32; Gal 2:16), and "not by the law of righteousness" (Rom 9:31); and there is "not a righteousness of our own that comes from the law" (Phil 3:9), it is "not our own righteousness" (Rom 10:3), and "it is not from works that we have done in righteousness" (Titus 3:5).

16. And in this manner "no-one is justified" (Rom 3:20; Gal 2:16), not Abraham the father of all believers (Rom 4:2), nor David, the man after God's heart (Rom 4:6), nor Paul that chosen vessel—even though in everything his conscience was clear (1 Cor 4:4; Phil 3:8–9)—nor any of the saints (Ps 143:2). But finally, there are those who justify themselves, but who do so wrongly (Luke 10:29 and 16:15). Expressed by its opposite, righteousness comes "apart from works" (Rom 4:6) and "apart from works of the law" (Rom 3:28). Justification excludes every righteousness that is according to the Law, whatever sort it might be and to whomever it might belong; and so it also excludes any boasting (Rom 3:27; 1 Cor 1:31).

17. And we assert (to put it positively) that as far as we are concerned we are justified "freely" and "by the grace of God" (Rom 3:24); to some extent this makes up the material cause of justification, which is put directly over against what our works have deserved or merited (Rom 4:4–5 and 11:6). And so it is granted to us not just apart from any merits but even despite our demerits (Rom 3:23 and 4:5–6; Eph 2:8).

18. And indeed [the material cause] is the "righteousness that belongs to God" (Rom 1:17; 3:24–25; 2 Cor 5:21), "that is apart from the law" (Rom 3:21), and "that is by God" (1 Cor 1:30) and "from God" (Phil 3:9). That is to say, it is not the righteousness whereby God is righteous in himself, but the righteousness that He has prepared and gives or imputes to us (Rom 5:15). It is directly opposite the righteousness of the Law, or our own proper righteousness (Jer 23:6; Rom 3:21–22 and 10:3; 2 Cor 5:21; Phil 3:9).

19. And this is the righteousness of Christ, who is "our righteousness" (Jer 23:6 and 33:16), whom "God has made righteousness for us" (1 Cor 1:30). It is the "righteousness of God in Christ" (2 Cor 5:21) in "whom we are made righteous" (Gal 2:17). And it comes "in the name of the Lord Jesus" (1 Cor 6:11), "through Christ" (Rom 5:11), "through the grace of Jesus Christ" (Acts 15:11), "through the redemption made in Christ" (Rom 3:24) and "in the blood of Christ" (Rom 5:9). It is that very righteousness which comes by the satisfactory work of the Son of God—seen in all its fullness (both active and passive) as obedience placed over against disobedience—by which we are justified. It is placed opposite to a righteousness from the Law, and to our own, inherent righteousness (Phil 3:9).

20. And yet the Law, or the righteousness of the Law and of works, is not placed over against the righteousness of God in Christ, or over against Christ's righteousness simply as its opposite. For we are not justified contrary to the Law, for Christ has fulfilled it both by suffering the punishments owed for our sins, whereby he put an end to our guilt, and by presenting all righteousness and obedience to the Law, whereby he fulfilled what is required for eternal life. But the Law is opposed to righteousness in a certain respect, to the extent that the full payment for it was made by the Son of God for us and not by us ourselves, which was an additional requirement of the Law (Rom 8:3–4; Gal 3:13 and 4:4–5).

21. The form of justification is in its application from the side of God towards us, or in the bestowal and placement [upon us] of God's gratuitous righteousness in Christ, or in the *logismos*, that is, the imputing of righteousness (Rom 4:11), since "God does not impute to the sinners the sins that they have" (Ps 32:1; Rom 4:8; 2 Cor 5:19) but "He forgives them their sins and remits them through Christ" (Acts 10:43 and 13:38–39), and He "imputes [to them] the righteousness they do not have" (Rom 4:3; 1 Cor 1:30; 2 Cor 5:21). This alien righteousness of Christ becomes our own, and so we

are made righteous in the presence of God (Rom 5:19). The form of justification is also in the declaration and pronouncement by God himself, whereby He considers, deems, and judges someone righteous in his sight as well as in his own conscience, where God establishes his judgment-seat (Rom 4:2 and 8:33–34).

22. And this imputation is not some imaginary invention, but it has its proper place in the concept of equity and in legal right which has established that a creditor has the same right towards the one who guarantees the surety as he does to the debtor. Since imputation is a relational term, it has as its basis something that is not inherent in the person to whom it happens (i.e., some deed); as end-point a reward; and as relation imputation according to what is owed—as if there is something within us that by virtue of its own full or partial worth is imputed for righteousness—as the word appears to be used in Rom 4:4 (unless we want to understand the word in a different sense that would fit and match the topic). But the basis is situated in the judgment and will of the God who imputes or ascribes [the righteousness], and not in us (for in us, on the contrary, the foundation evokes wrath instead of righteousness, if God should enter into judgment with us); the end-point is the righteousness of faith or the merit of Christ; and the relation is an imputation which comes not by what is owed but by grace, in such a way that it is equal to being fully paid. Rom 4 uses it ten times in this way, and there the former meaning of imputation is explicitly removed from the matter of justification.

23. And by this point it should not seem strange that the righteousness of Christ has the character not only of a meritorious cause but also a material and even formal one, since it works in different ways, namely as that cause because of which, in which or by which, and also through which we are justified.

24. And as to the application, it is by the Holy Spirit that it comes about (1 Cor 6:11), namely as a gift of faith. For it is the Spirit himself who ingenerates it through the ministry of the Gospel (called "the ministry of the Spirit" in 2 Cor 3:8), and he confirms and increases it through his Word and sacraments (Phil 1:26; Gal 5:5). For this reason, he is called also "the Spirit of faith" (2 Cor 4:13), by which faith we appropriate God as gracious, Christ as Redeemer, and we appropriate his righteousness, and from it life eternal (John 1:12, Rom 9:30)

25. And for our part, we are made righteous, and God makes us righteous "by faith" (Rom 5:2; Acts 26:18), "from faith," and "through faith" (Rom 3:30). I say "by faith in God" and "by faith in Jesus Christ the Lord" (Acts 26:18), "out of faith to faith" (Rom 1:17), and even by way of exclusion, "by faith without works," or by way of its opposite: "By faith and not by works of the law." And "by nothing except by faith" and "only by faith," that is, by faith alone (Rom 3:28 and 30; Gal 2:16; Luke 8:5). Therefore, this righteousness is even called "the righteousness of faith" (Rom 4:11–13), the "righteousness of God by and through faith in Jesus Christ" (Rom 3:22 and 9:30), the "righteousness that comes from God in faith" (Phil 3:9). And that faith and the righteousness from faith similarly is placed opposite the Law, works, and also merits.

26. So then 'faith' does not merely denote the doctrine of the Gospel, the habit and action of the mind (that is, a bare rational knowledge of God, Christ, and the Holy Spirit), but bound up with it is the act of the will (Eph 3:12, 17), namely trust in God and Christ and the promises about the forgiveness of sins, righteousness, and life eternal. And faith appropriates these real, good, and life-giving things not just in general but in a particular way, to oneself individually, and even though they are external objects faith makes them one's own (Matt 9:2, Rom 4:20–21). That kind of faith is commonly called "faith that justifies." But whenever 'justification' is assigned to knowledge (Isa 53[:11], John 17:3), then as an expression of a part for the whole and by a common Hebrew manner of speaking it includes also trust.

27. Therefore our justification is "by this faith, out of faith, and through faith." The apostle even states that "faith is imputed for righteousness" (Rom 4:3, 5, 6, 9, 11, 22, 23 and 24). But faith does not act from its own initiative and by itself, like some quality in the proper sense, or motion (whether active or passive). Nor does it act as some work that is good and of exceptional value, as though faith itself were righteousness or a part of it—or even, by the appraisal and evaluation of God, in the place of righteousness. But faith acts in a secondary place and following something else, so that it is really the mode, means, and instrument, or 'the eye and hand' whereby we are made partakers of Christ and his righteousness. Indeed, faith justifies in relation to its object, Jesus, his righteousness and his promises of grace (Phil 3:9).

28. And we are justified by faith "alone," for it is not possible in any other way to appropriate God's promises, the forgiveness of sins, the alien

righteousness, and thence eternal life. Nor can one point to any other instrument, either from all of Scripture or the whole of the natural world. For these things are received not by love or good works, but for them God has appointed only faith.

29. But true and living faith is not something all on its own, unaccompanied by obedience or good works or love (Gal 5:6); for faith comes about by regeneration, which entails repentance together with faith. And faith coexists alongside repentance, and Acts 15:9 states that "our hearts are cleansed" by faith. And so while our justification comes by a faith that is not apart from works, yet it is apart from works that we are justified.

30. And so all of the following [statements] are connected closely with each other in a most excellent way: "It is God who justifies," "by his grace," "freely," "graciously," and "on account of and through Christ" and his "obedience," "righteousness," "by the imputation of righteousness" and "by faith." The one posits the other, or advances it, or infers it. At the same time, placed opposite to them and yet in their own order, are [the statements that] we are saved or justified "by ourselves, out of the law, and through the law, our works and our own proper righteousness," "by what is owed to us and what we have earned." Indeed, God's gracious justification does not conflict with the merit of Christ and its imputation by God; nor does faith conflict with these. For they are subalterns and that is why the justification of man by God's mere mercy is not prevented from being gracious and Christ's intervention from being meritorious. And through it [i.e., God's free justification] nothing is excluded except our own works, not those of Christ. Nor is God's gracious imputation something absolute, but it is the imputation of righteousness, namely the righteousness of Christ. And faith is judged not by its own worthiness but by the worthiness of its object. Or if the word 'faith' says something other than Christ's merit, it only points to the manner in which the merit of Christ is perceived.

31. Therefore the judgment and justification of God differs so much from that of men. It is abominable in the sight of God that the wicked is justified by the judgment of men (Exod 23:1; Deut 25:1; Prov 17:15), because it happens contrary to the Law. In the case that God justifies the ungodly, the judgment is in harmony with righteousness, because it happens according to the Law while Christ intervenes with a righteousness whereby, he makes satisfaction to the Law, and that righteousness becomes our own by

imputation and faith. Therefore, the apostle says "by faith," or "by the righteousness of faith, the law is not overturned but established" (Rom 3:31).

32. As to the goal of our justification by God in Christ through the Spirit and in faith, it is, with respect to God, the glory of God, so that God in justifying us may show himself to be merciful in Christ and powerful in the Spirit. For an amazing combination of mercy and justice is conspicuous here (Rom 3:26), as is God's extraordinary power (Rom 1:16; 2 Thess 1:11). With respect to us, however, the goal is our very salvation and eternal life (Rom 1:17 and 8:30; Titus 3:7).

33. The justification that arises from these causes, as it is an existing effect, likewise produces various fruits and [other] effects, and these include pacification both with God and in the conscience, and access to this grace, perseverance in the same, a hope that exults in life eternal, a boasting in the midst of hardships, and a boasting in God, etc. (Rom 5:1–2, 11, and 3:27; 1 Cor 1:31).

34. The subject or the object of justification is the sinner and the ungodly (Rom 4:5), that is, the sinner in and of himself, in his own nature, yet one who lives "out of faith" or "a believer" (Rom 3:22, 26; Acts 13:39); indeed, one who is elect and called according to God's decree (Rom 8:28,30).

35. The proper adjunct of justification, its proper affection, or, as others put it, the proper and necessary effect of justification, is sanctification (Acts 15:9) and the good works that flow forth from it, and the love of God and one's neighbor (Gal 5:6; 1 Tim 1:5; Titus 3:8). Although these good works are imperfect, yet because they are undertaken by the norm of the Law and because by that faith they are pleasing to God in Christ, they go by the name of 'righteousness.' And thereby we, too, are called 'the righteous' (Acts 16:35; 1 John 2:29 and 3:7, 10) even in the sight of God, on account of our sincerity and integrity. And we are called 'perfect,' each according to his measure and manner (Luke 1:6). And the righteousness is even called 'our righteousness,' as a righteousness that inheres in us, having been effected in us by the Spirit of God. But it is not identical to the righteousness of Christ, which is imputed to us by faith, nor is it a part of it, since it is distinguished from it (Eph 2:9–10). For in the believers there exists no righteousness of works (Rom 3:20; Gal 2:16). And yet there are works of righteousness in them (Titus 3:5).

36. In fact, justification, salvation, and occasionally even life eternal are attributed to the works, although it is not attributed in the proper sense (Jas 2:21, 23; Matt 12:37). It is attributed because there must be a coherence between justification and the works, and because of the testimony and declaration of faith, that is to say, whereby justification means the manifest proof and declaration (Jas 2:18), also to the external human judgment (Rom 4:2; 1 Cor 4:3–4).

37. In sum, God the Father justifies us as judge (to be sure), but He is seated on a throne of grace, and He does so by remitting sins and imputing righteousness. It is in Christ that we are justified, as he performs the satisfaction on our behalf and acts as our advocate. We are justified through the Holy Spirit, in that he is the one who grants faith and seals this grace in our hearts; and he does so by the preaching of the Gospel as the means of God's power. We are justified by faith, which appropriates the righteousness of God himself and of his Son and makes it her own. And lastly, it is by good works, as they display and declare the righteousness of our faith.

Antitheses of the Papal Teachers and the Socinians, Which We Reject as Contrary to the Truth

Ant. 1. The papal theologians, on the other hand, do not take the word 'justification' as a forensic term for the action of God as judge that relates to an object in the absolution of his guilt. But they understand the term in its grammatical sense and as a proper Latin compound word for the motion towards righteousness or a super-physical action of God whereby He works upon the subject by infusing and imparting the quality of righteousness, or whereby He makes and establishes the just out of the unjust. And so, by mixing up justification with regeneration and sanctification, they hold the view that God justifies effectively (contrary to the use of the word in this matter, at least in sacred Scripture)—and that is 'the first lie.'

Ant. 2. However, we do not think that they are excluding altogether that first [forensic] meaning of justification here, but they consider it too as the second, subsequent one, namely that the one who has already been made righteous and lives justly is also justified by God; that is, God absolves him. But there are some who limit this to the final act of the final judgment, although it is also and especially taken in this sense of justification in this life.

Ant. 3. They state that some kind of preparation must precede that justification, a preparation made partly by God and partly by us, that is, by the powers of human choice whereby man both wills and does what is within himself. And they say that these preparatory works deserve justification by the merit of congruity (although they say that this is not properly merit, and some even disapprove of the term, while like the others they do retain the substance of it). For it is congruous with God's kindness that He lends support to the one who does what he has within himself. But that is so far from being any reason for merit that the apostle declares: "Whatever is done without faith is sin" (Rom 14:23) and "no-one is able without faith to please God" (Heb 11:6).

Ant. 4. They think that justification itself follows upon this ordinary preparation, and they divide it into primary and secondary justification, or unfinished and finished, incomplete and complete justification. But justification is one single act that occurs in an instant, although it has its own application, continuation, and feeling, which come about by degrees and repeatedly (Rom 8:30). For this reason we daily pray "forgive us our sins" and we confess "I believe in the forgiveness of sins."

Ant. 5. They call it the primary justification whereby God makes an unrighteous person into a righteous one by infusing a new habit, and He turns the wicked into good by driving out the iniquity of his guilt and bestowing the uprightness of righteousness. But this is an act of regeneration, not justification.

Ant. 6. They posit that this [primary] justification entails two things. Firstly, the forgiveness of sins, as an act that precedes. And thereupon it entails the infusion of the habit of righteousness, whereby a man is formally rendered righteous, while he obtains the ability of doing works well and he becomes inclined to love and to other good works. However, the act of justification is not an internal act but a truly external one, and its form is in the forgiveness of sins.

Ant. 7. But the justification that they call secondary is the one whereby a man, having been equipped with those qualities, actually does become a righteous man by the acquisition of righteousness. That is to say, by performing works that are just man becomes increasingly righteous; that is to say, hereby his justification grows by his good works and finds its completion and fulfillment in him. And so he merits a greater righteousness and life eternal, and he does so through the merit of condignity because Scripture calls life eternal a reward. But in fact Scripture everywhere rejects justification by works. And the word 'merit' is also foreign to Scripture, and life eternal is received as a gift and by the right of inheritance (Rom 6:23 and 8:17–18); it is for this reason that life eternal is called a reward, though not in its proper sense.

Ant. 8. And they place [secondary] justification first and primarily in love, and thereafter among the other works. Love, however, is an effect of faith and consequently it is an effect of justification (1 Tim 1:5).

Ant. 9. They also want to think that God has established a twofold order or degree for righteousness, and so also for justification. The first one is "necessary, in the observance of God's precepts," in keeping with that statement: "If you would enter life, keep the commandments." And the second order, which is not so much necessary but "advantageous and useful" for a higher degree of blessedness, is "observance of the evangelical counsels," in keeping with that saying (as they would have it): "If you would be perfect, go and sell all that you have and give it to the poor, etc." And it is especially among these things that they place the 'merit of supererogation.' However, the one is to deform the Gospel into Law, while the other is to invent a more perfect righteousness over and above the Law.

Ant. 10. Thus, they think the apostle's statement that "God justifies the sinner and the ungodly" does not mean forgiving a guilty person his sins or being clothed in an alien righteousness (the righteousness of Christ), but from a sinner being made righteous as a disposition and personally. They do admit that no-one can be justified without the forgiveness of sins that is done for the sake of Christ's merit, however they do not consider that to be justification in the proper sense but as a prior justification, or as some put it, 'conjoined justification,' and others, 'subsequent justification.' But this is contrary to the apostle's clear statement, "but to the one who does not perform works but trusts in God who justifies the ungodly, faith is counted as his own righteousness" (Rom 4:5).

Ant. 11. They think that the apostle's statement [in Gal 2:16 and Rom 3:28], "we are not justified by works of the law but apart from works," is about the works of the ceremonial law, or even the moral law (performed, however, before conversion), and that are not yet works of the Gospel. But that is contrary to the examples of Abraham and David (Romans 4).

Ant. 12. They do admit that we are justified "by grace" and "by the grace of God," but they understand the word grace to mean an undeserved act of God whereby he forgives us our sins and infuses the habit of love; or they take it to mean the gifts that are infused through God's grace and mercy; they call this grace habitual and inherent. And by that they mean the theological virtues of faith, hope, and love. But in so doing they confuse grace with its effect, since grace means God's mercy (Eph 2:4) and is opposed to what is owed or merited (Rom 4 and 11; Gal 5:4).

Ant. 13. They do not understand the term "righteousness of God" to be the righteousness that Christ himself has presented and God bestows on us, but a righteousness that God infuses in us and that is inherent in us. But to the contrary, Phil 3:9 places the righteousness of God over against our righteousness.

Ant. 14. They do admit that we are justified "through and on account of Christ, by the merit of Christ and his righteousness," such that the righteousness whereby we are justified emanates from Christ and that the satisfaction is indeed applied to us, but that his merit and its application are not the proximate, full, and non-mediated cause, but a more removed one whereby God is moved to infuse the habit of love and of the other virtues in us, whereby, as the proximate and non-mediated cause, we are justified. Or they say that by his death Christ has obtained that we should be clothed with inherent righteousness and love, by the merit of which we obtain life and salvation. But in so doing, with their own satisfaction and their own merit they actually make Christ powerless.

Ant. 15. They do not take the "imputation of righteousness" or "of faith unto righteousness" to mean a reckoning by God whereby instead of the righteousness of the Law which we should have within us, He imputes Christ's obedience and the righteousness that Christ offered on our behalf, and so reckons us as just (which imputed righteousness they clearly deny), but they want that the inner renewal, faith, and works, or the inherent righteousness, although it is not perfect in itself nor of itself meritorious of life eternal, to be considered as such. To do so is to overturn Paul's entire teaching about the righteousness of God, Christ, and faith, and to put in its place the works and merits of men.

Ant. 16. When Scripture says that it is "by faith that man is justified," they take it to mean that it is some unfurnished, general, and implicit understanding whereby man is persuaded that the Christian religion as a whole and the articles of the faith are all true. And consequently, they exclude from faith trust and the special certainty of salvation, which they understand to be no more than moral and to come from a particular revelation alone. And to do so is to overturn the idea of faith as Scripture takes it, as well as its nature and strength.

Ant. 17. And next, they do not take our justification by faith as such (because faith resides in the intellect and is common even to many wicked people, while righteousness is in the will), but they take it in the sense of a part representing the whole and as a metonym (i.e., initially, partially, principally), and insofar as that act of justification is formed by love and made alive by the other virtues and good works. And consequently, they do not locate the mode whereby justification is applied in faith only, but also in works. But in fact faith is not formed from love. For the one quality is not the form of another. Nor do faith and works concur together for this act.

Ant. 18. And so they make the first justification gratuitous while the second is meritorious of salvation, although it is by the strength of Christ's suffering, or (as some Jesuits say) insofar as our works have been washed by the blood of Christ.

Ant. 19. In sum, they want "God to justify effectively" by acting in the subject; they want the "free choice" to act as a co-cause, the "suffering of Christ" as the meritorious cause, namely so that we are able to merit. They take the "habitual grace of God" in the sense of a formal cause, the "sacraments" as instrumental and as effective by the work performed, the "priest" as ministering and even acting in a judicial sense. They want "faith" to be a beginning cause, and lastly, "good works" to be a cause that perfects and makes complete. And on this point they make up a three-fold righteousness: inborn, infused, and acquired, and to each of them they attribute its own proper parts.

Ant. 20. Therefore, the foremost point of debate between the papal teachers and us is: "What is the principal, proximate, and complete cause of our justification?" Or better: "On account of what thing, and by what thing is it that we, as we stand before God's most irreproachable and perfect tribunal, are considered and judged to be perfectly righteous?" Is it an infused habit of love and the exercise of the other virtues? Or is it actually the imputation, that is, the participation, of the merit and satisfaction that Christ has given, so that Christ's righteousness is ours through faith? The former is their claim, while we steadfastly affirm the latter.

Ant. 21. The ungodly teaching of the Socinians is no different from these, insofar as it concerns the thing whereby we are justified; for like them they hold that it was our own obedience—except that they deny that the meritorious cause of justification (on which nearly all Christians agree) is the satisfaction made by Christ, which they claim is not necessary or likely, and even impossible, and they make up a metaphorical redemption, one that has no price.

Ant. 22. In fact they wrongly define faith not merely as trust but also as obedience to Christ's precepts.

SOURCES

Augustine on *Psalm 130*

"If you should mark transgressions, O Lord, who would stand?" [Ps 130:3]. He did not say "I shall not stand" but "who will stand?" For he observed that nearly all of our human existence is dogged by our own hounding sins, that our consciences are being accused by our thoughts, and that a clean heart which trusts in its own righteousness cannot be found. And so if a chaste heart that relies upon its own righteousness is not to be found, then the hearts of everyone must place their trust in the mercy of God and must say to God: "If you should mark transgressions, O Lord, who would stand?" What hope, then, can there be? "But with you there is forgiveness" [Ps 130:4]. And what is that forgiveness, except that of a sacrifice? And what sacrifice is there except one that is offered on our behalf? It was the outpouring of innocent blood that blotted out the sins of all who were guilty, and the payment of so great a price delivered all the captives from the hand of the enemy who held them fast. "Therefore, with you there is forgiveness." For if there were no forgiveness with you, if you should choose to be only a judge and not wish to be merciful, and if you should mark and search out all our iniquities, who could stand? Who could stand before you and say "I am innocent?" Who could stand in your judgment? Therefore, there is only one hope, because forgiveness is only with you.

Bernard of Clairvaux, *Sermon 23* on the *Song of Songs*

Man's righteousness is forgiveness by God. And while the righteousness of God consists in not sinning, the righteousness of man is that sin is not imputed to him.

Bernard, *Epistle 190*

The alien righteousness was allotted to man because he lacked his own.

ON GOOD WORKS

President: Johannes Polyander
Respondent: Johannes Backerius

Good works are 'the actions of regenerate people that come about according to the precept of God's Law, out of faith that works through love, for the confirmation of our election and calling, for the upbuilding of our neighbor, and to the glory of God.' Following a typically scholastic structure, the disputation moves from this definition (1–3) to the efficient and instrumental causes of good works (4–10), and then to the subject-matter (11–14), form, (15) and goals (16–18) of good works. So-called good works of the gentiles are contrasted with true good works (19–22) and the properties of good works that are non-essential are explained (23–31). Romanist teachings of good works are refuted at some length (32–50). Whereas the primary efficient cause of good works is God himself, the secondary cause may be those whom the Holy Spirit has regenerated (6–8). Only the works which God himself has commanded can be considered 'good' (11–12); and these works in all of their parts must agree exactly the rule of God's Law (15). However, good works cannot be meritorious because of their own inner worthiness, for even the very best works are imperfect. But God deigns to accepts these works for the sake of Christ, whose perfect righteousness covers our weaknesses, and who presents these works to the Father as fruits of the Spirit (36). Therefore, the disputation concludes that our merit is the compassion of God (50).

1. The fruits of faith that befit repentance are the holy, good works that are born from the seed of regeneration and grow from the root of justifying faith, which was explained very recently.

2. Good works are the actions of regenerate people that come about according to the precept of God's Law, out of faith that works through love, for the confirmation of our election and calling, for the upbuilding of our neighbor, and to the glory of God.

3. We should not apply this definition of good works to our first parents in their state of innocence nor to their offspring—Jews as well as gentiles—while they are in the state of corruption. We should not apply it to our first parents, because their works before the fall into sin proceeded not from justifying faith but from the original righteousness with which they had been created. And we should not apply it to their offspring, for since they were deprived of that original justice through Adam's fall into sin and they lack the faith that is rooted in Christ, they are not capable in themselves of producing fruits that are truly good.

4. The efficient cause of works of this sort is either primary or secondary. The primary or principal cause is God alone. For as He alone is God, so it is from him alone that every good gift first comes down (Jas 1:17). And He may be considered as the cause either absolutely or relatively. We may consider him as the relative cause in as much as the three divine persons are connected in essence and coordinated on equal terms for producing these [inner] works as well as the other ones that we call outward.

5. And so although it is God the Father who with the Son softens the natural man's heart hardened in wickedness, and bends it towards a new obedience that conforms to his Law, yet the Holy Spirit is in no way subservient to the Father and the Son in this action as an instrumental cause to a principal cause or as an inferior cause to a higher one; but he concurs with both of them for this action by a power that is co-equal to theirs. At the same time, because the Holy Spirit is the last person in this action according to the order of the divine persons and the one closest to us, for that reason the apostle calls our good works his fruits especially (Gal 5:22; Eph 5:9).

6. The secondary cause is the person who has been renewed by the Holy Spirit, who brings forth good works from his own heart as from the proper principle or starting-point, and he does so from his own personal store-house [Matt 12:35]. Hence those who are reborn are called God's work created in Jesus Christ for the good works which God had prepared beforehand, that they should walk in them (Eph 2:10).

7. This cause depends so much on the first one that no good work can be started or completed without it. To be sure, the good works God begins in us He also completes, and just as the Holy Spirit by his preceding grace bestows new strengths on us so that we become willing and able to do good works, so by his subsequent grace He brings it about that we do in fact work

well. Augustine skillfully describes the two graces with these words: "It is certain that we who have been reborn will what we will, but He who works the will sees to it that we do will. It is certain that we do what we do, but He who works to bring it about is the one who sees to it that we work" (Augustine, *On Grace and Free Choice*, chapter 16).

8. And so we should attribute good works only to the Holy Spirit, insofar as the Spirit of God works them in us not by our power but by his own. But insofar as he works them so that we, too, perform them, then we should call them also our works, as Augustine rightly points out (Augustine, Sermon 93, *On the Liturgical Season*). On the other hand, since the wicked deeds that are mixed in with our own works are not brought about by the Holy Spirit but flow forth from the carnal vices clinging to us in this life, we should not attribute them to the Holy Spirit but only to ourselves, as Augustine points out in the same passage.

9. The instrumental cause is either internal or external. The internal instrumental cause is faith, through which God cleanses our hearts and engrafts us into Christ like branches onto the vine, so that rooted in him we should bring forth much fruit (Acts 15:9; John 15:5; Col 2:7). Therefore Jas 2:22 says that Abraham's faith was the 'handmaid' to his works; persevering in the faith in Jesus Christ is linked with the keeping of God's commands (Rev 14:12).

10. The external instrumental cause is the preaching of the Word, and by administering it God exhorts and drives us on towards the newness of life that befits our faith. Thus Christ compares the preaching of his Gospel with a seed, and those who have been reborn with good and fertile soil, in Luke 8:15, where he affirms that they keep the word that they have heard in hearts that are good and honest, and by perseverance bring forth fruit.

11. The subject-matter, which at the same time is the rule for determining works that are good, is whatever God our lawgiver prescribes for us in his Word, of which the moral Law is a summary, the indicator of the good that God commands and finds pleasing, and of the evil that He forbids and finds displeasing. In the Old Testament God explained it clearly through the prophets, and in the New Testament He did so through Christ and his apostles, and He adapted it perfectly because of varying circumstances to the general instruction of his church as a whole and to the specific instruction of certain people.

12. And just as God is the one and only lawgiver who is able to save and to destroy (Jas 4:12), so too does He demand for himself every right to put before us, his creatures, the rule for piety, honesty, and righteousness (Deut 12:32): "Be careful to observe everything that I command you, and you shall neither add nor subtract from it." And Ezek 20:18–19: "You shall not walk in the statutes of your parents, nor keep their laws. I am the Lord your God; you shall walk in my statutes and keep my laws." From these it is clear that we must perform only those works which God himself has commanded, and we must consider only them as good.

13. Therefore it is right not to reckon among the number of good works those that according to the traditions of papal teachers are done from good intentions, or from self-willed worship [Col 2:23], even though they possess some wisdom or humility of heart and are crowned with the impressive title of apostolic and ecclesiastical instruction (Isa 29:13; Matt 15:9; Col 2:22–23). Works of this sort are the monastic vows and fasting, adoration of saints or pilgrimages to their shrines, and similar works; these have no real connection at all to works of piety.

14. For all the works of piety that God's Law has prescribed lead to the adoration only of God, but worshipping and calling upon saints leads also to a superstitious veneration of creatures. Added to that is the fact that everyone, all individuals included, is required to present all the works of piety commanded by God's Law; they are absolutely good and necessary. But the vows of monks (as the papal teachers themselves admit) are arbitrary and preeminent only for a few people who voluntarily bind themselves to doing them, notwithstanding the fact that it is with the promise of greater merit and reward that they are commanded to do them.

15. The form of good works is their integral conformity, or their exact harmony and congruence, with the rule of God's Law in all of their parts, insofar as their inner soundness and also their outward appearance is concerned. For since God knows the hearts and judges according to the truth, and since his Law is a spiritual one—not just pertaining to words and deeds but also to thoughts and desires—our actions should conform to the Law of God (Rom 2:2, 7, 14; Phil 1:10).

16. Good works have three goals. The first of these concerns us, namely, the testimony of our thankfulness towards God, whereby both our election and calling are confirmed in us (Rom 12:1–2; 1 Cor 6:19–20; 2 Pet 1:5, 9 and 10).

For it is by our good works that we are rendered more certain of our election and calling unto salvation, as the works are like sacrifices acceptable to God, and like undoubted marks of justifying faith, as Peter's word of encouragement makes clear: "Therefore, brothers, be eager to make your calling and election firm, for if you do this, you will never stumble" (2 Pet 1:10). And there is also Christ's promise in John 15:8, where the hearers of the Gospel are assured that by the fruits of good works they will know more certainly that they are his genuine disciples, vine-branches forever engrafted into Christ.

17. The second goal of good works is the upbuilding of our neighbor, whether he is a believer or unbeliever. For when in doing good we cause no offense to others, that is, when we lead the way for others without being a stumbling-block and we show openly that our faith is sincere, then the believer is confirmed in the same faith as we are. The unbeliever, however, is either won over to it or he is put to shame by it, if he nonetheless reproves our good walk in Christ (1 Cor 10:32[, 1 Pet 3:16]). Lactantius sums it up elegantly when he says: "When unbelievers see that they and their people do those things which we have said, but that ours practice only that which is just and good, if they had any sense they might have perceived from this that those who do what is good are pious, and moreover that they themselves, who commit wicked actions, are impious. For it is impossible that they who do not err in every action of their lives, should err in the main point, that is, in religion, which is the chief of everything" (*Divine Institutes*, book 5, chapter 9).

18. The third and final goal of good works, and the one to which the other two are subordinate, is the glory of God. For God has placed the regenerate in this world and in the midst of a crooked generation, not only so that they themselves might be blameless and sincere when they bring glory to God with their works and with their speech, but also so that like shining lights they might by the light of their good works incite all others to bring glory to God (Matt 5:16; Phil 2:15; John 15:1[–8]). An unbreakable bond unites this goal to the preceding ones, and together with them it comes in due order in the wake of good works; for this reason it is called by the same name as they are, sometimes their fruit, or their use, or their effect.

19. When the moral and civil virtues of the gentiles are put to the test in light of the definition of good works as we have fully explained it, then there is no

way whatsoever that we can applaud them as works that are good in God's sight—nor should we, because no part of that definition applies to them. For their virtues do not proceed from the Spirit of regeneration, since they are carnal, nor do they proceed from justifying faith (without which it is impossible to please God), since they either ignore or reject the righteousness of Christ. Nor do those virtues proceed from true love, since love is the 'hand of faith' whereby faith does what God demands in his Law. And the gentiles do not perform these works for the sake of God, who is the general goal that also is connected to the eternal well-being of those who do the works. Instead, they do them for some specific goal that ceases along with their life in this age, that is, for personal gain, to win popular acclaim, or to obtain civic honors for themselves.

20. And yet the virtues of unbelievers are not absolutely wicked, or wicked in and of themselves; they are wicked in a certain respect, and by accident. For they are good in a material way and when they are considered simply in themselves. But it is from the root on up that they are wicked, and so too in their form. From their root, because they emanate from a heart that is wicked and impure; in their form, because they are performed differently than they should be.

21. It is for this reason that Cyprian calls the virtues of pagan unbelievers false virtues, and Jerome calls them corrupt, while Augustine, with an eye to Paul's statement in Romans 14:23, calls them "sin itself," when he says: "Regardless of how much we predicate about the works of unbelievers, we know that the Apostle's saying is true, that whatever does not come from faith, i.e., from God's command and resting upon Christ's righteousness, is sin. If a gentile should provide clothing for the naked, is it then sin because it was not done out of faith? Yes indeed, to the extent that it was not done out of faith it is sin. It is sin not because the very act of clothing the naked is a sin, but because in work of this kind the boasting is not in the Lord; it is only the impious who denies that it is sin" (Cyprian, *On the Virtue of Suffering*; Jerome, *Commentary on Galatians*, chapter 3; Augustine, *On the Palestinian Proceedings*, chapter 14, and *Against Julian*, book 4, chapter 3.)

22. To be sure, in other respects those deeds are partly good and partly wicked. Good, because by the power of the Spirit who restrains the corruption within them they are useful for the respectability of the present life, for obtaining temporal happiness, and for the mitigation of everlasting

punishment. But they are evil because they are of no use for obtaining everlasting life. Augustine illustrates this with the example of the Romans, in his *Letter to Marcellinus*, where he says: "The early Romans established the Republic and advanced it with virtues, even though they possessed no true piety towards the true God. And in this very opulent and illustrious Roman empire God shows that even without true religion civic virtues are capable of so much that one would understand that when the true religion is added people would become citizens of another state where truth is king, love is the law, and eternity is the way of life." And in *Against Julian* book 4 chapter 3 he writes: "Fabricius will receive a lesser punishment than Catiline, not because the former was good, but because the latter was more evil; and Fabricius was less wicked than Catiline, not for having real virtues but for not deviating as much from real virtues."

23. Good works possess three adjunct properties: necessity, integrity, and dignity.

24. Necessity is considered an attribute of good works in many ways. Good works are called 'necessary': 1) by the necessity of the divine command; 2) by the necessity of the means ordained for God's glory and our salvation; 3) by the necessity of the worship and obedience we owe to God out of our natural obligation; 4) by the necessity of a good and tranquil conscience that is rightly conscious of its own salvation and calling unto salvation; 5) by the necessity of the duty to show love to our neighbor.

25. The papal teachers add the necessity of efficiency to the preceding ones, but we repudiate it as false because good works are necessary neither for the beginning of salvation (which consists in the forgiveness of sins and our reconciliation with God) nor for its consummation, which finds its place in eternal glorification and the full fruition of the future immortality, as if they were efficient causes. For they follow our justification in the sight of God through faith and they precede the inheritance that has been prepared in heaven for us only as a way and a required condition in the inheritors.

26. And it is not possible to prove the opposite from those very places in sacred Scripture which the papal teachers misuse to spread abroad their own fabricated opinion. Some of the passages show the quality or condition required of those who are promised eternal life (Heb 10:36, etc.). Other passages show the mark and way of faith whereby one reaches eternal life (as in Matt 25:35; Jas 1:25 and 2:14). And other places point out the fruit and

effect of the salvation that has begun and that consists in the forgiveness of sins (as in Luke 7:47, etc.).

27. The integrity of good works is that by which we, from an entirely pure heart and with all our strength, present everything God demands from us in his Law. By another name this is called the perfection of the integrity and the parts.

28. Neither sacred Scripture nor experience recognizes any other perfection, such as the perfection of degrees. For both of them testify that the good works of even the most holy men in this life are found to be imperfect, spotted with a variety of blemishes if they are examined in light of the perfection which the Law of God demands from us.

29. Scripture declares that the works of holy, believing people are not perfect for three reasons especially. 1) On account of the state and the mode of their regeneration in this age, which is such that it grows in small increments daily, and the works do not reach the final degree of perfection until after the last breath of life has been taken. 2) On account of the remnants of depraved concupiscence that continually clings to them by the vices of the flesh. 3) On account of the constant struggle between flesh and spirit, which is like that of enemies fighting with each other on the same battlefield; from their mutual conflict mixed actions arise, which are called either works of the spirit or of the flesh, because of the quality at which these works aim.

30. For these reasons the prophets and apostles testify everywhere that no entirely pure man is to be found who fulfills the precepts of the Law to the level that it requires (Ps 143:2; Rom 7:7–8; Rom 8:3; Jas 3:2).

31. But those who support perfectionism [in the degrees of good works], in particular the papal teachers, maintain the opposite view when they assign so much power to the regenerate that they are equal to fulfilling the Law of God, yet also are capable of achieving even more works, ones much more arduous than the Law's demands—that is to say, works of supererogation.

32. In order not to appear to be speaking without Scriptural support, they bring forward very many prooftexts from it, which they wrongly draw up into these three conclusions: 1) It is possible for saints in the 'arena' of this life to keep the Law. 2) The works of the flesh, which are mingled with the righteous works of the saints, are not deadly sins incompatible with the Law, but they are pardonable sins committed outside the Law, and therefore they do not

impede the compatibility of their righteousness with the Law. 3) The saints are capable of performing even more and greater works than they are bound to do by the precepts of the Law.

33. With the following arguments we shall demonstrate that they incorrectly are citing those prooftexts with which they struggle to prove their first conclusion. The first is that not one of the places they adduce deals with keeping God's commandments, or the general righteousness of the saints that corresponds to God's Law precisely according to the perfection of the degrees. Instead, some places testify to the zeal and effort of obedience in general, or of righteousness that has been undertaken yet is incomplete in degrees, but which conform to the Law insofar as sincerity of heart and all the elements of obedience are present (Josh 11:15; 1 Kgs 14:8; 2 Kgs 23:25; 2 Chron 15:12; Ps 119:11; Luke 1:6; Acts 13:22). Other places deal with the specific righteousness of the saints, or causes (Ps 7, 27, and 119), or deeds of righteousness (Ps 106:30). The second argument is that some places deal with the duty of those people who are held to aspire to the perfection of universal righteousness (as in John 14:21; Rom 13:8; Gal 5:14; Col 4:12). And other places deal with the greater progress of those who have surpassed others either in knowledge of the faith (1 Cor 2:6; Heb 5:14) or in the exercise of it (Phil 3:15; Jas 3:2). And the third argument is that they encourage us promptly to endure the cross and to carry out God's commandments eagerly (Matt 11:30; 1 John 5:3).

34. A comparison of the testimony of the apostle John (1 John 3:9) with the one which follows (1 John 5:8) shows how wrong the papal teachers are in drawing their second consequence from it. For in the latter passage, wherein he interprets his own statement, the apostle indicates that the earlier passage should not be understood as concerning any sin whatsoever, but the sin unto death in particular, for he asserts that those who have been reborn are immune to that sin, otherwise the apostle's earlier pronouncement (in 1 John 3:9) would be contradictory with the previously made statement in 1 John 1:8 which asserts that no-one is without sin.

35. The third consequence they draw also rests upon a false foundation. For in no place does Scripture call Christ's specific commands (which are prescribed only for certain particular individuals because of their function or a special gift) 'counsels' that are more perfect than the commandments of the moral Law, nor does it anywhere apply the name 'works of supererogation'

to those works of piety, abstinence, or love that must be presented only by those people who have received them. It calls them 'duties' that are owed either to God (according to the first table of the Law) or to our neighbor (according to the second table of the Law), as we shall show in a later disputation, the one on vows.

36. We should assess the dignity of good works not by their merits (as the papal teachers would have it) but only by God's grace, as the Gospel teaches. For if God were to test them against the rigor of his Law, then because of their own imperfection they would be worthy of censure rather than his favor and beneficence. God, seated on his throne of fatherly grace, deigns to accept these works and to crown them with eternal glory for the sake of Christ his beloved Son, who covers all our weaknesses with his own perfect righteousness, and who on our behalf presents our works to the Father as fruits of the Spirit who is working in us through faith.

37. Besides the fact that their own imperfection clearly reveals that our works cannot merit anything in God's sight by their own inner worthiness, there are the four following arguments that can prove the same. The first of these is the fact that for the promised reward of the future life the proportion of those works is not at all equal, since they are finite and temporary while the reward is infinite and eternal.

38. If the apostle Paul asserts concerning this that the brief sufferings which the saintly martyrs endure for the sake of the name of Christ are outweighed in countless ways by the reward of heavenly glory (Rom 8:18), then we should make the same assertion even more about the same reward that is promised for our actions, which we must perform and which are less than the sufferings of the holy martyrs. And the claim by the papal teachers that the distinction between merit of congruity and condign merit can be rightly drawn up from this statement by the apostle is so far from the truth that it would be best for us to reject it altogether. For if there is no equal proportion between works and the reward of the heavenly kingdom, then good works have no merit, nor is the reward a compensation that is to be provided based on an assessment of a proportionate righteousness.

39. The second reason is that good works, to the extent that they are good, proceed from the Holy Spirit (as we have declared earlier in thesis 7) and therefore they are not properly our works but gracious gifts of God that were brought forward by us. They are acceptable to God because we have them

not from ourselves but from him, and we, as instruments of his Spirit, present them to God, as Augustine has rightly noted (Sermon 39, *On the Liturgical Season*).

40. The third reason is that our works are owed, and it is by right that God requires them of us, as He is the supreme and only Lord to whom we owe ourselves and all that we have. If our works are owed to God as our Lord, then surely we can earn nothing from God by them; but if on the contrary they are meritorious, then they are not owed to him by his right of lordship. But in fact they are owed to God by his right of lordship, and Christ shows this by the parable of the slave: "Will the master thank his servant because he did what he was told to do? I think not. So you also when you have done everything you were told to do, should say 'we are unworthy servants, we have only done what we ought to have done'" (Luke 17:9–10).

41. The fourth reason is that with our works we do not bestow on the Lord God anything that by its priority lessens his goodwill in such a way that He gains some benefit for which He should consider himself under obligation to us. Christ links this reason to the immediately preceding one (Luke 17:10) when he says that it is in this regard that we are God's unworthy servants. And Job 35:7 presents the same thought for us to read: "If you are righteous, what do you give to God? Or what does He receive from your hand?" And Job 41:2: "Who has come before me, says the Lord, that I should repay him? Whatever is under the whole heaven is mine." And similarly Rom 11:35: "Who has ever given to God that God should repay him? For from him and through him and to him are all things."

42. To these reasons we may add that the very word 'merit' itself is just as strange as 'doctrine about merits,' and it is used nowhere by God's inspired scribes. And although Jesus Sirach is not counted as one of them and therefore in our view not a self-authenticating witness, yet we shall point out that the [Greek] word *erga*, which he uses in Chapter 16:13, means 'works' and not merits, as the papal teachers think, who prefer to follow the bad rendering of the Latin translator than to cling to the authentic meaning of the text taught by us. This is clear also from the passage in Heb 13:16, where, for the sake of constructing their 'merit of condignity' they would rather, in line with the ancient translator, explain the verb [in the second clause of Heb 13:16] as 'to earn,' than—as we do—'to be cherished,' even though this latter

word expresses the meaning of the apostle better than the former. No-one who is skilled in the Greek language—and also orthodox—would deny it.

43. It is no less absurd to adduce the word 'wages' (which occurs very frequently in the sacred writings) in order to lend support to that same merit [of condignity] since the Gospel nowhere promises the salvation of our souls, or eternal life, as wages owed for our good works but as an undeserved and gracious reward. And for that reason, it is sometimes called the "goal of faith" (1 Pet 1:9), the "gift of God" (Rom 6:23), and again, "the inheritance that is kept in heaven for us who are co-heirs with Christ by the grace of adoption" (1 Pet 1:4).

44. Moses looked forward to that reward with the eyes of faith whereby he relied upon the expiatory reproach that Christ bore, in keeping with God's gracious promise made to Abraham and his seed, and he considered the riches of that reproach of greater value than the treasures of the Egyptians (Heb 11:26).

45. As we journey in the rugged desert of this life we may cast our eyes upon the same reward, so long as we look upon it not as a payment in the way that hirelings do, but as an inheritance that will be assigned to us for free by our Lord and heavenly Father, as befits slaves who have been adopted as sons, and who temper the troubles of this present life by the sweet solace of this expectation.

46. In 1 Cor 9:24 the apostle presents that same reward to us as the prize of an imperishable crown, so that, by looking at it we should be driven more eagerly to run our race until the end. And Phil 3:14 shows what kind of prize it is: it is the prize of the heavenly calling of God who supplies us with the strength in Christ Jesus for the valiant and steadfast completion of our race-course. Since God's calling is free, then its effect and its scope must also be free—that is, the prize of the eternal crown.

47. And this does not conflict with the fact that the same apostle defines that imperishable crown as the crown of righteousness that has been laid up for him in the heavens and that Christ the righteous Judge will bestow on the day of his glorious coming (2 Tim 4:8). For Paul does not mean that Christ must give that crown to him following a rigorous appraisal of his works, for he flatly denies that he was justified by that (1 Cor 4:4), even though he was not aware of having committed any misdeed. Rather, he means that—

according to the analogous rule of truth—[the crown] corresponds to the quality of any work whatsoever (good or bad), which in other, parallel passages is explained distinctly and antithetically (or, in comparison with what is opposite to it). This occurs in Rom 2:[6]–8: "God will repay each person according to his works. To those who are persistent: the glory of good work. But for those who are contentious and do not obey the truth but unrighteousness there will be fury and wrath, etc." And: "It is just in the eyes of God to repay with affliction those who afflict you, and to give relief, together with us, to you who are being troubled, when the Lord Jesus will be revealed from heaven" (2 Thess 1:6–7).

48. And from this sort of relation to the works of believers as well as unbelievers it is not right to conclude that the works of either are meritorious, since Christ repays the works of unbelievers with the punishment for unrighteousness by the law of the highest right, but the works of believers with the crown of righteousness according to the Gospel of his covenant of grace, so that he might reveal his righteousness by the trustworthy payment of the promised blessedness no less than his mercy by the favorable declaration of it (Heb 6:10 and 10:23; 1 John 1:9).

49. When the orthodox fathers employ the words 'merit' and 'to earn' 1) they understand the word 'merit' in both ways, as merit for a good work or merit for a bad work. This is seen in *Epistle* 40 of Augustine, where he makes a distinction between the evil merit of the impious and the good merit of the pious. 2) They understand the word 'to earn' as 'to obtain' or 'to acquire,' as in the *Proceedings of the Council of Carthage*, cognition 3, article 258: "let us leave aside how much shedding of Christian blood was done by Leontius, Ursatius, Macarius, and the other executioners whom they *obtained* from the rulers of the world to slaughter the saints." And from the *First Sunday of Advent*: "O Lord, we beseech you to summon forth your power and come, so that by your protection we may obtain escape from the dangers that threaten us sinners and salvation by your deliverance." 3) So that no-one should misuse those words and devise for good works an innate meritorious worthiness, they sometimes state that good works are worthy more of God's sympathy than of a payment of life eternal. See Augustine on Ps 49 and 61, and Bernard, Sermon 67 on the Song of Songs.

50. For this reason the papal teachers deserve to be judged more severely, because by badly twisting the words not only of sacred Scripture but also

those of the ancient church fathers, they feel no shame in conjuring up their doctrine of the merits of good works. And as for us, we bid them farewell, and in keeping with the arguments made earlier, we conclude with Bernard that our merit is the compassion of God.

DISPUTATION 35

ON CHRISTIAN FREEDOM

President: Andreas Rivetus
Respondent: Jacobus Henricus

Christian liberty is treated in the Synopsis from the perspective of the saving work of Christ that was delineated in earlier disputations. The satisfaction for sins that Christ has obtained for us and our consequent justification are the basis on which Christian freedom from slavery to sin arises. Locating Christian liberty within the process of sanctification by the Spirit, the disputation rejects the idea that any lawlessness is permissible (1, cf. 47). This subject is important, for without Christian freedom 'we will not be able to rightly know Christ, the true Gospel, nor inward peace' (2). The freedom in question is, like its opposite, slavery, spiritual in nature (4). It is the condition of those set free by the grace of Christ whereby their consciences are no longer enslaved to sin, the power of the devil, and the curse of the law (7). Thus all who believe are free from sin and guilt (11–12), free from the demands of the moral law (13–16), and free from any human traditions that seek to restrain believers' consciences (17–19). Theses 20–23 articulate the nature of the freedom that believers enjoy in light of the Christ who has been revealed in the Gospel. Believers have been set free from Old Testament ceremonial laws (28), forensic laws (29), and political laws (30–31). What follows is a treatment of the so-called adiaphora, or 'indifferent things' that are judged to be good or bad not in or of themselves but from the circumstances of their use (33); they are restricted by the law of faith and love (33–36). The form that Christian freedom takes is the 'undoubted conviction and full assurance in the hearts of believers about their sonship' produced by the Holy Spirit (41). Goals are a good conscience, joy, and the praise of God's grace (42). Those enjoying the freedom of grace look forward to the freedom of glory in the life to come, to which belongs the soul's immortality and the resurrection and the glorified state of our bodies (43–44). There are many benefits of this doctrine, in keeping with the various degrees of freedom (45–46).

1. In the preceding disputations we treated the redemption that is obtained through Christ, and its application by saving faith for all who through Christ's merit have been redeemed from slavery to sin and death; and also the sanctification of those who have been justified and their thankfulness in the exercise of good works. In fitting order, therefore, it follows that we now undertake an investigation into the true Christian, or evangelical, freedom that is shared by all to whom the fruits of Christ's suffering belong.

2. We acknowledge that the need for having this doctrine is such that if we do not keep it then we will not be able to rightly know Christ, the true Gospel, nor inward peace in our souls, nor to perceive these things with earnest awareness in our hearts. Nor could our conscience undertake anything without hesitation, nor could the power of justification be sufficiently understood. Therefore, we must make every effort not to suppress a part of doctrine that is so necessary; and we should also make every effort to explain it so as to cut short any opportunity for criticism or arrogance for those who misuse the name of freedom in order to hurl themselves into unsound activities of lust and unbridled abandon.

3. In terms of kind, the nature of freedom should be distinguished from its opposite, namely slavery, which means a certain state of vile and wretched subjection, whether that subjection is voluntary or forced. It is hence that men are divided into 'slaves' and 'freemen,' the former of which had come under the power of another person according to the rule of law either by the right of war, by birth, by just sentence of condemnation, or by purchase. But the latter were born free and never had served as slaves. The Jewish people proclaimed themselves to be of this sort: "we are the seed of Abraham and we have never served anyone; how can you say: 'you will be set free'?" (John 8:33). Occupying a middle position between these two were the 'freedmen,' who had ceased to be slaves, and whom their masters had set free from their rightful servitude.

4. We are not dealing here with the question of that civic and corporal slavery, nor with its opposite, civic and corporal freedom. But we do use some terms and expressions from those realms in order to explain the slavery and freedom that are spiritual. Concerning that spiritual slavery and freedom Christ says: "If the Son shall set you free, you will indeed be free" (John 8:36). Since this spiritual freedom has its origins in manumission and liberation, it

follows that no-one is born free but becomes it, and that no-one is spiritually a pure freeman but all people who enjoy that freedom are freedmen.

5. This manifold spiritual slavery came about after the first man abused his natural freedom and so lost it for himself and his posterity, and became a slave to what he obeyed by abandoning God, namely sin, to which everyone is kept enslaved by both the guilt of condemnation and by dominion. As a consequence, Satan's sovereignty and domination came over the sons of rebellion (Eph 2:2), a sovereignty that would not exist if it had not arisen from sin. This slavery was followed (so to speak) by its declaration or manifestation (itself also called slavery) when God renewed the force of the moral law and demanded that it be kept carefully—the law which had been nearly obliterated (or at least mainly hidden) from the hearts of men. God did so in order that man might recognize the tyranny of ruling sin from the fact that he would have to abandon all hope of fulfilling the requirements of that law. The ceremonial law was added to it, and by it the condemnation that man deserved was sealed with various types whereby he, convicted of his guilt, would await the ultimate accursedness unless he should be redeemed by being set free.

6. The servitude to empty pride and wretchedness in this and the future life was added to this slavery of sin to which the law bore witness. And opposite to this manifold slavery is placed a triple freedom, namely 1) The freedom of our nature, or innocence, such as Adam had; 2) The freedom of grace, which believers receive in this life as participants in the heavenly calling; 3) The freedom of glory, whereby they will, after this life, be set free from every [form of] slavery to corruption and wretchedness.

7. We ascribe the name 'Christian freedom' especially to that intermediate freedom, which is the freedom of grace granted in Christ to all "who throughout their whole lives were held in slavery by their fear of death" (Heb 2:15). And we describe [that Christian freedom] as the condition of people who have been set free by the grace of Christ, a condition whereby their consciences have been released from slavery to sin, the tyranny of the devil, and from the precise demands and curse of the moral law, and from observing the ceremonial law; and after shaking off the yoke of human traditions, they conduct 'intermediate things' safely without reproach by applying knowledge of faith and practical judgment of love, so that they who have not received "a spirit of slavery unto fear" but a spirit of sonship (Rom

8:15) may serve God willingly and eagerly in soul and in body, "for the praise of his glorious grace" (Eph 1:6) and their own eternal salvation.

8. The chief efficient cause of this freedom is God the Father "who has made us to share in the inheritance of the saints in light" (Col 1:12). It is also the Son, the Mediator between God and man "who has set us free" (Gal 5:1); and the Holy Spirit, 'fellow-worker' with the Father and the Son, who brings freedom with him wherever he dwells (2 Cor 3:17). The principal impelling cause is God's grace and love for mankind in Christ (Luke 1:72 and 74). The initiating cause is the merit and satisfaction of Christ in whom we have "freedom from sin" (Rom 6:22) and a "ransom from the empty way of life inherited from our fathers," a ransom "which was not made with silver or gold but with his precious blood" (1 Pet 1:18[–19]), which excludes the merit of any human work.

9. There are two aspects to the efficient instrumental cause: from the side of God it is the true Gospel whereby freedom is offered through the preaching (Jer 34:15), and John 8:32 ascribes liberation to it. Accordingly the preaching of the Gospel is called "the ministry of reconciliation" (2 Cor 5:[18–]19). For man, however, the necessary instrument, which is ingenerated by the Spirit and the Word, is a living faith, "whereby we have access into this grace in which we stand" (Rom 5:2).

10. The matter in which, or the subject [of Christian freedom], is everyone who believes in Christ and who takes refuge in him as his liberator, whether Greek or Jew, male or female, etc. (that is, of whichever gender, state, nation, etc.) in the church of the New Testament. For it is to the members of the church that 'Christian freedom' in all of its degrees properly belongs. And if all of the degrees are to be grasped fully, then before Christ was revealed no-one could be a member. But if we consider the primary, foremost degrees, the ones that are altogether necessary for salvation, and the very substance of freedom, then we do not deny that freedom had been communicated to believers under the Old Testament, albeit not to the extent that was revealed with Christ's appearance. And that freedom in its own way could even be called 'Christian' freedom, for those who were at that time bearing "the reproach of Christ" (Heb 11:26) realized that Christ was the author of spiritual freedom too; and because they were participants in it with us, some not inappropriately have called this freedom 'shared' in order to distinguish

it from the freedom that concerns the fullness of grace, which is called Christian freedom in particular.

11. The matter concerning which, or the object of the two freedoms (the one that is shared and less complete, and this more complete one), is manifold, and from its variety also diverse degrees (or parts, as others prefer to call them) have been arranged. For 1) it has sin as its object, and the guilt thereof, that is, the dominion of the devil and so his tyranny. [All believers] acquire that degree of freedom from the primary slavery, since through the remission of sin it is not imputed to them, and through the mortification of the flesh it no longer reigns over them. And they acquire it also through the immunity from the second death, because "the law of the Spirit of life through Jesus Christ has set us free from the law of sin and death" (Rom 8:2), and so "there is no condemnation for those who are in Christ Jesus" (Rom 8:1).

12. The fact that sin still dwells in those who believe and remains active in them (1 John 1:8) is not a hindrance to this freedom because the guilt for it has been removed and its powers have been diminished, in order to do away with its kingdom (Rom 6:12). For through the granting of the Holy Spirit the consciences of the pious are set free from sin to the extent that they are no longer slaves to it, but they are soldiers and servants of righteousness (Rom 6:14[,18] and 7:22). Therefore, though the war is not yet over, it is enough that the victory has been obtained from the enemy. And since we have dealt with this matter in the doctrines of repentance and justification, we do not need to pursue it further.

13. 2) The same freedom has a function concerning the moral law, insofar as "by it the feelings of sin are at work in our members to bring forth fruits unto death" (Rom 7:5), since it presents no hope at all of salvation for the sinful man other than in a very precise observance of the commandment "do this and live" (Luke 10:28). This very harsh requirement of fulfilling the entire law was linked to the same law's curse if we did not keep it perfectly (Deut 27:26; Gal 3:10). This yoke was very heavy and unbearable, and Christ broke it, having transferred both obligations to his own person: the curse that came for not fulfilling the law as well as the requirement of fulfilling it. And by the transference he both fulfilled the law perfectly and was made a curse for us (Gal 3:13). "And by sending his Son God condemned sin in the flesh so that the righteousness of the law might be fulfilled in us" (Rom 8:3–4).

14. Accordingly we teach that the law is not superfluous, but we rather state that what it teaches remains unaffected, and that all should obey it; and we know what freedom really is only when we serve God according to the prescript of his law. Therefore, in Scripture 'to be free' and 'to serve God' are in fact the same thing, although they are worded differently (1 Pet 2:16). And Paul, in Rom 6:18, locates Christian freedom in the 'servitude to righteousness.' Therefore, part of the freedom is the fact that in us it is brought about that we, gifted with the Holy Spirit, fulfill the law for a large part, although not in its entirety. And because through the weakness of our flesh we either omit [to keep it], or on the other hand commit [sin against it] it is not considered as an omission or a commission, because the perfect fulfillment of the law—which is in Christ alone—has been imputed to us.

15. Therefore even if those who have been born again are free from the law insofar as it is a means for obtaining justification by it, or insofar as it condemns, [the law] is nonetheless of use to them since it teaches what those good works are wherein they ought to walk. And it guides them to stay within the boundaries of the right way, while it denounces the old remains of the flesh, chides them for the imperfection of the obedience that was begun in them, and provides convincing reasons for being humble, so they are not swept along to a persuasion of their own righteousness.

16. Therefore just as we reject the ravings of the Antinomians, who are of the opinion that the moral law ought to be proscribed and eliminated from the Church (we say that if the teaching [of the moral law] is not preserved undiminished in the Church, then its purity and integrity cannot stand firm, nor the articles about justification, the doctrine of good works, original sin, or free choice), so too do we have the right to complain about Bellarmine's dreadful slandering, which falsely alleges that we situate Christian freedom in the fact that the man who has been justified by faith is in his conscience not subject to any law at all, but is free from the requirement to fulfill the law and he considers everything as indifferent, as neither prescribed nor prohibited (Book 4 *On Justification*, chapter 1 and 5).

17. 3) It has also been a part of the freedom common to all believers, and it will be so until the end of the age, that they have consciences that are free of every yoke of human traditions in matters pertaining to the worship of God and in matters which involve religious actions (which are called 'elicited acts'). For it belongs only to God to prescribe matters that pertain to religion, and

it is for this reason that in matters of worship we should pay attention only to his Word and not to human traditions. For to no-one has God granted authority (whether it be autocratic or legally bestowed authority) over the consciences of other people, when it concerns worship in which God alone binds the conscience in a non-mediated way, as He "alone is the lawgiver who is able to save and to destroy" (Jas 4:12).

18. But since we are speaking about the strictly spiritual government, which we claim belongs entirely to God alone (since it pertains to the spiritual kingdom in which God does not allow a vice-regent), we do not want what we say about spiritual freedom to be wrongly drawn into the realm of politics, as if Christians who are free according to the spirit are therefore exempt from every kind of service to the flesh. For we reject the fanatics who under the pretext of Christian freedom cast off every form of civil obedience, because God through Paul teaches us to obey the magistrate, "not only from fear of punishment, but for the sake of conscience" (Rom 13:1 and 5).

19. However, it does not therefore follow that the consciences are bound in a direct, non-mediated way by political laws that are strictly human laws and not found among the laws of God (which the papal teachers contend), because it is what we must do by God's command that strictly and of itself binds the consciences non-mediatedly, although no command or consideration of any creature is added to it. The subject-matter proper to human laws is not of that sort—human laws which we nevertheless admit do bind the consciences in a mediated way, by force of God's general command, which bids obedience towards the magistrate. For since human laws are not binding in principle and of themselves, but secondarily and through accident, the teaching that Bellarmine defends is false, that "the civil law is no less binding than the divine law, and that all laws that have been made by any one at all (whether God, an angel, or a human being) are binding in the same manner" (*On the Members of the Church Militant*, book 3, chapter 2).

20. So much for now about the degrees and elements of the freedom of God's children that all believers in every age share (whether they believed in Christ yet to come or now believe in Christ as having been revealed), although these stages and elements have been communicated to a greater or lesser extent. Particular to the freedom that befits the times of the New Testament is the release from the dispensationary slavery to the ceremonial law, and in keeping with the law's diverse aspects it has many facets. For in the first place,

the law consisted of the fact that it was a sign of the sinner's verdict and a written record of our indebtedness (Gal 3:21), laid upon us "until the time of restoration" (Heb 9:10), the time that was fulfilled when "Christ blotted out the written record of ordinances against us and took it away" (Col 2:14). For when the verdict was taken away by him, it was no longer necessary that the sign of our verdict stay.

21. Moreover, since the ceremonial precepts are concerned especially with the worship appropriate to the Israelite nation for an outward sign of the mysteries of the coming Christ (Col 1:27; Heb 8:4 and 10:1)—for which reason Moses had been ordered to make everything "according to the likeness and pattern shown on the mountain" (Exod 25:40)—when he did come in the body, the shadow disappeared, and when the prototype came, the type yielded its place, and it now is no longer possible for the mystery of redemption to be truly signified as something yet to come either in word or in deed, for in the outward sign of the deed there would be the same lie as if someone were to say "Christ is still going to come and to die, etc."

22. Indeed, if we take a look at the same rites, because the church of the Jewish people in the time of its infancy (which needed a tutor and pedagogue) was kept in custody under the elements of the universe (Gal 4:3) in hope of the coming Messiah, so that it might be led to believe in him and be led to him, [we see that] the same Apostle who taught this use of the ceremonial law also pointed out that "in the fullness of time his Son was sent forth, etc., to redeem those who were under the law" (Gal 4:1 and following), "so that you are no longer slaves, but sons and heirs through Christ" (Gal 4:7).

23. And lastly, if we consider the other use of the ceremonial law, namely that its rites were the marks of what it professed, the signs and tokens that set the Israelite people and its ecclesiastical form of government apart from all the other peoples, which like an enclosure or a dividing wall distinguished the Israelite nation from the idolatrous forms of worship of the other peoples (Gen 17:13 and 14; Deut 4:8; Eph 2:14), there was no longer any place for this aspect of the law after "the people who once were far off were brought near by the blood of Christ, who is our peace, who has made both one, and has broken down the middle wall of partition" (Eph 2:13 and following).

24. Therefore in former times the ancient heretics were rightly condemned who thought that this law has not ceased but ought to be preserved in perpetuity along with the Gospel: Cerinthus (as witnessed in Epiphanius

Against Heresies 28 and Augustine *Against Heresies* 8), Ebion (as witnessed by Irenaeus book 1 chapter 28) along with the Ebionites and those who were called the Nazarenes (in Epiphanius *Against Heresies* 18 and Augustine *Heretics* 9). The fact that after Christ's resurrection Paul circumcised Timothy (Acts 16:3) does not help their view, nor the fact that on the advice of James he, together with others, purified himself according to Jewish ceremony (Acts 21:26)—an affair wherein Paul showed no prejudice against Christian freedom, as he showed himself to be a forceful defender of it elsewhere, over against the unwise behavior of Peter (Gal 2:14).

25. At this point we must therefore apply the distinction that the 'School of Theology' derived from Augustine, namely that after Christ the ceremonial things could have been observed until such time as the Gospel was sufficiently spread among the Jews—not, of course, as outward signs that foretold that Christ was yet to come, or from the notion that it was necessary for salvation, but as commands proceeding from a good source that by Christ's suffering were put to death and emptied of meaning, but which are to be carried to their graves and buried with due respect. But after that time it was no longer permitted to observe them, nor should anyone observe them now unless he wishes to be seen as a 'violator of the tomb.' But at that time they were dead indeed, but only in the sense that we stated, although they were not yet deadly, so that the two nations might grow together. (But later they would be both dead and deadly.)

26. Nor should anyone state that he is removing the signification and abandoning all necessity, and so (as Cajetan does) excuse the superstition of the Ethiopians who maintain circumcision for the sake of imitating Christ, and not for what it signifies. For even other people of that same school rightly sense that this cannot be right, not only because of the stumbling block but also because that religious observance (both as an outward sign of the coming Christ and as a means) flies in the face of the truth and perfection of the Gospel whereby it was Christ's will that this religious practice should be made obsolete. Not only because it functioned as an outward sign of the things that were to come, but also because it belonged to the manner of worshiping God that was but a shadow and not perfect. If one were to examine the majority of the papal ceremonies by this standard, they would be no less deadly at this (current) time, and all the more so because they were brought in by men for worship and from the notion that they are necessary.

27. Yet we do grant that there is great value in knowing the ceremonial laws, even though Christians are free from them. For just as the things that the prophets foretold about the coming of Christ may have been fulfilled, yet are read in the church with great benefit, so too the Levitical ceremonies are examined and explained no less usefully, so that from an understanding of how Christ and all his benefits had been prefigured in them we derive the strengthening of our faith. What Christ said to the Jews in John 5:46 is relevant here: "If you believed Moses you would believe me, for he wrote about me." By this he meant not just the explicit words of the prophecies but also the ceremonial rites and figures that foreshadowed Christ. In this manner it is from the rite of sacrifices for sin that we today defend the doctrine of Christ's perfect satisfaction, over against the modern-day antichrists.

28. From the things that have been stated about the ceremonial law given to the Israelites we should judge Christian freedom concerning the judicial laws of Moses, which, because they were given by Moses and to such a nation, they neither affect nor bind Christians. And yet we should note that mixed in with those laws were some ceremonial elements, and these are entirely out of date for our time, either because of what they are, or by analogy. A commandment of this sort is the one about the corpse of someone who has been hanged, that it must be buried on the same day lest the land should be polluted which Jehovah our Lord had granted to the Jews as a possession (Deut 21:22 [and 23]). We should place this commandment in the company of those with similar ceremonial admixtures that pointed to Christ and were intended as proper types of him; consequently, these are, in our time, deadly.

29. As far as it concerns laws that are in no way ceremonial, we need to make yet another distinction. For firstly in forensic law there are some commandments that are not at all subject to change. For whatever has been sanctioned for the common good according to universal principles of nature and common sense in moral law (whether by command or prohibition, reward or penalty), that of itself remains permanently, and even though it is not by the force of Moses's government that we should keep it; yet to the extent that it is marked by law and common reason and pertains to the law of nature, no occasion or condition can come about to loosen it, nor could anyone have reason to speak against it or resist it successfully. Consequently Christian freedom does not extend to this point.

30. Other laws are purely and absolutely political, and thus common; and though these do not change in nature or substance, they do sometimes exist in themselves for themselves, and at other times by analogy (by which a judgment can be made about the most similar cases). But depending on the circumstances, they undergo very many changes and they vary according to the time, place, persons, deeds, means, causes and the things that support them (whether in the past, present, or future; public or private). Many laws of this sort that in such circumstances have the character of a private right had been set up by Moses, which had been determined by a particular right (in the manner of the Jewish republic), that is, of persons, actions and a specific goal; and it is certain that Christians are free from them.

31. But if there are laws of the mixed kind, being both moral and political—and there are a few—then we must distinguish between the ethical and the political as follows: we consider anything that is moral to be permanent, but whatever is political is not binding as far as its specific decisions are concerned. But if we ponder these things carefully, then the arguments spontaneously collapse which the Anabaptists and some other fanatics have constructed to eliminate Roman laws or any other laws whatsoever from Christian states, in order to foist upon judges the requirement of passing judgment in civil cases according to the forensic laws of Moses. The experts rightly consider this idea not only dangerous and confusing but also wrong and foolish.

32. It remains for us to treat the other degree, or part, of freedom that is properly Christian, the part which deals with the exercise and use of things that are indifferent, or 'middle matters.' These are things which by their own nature are neither good nor bad in a moral sense, and which neither have been prohibited nor commanded by any law, and so they are things that anyone could use in the right way, or the wrong way, or plainly not at all. It is very important to understand this part in order to remove any feeling of despair or superstition about them. For whenever people's hearts are tied up with doubt, controversy arises over whether it is the will of God (and his will should show us the way in all our actions) to use these or those things. Unless help is offered, it is easy to fall into all manner of superstitious ideas. In this way, once a scruple has befallen someone in the use of wool or linen, he will thereafter not be entirely sure about hemp, either. Or if someone should lack the light of God's Word and still not be affected by any scruple, he may out

of profane carelessness cast off his reverence for God and will cause the way that he otherwise will not see as unencumbered to become his own ruin.

33. Therefore since indifferent things are judged to be good or bad not in or of themselves but from the circumstances of their use, we must ponder carefully what in matters of this sort should be left to our freedom. For although it seems that Paul subjected everything of this outward kind to our freedom (Rom 14:14), it was still God's will to restrict this freedom with a double law: the law of faith and love. The first of these is required for the fact that the reason for the freedom in our hearts is with God, so that we are rightly taught and sufficiently established in the lawful use of things that are indifferent, and so that we do them, or dare to do them with a conscience that doubts nothing. For that which of itself is not common or unclean, to him who considers that unclean it does become unclean (Rom 14:14).

34. And so those who are not yet certain about the freedom they have, and so hesitate or doubt in using it, or are laboring under some superstitious idea, for them the use of things that otherwise are indifferent is not indifferent or allowable because what they are doing is done by them not out of faith (Rom 14:5, 14, 22 and 23), and since their hearts are wavering and their consciences doubting [cf. Jas 1:6–8, 17], they are unable to receive God's good gifts with a giving of thanks that comes from the heart that acknowledges God's beneficence and goodness in his gifts—which is still the only way whereby the things God created are made holy for our use (1 Tim 4:[4 and] 5).

35. The lantern of this faith which lights the way not only investigates the nature of the thing that is called 'the middle thing' and reveals whether or not it is middling in and of itself. But also, while it cleanses their hearts (Acts 15:9) it guards the mind and conscience against uncleanliness and sees to it that such things are not wantonly longed-for, conducted in pride, or extravagantly poured out, and that these vices do not befoul whatever in itself is permissible. And it sees to it that they who are clean make pure use of God's gifts with a pure conscience, "for whom all things are pure" (Titus 1:15), who "whether they eat or whether they drink, or whatever they do, they do everything to the glory of God" (1 Cor 10:31).

36. Freedom in matters of this sort is moreover kept in check by the law of love, which demands that we take into account our weaker brothers who have not yet been instructed sufficiently about the privilege of their own freedom, in order to guide their comprehension (and to do that for as long

as they can be taught) and to attend to their upbuilding. For not always do "all the things that are allowed also build up" (1 Cor 10:23). For this reason, the same apostle said: "If what I eat is a stumbling-block for my brother, I shall never eat meat again, lest I cause my brother to stumble" (Rom 14:22; 1 Cor 8:13). But in this matter, it is the responsibility of the weaker and uninformed brothers to leave untouched the rights and freedoms of those who are stronger, and not to condemn him who, knowing his own freedom, does eat (Rom 14:15).

37. But while we should yield to the weak for the purpose of edifying them, to those who are stubbornly superstitious or who are lying in ambush with evil intent we must give up nothing that might lead them to prejudge our freedom, so that we do not by our abstinence confirm them in their evil superstition, nor should we otherwise prejudge those who are strong and well-taught in their own freedom. Accordingly, Paul chided Peter very severely because, when he withdrew himself from the gentiles in order not to offend the Jews, he confirmed the Jews in their stubbornness and offended the gentiles by his hypocrisy (Gal 2:11). But in these two cases Paul displayed an illustration of Christian wisdom: when he circumcised Timothy out of consideration for the weakness of the Jews (Acts 16:3), and when he did not wish to circumcise Titus after he saw that he had to defend Christian freedom over against those who were stubborn and lying in ambush (Gal 2:3–4).

38. But at the same time that faith determines what is allowed in these things it also teaches that our freedom always remains undiminished, even though we accommodate ourselves to our weak brothers. For faith makes a distinction between freedom itself and the use of freedom, and since the freedom is in our conscience and looks to God, while the use of it is concerned with external things in which the handling of it is not with God only but with people, it judges that among people "not all things are expedient, though all things are allowed" (1 Cor 6:12) and that we must not use our freedom "except for building up" (Rom 14:19).

39. In this way we acknowledge that even the freedom of our consciences is not hindered, because when some political law or ecclesiastical regulation restricts the use of the middle things it is not the freedom itself but only the outward deed that is bound. For strictly speaking it is only God who binds the consciences, as we have said. And yet on occasion a magistrate can, for the good of the nation, order or forbid something to be done that of itself is

an intermediate thing. And the church may decide something of a similar substance for the sake of good order—in such a way, however, that it does not assume for itself any power over the conscience. This case excluded, no one would resist such regulations out of a desire for rebellion without sinning or rightly oppose them—who, whereas he would prefer to guard his conscience, would rather endanger it since it would suffer harm on account of the rebelliousness.

40. But while the magistrate or the church prescribes those actions (if, at least, they are not abusing their rights or transgressing the boundaries of their jurisdiction) and have as their intention not to make the middle matters simply necessary but only because it is on the supposition of the circumstances that they are being commanded or forbidden, then the person will not be committing a sin who, when those circumstances cease to exist, while avoiding an instance of being condemned or scandalized, reverts to using his own freedom, especially if the sword of necessity threatens. For we do not think that regulations of such a sort then retain the power of binding or obligating. But if people extend their own rules to include things that of themselves are good or evil, we don't hesitate to affirm that we should consider this action to be over and above [their right], because there does not exist any cause of danger or offense that we should neglect what God commands or with impunity do what God prohibits us to do, and for this reason we should not, for the sake of our neighbor, offend God (Matt 5:29–30 and 10:37). Nor should we obey the magistrate who makes some rule contrary to God's Word or who does violence to our consciences (Acts 4:19, 24 and 5:29).

41. Until now we have spoken about the objects and degrees, or parts, of Christian freedom, wherein we considered the things that were needed to explain its subject-matter. From these it is easy to see what we should think about the form of Christian freedom. This form exists in having and enjoying those good things by the witness of the Holy Spirit with which He seals that undoubted conviction and full assurance in the hearts of believers about their sonship whereby they have been turned from slaves of the devil into sons of God, and are protected against all the temptations and attacks of sin, the law, and condemnation, and are made certain about their exemption from every bygone slavery (Rom 8:14–15 and following; 2 Cor 1:22; Gal 4:6–7; Eph 4:30).

42. The proximate goal is the tranquility of the consciences of Christians (Luke 1:74; Rom 14:5), who "having been released from sin and become servants of God, have their reward unto holiness, while the goal is life eternal" (Rom 6:22). Therefore, for those who have been granted freedom there follows, as virtues that necessarily accompany them: peace, righteousness, a good conscience, and the joy of the Spirit (Rom 14:17). But the highest goal is the same as the one for God's other benefits: "the praise of his glorious grace" (Eph 1:14).

43. But because that freedom of grace is distinguished from the freedom of glory, those who in this life enjoy the first kind do not yet actually possess the second one; but as children of God they do have the right to it, as they have become his heirs, and are co-heirs with Christ (Rom 8:17). For they are children of the resurrection and sons of God through the Spirit, who is "the pledge, the seal and first-fruits of that inheritance" (Luke 20:36; Gal 4:6; 2 Cor 1:22). In Eph 1:14 the seal of the Spirit "who is the pledge of our inheritance" is said explicitly to have been made "until we acquire possession of it."

44. To this inheritance belongs also the blessed immortality of our souls, as well as the resurrection and the glorified state of our bodies. Although the slavery to corruption and even death itself still keep our bodies bound up in chains, believers do look forward, along with their souls, to the "freedom of glory" and "the redemption of our bodies" on the day when Christ with open hand will declare that they have been redeemed by him. Meanwhile they rest secure in the hope of this freedom "until they, whose lives for a time have been kept safe with Christ in God, when Christ appears will also appear in glory with him" (Rom 8:21 and 23; Gal 5:17; John 6:44; Col 3:3 and 4).

45. From what has been said it can be determined what is the manifold use of this doctrine, following the various degrees of freedom. From the first [two degrees] those who believe possess the fact that their consciences have been put at ease, and they are no longer terrified by the threats of the law, and without compulsion they take delight in the obedience of sonship by the guidance of the law (Ps 1:2). And they are also confident that their acts of obedience, although they are immature and still not perfect, do not displease their benevolent Father, but are acceptable to him in his love.

46. From the two last degrees they reap the benefit that they know their consciences have been released from the power of all people (1 Cor 3:21 and

7:23); and that with true worship (namely, spiritual) they learn to serve God instead of creatures, so that they do not give in to themselves or other people for evil. And that harmony in the church is maintained, while Christian freedom is preserved in indifferent things. And that they are employing God's gifts out of faith for the use to which God had given them, and to guide that use in love for the upbuilding of the neighbor and the general wellbeing.

47. It is also clear that this freedom does not constitute exemption from all laws (both divine and human ones) and that it is not a license for living by the feelings of one's heart and of indulging the sinful desires of the flesh, nor a release from civic responsibility, duties, and payments. For there is nothing to prevent those who are free spiritually from serving with their bodies (1 Cor 7:21); "servants obey your earthly masters, as to the Lord" (Eph 6:5). Therefore, Christians are subject to their kings and magistrates, as before (Rom 13:1), and they seriously condemn all those who under the pretext of Christian freedom attempt to shake off the yoke of magistrates and who enslave themselves to the devil by "turning their freedom into an opportunity for the flesh" (Gal 5:13).

48. The things that the Jews have dreamed up about the temporal kingdom of the Messiah are also in conflict with Christian freedom; nor is the freedom affected by the magnificent arrogance of the Stoics, who paradoxically and illogically make only their own wise men to be free, even though they are possessed by vanity and presumption. Augustine gave this paradox a special status in the church with the following words: "The good man, although he is a slave, is free; but the bad man, even if he reigns, is a slave, and he is a slave not of one man but, what is far more grievous, of as many masters as he has vices" (*City of God*, book 4 chapter 3).

49. But of all people it is the papal teachers who most dangerously affect this very gratifying doctrine, and also the Socinians who are of like mind with the papal teachers, as well as the others who refurbish their teachings; because, not being content with the uses of the law as we described them earlier, they turn the Gospel into a demanding law for us and they present Christ as a second Lawgiver who does not so much fulfill the law of Moses by his own obedience as to perfect it by means of adding new precepts, in order that believers should seek righteousness in the keeping of the law and hope to gain eternal life through it. But Christianity is overturned by this teaching

since it hides from view the office of Christ, and especially takes away his benefits, and completely overturns the foundation of our salvation and the comfort of our consciences.

SOURCES

[Pseudo-Augustine] *Question 61 on the Old and New Testament*
It has been commanded that these things which are not dangerous should be observed in such a way that they would not be harmful if they are admitted out of necessity, because they have been commanded not for salvation but for their reverence. But that which is entirely unallowed and also not mitigated by any kind of necessity that would not make its admission a hindrance, that is never permissible.

Bernard, *Treatise on Grace and Free Choice*
Since a three-fold freedom is set before us, freedom from sin, from misery, and from necessity. The last one of these is bestowed on us in the state of nature; by the first freedom [from sin] we are restored by grace, while the second one is kept for us in the fatherland [Heb 11:14–16]. The first is called the freedom of nature, the second one is called freedom of grace, and the third, the freedom of glory. The first possesses great honor, the second great virtue, and the third, last virtue, possesses the pinnacle of delight.

ON THE RELIGIOUS
PRACTICE OF INVOCATION

President: Antonius Walaeus
Respondent: Antonius Delienus

Invocation, or prayer, is a human duty through which God communicates his benefits to his church and by which at the same time we repay our gratitude for these benefits (1–2). Only God should be invoked, as He is the greatest giver of all good things and averts evil (4); only He examines the heart, and only He is trustworthy as the almighty Lord who knows all our needs (5). In disobedience to the command of God, Roman Catholics pray to angels and deceased saints (6–11). We should call upon God alone, not just in his essence, but also according to the divine persons individually (12–14). Weak and sinful people need a mediator to get access to the holy God: Christ, through the merit and efficacy of his death, is the only one who is able to intercede for us (15–19). Repentance, humility, filial fear of God, true faith, and a true desire are necessary aspects of prayer (21–28). Prayers that are offered in public should be heard and not silent, as is the practice among some Anabaptists; they should be understood by all, and not spoken in a foreign or ancient tongue (31). The words of prayer should not be repeated needlessly (32). So-called 'form prayers' are lawful and very useful (33) but praying freely is fostered (34). Attention is paid to the variety of physical bearing during prayer, and to gestures, location, and time (35–43). Our prayers should focus on people of all kinds and on God's (already received or future) benefits (44–52).

1. Since up to this point, we have given a treatment of God's benefits to the Church, it now follows that we should treat next our own remaining duties, and the means through which these benefits are communicated to us.

2. Among the foremost of our duties and the means of this communication is the true invocation, or adoration, of the true God. This invocation is like a

key whereby we unlock the treasuries of divine benefits, and repay to God the debt of gratitude from our faithful hearts, in the same way that David links the two together: "Offer sacrifices of thanksgiving to God and render your vows to the Most High and call upon him in the time of trouble and I shall deliver you, that you may glorify me" (Ps 50:14 [and 15]).

3. For a succinct treatment of this doctrine of invocation that is so necessary we should explain: 1) who is to be invoked; 2) through whom he should be invoked; 3) how he should be invoked; 4) what should be the object with which true invocation deals.

4. All the rules of invocation taught in various places of Scripture instruct us that, as the greatest giver of all good things and who averts evil, we should call upon God alone, namely the Father, Son, and Holy Spirit. These rules are summarized in Christ's words: "You shall worship the Lord your God and him only you shall serve" (Matt 4:10). The same is taught by all God's promises, the summation of which occurs in the Apostle's saying (Rom 10:13): "Whoever calls upon the name of the Lord shall be saved." And lastly, the same is taught in the Old and New Testaments by all the examples of the saints, none of whom ever directed his prayer to anyone other than the true God. In the same manner Christ himself instructed his disciples to direct their prayers to none other than "our Father who is in heaven" (Matt 6:9).

5. The same is shown also by the requirements that must be met in the one who is going to be invoked. For he should be someone who examines the hearts, so that he can tell apart the ones who worship in Spirit and truth from those who are hypocrites. Solomon (1 Kgs 8:39) and Paul (Rom 8:27) bear witness that it is only God who meets this requirement. Secondly, he should be the kind of person in whom we can place our trust, not just as a bountiful and kind-hearted father, but also as an almighty Lord. The prophet Jeremiah (17:7) and also the apostle Paul (Rom 10:14) teach that we should place this trust in God alone. And lastly, he should be someone who knows the general and specific needs (both internal and external ones) of all those people throughout the whole world who call upon him. And this requirement is met only by the omniscient and omnipresent God, as seen in Ps 139:2, Matt 6:32, Heb 4:13, etc.

6. There is clearly nothing that can be brought in to contradict the first two requirements. And what the papal teachers put over against the third requirement is foolish and beside the point: the 'mirror of the Trinity'

wherein all these earthly things shine forth. This is foolish because their claim is made apart from Scripture (and therefore as easily rejected as it is stated), and because it is by an act that is voluntary and of free choice and not by a natural and necessary act whereby the objects of divine knowledge are communicated to the blessed ones. For even the "angels who always behold the Father's face" (Matt 18:10) still "do not know the day of judgment" (Mark 13:32); "and to the principalities and powers in the heavenly places the manifold wisdom of God is made known through the church" (Eph 3:10), and "no-one in heaven or on earth or under the earth was able to open the book (that is, the book of God's providence concerning the church) nor to look into it, except the victorious Lion of the tribe of Judah and the root of David" (Rev 5:5).

7. The argument that others bring forward, that these things are revealed through angels or through believers who have departed from this world into heaven, does not match their hypothesis. For they confine deceased believers to the fires of Purgatory for a period of time, away from the sight of God. Secondly, neither angels nor dying believers know our inward needs, since they are not 'knowers of the heart' [Acts 1:24, 15:8]; nor are we always in the presence of the angels or the departing saints, nor they with us. For following their death, these saints are occupied with their own salvation, while the angels for the most part spend their time in their own abode, that is, heaven (Gen 28:12; Luke 1:19, etc.).

8. Nor are they helped any further by this last thing that they fabricate: that God reveals and commends the needs and prayers of believers to the saints in heaven so that they in turn reveal and commend them to God. For there is no need whatsoever for this detour circumventing Scripture; for the access to God in Christ that lies open for us is the same as the one that was always available to believers before any saints were received into heaven. And this is invincibly refuted by those places in Holy Scripture wherein the ones who have died are deprived of this knowledge of particular things of this life, as can be seen from Job 14:21, Eccl 9:2, 2 Kgs 22:20, Isa 64:2 [probably Isa 63:16 or 64:6], etc.

9. This being the case, it follows that when they call upon angels or the deceased, the papal teachers not only contradict the commandments of God and the examples of all the saints, but also they commit blatant idolatry when

in their prayers they ascribe to them things that God willed to keep for himself alone.

10. And also the little difference in meaning between *latreia* ('due service') and *douleia* ('bondage') does not excuse them from the charge of idolatry, because Holy Scripture conveys the idolatry of the gentile and Jewish peoples no less with the word *douleia* than *latreia*, as can be seen in Gal 4:8.8 Indeed, if we must make a distinction between those two terms, then it would be one of increased submission in *douleuein* compared to *latreuein*, since the latter term is used for any and all who provide a service, while the first is properly used of slaves.

11. This difference in the words' meaning introduces a much smaller distinction in the actual matter. For besides the fact that it is obvious (however much they explain it away) how in this invocation of theirs they ascribe divine properties to created beings, there is the additional element that very many of their prayers to the saints are conceived and pronounced with the same words (and the same sentiments) that Holy Scripture teaches should be used in our prayers when we beseech God. This is clear from the expressions in, among others, their 'Little Garden of the Soul' and the 'Marian Psalter' that are taken nearly verbatim from the Psalter of David.

12. When we state on this point that we should call upon God alone, then we are thinking of God not just in a general sense and in his essence, but also according to the [divine] persons. And although Holy Scripture more frequently puts forward the name of the Father in invocations, because the other persons owe their origins to him, and because in the work of our redemption he occupies the primary position, even so there are passages and examples from Scripture that demonstrate that it is possible to call upon the other persons individually, too.

13. For when the Father brings his only-begotten Son into the world, He proclaims this order about him: "And let all the angels of God worship him," as the apostle in Heb 1:6 testifies from Ps 65:6 [apparently Ps 97:7]. Indeed, "therefore he has received the name above every name (even as the Mediator) that at the name of Jesus every knee should bow" (Phil 2:10). And for this reason also Christ's Church throughout the world, and the individual apostles, very often call upon his name in particular, as can be seen from Acts 9:14, 1 Cor 1:2, Rom 1:7, 2 Cor 1:2, Gal 1:3 (etc.), 2 John 1:3, Rev 1:5, etc.

14. All the properties that we stated above as required for genuine invocation show that also the Holy Spirit can be called upon individually. This is shown moreover by the example of the apostles and the first church, as in 2 Cor 13:13, Rev 1:4, and likewise in Acts 4:24 when compared with Heb 3:7 and Acts 28:25 in comparison with Isa 6:3, etc.

15. The second question that we undertook at the beginning to answer is: by whom ought this prayer to be made. For since God is a consuming fire and his eyes are so pure that they cannot stand to look upon iniquity (Hab 1:13), it follows that weak and sinful people must seek a mediator through whom the access to the throne of grace is opened (Heb 4:14, etc.).

16. We think that this mediator should not be sought among angels (as the Platonists once contended) or among deceased saints (as formerly the Antidicomarianites thought, and now the papal teachers who follow them think), because the sort of properties that are required in this mediation do not belong to any one of the angels or the saints who have been received into heaven.

17. For neither angels nor deceased saints were chosen by God for this part of the priestly office, "since no-one takes this honor upon himself, but only he who is called by God, as was Aaron" (Heb 5:4). Nor are they able to appease God's wrath by their own merits and death, or to open for us the access to the throne of grace, as they owe their salvation to nothing other than God's mercy and Christ's mediation (Col 1:20). And not being in all things of like nature with us [Acts 14:15 and Jas 5:17], they cannot know all our needs, or be touched by them in their feelings, as they are not affected by the circumstances of even their own surviving children (Job 14:21), nor do they see the evils that befall their subjects, or their own household (2 Kgs 22:20).

18. But it is only of Christ that the Father swore: "You are a priest forever after the order of Melchizedek, etc.," and therefore He is able to the utmost "to save perfectly those who draw near to God through him" (Heb 7:25). And it is He who through the merit and efficacy of his death "has opened for us a new and living way, and freedom to enter into the heavenly sanctuary" (Heb 10:19). Lastly, it is He who in every respect has been tempted as we are, yet without sin, who can sufficiently be touched with the feelings of our weaknesses (Heb 4:15).

19. Therefore Holy Scripture testifies about no-one else but Christ that he is interceding on our behalf at the right hand of the Father (Rom 8:34), and because "as our high priest he has entered into heaven itself now to appear in the presence of God on our behalf" (Heb 9:24) and because "in him we have a just advocate with the Father" (1 John 2:1). Even Christ himself asserts about himself alone that "I am the way, the truth, and the life, no-one comes to the Father but through me" (John 14:6); and again: "whatever you ask of the Father in my name I shall do it, so that the Father may be glorified in the Son" (John 14:13, etc.), and: "Truly, truly I say to you, whatever you ask from my Father in my name, he will give it to you" (John 16:23).

20. All these things do not, however, prevent the souls of the blessed who are in heaven in the company of the angels themselves from yearning for the coming of the kingdom of Jesus Christ with constant prayer, and from seeking the deliverance of the militant church here on earth, as is seen from the illustration of it in Rev 5:8 and 6:10. And like the believers living on the earth, they solicit God with one accord through the only Mediator Jesus Christ not only for themselves but also for their brothers and their needs, because they are fellow-servants of one and the same master, and members of the same body under the same head. In their eagerness for God's glory and the law of common love, they have been restricted by God, in keeping with their state and knowledge, to fulfilling these reciprocal duties, as is shown by the very many instances and commandments of it that one meets in Scripture.

21. After this explanation of the first two elements, the third one now follows: in what way this invocation should be made so that our prayer may be pleasing to God and salutary and fruitful for us.

22. To this mode we relate the legitimate inward form and disposition of the prayers and the people praying, and also their outward form and disposition.

23. A true and genuine sense of repentance in the one who is going to pray is required before all else for the internal disposition of the prayers and the one praying. And this is not just that general and first repentance, but that particular repentance from sins that have been committed. And it is just as Scripture testifies: "God does not heed sinners" (John 9:31), and many "ask but do not receive because they ask wrongly, so that they may spend it on their own pleasures" [Jas 4:3]. And so [God] warns his people to "put away the evil of their own doings," if it wishes its prayer to be heard (Isa 1:16), and

the apostle John asserts: "If our heart does not condemn us, we have confidence toward God, and whatsoever we ask, we receive of him because we keep his commandments and do what is pleasing to him" (1 John 3:21 [and 22]).

24. On this point Holy Scripture advises us especially to be reconciled with our brothers, and to forgive from the heart those wrongdoings which have been committed against us, as Christ instructed both generally (Matt 5:23) and specifically in the prayer for the forgiveness of sins (Matt 6:12), and most broadly in the parable of two debtors (Matt 18:23 and following).

25. The second element necessary in prayer is "true humility accompanied by child-like reverence" in the one who is praying, in view of both our own state and the majesty and kindness of the one we are beseeching in our prayers, as is clear from the examples of the saints Abraham (Gen 18), David (2 Sam 7), Daniel (Dan 9), etc. It is clear also from what Christ expressly teaches in the parable of the Pharisee and the tax-collector with this exclamation: "Everyone who exalts himself will be humbled, and he who humbles himself will be exalted" (Luke 18:14). And so also the apostle Peter testifies that "God resists the proud but gives grace to the humble" (1 Pet 5:5). And therefore, Christ warns us to so make our prayers that we consider the fact that the one whom we are calling upon is "our Father, who is in heaven, and to whom belongs the kingdom and the power and the glory" (Matt 6:9, 13 and 15).

26. True faith is the third element required here, and not merely the faith with which we generally believe in God and Christ the Mediator—for "how shall they call on him in whom they do not believe?" (Rom 10:14). But we also "place firm confidence in him," that we shall receive the very thing we ask for in accordance with his will. For whoever does not possess this confidence distrusts God's promises, which are both numerous and very clear on this point. And therefore, the apostle James warns us: "If any of you lacks wisdom, let him ask God, who gives generously to all; but let him ask in faith, and without doubting" (Jas 1:5 [and 6]). And Christ himself warns us even much more clearly: "Therefore I say to you, whatever you ask for when you pray, believe that you will receive it and it will be yours" (Mark 11:24).

27. And the final requirement is a genuine endeavor of our heart, towards the one whom we are calling upon, and the one through whom we call (as is clear from the preceding). But it is also a burning desire that arises from the awareness of our need, and a constant right attitude towards the very thing

that we are beseeching in accordance with God's will. For this reason, the prophet David testifies not only that he is lifting up his soul to Jehovah (Ps 25:1, and many other places) but also that he is calling on Jehovah from the depths of sorrow (Ps 130:1) and that he is pouring out his meditations before him and disclosing his own anxieties before him (Ps 142:2, etc.). And therefore, he likens his prayer to the evening offering and incense—which, though the winds often blow it away, in the end it will reach up to heaven (Ps 141:2). And in Ps 123:2 he states: "Behold, as the eyes of servants look to the hand of their masters, and as the eyes of a maidservant to the hand of her mistress, so our eyes look to Jehovah our God, until he grant us his grace."

28. And here is that Spirit of grace and supplication whom God through Christ in the new covenant promises to pour out on the house of David and the inhabitants of Jerusalem, "that they may look upon him whom they have pierced" (Zech 12:10). And here is that "Spirit of adoption through whom we cry, 'Abba, Father,' etc." (Rom 8:15), and who intercedes on our behalf with groans that cannot be uttered, etc., and in harmony with God's will (Rom 8:27).

29. The external mode of invocation exists partly in what we say, partly in our physical gestures, and finally, partly in some other circumstances.

30. Outward speech is not absolutely necessary for prayers that are private, since also internal discourse and merely the groans of the heart are sufficient for God, as can be seen from the example of Moses (Exod 14:15), Hannah (1 Sam 1:13), Nehemiah (Neh 1:4), etc. In other respects it is customary to use outward speech more frequently as witness and aid to internal feelings— even wailing when in great difficulties, like the very many instances of it in the Old and New Testament, even of our Savior (Heb 5:7).

31. We do hold that for public prayers which we share with many other people or in which the minister of the Word leads the church it is altogether necessary that the speech of the one leading in prayer be outward (contrary to the Anabaptists) and that it be understood by the one leading as well as the others (contrary to the papal teachers). For if not, people could not possibly be of one and the same mind towards the same prayer—something that Christ expressly requires on this point (Matt 18:19). And then neither the hearer nor he who occupies the place of the uninformed can say 'Amen' to that sort of prayer, as the apostle notes in very clear terms (1 Cor 14:15–16).

32. We must studiously avoid all vanity in the very form of speaking, and also all repetitions and verbosity, as Christ warns (Matt 6:7), although with that repetition we should not understand the reiteration of the same or similar words if that happens to break out from the distraught feelings of the heart, since even the saints on occasion permit such reiteration in their prayers, including also Christ himself when he was greatly troubled (Matt 26:39 and 42), and when he was hanging upon the cross (Matt 27:46). But what we should understand by that kind of repetition are the vain and empty repetitions [Matt 6:7] that are unnecessary and superstitious, and the rehearsing of the same prayers that are repeated up to a specific number; this was prevalent among the gentiles of former times, and it is prevalent today among the papal teachers. Christ criticizes this practice in the Pharisees and scribes, who under pretense of making long prayers were devouring widows' houses (Matt 23:14; Luke 20:47).

33. At this point the question often arises whether it is permitted in prayers that are public or private to use previously composed sets of words. It is our contention that so long as they are spoken from the heart with due intent, the formulae are not only lawful but very useful. For it has not been granted to each and every Christian to compose fresh sets of words that are suitable, and in large gatherings the attention of the hearers is helped considerably by sets of words that are familiar to them. For this reason even God himself prescribed the form of blessings for the priests in the Old Testament (Num 6:24 and following). In fact, when Christ was hanged on the cross he used the form of prayer that had been observed previously by David as type (Matt 27:46). And Christ's disciples asked him to teach them how to pray (Luke 11:2), just as John had taught his disciples; and Christ responded to them: "When you pray, say: 'Our Father who is in heaven, etc.'" It is clear from the context of these words that Christ's prayer is not just the norm for correct prayer but moreover the correct form of praying. And the whole early church always considered this to be beyond debate.

34. Yet at the same time we acknowledge that it is very useful and almost even necessary that all the more advanced believers, and especially the shepherds of the church, foster in themselves the gift of praying freely, even without a set of words that were made previously, so that they will be able to make prayers of supplication and thanksgiving that are fitting to the immediate situation and to needs that suddenly come up. We read that holy men, and also the prophets and apostles, did this frequently in this way. It

will not be difficult for us to do likewise, by observing the method that they employ in their prayers, and the required practice which this method involves.

35. One can observe a variety of physical bearing in the prayers of the saints. Moses fell upon his face (Deut 9:18); David was stretched upon the ground and clothed in sackcloth when he prayed for his infant son (2 Sam 12:16). Job was seated in ashes and dust (Job 42:6); the Israelites were standing (Neh 9:5); Ezra and Paul were kneeling down (Ezra 9:5 and Acts 20:36). Solomon prayed on bended knees and with hands outstretched (2 Chron 6:13); Christ with eyes lifted up towards heaven (John 17:1), while the tax-collector prayed with his eyes cast down to the earth (Luke 18:13). And while men pray with their heads uncovered, women do so with covered head, according to the apostle's instruction (1 Cor 11:4).

36. A comparison of all these things with each other makes it clear that a certain amount of freedom was given for various gestures, but that at the same time we should adopt the kind of postures that are best suited to every nation's own customs and that promote rather than hinder the attentiveness of our soul. We should avoid every form of vanity in those postures, but also carelessness and pride; and the gestures should convey, without pretense and in a most suitable manner, the inner disposition and ardent longing of those who are praying. Yet the saints most frequently employed the bending of the knees, and so that gesture was sometimes used in the absolute sense for the prayer itself, as one can see from Rom 11:4 and 14:11, and likewise in Eph 3:14. And in the same vein the apostle links the stretching forth or lifting up of hands to the injunction that they should pray everywhere (1 Tim 2:8).

37. The circumstances to which we must also pay attention in prayers are location and time.

38. As for location, during the time of upbringing that is the Old Testament, any location was permitted [for prayer], for God did hear the prayer of Jacob and Hezekiah when they were upon their beds, and Job sitting upon the ash-heap, Samson in the temple-court of the Philistines, and Jonah from the belly of the whale. Yet at the same time believers were also restricted to certain specific locations as sanctuaries of God's presence, both before and after the law was given (Gen 4:14; 28:16; and 35:1; Exod 3:12, etc.). These were either locations according to regulation, like the tabernacle and the temple (to which also Daniel turned in his prayers from exile, in Dan 6:11), or extraordinary

ones, which the prophets designated apart from a regulation (Josh 8:30; 1 Sam 14:36; 1 Kgs 18:36 etc.).

39. In the New Testament, however, as the prophet Malachi (1:11) had foretold and as Christ testifies: "The hour was coming and now is, when the Father shall be adored neither upon the mountain, nor in Jerusalem; but the true worshipers will worship the Father in Spirit and in truth" (John 4:23 [and 24]), and therefore the apostle orders that "men lifting up holy hands without wrath and dissention to pray in every place" (1 Tim 2:8).

40. Christ warns us that for praying privately we should seek out hidden places, ones that are removed from on-lookers (Matt 6:6), so that we do not appear to be longing for the close attention and praise of men (which, as Christ in the same passage clearly states is what hypocrites do), and moreover so that our own attentiveness thereby is less interrupted. It was for this reason that Christ selected lonely places to pray, as is seen from Matt 14:23, etc. But in public and shared prayers we should not neglect to gather together, as the apostle cautions in Heb 10:25, since it is to the assembly of believers and their oneness of heart that Christ gave this promise: "When two of you upon earth agree concerning anything they shall ask, it shall be done for them by my Father who is in heaven; for where two or three are gathered in my name, there I am in their midst" (Matt 18:19–20).

41. For this reason those pilgrimages that the Roman Catholics undertake to the tomb of our Lord or to other, far-flung places for the sake of prayer are altogether superstitious, since God now gives equal hearing to the prayers of believers wherever they are. And this sort of people, contrary to the commandment of love, expose themselves to unnecessary dangers, and often, under the pretext [of going to pray] they unfairly let down those people whose care has been entrusted particularly to them. And there is also no superstition lacking to the actions of those who for the purpose of making private prayers made it their custom to visit churches and sacred buildings when empty of the gathering of believers, even though other more private places were available to them. This is superstitious because Christ explicitly condemns this religious practice among the hypocrites, in the passage cited earlier (Matt 6:5–6, etc.).

42. The time suitable for prayer is any moment at all when faith, hope, love, and our sense of need (public as well as private) remind us that we ought to pray. For this reason, Christ, too, commands his disciples that "they should

always pray and not lose hope" (Luke 18:1), and the apostle that "they should pray without ceasing" (1 Thess 5:17). And yet that is not a reason to commend the doings of the ancient Euchites or some monks nowadays, who profess that they spend their whole life-time chanting and praying. Prayer ought to be an aid and not a hindrance to the other works of love for God or the neighbor.

43. Meanwhile, we readily acknowledge that we should assign certain days for public prayers, and for private ones a certain time of the day, to assist us in our carelessness and weakness, as in the case of David (Ps 55:18), Daniel (Dan 6:11), and Peter (Acts 10:9). But it should be done in such a way that all superstition stays away, and vainglory [Phil 2:3], or scruple of conscience if strong necessity or individual or public charitable deeds demand an interruption to prayer, since in this matter Christ or the apostles handed down no precise rule, and since even the groanings alone of the heart to God could take its place, as we have pointed out earlier in thesis 30, and as the exiled church of Israel in Babylon showed (Ps 137).

44. The last that remains for us to explain is the object around which our prayer should turn, and it is twofold: either the person for whom we pray or the thing for which we ask in our prayer.

45. As far as the person is concerned, we should pray not only for ourselves or those who are dear to us, but also for anyone at all (1 Tim 2:2)—even for our enemies and persecutors, as Stephen displayed in an exemplary way (Acts 7:60). The only exception is for those who sin against the Holy Spirit with the sin unto death; we are forbidden to pray for them (1 John 5:16). But in particular it is recommended in Scripture that we pray for kings and those who are placed in prominent positions (1 Tim 2:2), shepherds and overseers of the church (1 Thess 5:25; Heb 13:3, etc.). Also commended for prayer is the church itself and all the saints, those who are imprisoned or subjected for the sake of Christ's cross (Acts 12:5; Heb 13:3), the sick and the oppressed (Jas 5:14). And we should pray for brothers who commit sins that do not lead unto death (1 John 5:16).

46. The things for which we call upon God are the divine benefits offered [to us] that serve God's glory or the needs and wellbeing of people; and that we have received in the past, or that we are to receive in the future.

47. It is by the apostle's injunction that we should give thanks to God for the benefits that we have received in the past: "Give thanks always for everything to God the Father in the name of our Lord Jesus Christ" (Eph 5:20). And we should do so not only in times of joy and gratitude, but also in sad and difficult times, whenever God decides to train or try us by them, as in the case of Job (chapter 1:21) and the apostles (Acts 5:41).

48. The prayer for future benefits, whether they are shared in common or individual, are of two kinds: the prayer to ward off those evils we should fear, or the prayer of supplication for the good things that we should hope for. These benefits are bodily or spiritual, and both are also either absolutely necessary for our salvation and the glory of God, or they are necessary for another reason. Therefore, we posit that the ones of this latter kind should be asked for conditionally, and as the former are absolute, we should ask for them without condition.

49. Here the question arises, whether it is not permitted for us or other people to pray God to ward off anything good, or to invoke anything evil. We reply that there are certain bodily and spiritual goods which, because the holy men deemed them to be beyond their own capabilities, they sometimes humbly prayed to avoid them (as is clear from the examples of Moses in Exod 3 and Jeremiah in Jer 1), or because they feared that they might abuse them, in the way that the wise man prayed equally to ward off too many riches and poverty (Prov 30:8–9).

50. In the Scriptures various examples may be found of imprecations wherein the saints cursed the day that they were born because of the severity of the hardships that have come over them (Job 3:3 and Jer 20:14)—but it rather seems that these prayers arose from their own frailty. Or these imprecations were made to declare their own innocence, and with the proviso that if they had committed one thing or another, they wish God to punish them. Of this sort of imprecation there are many examples in sacred history. But [they never called down curses] from Satan or hell, like the gentiles and the papal priests do, who are impiously accustomed to invoke curses upon themselves. And, lastly, the saints offered imprecations as a special testimony of their own eagerness and zeal for God's glory and the safe-keeping of other people, for whose sake they at some time put off even their own salvation, as we see in the case of Moses (Exod 32:32) and Paul (Rom 9:3).

51. And there are also various examples of imprecations against other people, that is, against those who are upright, or against the unrighteous. Against the upright, to set them straight by chastising them if they do not heed warnings, as in the example of it in Job 34:36. There are very many examples, in both the Old and the New Testament, of imprecations against the unrighteous, the enemies of the Church and God's glory, as is seen in 2 Tim 4:14: "Alexander the metalworker did me much harm; the Lord will repay him according to his deeds" and in Rev 6:10: "How long, O Lord who art holy and true, do you not judge and avenge our blood on those who dwell upon the earth?"

52. But believers should not follow these examples rashly, unless the signs of such stubborn and incorrigible hostility are very clear. And otherwise, we should heed the warning of the apostle James, always in the case of private offenses "not to grumble against one another" (Jas 5:9). And the warning of Christ: "Bless those who curse you, and do good to those who hate you, and pray for them who treat you despitefully and persecute you, that you may be children of your Father who is in heaven" (Matt 5:44 [and 45]). To him be the glory and the praise forever. Amen.

ON ALMSGIVING AND FASTING

President: Antonius Thysius
Respondent: Johannes Westerburgh

Almsgiving and fasting are important acts in the life of the Christian that arise in response to the command to love one's neighbor (1, 4). Almsgiving consists in deeds of charity performed in faith and love, and 'in the hope of obtaining a divine reward' (3). The foundations for almsgiving are the inequality of possessions (5–9) and the bonds between people (10–11). Next, the disputation identifies the persons concerned (13–25) and the things that are shared (26–27). What it means to give or to receive is defined thereafter, and distinctions are drawn between giving freely and lending at interest (28–35). In sum, almsgiving, to which several promises are associated (37–38), is characterized by 'sympathy, benevolence, and beneficence of every kind towards the poor and helpless' (36). Fasting and vigil-keeping are the subject of the second part of this disputation (39–59). As a form of self-discipline, fasting consists in the abstinence from food and drink to help the believer focus upon prayer (39). After defining the term (39–41), the disputation identifies several characteristics of keeping vigil. It does not arise from the human will but as a divine ordinance (42). It is of a 'free disposition according to circumstances' (43; 44–47). It is not limited to particular times or occasions (46) and it does not bind the conscience (47). It consists in restricting or withholding oneself from food and drink (48–49). Indeed, it is non-essential in and of itself (50); it has certain goals (51–53), a particular manner (54–55), and produces various results (56). The disputation closes with a discussion of vigils (58–59), which are meant freely to take a part of the night to pray and meditate on the return of the Lord.

1. Among good works the outpouring of prayer to God stands out as an important duty of faith, although as far as it is poured out for other people, prayer also relates to the love towards our neighbor. In the same way, the giving of alms is an outstanding example of love for our neighbor, and when

accompanied by the practice of fasting it adds no small weight to the words of prayer (Matt 6:1, 5, 16; Acts 10:2, 3, 4). And with the help of God, in this disputation we shall undertake to treat these two.

2. The word *eleēmosynē*, which comes from 'having compassion,' means 'mercy' in Latin; that is, the sense of affection whereby the plight of other people touches us. But it also includes the effect of it: averting evil from our neighbor and helping him. The word is used for every 'act of kindness,' so that it is the gentleness of compassionate feeling (Jas 3:13), but especially for the support and aid that help the needs of the poor.

3. Almsgiving is an act of charity towards the neighbor, whereby someone who is devout, merciful, and sympathetic to the misery of another, someone who is kind and beneficent, comes to the aid of those who are truly poor and need the supports of this life. He does so from his own goods and in proportion to his financial resources and their current need, out of true faith and burning love for God and his neighbor, all in the hope of obtaining a divine reward.

4. And so we relate almsgiving to the love we have for our neighbor, that is, to the second part of the worship of God. But this love frequently includes the entire service and piety toward God (Matt 7:12; Rom 13:8–10), since the second table of the Law is connected to the first (Jas 2:10–11) and shown to be so by this love (because hypocrites frequently go undetected by the outward show of the first table's divine worship: Hos 6:6, Matt 9:13). In the same way 'almsgiving,' which is a particular act of love towards the neighbor, a very high degree of love and not its last part, stands for love, and *par excellence* is given the name 'righteousness and love' (Dan 4:27; Heb 6:10).

5. The premise for almsgiving is ownership of goods and inequality in possessions. For God, at the time of the first creation, although He created the world and everything in it for the use of all mankind in general, He gave Paradise to Adam in particular (as the first created human and begetter of all mankind) like a basilica to an emperor; and after the fall, it was to him that He gave the edict: "In the sweat of your brow you will eat your bread." But after the flood, the peoples and lands were divided (with God so disposing it) among the three sons of Noah. And also assuming a place of their own were the taking and giving of possession, the transmission of inheritance, and the acquisition by the right of war or other means. And the ownership of things is based on a common law, both divine and human.

6. The origin of rich and poor comes from this inequality of ownership. God declares that He is the Creator of both rich and poor (Prov 22:2), and Christ states that we shall always have the poor (Matt 26:11). Nevertheless, since riches do not make anyone acceptable to God, so too poverty is not a cause of shame for anyone, since in his own person Christ has sanctified it (2 Cor 8:9). And piety approves rich and poor alike (1 Tim 6:17–18; Matt 5:3) so long as the rich person does not confide in his riches but rejoices in his humility and the poor does not despair in his poverty but rejoices in his exaltation (Mark 10:24; Jas 1:9–10).

7. And the apostles did not abolish ownership of goods, or inequality of ownership, at the beginning of the Gospel-era, by their sharing of goods (Acts 2 and 4): "All who believed were together in one place and held everything in common." For their sharing was not a universal sharing by each and every Christian, nor was it a sharing of all their goods, nor was it presented as precedent, and perpetual law. But it was a special case in the church at Jerusalem, and it was in response to the state of the church at that particular time, done by the voluntary gathering of certain people and goods, as is clear from chapter 5:4. Moreover, it states clearly that Christ owned a purse (John 12:6 and 13:29); and the apostles and the believers, too, had their own purses. Hence the giving of alms also had its proper place.

8. And so [the sharing of goods recorded in Acts] is not a basis for the communism of some of the Anabaptists, which in reality removes all ownership and possession and consequently also the practice of almsgiving among believers. Nor is it a basis for 'the common life' of certain monks who profess by a special rule that they renounce property, ownership and any contact with money. Hence the proverb: "A monk who has an obol, isn't worth an obol."

9. Nevertheless, though sharing goods among Christians does not happen by possession, yet it remains by use, and this is fixed by a law of God forever (Deut 15; Mark 14:7). And this law is not, as some of the Scholastics would have it, an action only of someone's unbound will (and so only an encouragement to charity) but an ordinance of God's precept or law that, subject to the charge of sin, binds the conscience and that is free only with respect to some of its circumstances.

10. And so [sharing goods by use] is based upon God's wise counsel and will, which so governs and variously arranges everything that He bestows more

upon one and less upon another and has brought together poor and rich (Prov 22:2), whom He joined together by a natural bond and the bonds of common blood and politics (as man is a civil and social creature) so that the one would offer a hand of support to the other and so the abundance of the one would assist the other in his need (Isa 58:7; 2 Cor 8:13–14). This all the more so because while God kept the absolute and highest dominion for himself (Ps 24:1; 1 Cor 10:26), He did grant the use to the wealthy man and established him as the distributor of his gifts, in order to disburse them faithfully also to the poor (Luke 16:10–12). And although the wealthy had the duty to do this, God added promises of rich reward and interest from the Lord so that it might be conducted much more faithfully (Prov 19:17), and He added serious warnings, should the task be ignored (Prov 21:13).

11. A uniquely Christian bond is added to our natural and civil bonds. By this bond the believers, as members of a mystical body, are united into one body under Christ their head and have God as their common Father, and Christ, God's first-born Son, as their Brother. Having been adopted by God into sons and regenerated by his Spirit, they are brothers of one another, and through Christ they become heirs of everything, and by Him they are obligated more stringently to the special debt of offering assistance. Hence Christ, too, declares that what is done for His poor is done to Him (Matt 25:40).

12. For a more complete treatment of almsgiving we should also consider: the persons (who and for whom), the thing (what and how much should be shared), the act of sharing and the way it is done, and also the promises that are joined to it.

13. As far as the person giving is concerned, this is a virtue and generosity that all devout people share, to the extent that everyone, at least in their affection, should be ready for every duty of charity and to offer what he can to his neighbor, as his modest means allow. This virtue belongs also to those of slender means and goes as far as paying one or two small coins—like that widow who from her poverty put in her entire livelihood (Luke 21:4). Indeed, it extends to giving a drink of cool water (Matt 10:42); and for this reason the thief is ordered to work with his hands, so that he might be able to provide for him who has need (Eph 4:28). And in God's eyes, this duty is not assessed by the amount or the outward price, but by the affection of the heart, and the readiness of the soul.

14. But [this virtue] is peculiar to the pious people who are wealthy, whose goods God has increased, whose riches and abundance ought to serve the needs of others, and they should do so out of their abundance (Mark 12:44). They are bound to give "what they have left over," or from what they have (Luke 11:41). In fact, if it should be of use, then they can be "willing beyond their means" (2 Cor 8:3), as much as a tenth (Luke 18:12) of their goods, even up to a half (Luke 19:8).

15. And yet they should not pour forth all their resources to the point of their own financial demise (2 Cor 8:12–13). For the faith bids the believer to provide also for himself and those dear to him (1 Tim 3:4–5), and well-ordered love demands it (Matt 22:39). And it is characteristic of Christian prudence to reserve for oneself a source, that a kind of river of generosity may flow perennially, from which one can draw for others—unless it happens that a specific commandment (Mark 12:41) or a pressing need (1 Cor 13:3) demands otherwise.

16. When, in Luke 12:33, Christ speaks these words, "sell your possessions and give alms," he does not order that selling is a must; he is declaring more the attitude that should affect believers, than that they should perish from poverty as poor people. In other words, what he says in an absolute sense we should understand in a relative sense. Or when in Matt 19:21 he says to the rich young man, "if you wish to be perfect, sell what you have and give to the poor," then he is not proposing a perfection for the perfect over and above God's law. Instead, he is adapting the universal law that we should deny ourselves everything—even our own lives, should God demand it (Mark 8:34, 36)—in a particular situation to his specific order for the unwell soul of the man, and he brings out into the open the hidden disease of his greed. As the subsequent account clearly reveals, the man shows by his proud boast in admitting he has fulfilled the law how far that is off the mark.

17. And as for those "to whom should be given," they are the pitiable people worthy of our compassion, that is, all who are poor. Taking the word 'poor' in the general sense, it stands for beggars who have no possessions and also for those who have very little and do not provide for themselves what they need to live, at least according to the present condition of life for a time (Ps 41:2; Isa 26:6). That is, they are people who lack the supports of this life, and need someone else's assistance. About these people Christ says: "Give to all who ask" (Matt 5:42). And that does not mean generally each and every

449

person who asks, but him who asks out of need, and such as are unable to repay (Luke 14:12).

18. But we do not consider among their number those who are fit, or wayfarers and professional beggars, who, having been dulled by their base and idle laziness, practice mendicancy and put the security of their livelihood on it, and by feigning a state of wretchedness, by means of various tricks and craftily thought-up pretenses with which they would arouse compassion, by going about in public, door-to-door, or showing up at busy crossroads, they ask for a small gift, and in this way they unfairly eat up someone else's bread. In fact, they often make a profit and a rich income from it, contrary to the law that had been made at the beginning, "in the sweat of your brow you shall eat your bread" (Gen 3[:19]), which Paul interprets, "if anyone does not want to work, he should not eat" (2 Thess 3:10–11). For they are not truly needy who, while they are able to feed themselves from the labor of their hands, actually rob those who are truly needy of what is owed to them. But these people surely are guilty of deceit and robbery, even sacrilege.

19. But we do not put in the same category those beggars who due to a lack of charity are forced to beg for help—since no provision is made for those who are poor in a legitimate way according to God's law (Deut 15:4)—out of necessity (which at this point does not consider the law) either at private houses, like the sore-covered Lazarus (Luke 16:20), or in the open street, like that blind man (Luke 18:35) and the cripple (Acts 3:2).

20. On the other hand, however, among them we do reckon those beggars who are healthy, those monastic beggars or mendicant orders, who by a new arrangement that goes against antiquity (which acknowledged only monks who worked and which considered 'the lazy bellies' as robbers; Socrates in [Cassiodorus,] *Tripartite Ecclesiastical History*, book 8), and who under the guise of piety, with remarkable superstition, [adopt] voluntary poverty and mendicancy, whereby they do away with their personal possessions, and gobble up those belonging to another, and live off the hard work and sweat of other people; in fact, under this very pretext of poverty they possess a vast amount of earthly possessions. And with a perpetual vow they willingly take this cross upon themselves and volunteer to undergo it. This is a cross that they ought not to assume upon themselves but which should be borne patiently if God had placed it upon them; and this outward curse of God (Deut 28:22), which people should pray Him to avert (and they should flee

from it, insofar as that is possible with God's curse), they put under the category of blessing, indeed of piety and sanctity, and works of perfection and of people who are perfect, and to this punishment they ascribe the greatest merits, even the merits of supererogation.

21. And yet in a well-established nation those mendicants should in no way be tolerated, since God's command, "and there shall be no needy among you," [Deut 15:4] is not just a rule posited about everyone's duty but to some extent it is also about mendicancy. And even the emperor follows this same law, in the *Codex Concerning Healthy Beggars*. And those who moreover conduct themselves in the church in a disorderly fashion—that is, contrary to God's order—should not, the apostle states, be given food or tolerated, but he prescribes that they should rather be reprimanded (2 Thess 3:6–13).

22. With the words "those who ask" [Matt 5:42] are meant those who ask for good reason, and who are compelled to ask, and so who upon thoughtful inquiry and investigation are considered deserving of mercy and generosity. Foremost among their ranks are: 1) widows and orphans (Exod 22:22), 2) foreigners (Lev 10:18), 3) the weak and infirm, among whom are counted the lame, deaf, blind, dumb, leprous, etc. (Matt 25:36; Luke 14:13), 4) those who are weak on account of age, like infants and the elderly (1 Tim 5:3, 16), 5) those who ask for various reasons not their own fault, like people who have been driven to poverty by shipwreck, floods, fires, robbery, attacks of enemies, etc.; and we add to them the bashful poor who do not dare to admit their needs. And lastly, it includes 6) those who for professing the Gospel have been stripped of their financial means (Heb 10[:34]). With these people we link those who have been captured by enemies, especially enemies of the Christian religion. Some of them are physically feeble, others robbed of the ability to obtain a living, and still others who are not able to provide enough for themselves regardless of however much they do. These people should be assisted each according to his or her need; some completely, others partially, and again some others only for a period of time.

23. And so you should understand the words "everyone who asks" [Matt 5:42 and Luke 6:30] to mean any such person (without discrimination), whether he is a foreigner or a citizen and compatriot, stranger or relative by blood, friend or foe, believer or unbeliever (Matt 5.34, 44 and Luke 6:27, 32). In short, "every neighbor." And therefore our neighbor is anyone at all who is in need of our help in light of the state he is in, and for whose help and

assistance we are given the opportunity and the means, as Christ teaches (over against the Jews) in the parable of the wounded man (Luke 10:30).

24. But at the same time we should, depending on the degree of affinity and fellowship, exercise greater generosity towards those who are our own, namely our relatives, than to strangers (1 Tim 5:8, 16); and towards members of the household of faith and the saints rather than the gentiles (Gal 6:10); it is this especially that 2 Pet 1:7 calls "brotherly love." But while we should begin with those who are own, we ought not to stop with them.

25. We should not consider among this group [of all who ask] the "pastors and teachers of the churches," as some have thought. For what is paid to them are not alms but remuneration for work that is done (Matt 10:10; 1 Cor 9:4, 7; 1 Tim 5:18). And as to the fact that it says some women ministered to Christ from their own financial resources (Luke 8:2,3), although they displayed exceptional generosity, yet what was done and confirmed by those women themselves is what Christ generally taught and instructed his own to do (1 Cor 9:14).

26. So much concerning the persons. As for the actual "thing that is to be given," it consists not only of payment but of any help and work that lightens human need as Christ designates them: breaking bread for the hungry; giving a drink to the thirsty and clothing to him who is cold, shelter and hospitality to the stranger; and similarly, offering ransom for the captive, and care for the sick (Isa 58:7; Matt 25:35; Luke 3:11 and 14:12). Elsewhere these are summed up as "food and shelter" (1 Tim 6:8).

27. One should not, however, give away what belongs to someone else, or what has been obtained unjustly—that is robbery. And therefore, the following text does not apply here: "Make for yourselves friends by means of unrighteous Mammon," [Luke 16:9] since that should be taken not so much as being about wrongly obtained wealth (since it is God's will that our generosity should flow forth from a source that is pure) as about people's very frequently unjust abuse of it.

28. Then again, regarding the one who gives, the mode of the actual communion and imparting with the poor is that with respect to the goods everyone should not only give according to his own financial means, but also sincerely and secretly—for God and in his presence—with respect to his intention: not hypocritically and for self-advancement, that is, by false display

in the open to be seen by men for the sake of one's own glory (Matt 6:1, 2, 4). It should not be done under pressure, on the command of other people, by obligation and with a heavy heart; but willingly, readily, promptly, and with a cheerful heart. Otherwise it would not be pleasing and acceptable to God (Rom 12:8; 2 Cor 8:12 and 9:7). It should not be done from a desire and hope of receiving financial gain, but graciously, for the former would not be humane or charitable, but the professional pursuit of financial profit (Luke 6:33). It should not be done sparingly, but bountifully (2 Cor 9:6). And lastly it should be done out of faith in God and Christ (1 Tim 1:5), and out of love towards our neighbor (1 Cor 13:3). For in this way that deed is both of will and power (Mark 14:7) and so that it should nevertheless be governed by the rule of love.

29. But regarding the one to whom it is given, it should be administered according to the need that each person has; that is, by a certain equality and geometric proportion. It should be done with discernment of the person, cause, place and time; or when, to what extent, where and in what way. In these things prudence and circumspection very much should be kept in view (2 Cor 8).

30. In their turn, the poor who receive alms have the duty to be content with their lot and should not ask unless they are truly needy, and ask only to the extent that they are needy. And with an equally cheerful heart they should accept the little that is given from a cheerful heart. And they should always think that what is sufficient for sustaining natural life is much, and great, and they should thank God for causing pious people to arise who care for them.

31. This care of the poor is either private, for individuals, or it is public, when for all the needy people taken together who have been driven by want into this category. In a nation, a devout magistrate provides the care, or in the church its leaders. And the care is provided through serious, careful, suitable men who have been approved also by public testimony, with the support of the spontaneous munificence of religious people, after a collection has been taken from everyone, man for man, and person by person, for common use and openly, faithfully and wisely, in accordance with the need of each poor person.

32. The nation appointed almoners for this purpose, while the church appointed deacons and the deaconry (i.e., for the poor; Acts 6:1), as well as the Gazophylacium, or 'sacred treasury,' not only for the church's business

but also to provide support to the poor (Luke 21:1). And for this reason the church's treasury goes by the special name of treasury for the poor. And hence our pious ancestors devoutly undertook everywhere to build guesthouses, hospitals, homes for the aged, orphanages, nurseries for children, homes for the widows, etc. If a common and universal concern for the poor is added to these, then the care for the poor will lack hardly anything at all. Yet on this point we reject the thinking of those who under pretense of individual and voluntary care for the poor cause the public care to be overthrown, and vice versa.

33. And connected to almsgiving, in fact included in it, is giving a loan, which is paid to those who are not altogether needy, but needy for a short period of time. And we must care for such people by giving a loan, which should be done without interest, according to that statement in Deut 15:8: "Open your hand, and you will lend him sufficient for what he is in need." And the Psalmist: "The just man shows mercy and lends" (Ps 37:26); which Christ repeats: "Give to him who asks, and do not turn aside from the one who would borrow" (Matt 5:42; Luke 6:35). And in Luke 6:35 it says: "Give a loan, expecting nothing in return." That is to say: expect in return nothing more than the principal amount, and not even the same amount, as is clear from verse 34. In fact, if the situation demands it, don't expect back even the principal; i.e., give from a heart that purely does what is good—which (by some exaggeration of the wording) has the sense of being taken comparatively, as are also the other things in the same passage.

34. And yet to those in need it is permitted to lend by way of a pledge as security for the principal amount (Exod 22:26; Deut 24:10), but it is not right to lend for a profit or premium. In fact, in Scripture the one kind of profit-making that is prohibited is only in the case of an arrangement with the poor and oppressed. And for that reason, also the Hebrew word *neshekh* ('interest') is the word for biting and gnawing, and it is mentioned nearly always when it deals with the poor and the oppressed (Exod 22:25; Lev 25:35–37; Prov 22:7). But lending at interest, which is practiced on those who are of moderate means or wealthier, when collected according to the law of love and fairness, is a kind of legitimate contract and belongs to monetary gain.

35. Hence the lending to the poor for financial gain that is practiced in the form of a pledge, and that is permitted by the magistrates in Christendom to a certain degree because of something good, is clearly cruel and harsh.

Because of the lending at interest itself, and because of the amounts of it, a well-established nation ought to have no place for anyone to practice this. And just as it is not granted to the Jews to shame and oppress Christians by practicing usury over them with impunity (Deut 23:19–20 and 28:13, 44), but, instead, so too as one must look after the poor by means of public almsgiving, should public authority and management look after the needs of some people by furnishing an 'altar of love' (as it is called) without any pledge. And one should not accept anything more than the amount of the money that has been taken for that use (if it cannot come from the public purse in any other way) and a reimbursement for the costs. In no way should such lending result in profit.

36. In short, included in almsgiving are: sympathy, benevolence, and beneficence of every kind towards the poor and helpless.

37. And for this goal the Lord promises to those who bestow pity upon the poor "a rich reward and recompense" (Prov 19:17), a "reward and a prize" (Matt 6:4 and 10:41; 2 Cor 9[:12]). It is declared that "they are lending unto the Lord" (Prov 19:17), that "they will be blessed" (Prov 14:21; Luke 14:13 [and 14]), that "blessings will be given to them" (Prov 12[:12]), and that "they will be like well-watered gardens, and like a fountain of water whose springs will never fail" (Isa 58:11). The good things of this life are promised to them—both bodily and temporal things (2 Cor 9:8–11)—and also spiritual, eternal things. These include the breaking-off and forgiveness of sin (Dan 4[:27]), cleansing (Luke 11:41), perpetual righteousness (Ps 112:9), a treasure safe in heaven (Luke 12:33 and 18:22), entry into the heavenly tabernacle (Luke 16:9), the possession and inheritance of life eternal (Matt 25[:34])—and that by God's righteousness (Heb 6:10).

38. In these promises almsgiving is not established as the cause of such great goods, but as their antecedent, because these goods happen to such people, and the explanation of their origin arises not from cause but from effect, or from the proper adjunct, and if some reason as a cause is indicated, it is done not by itself but by accident, with respect to the conjunction of this love with faith, and to God's reckoning. For, in fact, hearts are cleansed by faith (Acts 15:9). The remission of sins, the washing-away, and life eternal are merits of Christ, and life eternal is a gift from God, and the inheritance of sons is from God, and is traced to God's good pleasure (Luke 12:32; Matt 25).

On Fasting and Vigils

39. Thus far, then, about almsgiving. What follows is a second thing that is related to prayer conducted on special occasions, and is its frequent companion, namely, religious fasting, which is a more rigorous sort of self-discipline, or act which God prescribes in general that is voluntary in its circumstances whereby a stronger believer, because a more important and urgent need to pray arose, abstains from all food and drink, and all the customary trappings of life, beyond what is usual and for a certain period of time—as long as the natural strengths permit—at least for a day, in order to arouse and assist the soul and spirit in prayer, but that is especially undertaken and done religiously in humbling ourselves before God with repentance for sins, out of true faith, and either privately or publicly.

40. In calling it 'religious fasting' we distinguish it from the 'natural fasting' that is done for the purpose of maintaining or recovering bodily health. And we distinguish it from 'civil fasting,' which is when we are focused on some business or other, find ourselves in trouble, and we shun the needed refreshment (1 Sam 14:24; Acts 23:14, and 27:33). And it is different also from 'forced and necessary fasting,' such as hunger, famine, and lack of food and drink, whether it is brought on by God or human beings (Matt 24:7; 2 Cor 11:27). And so what we mean is the fasting that is done for religious reasons.

41. And yet what does not properly come into consideration here are sobriety, frugality, and moderation in the standard of living, as they are commanded to all believers throughout the entire course of their lives (Rom 13:13; Luke 21:34; 1 Pet 5). And as moderation is daily and lifelong, so also it is not properly considered fasting. Also not strictly fasting is the poverty, austerity or frequent fasting that is done according to a special calling for a particular lifestyle, such as that of John the Baptist, whose lifestyle was not at all common with others, since he fasted many times—besides the fact that he abstained from everyday foods (Matt 3:4 and 9:14). This is 'extraordinary fasting.' And also not relevant here is 'miraculous fasting' that comes by the special working of God—such as that of Moses (Exod 24:18 and 34[:28]), Elijah (1 Kgs 19[:4 and 5]), and Christ (Matt 4[:2])—and that thus cannot be imitated.

42. Therefore concerning religious fasting that is common to all believers we draw up the following propositions from its definition. [1)] The first is that

the practice of fasting as such is not self-willed or spontaneous worship, but something that has been established by God and that has been observed and a rule that will be exercised forever in the church (Joel 1:14 and 2:15; Matt 6:16 and 9:15). Accordingly, the outward, bodily fasting was not made obsolete in the New Testament along with the other ceremonies of the law, as if it retained only a figurative and spiritual meaning—that is, abstinence from sin, so that the mouth 'fasts' not from food but from base words, and from devouring and cursing one's neighbor; so that the hand 'fasts' from theft, the feet from every unlawful thing, and the eyes from what is not chaste, and the ears from disparaging slander, etc. (Isa 58:6; Jer 14:12; Zech 7:5).

43. [2]] But this divine ordinance is of such nature that while it is indeed general, it is of a free disposition according to circumstances. In fact in the Old Testament there was only one fixed and regular, annual fasting by divine prescription: on the tenth day of the seventh month before the feast of Atonement, in the house of the Lord every year there would be a solemn fast, and it was celebrated until evening (Lev 16 and 23). And by institution of the Church, dwelling in the Babylonian captivity, there was a fasting in the tenth month, to commemorate the siege of the city of Jerusalem, one in the fourth month for the city's capture, in the fifth for its destruction, and lastly, in the seventh month for the slaughter of Gedeliah that was followed by many disasters (2 Kgs 25; Jer 52; Zech 5:3 and 8:19). Added to these is the fast initiated by Mordecai, the one taken up by the Jews for the 'fast of Esther' (Esth 9:31–32). These have been abolished, the former for being ceremonial, and the latter ones for being temporary, appropriate for that people during particular period (Zech 8:19).

44. But in the New Testament Christ and his apostles did not set any certain time at all for fasting, but left it free, as also Augustine testifies (Epistle 86). And that fasting should be used (as the Orthodox state in Tertullian's book *On Fasting*) in a manner that is indifferent, by personal decision, and not by the order of a new discipline, and suited to everyone's time and cause—that is, suited to the degree of strength of each person. As to the time, mostly a time of mourning; as to the occasion, one that befalls and presses, one of a graver necessity (Matt 9:15; Mark 2:20; Luke 5:34), whether public or private, present or looming. And it should be done for the sake of obtaining some spiritual or bodily good, or for the sake of averting evil, and without the superstitious observance of time and days.

45. Accordingly, it follows from the reason for and keeping of fasting, that some are private, others public. The former is undertaken privately in a matter that is personal, either for oneself or for another (Dan 9:3 and 10:3; 1 Cor 7:5; Acts 10:30). The latter is done in public and is proclaimed by the overseers of the church, and kept publicly (Ezra 8:21; Acts 13:2–3 and 14:23).

46. And therefore the papal teachers are making a serious mistake, who contrary to Christian liberty, tie fasting to specific times and days, and, outdoing Judaism, have burdened the church with many fixed fastings for no pressing reason, and they bind the consciences to observe them as if by a required law—such as weekly, by fasting on the fourth and sixth day of the week [i.e. Wednesday and Friday]; and likewise on the Saturday after that (especially in the Roman church). So too the imposed annual fasting at the forty days of Lent and (only for clerics) from the fiftieth day before Easter; and also the fasting of the four seasons (March, June, September, and December), and very many other ones, like the yearly Vigils for the feasts of the Apostles and the other saints.

47. Some of these, namely the weekly fasting and the four Ember days, derive their origins from Jewish custom, and have been changed only in their reason (Luke 18:12; Zech 7). The one for Lent, however, was introduced as a vain, foolish, poor imitation of Christ's miraculous fasting, which we should marvel at but not copy. And although the ancient church did employ it, yet it varied and was free, so much so that there was a great diversity and dissimilarity both in its duration and its observance—one, two, several, and forty days (Eusebius, [*Ecclesiastical History*,] book 5, chapter 26; Socrates, [*Ecclesiastical History*,] book 5, chapter 21; Nicephorus, [*Refutation and Overthrowing of the Definition of the Synod of 815*,] book 1, chapter 34). But the papal teachers make the observance of fasting necessary and binding upon the conscience.

48. [3)] Fasting consists in the cheating of the natural appetite, in a restraint that is more severe than is customary, or in an abstinence from all food and drink altogether, as much as our human powers permit—for instance, usually from one evening until another evening (Lev 23:32), but sometimes it continues until the third day (Esth 4:16). Or from morning until evening, especially in a fast of many days, like a week (1 Sam 31:13), or three weeks (Dan 10:2) when in the evening they ate food, but only a little, and sparingly.

In this way Daniel abstained from meat and wine, and even tasty bread—but he did so freely (Dan 10:3).

49. And furthermore the papal teachers do not fast at all, since in the first place they define fasting not so much by abstinence from all food and drink as by the foolishly superstitious discrimination and selection of foods (1 Tim 4:1–3) or of meat. And at Lent it is abstaining from everything that comes from an animal; for example, milk, butter, cheese, eggs (whereby they think they become unclean). And by contrast, [it consists of] the use and even greater use of fish (often well-seasoned with spices), or very tasty fruits, including the most dainty delicacies; or of legumes that produce much flatulence. And it likewise consists in not being self-restrained in the drinking of wine or spirits, whereof they make extravagantly abundant use. And then also they fast not by abstaining from food and drink for the whole day, but they still fill their stomachs every day while postponing breakfast only once, which very many of the ancients sought to do their whole lives. And they foist this law upon the people's consciences, as a necessary law, nor do they grant an exemption to this, unless upon receipt of money.

50. [4]] And finally, in and of itself fasting is a 'middle thing,' and indifferent; that is, by itself it is neither something good nor something evil. "For the kingdom of God is not meat and drink, but righteousness and peace and joy in the Holy Spirit" (Rom 14:6, 17; 1 Cor 8:8). But in its use, fasting is properly and foremost an outward or bodily exercise, and an aid for training, nurturing and fostering piety. And it is a mark of penitence, that in and of itself is of no, or very little, advantage (Col 2:23; 1 Tim 4:8). But it is advantageous by accident with a view to a more excellent goal, insofar as it concerns piety, prayer, and repentance. For this reason the recommendation to fast is related to righteousness (Matt 5:6).

51. And so the goal of fasting is that, after our wanton and languid flesh has been halted by this lack of food, our heart and soul become so disposed and incited that they are rendered more free, unencumbered, and zealous than usual to offer prayer unto God, to undertake spiritual meditation, and to pour out prayers that are more efficacious than ordinarily. Hence Scripture often links fasting with prayer (Joel 1:14; Neh 1:4; Matt 6:5; Luke 2:37; 1 Cor 7:5), even apart from the link to special penitence (Acts 13:2).

52. The highest goal, however, is in the penitent's prayer, for the affliction of the flesh and for humbling the entire man before God (Ps 35:13), so that it

becomes a testimony and symbol of serious repentance and of true grief arising over sin (Joel 2:12). For this reason fasting is also called an affliction; and the statements 'to afflict oneself or one's body or soul' is used for fasting (Lev 16:29; Isa 58:3; Ezra 8:21 and 9:5). And therefore, the cause is usually grief, and an occasion for grief (Matt 9:15). And so contrariwise, in times of formal festivities it was the custom with joy and delight to eat more lavishly, and with pleasure, and to deliver portions to the poor, and in the presence of the Lord to have pleasure, as a testimony to their thanksgiving (Ps 116:13; Zech 8:19; Ezra 6:21–22; Neh 8:11,13).

53. In former times people added to that fasting a variety of gestures and ritual actions to indicate their contrition and grief. These included the tearing of garments (Joel 2:12–13), wearing clothes of mourning like sackcloth and goat's hair (Ps 35:13), being seated or cast down in dirt and ashes and sprinkling these on one's head, befouling and hiding one's face (2 Sam 12:16), neglecting to wash and anoint oneself (Matt 6:16), bending one's head downward (1 Kgs 21:27; Isa 58:5), pouring out water (1 Sam 7:6), pulling out one's hair and beard ([LXX and Vulgate editions of] Ezra 9:3; Esth 14:2), weeping, wailing, and howling (Joel 2:12). In fact, in more serious times of grief even children and herds were called to join the fasting (Joel 2:16; Jonah 3:7). The Jewish nation either shared nearly all these things with the peoples of the near East, or they were proper to that nation, or those things were meant for the pedagogical teaching of that people [Gal 3:24–25]. Christ liberated his people from them, in keeping with the thing, place, and time.

54. What is clear from these goals (and connected to them) is the mode of fasting: it should not be done hypocritically or for reasons of ambition, i.e., with an outward appearance, boasting, or pretense for the reputation of being holy (Matt 6:16–17). Nor should it be done superstitiously, i.e., out of habit and to honor saints; but with faith, fear of God, and love for the neighbor, and to God's glory.

55. When it is undertaken and done in this way for these goals, fasting pleases God, as a work that is good to do. Without these goals, however, fasting displeases God—no matter how much affliction and chastisement of the body accompanies it. It is for this reason that God especially urges spiritual fasting in place of it, as it should be part of the physical fasting, and the physical fasting should be valued by the spiritual one (Isa 58:5–6; Zech 7:5,9).

56. Because fasting is linked to something else—i.e., to the prayer of faith, that is, made out of faith and accompanied by repentance—the prayer for the aversion of God's wrath is attributed to fasting (Deut 9:18; Jonah 3:9), and also the reward and retribution by God (Matt 6:18). And moreover, in view of some sort of self-humbling, fasting also brings about a decrease of temporal punishment (1 Kgs 21:27–29). In fact, even the power to cast out demons is ascribed to fasting (Matt 17:20–21).

57. And therefore the papal teachers are making a serious mistake, for when they fast either for appearance's sake or become depressed in their hearts from their excessive abstinence, they make the claim that fasting or this emptiness of the stomach and intestines, and this bodily affliction is in itself a form of worship to God and a good work; that it renders their prayer pleasing to God, is satisfactory for sins, meritorious of righteousness and eternal life, and also appeases the wrath of God, justifies man in God's presence. In fact they claim that by it even souls are set free from Purgatory (Lombard, [*Sentences*,] book 4, chapter 15). All this is contrary to the obvious testimony of Scripture that we produced earlier in theses 50 and 55.

58. Vigils are also included under fasting, and they, too, are often combined with prayers (Matt 26:38, 41; 1 Pet 4:7). And by 'vigils' are meant not only the vigils of the heart and soul, whereby we are always readied and equipped for prayer and for the Lord's coming, in contrast with the security in the flesh (Matt 24:42; Mark 13:35; Luke 12:39; 1 Thess 5:6; Rev 3:3 and 16:15). But included also are the bodily vigils, whereby we freely take some portion of the night (as needed) to pray and meditate on the Lord's coming. This is what David testifies about himself (Ps 119:55, 62), and Christ led the way in doing (Luke 6:12), and the apostles reinforce (Col 4:2; Acts 16:25)—namely, that we should keep watch lest we enter into temptation (Matt 26:38, 41).

59. In former times vigils were both a private and a public, fixed institution. The vigils of Easter, that is, in the night before the day of Resurrection, were celebrated by keeping watch throughout the night, with lights burning in both public and private places. Ambrose (Sermon 60) writes: "We fast on the Easter Sabbath, we celebrate the vigils, and we conduct prayers constantly;" and the reason that Lactantius ([*Divine Institutes*,] book 7, chapter 19) and Jerome give is: "Because it was on that night that they expected Christ to return as Judge." But, in keeping with Christian freedom, the ancient Church made this vigil obsolete as freely as it had been undertaken and kept.

60. So much for fasting. As for the Bacchanals that are celebrated before Lent by the Roman Catholics after the manner of the gentiles according to an evil custom, all Christians should detest and avoid them altogether, as the papists start this Lenten-fast of theirs with immoderate licentiousness and luxury.

SOURCES

Augustine, *Enchiridion addressed to Laurentius*, chapter 75

Now, surely, those who live very heinous lives and are not concerned about correcting their lives and habits, and who nevertheless amid their crimes and misdeeds continue multiplying their almsgiving, flatter themselves vainly with these words of the Lord: "Give alms; and, behold, all things are clean to you." They do not understand how far this saying reaches, etc. Should we interpret this to mean that to the Pharisees, who did not have the faith in Christ, all things are clean so long as they give alms (as they think they should be given), even though they have not believed and have not been reborn of water and the Holy Spirit? But all are unclean who are not made clean by the faith in Christ, of which it is written: "Cleansing their hearts by faith" [Acts 15:9]. And as the apostle said: "But to those who are unclean and to unbelievers nothing is clean; both their minds and consciences are unclean, etc." But no-one, however, gives any alms at all unless he gives from Him who does not need anything. Accordingly it says: "His mercy shall go before me." [Ps 59:10]

Augustine, *Letter 86 to Casulanus*

Thinking the matter over in my mind, I observe that in the Gospels and the Epistles, and in the entire document called the New Testament, there is a precept for fasting. But I do not find any rule definitely laid down by the Lord or by the apostles about which days we should or should not fast.

DISPUTATION 38

ON VOWS

President: Johannes Polyander
Respondent: Gerhardus Paludanus

A vow is a voluntary promise made to God 'of our own doing, and by faith, for the glory of his name and the upbuilding of our neighbor' (3). The structure of this disputation follows conventional scholastic progressions of thought: the origin of the word 'vow' (2); a definition (3); the difference between vows that are lawful and unlawful (4–7); sub-categories of vows (8–22); the cause of making vows (23). The disputation then focuses our attention upon the vow's subject, content, and object (24). The person who utters the vow is the subject (24–33); its content may be ordained in Scripture (as in Baptism or the Lord's Supper), or it may belong to the 'adiaphora' for which no content is commanded (34–49). God himself is the object of our vows (50–51). Inward and outward forms of vows are treated next (52), as is their goal, which is especially the glorification of God (53). Interested readers may wish to compare Polyander's discussion of vows with Walaeus's treatment of oaths in Disputation 20.

1. In his Word God no less prescribes vows for those who call upon his name and generously give alms to their neighbors than He prescribes fasting. Therefore, this disputation about vows is aptly joined to the preceding ones about calling upon God, almsgiving and fasting.

2. If we look to the derivation of the word, then *votum* ('vow') has the same meaning in Latin as *euchē* in Greek and *neder* in Hebrew.

3. When considered in a general way, a vow is a sacred and religious promise about things that have been commanded, or about indifferent things that have been placed in our power, for the sake of giving testimony to God alone of our intention and duty towards him, a promise that is made of our own doing, and by faith, for the glory of his name and the upbuilding of our

neighbor. In the sacred writings, however, vows are more frequently limited to intermediate things.

4. Although making vows is an ancient practice and was used by all heathen nations, yet it was only to his own Israelite people that the God of Israel once prescribed a pattern for them (Lev 27; Num 30).

5. Hence only the vows of the Israelites were lawful, while those of the other nations were unlawful.

6. Lawful vows are those that are made only to the God of Israel, in accordance with his law, in truth, with discernment, and in righteousness.

7. Unlawful vows are ones that either disregard God and are made to his creatures, or that are made to God but not to him alone, or not following the law and manner delivered by him, but falsely, rashly and unjustly.

8. Lawful vows are either moral or ceremonial.

9. Moral vows are those that bind each and every person to the obedience that the Decalogue prescribes.

10. Ceremonial vows are ones that some people make from a religious conviction, for some pious work that is arbitrary and not, in itself, owed.

11. We have the moral vows in common with the fathers who lived in the Old Testament; but ceremonial vows, which are figurative, were specific to them in times gone by, and they were aids of the principal worship that God demands in his moral law.

12. Even though moral works are of themselves, naturally, owed to God, nevertheless in a special way and by a special bond believers are obliged to fulfill them by means of their vows, both ordinary and extraordinary ones.

13. Ordinary vows are the ones whereby believers one and all bind themselves by promise and a solemn obligation to the perpetual observance of divine worship.

14. Extraordinary vows are the kind that on occasion, due to some pressing need, are renewed either by the whole Church or its leading members in order to confirm themselves and others in the true faith, like the vows of the Israelite people in the time of Joshua (chapter 24:23) and Ezra (chapter 10:5).

15. Both vows are either absolute or hypothetical and conditional.

16. Absolute vows are the pure and simple ones that are declared without any condition. David's vow in Ps 34:2 was of this kind: "I shall bless Jehovah all the time, and praise of Him will always be in my mouth." And Ps 101[:1 and 2]: "I shall sing of your love and righteousness, O Jehovah! I shall keep the upright way. when will you come to me? Without ceasing I shall walk within my home in uprightness of my heart, etc."

17. Hypothetical vows are the ones to which certain conditions are attached, whether of person, time, place, or some other circumstance. Such was Jacob's vow in Gen 28:20[–22]: "If God will be with me and watch over me on the journey that I am going to undertake, and will give me bread to eat and clothes to wear, so that I shall return safely to my father's house; and so if Jehovah will be my God, then this heap of stones that I set up will be as a statue to the Lord God, and of whatever you will give me I shall in all give a tenth to you." And such was Hannah's vow in 1 Sam 1:11: "Lord God of hosts, if you will at all regard the affliction of your maidservant, and will remember me and not forget your maidservant, but if you will give a male offspring to your handmaiden, then I shall give him to Jehovah all the days of his life, and no razor shall come near his head."

18. And vows are divided also into perpetual and temporal. Pious people bind themselves to fulfill the thing that was vowed throughout their whole life by means of the former, whereas they do so for some time of their life by means of the latter. Of the first there is an example in David (thesis 16), and of the latter in Paul (Acts 18:18).

19. And like the prayers that are often joined to them, so too the vows themselves are sometimes only conceived in the mind as it reaches out for God, as is seen in the case of Hannah (1 Sam 1:11); and at other times they are also uttered by mouth, as is seen in the case of the Israelite people (Josh 24:24).

20. And again, these vows are either public or private.

21. Public vows are solemnly performed either in a civic meeting (like Jephthah's vow in Judg 11:31) or in a meeting of the Church (like David's vow in Ps 34 and 101).

22. Private vows are made in a place apart, a place removed from others, like Jacob's vow (Gen 28:20).

23. Foremost among the causes that compel the making of vows to God is God's command in Ps 76:11: "Make your vows and render your vows to Jehovah your God, and let all who dwell round about Him bring a gift to Him who is to be feared." Second: the example set by the saints (Gen 28:20; 1 Sam 1:11). Third: the remembrance of benefits received from God, which caused David to say: "What shall I render to Jehovah? All his benefits overwhelm me. I shall soon repay my vows to Jehovah in the presence of his people." [Ps 116:12 and 14] Fourth: the hope of obtaining some new and special benefit that has been asked of God in prayer and that one expects will be obtained. It was on the basis of this hope that Jacob made a special vow to God (Gen 28), as did Hannah, too, the mother of Samuel (1 Sam 1). Finally: the serious purpose of the heart to check the lusts of the flesh against any depravity. Such was the vow of Job who stated that he made a covenant with his eyes that he would not look at a young woman (Job 31:1).

24. Moreover, Holy Scripture defines the vows of the pious by three circumstances; the first of these concerns their subject, the second their content-matter, and the third their object.

25. The subject that is capable of making vows is the human being with whom God has entered into a covenant of his grace.

26. That covenant of grace which God has established with believing parents applies also to their infant children; and accordingly, since these children, like branches of them, have been sanctified at the root, they are implicitly obligated by them in a joint vow of obedience. In former times the sacrament of this implicit obligation was circumcision, but now it is baptism.

27. In order to confirm this obligation God instituted a second sacrament, namely, Passover in the Old Testament and holy supper in the New Testament, so that the children who over time have attained the use of reason, no less than their parents should affirm the first promise of their obedience by solemnly repeating it.

28. We should make a distinction between this general vow, which God has prescribed for younger as well as older people, and certain specific vows. That general one ought to remain completely valid, nor can human authority detract anything from it. These special vows are void if the people who make them are not legally independent but are restricted by the authority of father, husband, or some other lawful authority (Num 30).

29. And therefore this first axiom of Bellarmine's, that "it is permitted to make such vows (i.e., vows of chastity, obedience, and poverty) at any point in a man's lifetime provided that he make use of his own free choice" is false, since these vows are neither general nor prescribed by God, but special vows and devised by men, as we shall point out in its place. See Bellarmine, the second book [of the Controversies regarding the Members of the Church], *On Monks*, chapter 35.

30. Bellarmine's second axiom, that "children are permitted, contrary to their parents' will, to enter religious life," is correct if the expression 'religious life' is understood to mean the Christian religion in the strict sense. But it is false if the expression is applied to a special condition of life that is 'religious' taken in an equivocal sense and that is actually superstitious (as Bellarmine makes it; Bellarmine, *On Monks*, chapter 36). For in this way, under the pretext of "religion" children are wrongly granted a violation of the fifth commandment about honoring one's parents.

31. And although the special vows, insofar as they are appendices of the ceremonial law, have been abolished in Christ, and for this reason there is no precept in the New Testament about them, yet insofar as they belong to natural right and are chains whereby all people are more tightly bound to moral works that by nature and in themselves are owed to God, we state that they are no less permitted to us than to our forefathers before the law about them was given.

32. We should refer Paul's vow (mentioned in Acts 18:18) to that ceremonial law, which had not yet been abolished entirely at the time of the apostolic age.

33. As far as the outward, voluntary practices of some Christians are concerned, ones of the sort that involve abstinence from customary drink and food or from other things which they think put them at risk of an occasion to sin, certain or ordinary prayers, and certain endowments of alms: It is not useless for them to undertake these and similar vows, provided that they are free of all superstition, and that it is from a serious purpose of a pious mind devoted to God that they complete these vows in order to foster true faith, repentance, sobriety, love, and other Christian virtues.

34. The content-matter of vows are either things explicitly commanded by the Word of God or things not explicitly commanded but arbitrary. The

former are holy and necessary in themselves, while the latter are 'adiaphora' (or indifferent) in themselves but become holy by their circumstances and useful for salvation insofar as they are related to the principal worship of God and serve its advancement.

35. The general vow of Christianity that begins at Baptism and is renewed in the Lord's Supper extends only as far as things that have been commanded in the Decalogue and the Gospel.

36. Special vows are the ones that concern things that have not been absolutely commanded in the Decalogue or the Gospel—such as celibacy, and abstaining from certain drink, food, clothing and other good things that have been given for man's use. Or they concern matters that have been commanded partly in general (as far as their substance is concerned) and partly not in specific (as far as the circumstances of time, place, people, and events are concerned). Vows of this sort are the set prayers, fasting, almsgiving, and similar duties of piety, and the public determination of them God grants to the church's judgment, while the private execution of them is granted to each believer's choice.

37. The former kind of vows about merely indifferent matters stood out in former times in the case of the Nazarites (Num 6) and were praised in the case of the Rechabites (Jer 35). The latter kind of vows is seen in other Jews; but nowadays both kinds are condemned if anyone binds himself or others with their enslaving yoke out of a notion of necessity that completely conflicts with the freedom that Christ has obtained for us (Gal 5:1; Col 2:20).

38. The pontifical teachers, in foisting Jewish-like vows on themselves or other people, take no account at all of the conditions of lawful vows while they themselves do approve of some of these stipulations.

39. The foremost of these conditions is that vows be made according to God's commands. But in the whole of Scripture there is no text about the three vows to which the Romanist monks are bound. And despite making efforts to prove individual vows from certain places of Scripture by twisting them into a meaning they don't have, Bellarmine produces not a single text with which to combine and so confirm them.

40. The second condition is that no vow should pose a hindrance to what God in his Word prescribes or permits. But this is what happens in vows of poverty, obedience, and celibacy.

41. For with their vow of poverty, or rather of mendicancy, monks are drawn away from the work that God commands everyone (Gen 3:19; Exod 20:9) and drawn towards idleness which leads to vice.

42. And what is more, with their vow of regular (or rather, irregular) obedience, those same monks put aside the vow of universal obedience that we owe to Christ alone, as the Father commanded: "Listen to him" (Matt 17:5). And instead they naively, and without any restriction to their own contrary opinion or judgment, pay heed to the particular and various human rules of this or that Prelate as though they are divinely ordained.

43. And lastly, with their third vow, the one about perpetual celibacy, monks are unfairly excluded from the apostle's general command: "Because of sexual immorality let every man have his own wife" (1 Cor 7:2). For even monks (as Bellarmine admits) are in danger of committing fornication, and they could lose the gift of chastity that they have vowed to keep, and at some time or other be overcome by temptation (Bellarmine, book 2, *On Monks*, chapter 9).

44. And the third condition is that the vows should not consist in actions that are evil in and of themselves—like the papacy's calling upon saints, the veneration of images and relics, the monks' idle mendicancy, and similar actions.

45. And the fourth condition is that vows should not cause a hindrance to a greater good. And this is what the vow of poverty does, whereby the wealthy renounce their own goods and deprive themselves of any ability to provide for the communion of saints through deeds of hospitality and kindness, wherein God takes great delight (Heb 13:16).

46. The fifth condition is that whatever is vowed should not stand in the way of the duty which everyone is bound to perform for his neighbor out of natural and moral law. Such is the abandonment of human community, and especially of one's neighbors, which monks vow to do: that they will not be forced to serve the needs of their own relatives, and so they actually deny the Christian faith which they profess with their mouth. For where there is such inhumanity, there can be no piety towards God.

47. The sixth condition is that to most of those making the vow the matter ought not to be impossible; a matter of this sort is the perpetual chastity of a

celibate life. It is with no small scandal that all of Christianity has been observing the violation of this vow in monasteries since several ages ago.

48. The seventh condition is that there be no foolish, comical, and useless things, like religious pilgrimages, the various kinds of monks' clothing, abstinence from certain types of food, etc.

49. The eighth condition is that vows should be entirely free of any notion of worship that is necessary, or meritorious in the eyes of God on the basis of work that is supererogatory. Bellarmine confirms his fellow-monks in this notion by means of the following definition of vow: "A vow is a religious promise made to God about some more excellent good." This definition of Bellarmine rests upon this false assumption: that in the Gospel Christ recommends to us some good that is more excellent than what God commands in his Law. We have abundantly demonstrated the untruth in this definition in our earlier disputations about the Law and the Gospel.

50. The proper object of vows is the same as for prayers, namely, God, to whom alone true worshipers have directed their vows, in accordance with his command (Deut 23; Ps 50 and 76).

51. And therefore we have every good reason to consider the papal teachers as sacrilegious idolaters for making also their vows to the deceased saints or to the heads of monasteries, for they ascribe the honor that is due only to their Creator to the creatures He has made.

52. The internal form of vows consists in the fact that, following prior considerations of the soul, vows are freely made and arise from a certain knowledge and confidence of the faith, without which they cannot be pleasing God. Their outward form is that they are expressed also in speech, and even though this is not necessary for God since He knows the hearts, yet the outward form is put to good use as a witness of our zeal and holy intent to offer vows to God, while also edifying our neighbor.

53. The highest and general goal of making vows is the glory of God; subordinate and particular goals include: 1) That we bear witness to God of our repentance for sins committed against him, as well as our gratitude for the benefits that we have received from Him. 2) That by means of this goad we are very much spurred to all the other duties of piety, love, righteousness, and mercy, that can proceed from us.

ON PURGATORY
AND INDULGENCES

President: Andreas Rivetus
Respondent: Guilielmus Soestius

Disputation 39 is unique insofar as its purpose is not to explicate a doctrine positively but to refute a false one, namely the Roman Catholic teaching and practice of purgatory and indulgences. Simply put, purgatory and indulgences deny the efficacy of Christ's atoning sacrifice, his work of complete satisfaction for our sins, and our justification in the sight of God (1). 'God has instituted no purgation except the blood of Christ and the grace of the Holy Spirit' (5). Scriptural grounds and arguments that support the rejection of purgatory are provided (10–36). The treatment of indulgences (37–54) begins with an expression of confidence that 'once the fire of purgatory has been extinguished, the smoke of indulgences vanishes by itself' (37). The disputation ends with an expression of gratitude to God for raising up Martin Luther, who was led 'to overturn the entire system of indulgences from its very foundations.' 'Thus it remains that we, acknowledging the true source of the forgiveness of sins, and then being washed in it, should abstain from sins, and bring glory to God the Father, in Christ the Son, and through the Holy Spirit forever' (54).

1. In the preceding disputations we treated the offices of Christ, his satisfaction for our sins, and the application of that satisfaction in the justification of man by true faith. We also treated the gratitude in sanctification and the works of sanctification by those who were made partakers of that justification, and the correct use of fasting, almsgiving, and vows, which the papal teachers misuse in order to establish a satisfaction by man apart from Christ. Having done that, it is right for us to append an elenctic disputation about purgatory and indulgences in which we shall demonstrate that these made-up human inventions are not based on any solid

foundation but take away from the merits and unique satisfaction of Christ and are harmful to the church of God—a part of which church (and that not the smallest part) they imagine undergoes temporary torment in the underworld.

2. To avoid attributing to our opponents anything of our own making, it is from their writings that first we shall present the state of the controversy, and distinguishing what they themselves consider certain and necessary to believe from the things that are less certain and debated, we shall direct our arguments especially at those former things. For they themselves give this warning: "Some teachings which we hold about purgatory are more or less certain, teachings that are not equally confirmed by all testimonies and arguments whatsoever at once, but by differing ones" (Gregory of Valencia, [*Theological commentary on*] Thomas Aquinas's [*Summa theologiae*], part 3, disputation 11, question 1, point 1, paragraph 4).

3. But they posit the following as the first and foremost meaning of the word, according to which they think that it is rightly proved that there is a purgatory by the testimonies which they are accustomed to adduce either from Scripture or the church fathers or the ecclesiastical definitions. And by [purgatory] they mean some place whereto those believers' souls migrate from the body upon death, being bound still by the liability of some temporal punishment or even by some venial sins, and experience torments relative to the reckoning of God's justice, until such time as they have completely expiated such sins and are able to obtain the blessedness of heaven (Gregory of Valencia, ibid., Bellarmine, *On Purgatory*, book 1, chapter 1).

4. And therefore we leave aside the controversies that the papal teachers have stirred up amongst themselves about the location of purgatory, whereof they admit even that their own church has made no definitive decision—although by the more accepted opinion (which they deem to be more true) they think that it is below the earth and next to the hell of the condemned. [And we leave aside the controversy] about the fire, which the majority think is fire in the proper sense (though others: improper); about the quality of that fire, namely if it is real and corporeal (which they affirm is their theologians' most solid opinion); about the support that the living give for the sake of those who are deceased (and similar things). What we shall examine is what they call that 'substantial' and primary meaning of the word ['purgatory'], and we shall test it by the rule of truth, since they hold that it is so necessary to believe

that teaching, that Bellarmine judges that he who denies it must suffer torment in the eternal fire of hell (*On Purgatory*, chapter 15). And [Francesco] Panigarola did not hesitate to say that there is no God if there is no purgatory (*Lecture on Purgatory*, held at Turin).

5. But as for us, we believe very firmly in the existence of God and we also steadfastly deny that this sort of purgatory exists—nor do we, for that reason, fear the punishments of the world below. For we know that God has instituted no purgation except the blood of Christ and the grace of the Holy Spirit, which is distributed to believers by the Word and sacraments in this life—unless, perhaps, someone should state that afflictions and chastisements purge away sins. They, however, don't do this by their own power, but only as occasions, that is insofar as 'sufferings are lessons' (to say it in this way) whereby we are warned through our weaknesses to take recourse in a doctor—a logic that cannot apply to the afflictions of the purgatorial fires after this life (as our opponents themselves admit).

6. Their assumption, that the catholic Church has always been of the opinion that such a purgatory exists, is completely false; and they consider that this assumption should be sufficient to preserve the claim of purgatory—although they have no testimony from Scripture or any other argument. And they carefully lay down this basis, for they are themselves aware that whatever they produce from Holy Scripture is dragged 'by the scruff of the neck' to support a matter foreign to it, and is not capable of making those people believe whose eyes have not been glazed over by the 'cataracts' of pontifical authority and the 'corneal blemish' of human traditions that wrongly claims for itself the authority of the catholic Church.

7. And so even though they twist some testimonies of Scripture, there still were some within the realm of the papists itself who were compelled by the truth to say that "one cannot readily produce any one Scripture-passage with which to compel an impudent person, whether he is willing or not, to confess that purgatory exists, even if there could be such a passage—although until now it has escaped the notice of the most careful investigators" (Bishop of Rochester, *Against Luther*, article 18). And hence it happened that in France the Jesuit Pierre Coton, when he was not able to persuade the living, tried to move Acheron, and he did dig up what until then had escaped the notice of the most careful observers—assisted as he was by a demon, to whom he put

SYNOPSIS OF A PURER THEOLOGY

the following question (among others): "What place is there in Scripture from which one could clearly prove purgatory?"

8. For obviously he knew what Peter de Soto states frankly in his *Lectures on the Institution of Priesthood* (On Purgatory, lecture 1), "that the authoritative passages of Scripture adduced by our teachers are less clear and less effective, and demonstrate less, and that therefore people should not use them to prove that purgatory exists." And likewise, "that it is neither necessary nor opportune to rely on the authority of the passage taken from Matt chapter 12[:32], that 'there will be no forgiveness either in this age or in the one that is to come,' because one could reply that this is said through some exaggeration and hyperbole." Nor does it hold on the basis of that well-known passage in 1 Cor 3[:13]—"and so as through fire"—that upon death there is some sort of purgatory, "because we should understand this sort of fire to mean that both those who build with gold and those who build with straw pass through it." And the same author says that "this reasoning very effectively argues that this passage does not prove a purgatory after death, or if it seems to someone that it can be proven nonetheless, then certainly on account of its ambiguity the meaning is less clear. And therefore, one should also not rely on that passage."

9. But the passage from 2 Macc 12, which Bellarmine and Gregory of Valencia place in the vanguard, contains nothing about any purgatorial fire or place where souls are burned, and it can be so explained that it is impossible on the basis of it (at least, from the deed of Judas) to prove assistance for the deceased. Yet what is more, "among the ancients there existed doubt about the authority of that book (whether or not it belongs to the canon), and in Augustine's time this appeared not yet sufficiently resolved," as the same de Soto says, and he asserts, "the doctrine of purgatory is more certain and evident than the authority of that book; and one should not prove what is more evident by means of what is less evident."

10. In order for us to demonstrate that this doctrine is not just an 'unwritten' one but even 'contrary to what is written' there is no need for us (although some of our opponents unfairly demand it) to make the case for the negative argument, word-for-word and literally from Scripture: "There is no purgatorial place for souls after death." It is sufficient if we show in many ways how that dogma of the papal teachers conflicts with Scripture and sound reasoning. Scripture does not put anything in the middle between

believers and unbelievers, good and bad, between those who enter by the narrow gate and those who enter by the wide one, the sons of eternity and the sons of the devil, the spiritual and the carnal, etc.; but everywhere it has established a direct opposition between these sorts of people (Luke 16:8; Matt 7:13; Matt 25:32; John 5:29; Rom 8:5, etc.). And therefore, it does not acknowledge that there are people in the middle, who are "neither altogether evil nor altogether good;" and when these are taken away, then purgatory is empty.

11. The same Scripture points out that there are only two lives, and Augustine also testifies "that the Church knows that God has proclaimed and pointed out to it the same two lives, of which one is in faith and the other in sight. The one is in the time of sojourn, the other in its eternal abode; the one is struggling while the other is at rest; the one is *en route* while the other has reached the fatherland; the one is actively working while the other has been rewarded with beholding, etc." (Treatise 124, on John). Paul clearly delimits and circumscribes the first of these lives within the boundaries of this current life (Rom 8:18; 2 Cor 5:10). And he evidently teaches that "what is seen is temporary, and what is not seen is eternal" (2 Cor 4:18). But since the state of souls after this life is unseen, it must be eternal. The Scholastics themselves understand by *viatores* ['sojourners'] only those people who are still enjoying the use of that light.

12. And, with the same apostle, we know that "if the earthly tent we live in is destroyed, we have a dwelling-place from God, a home not made with hands, eternal in the heavens," and not a temporal one in the realm below. And Ephraem [the Syrian] states: "Beyond these two orders there is no other, middle order; yet I do speak about one order above and another below" (Treatise *Regarding the Mansions of the Blessed*). And a little farther on, "Fleeing Gehenna precisely means to enter into the kingdom of heaven, just as to depart from heaven is to enter Gehenna. For Scripture also has not taught us that there are three regions." Correct, for "he who believes has crossed over from death to life" (John 5:24). And "from now on they rest from their labor who die in the Lord" (Rev 14:13). For what Bellarmine and others state is wrong, "that some die partly in the Lord and partly not in the Lord"—as if to say that someone who is still wandering beyond it has reached the turning-point.

13. And whenever Scripture presents teachings and examples of dying well, it does not strike any fear of torments and physical pain into the hearts of the pious; rather, it instills the fullest measure of hope and joy—which could not possibly happen if pious believers in Christ had to fear the flames of purgatory after their death, flames that are different from the fires of hell only in the length of time: "The righteous perishes and there is no-one who takes it to heart, and men of compassion are gathered away, etc. Peace will come, and he who walks in love will rest upon his bed." (Isa 57:1) And accordingly those who were going to die "sought to be dismissed in peace" (Luke 2:29) because those who were faithful unto death are promised the crown of life (Rev 2:10), but the punishment of the fire is not being prepared for them. And the apostle testifies that the crown that has been reserved for him after the struggle of this life is the same as the one reserved for everyone who cherishes Christ's coming (2 Tim 4:8).

14. If there was anyone who needed some satisfactorial purging upon death then surely it was the murderer who was converted upon the cross, who confessed that he was receiving what his deeds deserved (Luke 23:41). He ought to have suffered the purgatorial punishments for many hundreds of years after his death, and yet he heard Christ say: "Today you will be with me in Paradise." For the fact that some papal teachers assert that death undergone by this soul suffering death with a most patient mind and his admirable confession could have counted as just satisfaction (Bellarmine, *On Purgatory*, book 1, chapter 2)—this is why among the Jesuits there are some who call this murderer "martyr for Christ"—completely contradicts Scripture and sound reasoning. "For whoever suffers as a murderer, or thief, or evildoer" (1 Pet 4:15) certainly is not suffering for the sake of Christ.

15. Nor is it valid if someone were to say: "The privilege of a few does not make for a rule." For all believers receive the same promise, "that they will not enter into the judgment but have gone over from death to life" (John 5:24). "And the sun will not beat down upon them, nor will scorching heat," hence, "no purgatorial fires (Rev 7:16). And accordingly, as soon as the soul of Lazarus departed from his body, the angels carried it to the bosom of Abraham, where he enjoyed consolation (Luke 16:22). And therefore, he did not suffer the grievous pains of purgatory. Those who die in this faith "desired rather to be away from the body and to be present with the Lord" (2 Cor 5:8), "to depart and to be with Christ" (Phil 1:23). Indeed, they knew that the Lord "willed that those whom the Father had given to him would be

where he is, even with him, and that they might behold his glory"—and therefore not that they should be in the world below alongside the damned, suffering a similar fire for many years.

16. Scripture testifies that the time of this current life is the time for sowing, but that after this life is the time for harvesting (Gal 6:7) "when everyone will receive according to what he has done in the body" (2 Cor 5:10); that now "is the acceptable day of salvation" (2 Cor 6:2); that the Son of man forgives sins "on earth" (Matt 9:6). And, what is forgiven or loosed on earth, the same is forgiven and loosed in heaven (Matt 16:19). Therefore, since the forgiveness of sins and salvation is obtained (or lost) only in this life through faith that is kindled by the ministry of the Word and Sacraments, and since the effect of the things that are done on earth is to be looked for in heaven, the making of a purgatory outside the inhabited world and heaven makes no sense.

17. The very doctrine of purgatory cannot co-exist with the remission of sins. The Jesuits state that "in the next life there is no place except that of righteousness, namely, in the retribution of punishment or reward, in return for what has been merited or demerited in this life" (Gregory of Valencia, disputation 11, question 1, point 1). According to them, therefore, there is no place for mercy. But if someone says that the forgiveness of sins is not an effect of mercy, then he should be 'placed in the care of his relations and kinsmen.' For what the Jesuit adds that sins are forgiven, "only insofar as the payment of the penalty makes satisfaction for God's justice," is so foolish that it brings forth the blasphemous consequence that even Christ, who fully satisfied God's justice, had his sins forgiven him.

18. And no less absurd is their statement that with the remission of guilt a man is cleansed from sin, while after this life a temporal punishment is exacted from him. For Bellarmine himself admits that "the penalty which is owed" (or the liability of the penalty) "does not produce a stain but makes one a debtor" (*On Purgatory*, book 2, chapter 4). But where there is no stain what need is there for purging? And also, whatever is cleansed is taken away, for God takes away the stains which he purges. But, according to our opponents' assumption, in purgatory punishment is exacted unto the very last penny. Who has ever heard of someone who is purged from a punishment which he is forced to suffer in its entirety? For if someone says that those who are in purgatory sometimes are relieved from punishments

through the assistance of the living (even though this is not true) then it follows from that only that the help and deeds of satisfaction by the living are purgatorial, but not some fire which does not actually purge but from which those people for whom satisfaction is made are purged and set free, in which passive sense even the penalties the damned deserved would be purgatorial, because Christ has liberated those who belong to Him from these penalties by making satisfaction.

19. As a result of all this the most important basis of our opponents' contention collapses, upon which they argued that one must necessarily confess that after death there remains some time and place when, outside heaven itself and even outside the hell of the damned, souls make atonement for their liability of punishment and their venial guilt in order to be able to enter into the kingdom of heaven. For [they argue] the sort of people are found who, although they are in the grace of God, nevertheless are not granted immediate entry into the kingdom of heaven without making some additional expiation, since nothing gains entry there that is defiled in any way, and also since there is no church there that still has some "stain and wrinkle" [Eph 5:27]. But we state that there is not any stain or wrinkle that remains in those who die in grace, and the apostle's statement applies: "Whoever has died has been made righteous from sin" (Rom 6:7). And moreover, Bellarmine has admitted that the penalty that is owed does not brand a stain. He also admits that "in death the tinder for sin is taken away when all sense perception is removed" (*On Purgatory*, book 2, chapter 9). And where there is no tinder for sin, there no sin at all can exist, not even venial sins. For if the cause is taken away then its effect is removed.

20. And add to this the fact that the distinction which the papal teachers make between venial and mortal sins goes against the definition of sin, for sin is not just "outside the Law" but even "contrary to the Law" and so it makes one liable to God's curse, for which there is no forgiveness. But since those who die in grace are not under the curse, and are not liable to any sin, because no sin is by its own nature so minor (whether that be 'due to the lightness of its subject-matter' or 'due to the incompleteness of its working') that it does not deserve an everlasting curse, since all transgression of the law is worthy of death (Deut 27:26). But Christ has taught that even the smallest sin is proscribed by God's law (Matt 5:22). And there is no exception for any sin for which Christ did not pour out his blood, since it purges us from all sin (1 John 1:7). If the stain of sin is not wiped away by Christ in anyone before he

dies, then he will forever experience the punishment of being not in some place that purges, but in hell. For "the wages of sin is death" (Rom 6:23).

21. Nor is the other basis that they place in support of purgatory and indulgences (whereof we must speak below) any more solid, namely that following the forgiveness of mortal guilt and eternal punishment there is some temporal penalty that must be discharged, either in this life by means of works that make satisfaction for penalties, or in the life hereafter, in some purgatorial fire. For these words assume that there are some satisfactions for sin besides the satisfaction of Christ, and the consequences that are associated with it show sufficiently that this teaching is foolish and blasphemous, i.e., "that Christ's merit does not then deserve to be called perfect satisfaction" (these are the words of [Ruard] Tapper, theologian at Leuven, in the *Explication of Articles*, tome 1 article 6). They are contrary to the explicit statements in Holy Scripture which testify that it was upon him [Christ] that the iniquities of us all were laid, and that He has redeemed us from all iniquity (Isa 53:6; Titus 2:14; 1 John 1:7, and countless other places).

22. And there are a few who are convinced by these testimonies, who confess "that Christ has made the fullest satisfaction for the liability of guilt of both temporal and eternal punishment of all sins" (Bellarmine, *On Indulgences*, book 2, chapter 10). And they nevertheless add things to it whereby they actually take away what they concede in their words. For they want none of Christ's satisfactions to be of any help for those people who fall into sins after baptism, unless they themselves have washed away their own sins by means of their own satisfactions—as if Christ's satisfaction was presented for the purpose that we ourselves should make satisfaction for our sins. By means of this reasoning they foolishly want Christ's satisfactions to be applied to us by means of our own satisfactions. But Scripture has no knowledge of this mode of application besides faith and the sacraments, and sound reasoning finds it abhorrent. For who has ever heard that punishment is applied by punishment, and that Christ's satisfaction is applied by means of purifying fires and torments? In what way would mercy be applied through the execution of righteousness in us; how would the remission of debts be applied through the exaction of a debt, and pardon be applied by means of punishment?

23. They continue to advance their fallacies by ignoring the proofs of our refutation, when they try by means of the many arguments sought from

Scripture and human experience to prove that after He has forgiven guilt, God afflicts the pious in various ways, also for sins that had been committed and forgiven. For this is not the point that is turned into doubt; but the crux of the matter is the question whether it is to make satisfaction for our sins that God inflicts such temporal punishment (whether the satisfaction is in whole or in part) rather than "to demonstrate the misery which we deserve, to correct our faulty lives, and to exercise the needed patience." This is what we contend, while we steadfastly deny the former piece that is stitched onto it by the papal teachers. And we make the assertion that the temporal punishments imposed on David and others after they had sinned have to do only with their instruction and testing, but were not (either in part or in whole) a ransom-price for sin, because after sin is forgiven "the things that are punishments for sin before remission, after remission has been granted become the contests and exercises of the righteous" (Augustine, *On the Merits and Remission of Sin*, book 2, chapter 34).

24. And moreover we assert that those punishments that chasten or cleanse do not reach beyond the boundaries of this life, a fact that is clearly shown from the goal for which they are usually imposed, which is partly to improve our own lives, partly as exemplary warning for others and as a precaution for ourselves for the future also. It is impossible for these things to have a place among the deceased: "For God chastises in order to correct, and he corrects in order to preserve us," as Cyprian well puts it (book 4, epistle 4). And Cyprian also "realizes that there is no place at all for repentance after death, and no effect from making satisfaction" (*To Demetrius*, treatise 1). And accordingly, Cyril used to teach his catechumens that "it is in this life only that we have the time prescribed for repentance and forgiveness of sins" (Cyril of Jerusalem, *Catechism* 18). For this current life is the time for healing. "But when punishment is viewed as a means of curing, then occasionally it happens that some pious person is punished without guilt on his part (since this guilt really is forgiven him through Christ) but not without a reason."— a distinction correctly made by Thomas (*Summa theologiae* 2/2, question 108, article 4).

25. And finally, from the punishments God inflicts there is not any consequence at all for people's imposition or voluntary undertaking of satisfactorial punishments, for if God should demand them as satisfactions then He would punish twice for the same act, and contrary to the laws of justice He would receive double satisfaction. For it is to no end that they give

as their response that our deeds of satisfaction are "subordinate" to Christ's satisfactions, for things that are opposite cannot be subordinated to each other. And these are in fact opposites: perfect and imperfect satisfaction, a once-for-all and a manifold satisfaction. In fact, an "imperfect satisfaction" is no satisfaction at all, since the added term contains a contradictory element. But if they take satisfaction to mean the required fulfillment of some condition or other in order to partake of Christ's satisfaction (which [fulfillment] through metaphor could be called 'satisfaction'), that could indeed be tolerated, although one would have to be wary of misapplying the term. But when they claim that we make satisfaction for our sins to God in the "true and proper sense," then they cannot be excused under any pretext whatsoever. Christ, who "by himself has made purification for our sins" (Heb 1:3) did not share this duty with anyone else.

26. But the places cited from Scripture are either examples wherein fruits that befit repentance are required, or they are difficult deeds the pious have undertaken, etc. They are less relevant to the matter at hand because these works had been demanded of or performed by living people only, and not by the deceased. These deeds should never be understood as being about satisfaction in the strict sense, but about merely fulfilling conditions that are required in us; or they are even about God's fatherly chastening, as has been said, and not about judicial punishment. For "there is not any condemnation for those who are in Christ" (Rom 8:1). Since their guilt has been forgiven it could not have been just to inflict any punishment as such. And since there is such a close connection between guilt and its proper punishment, the sacred language has expressed both of them mostly with one and the same word (Lev 16:9); and where the debt has been forgiven, there every obligation is taken away.

27. That need to make satisfaction for the liability of temporal punishment and venial guilts before obtaining the blessed inheritance is clearly overturned by the state of those who are alive on that very last day, who will "be caught up to meet the Lord" (1 Thess 4:17). For they will be changed in a split-second, in the twinkling of an eye, so that it is impossible to imagine a time and place for any purgatorial punishments. Therefore since the preaching of the Gospel (and the true faith that takes hold of Christ's merit) happens all the time and maintains the same force, what reason can there be why those who have died in bygone ages as well as those who are dying daily should be burned and tortured by fire any more than those who will be taken on that

very last day? What the papal teachers object is a very foolish thing to say, i.e., that those people must be purged by the very great tribulation that precedes the very last day as well as the fire that comes down from heaven when they will be taken to meet the Lord. Firstly, because all people will share in that final tribulation, and so by its own very nature it will not be purgatorial but will relate to the state of the current life (which we are not dealing with at this point). And secondly, the fire that comes down from heaven will not be purgatorial, but it will come down as a punishment for the impious and unbelieving, as the apostle testifies (2 Thess 1:8).

28. This being the case, we rightly relegate the purgatory of the papal teachers to the figments and fables of pagans and poets, from whom it took its origin. For we do not believe that if any such thing was recommended by Plato (in his *Gorgias* and *Phaedo*) or Cicero (in his *Dream of Scipio*), and Virgil (*Aeneid* 6) or Claudian the poet and similar writers, or if it was hinted at by the Quran of the Mohammedans or the Talmud of superstitious Jews, that it must therefore follow that those authors either had learned it from the people of God or by the light of nature had deduced it from known principles—unless there is some common belief that "there is need of a purging from sins before anyone can enjoy blessedness." But because they have no knowledge whatsoever of the premise about the true purging from sins in Christ and its application by the teaching of the Gospel, it is no surprise if in this matter (just as in the true knowledge of God) "they have become futile in their thinking, and their senseless hearts have been darkened" (Rom 1:21). And those who copy such folly within the Christian realm, who after Christ was revealed to them are being willfully blind, are all the more "without excuse" [Rom 1:20].

29. For we have already shown that what they produce from the Scriptures (both the Old and New Testaments) does not make for solid proof in the eyes of some papal teachers of great renown. In Matt 5:25 and Luke 12:58 Christ gives instruction about "reconciling with your opponent while we are on the way, etc.," a passage which Bellarmine twists into proof for purgatory (*On Purgatory*, book 1, chapter 7, throughout the entire chapter). But in fact the Jesuits Maldonado and Barradas saw nothing of the sort. In the *Harmony of the Gospels* (volume 2, book 7, chapter 17) the latter follows the opinion of Chrysostom and relates these words to hurrying up to reconcile and to solving lawsuits. But the former, since he explains it allegorically, together with Augustine thinks that the particle 'until' does not signify (to use

Augustine's words) "that they will go out afterwards, but that they will never go out, because those who are in hell never make full atonement for the penalties they owed, although they are always atoning for penalties." And so they acknowledge that their own brother Bellarmine has with his great efforts achieved nothing but great trifles.

30. The same Bellarmine (chapter 8) presses the passage in Matt 5:22, "whoever is angry with his brother" etc., in order to show that some temporal punishments are held back so that they may be paid after this life. But Maldonatus shows from the books of the Jews that all of those punishments were capital ones, and that Christ is making a distinction in degree, not in kind. And therefore that those about whom Christ is speaking will be struck by the same hellish punishments as those who do not deserve the same degree of punishment. Manoel de Sá has a different interpretation, but one that is equally opposed to purgatory, so that the sense is: 'the Scribes' teaching condemns the murderer, but I condemn even the man who is angry; they call the man who says "Raca" or "you fool" before their council, but I consign him to hell.' About the other passages which they produce for this purpose we make the general statement that they are apocryphal and extra-canonical, or entirely unrelated, or forcefully twisted, or altogether distorted, and that there is not even a single one of them that represents the word 'purgatory' or that contains any definition of it at all. Let it suffice to have shown one example here; the remainder will become clear in the [oral defense of the] disputation.

31. And what they cite for the same purpose from the church fathers and the councils cannot constitute an additional article of faith besides Scripture; even so, we provide this general advice: 1) In this case the papal teachers cite many spurious writings. 2) Very many authors they themselves adduced either make no mention of purgatory, or if there are those who do bring purgatory to mind they depict it as entirely different than the papal teachers do. 3) Moreover, there is not anyone among the genuine, older writers of earlier ages who wished to push the teaching of some purgatorial place as an article of faith. Bellarmine himself admits (*On Purgatory*, book 2, chapter 1) that "many fathers thought that after this life all people—good as well as wicked—had to be cleansed, with the exception of Christ." Origen, who was among the first to light the fire of purgatory, has people purified in it who are miscreants, sacrilegious, who in the midst of their crimes put an end to their lives (witness Augustine, *On Heretics*, chapter 43). But Augustine did

hesitate and doubt, not only over the nature of the punishments but also over the matter itself: "It is unbelievable that something like this happens also after this life, and one could question whether it is so" (*Enchiridion*, chapter 69). And elsewhere: "I do not argue against it, because perhaps it is true" (*City of God*, book 21, chapter 26).

32. And although they posit it as certain and beyond debate, the consequence they draw is a foolish one, namely that all those who promoted prayers and offerings on behalf of the deceased believed in purgatory. And they put those people who deny the usefulness of prayers and offerings in the company of heretics. For even if it is true that the custom of praying for the deceased is an old one, it is no less certain that the ancients had different reasons for considering it useful. For even the Greek church, Alphonso de Castro says, "has that custom until today, and yet to this very day the Greeks do not believe in purgatory" ([*Against Heresies*,] On Indulgences, book 8).

33. And in fact the primary reason why they poured out prayers for the deceased stems from the very doctrine that nowadays the papal teachers themselves consider among the errors, namely "that so many and such illustrious ancient fathers as Tertullian, Irenaeus, Origen, Chrysostom, Theodoret, Ambrose, Clement of Rome, and Bernard did not agree with this line of thinking (which the council of Florence, upon extensive discussion, determined to be a dogma of faith), that the souls of the righteous enjoy beholding God before judgment day; but they taught the opposite line of thinking," as Stapleton admits (*On the Authority of* [*the Church Regarding the Holy*] *Scriptures*, book 1, chapter 2, section 5). And to these Sixtus of Siena adds Justin Martyr, Lactantius, Victorinus, Prudentius, Arethas, etc. (*Bibliotheca Sancta*, book 6, annotation 345). It is not surprising if in this "delay in the resurrection" (as Tertullian calls it) they considered the prayers for the deceased useful, because of this exile of all the souls and penalty of punishment of damnation (though not a punishment of the senses). And the fact that the papal teachers themselves consider the basis to be an unstable one, we—who have been taught differently by Scripture—should not copy a rite that has no usefulness and is even harmful to the saints.

34. The kind of proof from the appearances of souls reporting that they have been in purgatory, and who seem to be begging the living for help we relegate to forged fables, or to the dreams of the insane, the possessed, and those who have been afflicted by fevers. And we relegate them also to the often-

disclosed deceits of the devil, deceits whereby people deserve to be fooled who "do not consult with God but with the dead on behalf of the living" (Isa 8:19). A delirious Bellarmine himself offers us an instance of such blind folly in *The Sighing Dove* (book 2, chapter 9) where he retells a story from Bede about the vision of a certain Dryhthelm who had seen a valley filled with the souls of men whereof one side bristled with burning fires, and another with a raging hailstorm and icy-cold snows blowing everywhere. And there he saw wretched souls that when they could not bear the force of the heat would leap headlong into the middle of the cold; and then they would shiver in the cold and, in unhappy succession, return into the midst of the flames. He says, "I do not doubt that this account is very true because it agrees with Scripture, which says in Job chapter 24[:19]: 'they cross from ice-cold waters to excessive heat.'" The same author relates another story, more suited to old-wives and madwomen, about a certain Christina whom the angels carried to Paradise when she died, and God gave her the choice of staying with Him forever or returning to earth in order to complete the most grievous penalties for the sake of setting free souls from purgatory. She made the choice to suffer, with the stipulation that after she had amassed many merits she would return to God. And so thereupon she entered into burning ovens, was tormented, gave forth horrendous cries, and finally came out—unharmed. And during the winter she lasted six days and more under the waters of the Maas, when everything was frozen stiff with cold. What is more, all her limbs were unharmed when she was fastened to the wheel of a mill and turned around and around in a horrible manner, etc. What sane person does not see that those are the devil's deceptions? And still Bellarmine says: "Look, here we have trustworthy eye-witnesses, a man and a woman, who have seen the harshest punishments of purgatory, so that those who do not believe these things are clearly without excuse." For in this way "God has sent to them the power of deception to believe a lie, because they did not receive a love for the truth that they might be saved" (2 Thess 2:10–11).

35. And no less fanciful is the argument which they draw from utility, namely that whoever thinks that besides hell there exists the fiercest fire of purgatory and that whatever has not been erased by the works that were owed for penitence must be atoned for there, lives with greater zeal and caution, while the opinion that takes away purgatory instead makes men careless in avoiding sin and in performing good works. As though those people who are undeterred by hell-fire will care at all about an imaginary fire, and as though

that [imaginary fire] will not rather give an opportunity for sin to those who think that they can free themselves from those flames by the help of others. This help wealthier people can obtain for themselves by an easy business deal. And especially the 'Master of Sentences' himself doesn't fear to make the claim that "in purgatory the wealthy obtain forgiveness more quickly than the poor" (*Sententiae*, book 4, distinction 45, letter d). And Albertus Magnus says that "there can be so much assistance for any one person that he is immediately set free in a moment of time, and that therefore in this matter the wealthy man's state is better than that of the poor, as he has the wherewithal for assistance to come in his own behalf, whence Prov 13[:8] says: 'A rich man's wealth is his ransom' " (*On the Mystery of the Office of the Mass*, treatise 3, chapter 16). Hence it surely is not piety that is increased by this, but instead the incomes of the churches' clerics, who "in their greed exploit people with lying words" (2 Pet 2:3), and while those people stress purgatory, they themselves are living lives of debauchery. Not only do reports bear witness to the fact that this is happening at Rome (where the doctrine of purgatory is doing exceptionally well) but also experience itself speaks loud and clear.

36. This being the case, it is our conclusion that purgatory does not have any authority from Scriptures, not any credibility based on the testimonies of the fathers, nor any likelihood based on logical arguments, such as especially the papal teachers believed, in whose writings the components do not hold the building together, which is bound up in a variety of ill-fitting and contradictory elements. It will be obvious to everyone that this statement is true, not just from the things that we have said thus far, but even when one reads the books of our opponents (especially Bellarmine) wherein one scarcely meets one or two chapters which do not cite divers opinions and principles that very often even contradict the writings of the papal teachers. And while they are crossing swords with each other, we rest with grateful hearts in the sole satisfaction of Christ, stating with certainty that those who firmly abide in Christ as the author of life should not be afraid of any purgatorial fire after this life.

On Indulgences
37. Once the fire of purgatory has been extinguished, the smoke of indulgences vanishes by itself. For with the removal of purgatory scarcely anyone will be found who would accept indulgences, even if they were

offered for free. Accordingly, the bishop of Rochester in *Against Luther* (article 13) when he saw that the origin of indulgences is not certain and admitted that it was only lately that Christians had accepted them as true, he brought forward the following reason: "That the ancients make no, or very little, mention of purgatory, and that until this very day the Greeks do not believe in it. And as long as there was no concern about purgatory, no-one looked for indulgences, on which every evaluation of indulgences depends, and if that is removed, there will be no need for indulgences. And therefore, no-one can be surprised that at the start of the growing church there was no use for them, since it was so late that purgatory became known to the universal church." Gregory of Valencia himself admits that "since the practice of penitence was thriving more pointedly among the ancients, there was no great need to have the benefit of indulgences, but that later, when that fervor of penitence diminished, the use of indulgences began to increase" (*Treatise on Indulgences*, chapter 4).

38. And besides, there are others who even admit not only "that there are no clear testimonies in Scripture about indulgences, and they advise their fellow Catholics not to rely on things that are less certain, but they also add that they do not have certain testimonies of the early, primitive church, and that in this matter they do not have the apostolic tradition" but only the authority of the Roman church and of some (actually recent) councils—as may be seen in the writings of Peter de Soto, in his *Lectures on the Institution of Priesthood* (*On Indulgences*, lecture 1). Nevertheless, they push their doctrine about indulgences as an article of faith, and define it as "the exemptions from temporal punishments that in God's judgment are owed for actual sins after the guilt has been forgiven, through the application of the excess deeds of satisfaction of Christ and the saints, done apart from the sacrament by someone who has the lawful authority to do so" (Gregory of Valencia, volume 4, disputation 7, question 20.1).

39. If we explain this definition according to their intended meaning and point out the folly of each individual part, we shall untie an otherwise knotty topic in a few words. We shall give them the benefit as far as the name ['indulgence'] is concerned, because for the most part the name is understood in a more pejorative sense. Even so, they use it for this subject-matter in an inauspicious way, as in 'the loving indulgence of fathers makes their children slothful,' so that 'good fathers' have it in them to indulge their nature. "For indulgences came about in order to lighten the church of its poverty, which

is not lightened only by the will to give but by the gift" (Augustine of Ancona, *On the Sovereignty of the Pope*, question 30, article 3). Therefore, they give in order to receive, and they do not indulge for nothing. When they say that indulgences are "the exemptions from temporal punishments, etc.," the words expose the primary basis for this business transaction, i.e., concerning some temporal, satisfactorial punishments of a penitent man whose guilt has been forgiven by God's grace but to whom punishments are still owed and which must be paid either in this life or in purgatory. We overturned this basis above, in theses 32–35, so that this need not be done at this point.

40. But the gamble of the papal teachers gives itself away when they prove that after their guilt has been forgiven believers still remain subject to temporal punishments either by actually paying for them or by obtaining exemption by means of indulgences. When it comes to the point, they are compelled to admit that no exemption via indulgences is possible for penalties on the basis of the indulgences they sometimes show from Scriptures as imposed on some believers such as David and the like. But the artificial penalties of purgatory are either ones that people commanded, or have to command, or undertake willingly. Therefore, indulgences not only do not absolve from the liability of any mortal or venial guilt, but they also do not absolve from any natural penalties such as diseases, death, ignorance, concupiscence, and similar things. And they also do not absolve even from the punishments that can be inflicted by the outward, the litigious forums (ecclesiastical as well as political). But they can only remove the penalty that is owed in the hidden forum of one's repentance, according to Bellarmine (*On Indulgences*, book 1, chapter 7).

41. It is obvious from these observations that the many people who purchase these wares at a great price and who have been enticed by the lofty promises of "fulsome and the fullest indulgence" for all sins (often with the added phrase, "from punishment and guilt") experience what the proverb says, that "in exchange for their treasures they possess nothing but coal." For because those punishments that are mentioned in Ps 89[:32 and 33] ("If your sons sin, I shall punish their iniquities with the rod") and in Heb 12[:6] (when the apostle says, "we receive discipline from God") and also in 1 Cor 11[:32] ("God judges and instructs us") are inflicted upon us by God as the "external, criminal judge," Bellarmine grants that they are not taken away by indulgences (*On Indulgences*, book 2, chapter 1), but that only the penalty is removed "which is inflicted in the penitentiary forum, a penalty that we are

driven to fulfill only by the fear of God and the goad of our own conscience." From this the objection which Luther rightly had made becomes very obvious, namely that indulgences are harmful, not beneficial, since they hinder us from doing good works (fasting, almsgiving, prayers) and in fact dispel "the fear of God and the goad of our own conscience." For "by means of permitted indulgences man makes satisfaction for the penalties that were imposed in confession, so that in case the Confessor imposed upon him a discipline, fasting, almsgiving, or some similar works to be performed, if he obtains the indulgence he is not bound to undergo the penalties" ([Francisco de] Toledo, *Instructions for Priests*, book 6, chapter 24).

42. But so that the zeal of those who in the dispensing of indulgences seek something greater should not grow cold, they stoked the flames of purgatory in order to inflict terror. And so the following 'fear-factor' was added: if it should happen that someone dies before he has completed the penalty of ten years that has been imposed, he will be punished with the fiercest penalty in purgatory, but from there he would fly as a free man to heaven if, properly equipped with letters of the fullest indulgence, he should show them to the gate-keeper of heaven. Hence it is that indulgences are granted for many thousands of years, because even if this time by far surpasses a man's life-time, still for one mortal sin a penalty of seven years must be imposed and it can happen to many people that they have committed more than one thousand mortal sins, who according to the canonical rules should spend seven thousand years in penitence if they were to have lived that many years. In this manner provision is made for them, namely by granting indulgence for so many thousands of years that is not only equal to but even surpasses the penitence they should have fulfilled if they had done thousands of years of penitence. To have pointed out these ominous signs is to have refuted them.

43. In order to supply satisfactions for so many years and for such countless temporal punishments from another source, they also laid a second basis for indulgences, namely that of the "excess satisfactions of Christ and the saints," which the Roman popes, and the other bishops according to their lesser measure, keep locked up in their treasury, on the assumption that the satisfaction of Christ, being absolutely infinite, could not have received any equivalent created reward and had merited infinitely more than any reward that He had been given. [And also on the basis that] "many saintly men have suffered much more for the sake of God and righteousness than their liability

to temporal punishment required, to which they were subject for the wrongs they had committed," and they redeem even some others from their every guilt. They put all these things together and poured them into their mixer to fashion that lump from which they could dispense small pieces in the form of indulgences.

44. And as far as we are concerned, whatever slanderous charge they should make against us, we piously acknowledge that the satisfaction of our Lord Jesus Christ is a treasury of invaluable worth that has been entrusted to the church of God. From this treasury are dispensed upon people who are truly penitent and believe in Him, indulgences that are real and valid in the sight of God, or rather the fullest remission of sins, remission from every penalty and guilt of original as well as actual sins. But we do assert that the papal teachers do injury to this satisfaction of Christ when, in order to add the satisfaction of men, they take away the limitless quality of Christ's satisfaction, because they deem that "his satisfactions must be applied in a limited way so that something may be added to them when the sufferings of the saints are linked to them," as Bellarmine says (*On Indulgences*, book 1, chapter 4). But we state that this not only adds a finite thing to what is infinite, but nothing to what is entire, for it is false and foolish what they say about the sufferings of the saints, i.e., that they possess a double force. Of this double force one is "meritorious" while the other is "satisfactorial," and regarding the merit they have received their full reward, but not regarding the satisfaction. For the works of the saints have neither of these aspects. But even Durand rightly proves that they did not have the satisfactorial quality from the fact that it was not the saints' intention to transfer the fruit of their own sufferings unto others—an intention that would have been necessary, at least. But such an intention could not have existed for the saints, as it would have been a haughty and blasphemous one.

45. If the suffering of the saints were satisfactory for other people and together with Christ's blood formed the treasury, then the distinction would be taken away that the apostle makes in Heb 12:24 between Christ's blood and the blood of Abel, for then "the blood of Christ would speak no more eloquently than the blood of Abel" (Heb 12:24). For then either one could have obtained forgiveness of the punishment for sins. And Solomon would have written in vain: "If you are wise, you are wise for yourself; but if you are a mocker, you alone will bear the evil" (Prov 9:12). Nor would "anyone boast only in himself and not boast in another" (Gal 6:4). And there would not

have been any reason why God through Ezekiel (14:20) should say about Noah, Daniel and Job that "they did not set free their own sons and daughters, but by their righteousness they set free only their own souls." There never was any saint who would not have concurred with Tertullian when he asks: "Who has paid for the death of another by his own except the Son of God alone? And so, you who imitate him by forgiving misdeeds, if you yourself have committed no misdeeds, then suffer on my behalf. But if you are a sinner, how could the oil of your torch have sufficed both for you and for me?" (*On Modesty*, chapter 22). And who would not have joined hands with Augustine when he says: "Even though brothers would die for brothers, yet in the forgiveness of brothers' sins not any martyr's blood is poured out" (*On John*, Treatise 84).

46. And yet there should be no fear that the saints' sufferings are in vain, for they serve different uses and goals whereof no doubt can be raised. But they are in vain insofar as their satisfactory powers are concerned, and there is nothing troublesome about the fact that they are without such result if they are not applied to those who need [satisfaction]. For not even the papal teachers deny that the sufferings of all the saints who will still be alive on the Day of the Lord will be in vain. So too for the sufferings that at that time will still be left in the Church's treasury, because then there will not be any people to whom they could be dispensed, unless perhaps the papal teachers think that when purgatory is emptied out there will still be "some days of rest for the guilty spirits under the [river] Styx," or that these souls will emerge at last by the power of the satisfactions—a mad idea that once upon a time fooled some of them who found prayer for the dead appealing.

47. But the 'communion of the saints' does not require the communication of satisfactions for sin. For 'communion' is different from 'communication,' since communion presupposes some common thing whereto the people among whom the communion exists have an equal right. The same relationship does not exist for something that the one who does not need it communicates with someone else who does lack it. On the contrary, the communion of saints completely overturns the notion of this or that man's particular satisfactions, because just as our communion consists of the fact that we have the same God, the same faith, the same baptism, and the same Spirit, and not in the fact that we communicate to other people the Spirit, faith or baptism that is superfluous for us, so also the communion of the saints consists in the fact that they all have the right to the one satisfaction of

Christ. And so the argument from the 'communion of saints' is effectively turned around against our opponents.

48. Nor is it a more firm foundation that supports what they mean by the 'communication' that should have its place also among Christians, for the communication ought to be of those goods that can be communicated and passed from one person to another. But it is impossible to prove that the sufferings of believers are goods of this sort. Nor can any reason be brought forward why "the part of a good work that is meritorious cannot be applied to others"—a fact that Bellarmine admits (*On Indulgences*, book 1, chapter 2)—whereas the part of the same work that is satisfactory can be communicated. Add to this the fact that satisfaction is not some good in an absolute sense but relative to the one to whom satisfaction is made. Therefore, even if someone were to establish such participation and communication on the part of the members with the intention to make satisfaction, it does not for that reason follow that there is acceptance on the part of the 'creditor,' without which the application of the communication would be altogether useless.

49. Therefore the statement they make is false, that another's satisfactions applied by the church's prelates are "means" whereby the fruit of Christ's infinite satisfaction is drawn down to men insofar as the forgiveness of punishment is concerned, for they cannot show that Christ has instituted this sort of means. Moreover, since Christ's satisfaction "is applied in a limited way" so that the satisfactions of saints may in fact be added to it (as we have shown from Bellarmine), it is sufficiently clear from their doctrine that the saints' satisfactions are applied in the same way as Christ's satisfactions—and consequently they are not the applications of the satisfaction of another, but are properly and of themselves considered together with Christ's satisfactions to be of the same kind. The promoters of indulgences want that by the power of love, whereby the members of the church are united with one another, "the payment which one has made on behalf of another would be received in such a way on his behalf as if he himself had offered it." This surely cannot be done without imputing the righteousness of another. And since apart from and against Scripture they grant that imputation to the satisfactions of men, it is surprising that the same people still mockingly accept the doctrine of the imputation of the righteousness of Christ our head, from whose very close union with all his true members the communication of all good things flows forth unto the eternal salvation of the elect.

50. Only his sufferings have the power to make satisfaction, and as they are communicated to believers by means of imputation, as the only Redeemer he has claimed this for himself. But in "that he has suffered on our behalf and has left us an example" (1 Pet 2:21), namely that we should undergo suffering for the sake of others, "not by the mode of redemption but through the mode of example and encouragement, according to that" [saying] that if we suffer tribulations it is for your encouragement and salvation, says Thomas (*Summa theologiae* 3, question 48, article 5, point 3). It is in this sense that he understands the apostle's statement: "I rejoice in my sufferings for you and in my flesh I fill up those things that are lacking from Christ's passions for the sake of his body, which is the Church" (Col 1:24). Or "what is lacking" are the things that each and every member of the church must suffer following the suffering of Christ; this is the meaning approved by the Jesuit, Gabriel Vasquez (*Annotations* to the Epistle to the Colossians). But he considers the plainer meaning to be the one he pursues as follows in his paraphrase: "I, who now rejoice that I suffer so many afflictions for your sake, by having endured them to the full in myself in the Gospel-preaching fill up what was lacking to Christ's suffering, so that the fruit of it through the labor of the Gospel-preaching might reach the body of the church, when by hearing it everyone might individually receive faith and be justified." Therefore it is not so that thence some satisfaction might come about by the bestowing of indulgences.

51. Since a nonbeing is not susceptible to any relations, it would be superfluous to treat further "the church's authority in the collection" of such indulgences: whether the authority is given only to the pope and the bishops "by divine right" and to others only "by commission." And: whether indulgences are applied through genuine absolution or through a dispensation only from the treasury. Whether indulgences are applied in the same way to the living as to the dead, or whether to the living "through the mode of absolution" and to the dead only "through the mode of assistance;" or whether it is given only to those "who are in grace." And similarly, what is a "plenary" indulgence, a "Carena," a "forty-day" indulgence? And, whether for small causes not any great indulgences at all are granted, or whether they have any such value as the cause demands, and what is a just cause for granting them, concerning which the patrons of indulgences argue with each other. Nor is there any agreement between them about the value of indulgences, about the treasury, the sufficiency of a cause, the disposition

of the recipient, etc. And the teachers de Soto and Victoria do not deny that the "certificates whereby the fullest indulgences are bestowed in return for the smallest almsgiving contain an intolerable mistake," as Joseph Angles reports ([*Flowers of Theological Questions*] *on the Sentences*, book 4, [Question regarding Indulgences], article 2, difficulty 5).

52. Nor should it cause trouble if anyone occasionally stumbles across mention of indulgence in the records of the ancients, for even now Peter de Soto admits that the papal teachers possess no definitive testimony from the ancient church. The matter, then, is as follows. Those early fathers, especially in serious, public sins, would not absolve and reconcile the sinner until he had proved his repentance to the church with long, hard and difficult exercises. But if persecution was about to happen, the penitents would sometimes be absolved beforehand, so that they might go to their martyrdom with greater courage. The same would happen if someone already in the process of penitence found himself in danger of dying, or if such zeal of contrition were observed in the sinner that there was no need for a longer period of testing, or if an accompanying repentance was bound up with it. The church would aid such people by means of indulgences to relax the strictest severity somewhat. Not only the statement of the fathers but also Paul's (which the patrons of indulgences misuse) should be taken in this way: "Anyone whom you forgive I also forgive, for also I, if I have forgiven anything, did so for your sake in the presence of Christ" (2 Cor 2:10), namely, "so that the man who had been excommunicated should not be overwhelmed by overflowing grief" (verse 7).

53. What rendered the institution of the hundred-year Jubilee disreputable was that most shameless business-dealing in sacred matters as well as the consideration of its very founder, Boniface the Eighth (who "took office as a fox, ruled like a lion, and died like a dog"), as he used to thirst for "gold obtained from any place at all, more than one could say," as Platina attests. Driven by the same mad lust, Clement the Sixth followed in his footsteps and he "(it is doubtful whether by a lust for money or a desire for men's salvation) gave the sanction that the Jubilee should be celebrated every fifty years." And later, Sixtus the Fifth, whose ambition and cunning was known to all, reduced it to every twenty-five years. Clement the Eighth calls [the Jubilee] "the Lord's year of appeasement, the year of forgiveness and pardon, the acceptable time, and the day of eternal salvation" in the announcement-bull (which really was a boil!). Over against him we put forward the sure certificate of the Christian

Jubilee (Isa 61:2; Luke 4:19): "The Lord has sent me to proclaim the acceptable year of Jehovah," namely the most joyful preaching of the Gospel brought from the bosom of the eternal Father, in which is announced to all believers, the real penitents, the liberation from all sins and all penalties for sins, in every time and place.

54. And for that reason we should give our utmost thanks to God because in the time of our forebears, when He had allowed the business-dealing of indulgences to reach the acme of shamelessness when Leo the Tenth opened public market-squares throughout all the kingdoms of the world, He raised up Martin Luther, who at first was thinking of nothing else than to punish the unlimited abuses, gradually, in God's providence and by his enemies recklessly providing a cause, was led not merely to overturn the entire system of indulgences from its very foundations, but thence also, when his enemies took refuge in those commonplaces of proof for the pope's authority (and the like), by pursuing them was finally led to the point of tearing down usurped power of the pope himself, until little by little through his ministry that marvelous work of the reformation of true doctrine was promoted through him and others, which afterward in God's greatest goodwill was spread far and wide during our own times. Thus it remains that we, acknowledging the true source of the forgiveness of sins, and then being washed in it, should abstain from sins, and bring glory to God the Father, in Christ the Son, and through the Holy Spirit forever.

Corollary

1. We declare that the *Limbo of children*, whereto the papal teachers send the souls of infants who have departed from this life without the outward washing of baptism, does not rest upon any basis in Scripture or earliest antiquity.

2. We state that it is an invention alien to the truth and to reason that some people after this life are punished in hell by the punishment of damnation but are exempt from the total punishment of the senses.

3. It is an invention from a spirit of Marcionism that the patriarchs and all the saints of the Old Testament were detained in the world below, as Tertullian testifies (*Against Marcion*, book 4, chapter 34): "Both conditions, whether of the torment or of the relief which determines their state in the

underworld, are laid upon those who were obedient to the law and the prophets."

ON THE CHURCH

President: Antonius Walaeus
Respondent: Jacobus Bosschaert

This is the first of three disputations on Reformed ecclesiology (Disputations 40–43). 'Ecclesia,' or the Church, is defined etymologically as 'the meeting of those whom God in his grace calls out from the state of nature into the supernatural state of children of God, in order to show his glorious mercy' (3). In this regard the teaching of the Church relates to God's call to salvation. Also the elect angels belong to the same family of Christ (6). The following aspects are successively discussed: the parts of the Church and their mode and form (8–25); the division of the Church into the Church of the Old and the New Testament, and into visible and invisible (26–36); and finally, the privileges and marks of the Church (37–51). The triumphant part of the Church is in heaven and consists of believers from both the Old and the New Testament (9–21). The other part of the Church is still fighting against the flesh, the world, and Satan (22–25). It is necessary for believers to belong to this Church, to have communion with each other, and to be joined together by the bond of Word and Sacraments (24). The invisible Church (28–31) is the multitude of elect believers of which the inner form (consisting of true faith and holiness) is not seen by human eyes, by mortal people (28). The visible Church (32–36) is 'the gathering of those who through the outward Word, the use of the sacraments, and church discipline, are formed together into one outward body and fellowship' (32). Hypocrites and godless people are mixed in with it (35). As for the marks of the Church, a distinction is made between erring and committing heresy. When false teachings are promoted that 'do not ruin the foundation of the faith' (1 Cor 3:11), a church errs (38). Heresy occurs when the Church errs obstinately in the fundamental articles of the faith (39–41). A believer ought not to join a church that is heretical or schismatic (42). Positively, the marks of the pure, visible Church are 'the pure preaching, and reception, of the Word, sealed by the lawful use of the sacraments, and upheld by the true use of the keys (or church discipline), according to the institution by Christ' (45). In the last three theses the many marks of the Church that are employed by Roman Catholic teachers are shown to be applied in such a way that it proves itself a false church (49–51).

1. 'Ecclesia' is a Greek word that comes from *ekkalein*, which is 'to call out,' and it corresponds to the Hebrew words *qahal* and *'edah*, and strictly speaking means a meeting or gathering of people who have been called by some higher authority, not solely for a purpose or end that is sacred, but also for non-religious and political ones, as can be seen in Acts 19:32 and 39.

2. But we here take the word 'Ecclesia' in the sense of a meeting or gathering that is sacred, as Christians commonly understand it. Occasionally they use it for the place where they hold sacred gatherings, but examples of this meaning do not occur in Scripture.

3. In general the meaning of the word is defined as the meeting of those whom God in his grace calls out from the state of nature into the supernatural state of children of God, in order to show his glorious mercy.

4. In the Church of Christ it is beyond dispute that God is the primary author of this calling, since He alone can bestow the grace to which He calls, and ordain the means whereby this calling is to be made, just as the apostle says in Heb 3:4: "For every house is built by someone, but the one who has built all these"—and he is speaking about the Church of Christ—"is God."

5. The subject-matter, or object of this calling are only the creatures who have been made in the image of God, that is, angels and men. For although God is able to make sons of Abraham from stones, as Christ says in Matt 3:9, yet only creatures made in the image of God are of themselves and directly capable of receiving blessed immortality and heavenly happiness.

6. Only a few things are revealed to us in the Scriptures about the calling of some angels from the state of mutable nature to the immutable state of glorious grace. Nevertheless, because everywhere they are specifically called the sons of God, angels of light, angels of glory, and elect angels, and because they also recognize Christ himself as their special head (Eph 1:22), and because they call themselves our fellow servants, fellow-servants of the brothers, and even belonging to the brothers who have the testimony of Jesus (Rev 19:10), it follows that we should profess that they are members of that entire body, and our fellow-servants in the family of Christ. And consequently, through the particular working of the Holy Spirit under Christ

498

the one and only Head of his Church, they are effectively established in glory and grace. Therefore, the apostle declares that we, too, have come to the myriads of angels through the effective calling (Heb 12:22).

7. Yet even though this fellowship with angels is a source of glory and comfort to us, still we should give special treatment to the Church of human beings because that is of the greatest interest to us. And about that Church we must investigate: the parts of the Church and their mode and form, the division of the Church, and finally the privileges and marks of the Church.

8. When the parts of the Church are considered as a whole, the papal teachers determine three parts for it, i.e., one that is laboring in purgatory, the second that is triumphant in heaven, and the third that is militant here on earth. We recognize with pleasure the two latter parts of the Church; but in a prior disputation we have demonstrated sufficiently that their third one is from outside of God's Word and invented, for the sake of emptying out money-supplies and oppressing the souls of god-fearing people with spiritual slavery. And so, in what follows we need only to treat the other two parts.

9. All the places that show convincingly the immortality of the soul prove over-against the Socinians, Anabaptists, Libertines, and similar heretics that a large part of the universal Church is triumphant in heaven under Christ its head. For while "the body returns to the earth from where it came, yet the spirit returns to God who has given it" (Eccl 12:7). And although "there are those who can kill the bodies of the pious, yet they cannot kill their souls," as Christ testifies in Matt 10:28.

10. But this is clear especially from those places and instances that depict the happiness and blessed state of the deceased. As we see in Matt 20:8, where "all who labored in the vineyard, when their labor has been completed, receive their reward," in 2 Cor 5:1: "We know that if the earthly dwelling-place is broken down, we have another, eternal home in heaven not made with hands," and in Rev 14:13: "Blessed are the dead who die in the Lord, from this time forth they rest from their labors, and their works follow them."

11. But contrary to the papal teachers we must maintain that not only believers under the New Testament, after Christ's ascension into heaven, but also believers who died in the faith under the Old Testament, reached this part of the triumphant Church in heaven. They, on the other hand, think that

those people had been locked up in a subterranean limbo and from there they have been looking for the coming of the Lord.

12. The promises of Christ demonstrate this, as do other places in Scripture, and also very clear exemplary instances.

13. The promises are clear: "There is fullness of joys most pleasant in your presence, at your right hand forevermore" (Ps 16:11). "Blessed are the poor in spirit, for theirs is the kingdom of heaven" (Matt 5:3), and "Blessed are the pure of heart, for they shall see God" (verse 8). "Blessed are those who suffer persecution, for theirs is the kingdom of heaven. Rejoice and be glad, because great is your reward in heaven; for thus they persecuted the prophets, etc." (verse 10). Without a doubt these sayings of Christ were true already then when he declared them, and did not become true only when Christ rose from the dead and ascended into heaven.

14. The passages from Scripture which reveal the state of the pious who have died before Christ's suffering are no less clear. Such passages include Eph 1:10: "God unites all things both in heaven and on earth in Christ," and Col 1:20: "And through Christ all things were reconciled, both in heaven and on earth." Since this manner of speaking cannot mean those angels who were not reconciled to God through Christ, it follows that it must mean the saints dwelling in heaven before [the advent of] Christ, just as the apostle says in Heb 12:22 that so we "have come to Mount Zion and to the city of the living God, the heavenly Jerusalem," etc., and "to the meeting and assembly of the first-born who are enrolled in heaven."

15. Scripture also presents to us brilliant examples of this state: Elijah (2 Kgs 2:11) is said expressly to have been carried into heaven, and 1 Macc 2:58 confirms it. Moses and Elijah appeared on the mountain in the company of Christ and three disciples, in glory; and then they were taken away from before their eyes by a cloud (Luke 9:31). And from that cloud a voice came down: "This is my Son, etc." And Peter testifies to the fact that this voice came down from heaven (2 Pet 1:18). The angels carried Lazarus into the bosom of Abraham. But the Scriptures say nowhere that the angels carried believers to places under the earth, since their proper dwelling is in heaven. Matt 8:11 states explicitly that this bosom of Abraham, wherein the faithful recline, is heaven. Christ says: "I say to you that they will come from East and West and recline with Abraham, Isaac, and Jacob in the kingdom of heaven." And lastly, the same is confirmed by the example of the thief who

was crucified together with Christ, whom Christ promised that on the same day he would be with him in Paradise (Luke 23:43). The apostle asserts that Paradise is the third heaven (2 Cor 12:2 and 4).

16. From these passages it is clear that before Christ's coming the fathers were no less triumphant in heaven by the power of the coming Christ than under the New Testament now that they are reigning by the power of Christ after he suffered and was taken up into heaven.

17. In fact we assert from Scripture that the pious who have died under either of both testaments are not just enjoying some heavenly joy apart from the presence of God, as some of the great men used to think, but that they are fully enjoying true and unbroken blessedness in God's very presence. Even so we do not deny that some degree of happiness is kept aside for them until the last day, when [their souls] will be joined to their bodies.

18. This is demonstrated by very many places of Scripture, for also David locates the place of their true blessedness as the presence of God (Ps 16, 23 and 84). And Paul desires "to depart and to be with Christ" (Phil 1:23); and 2 Cor 5:8: "And so we choose rather to depart from the body and go to dwell with the Lord." The apostle testifies that Christ is with the Father, and on the Father's throne (Rev 3:21; John 17:5; Heb 9:24). Therefore, also throughout Revelation the deceased saints are placed together with the angels before the throne of God and the Lamb, so that they sing constant praises and give thanks to Him, as can be seen in Rev 4:8, 5:8, and 7:9.

19. However, it does not therefore follow that this part of the Church that is triumphant is therefore put in charge of the militant Church on earth, as in the dream of those papal teachers who put them in charge of kingdoms, provinces, cities and districts—even diseases, the arts, peace and war—like patron deities. For even if Holy Scripture does assign the angels some common ministry in these matters, it testifies everywhere that the deceased saints "enter into peace and rest from their labors" (Isa 57:2; Rev 14:13), "and that they do not arise or return again to their own home, nor does their place know them any more" (Job 7:10); "in fact, if their children increase, they are unaware of it, and if they are brought low, they do not perceive it" (Job 14:21). Likewise, "we shall go to them but they will not return to us" (2 Sam 12:23), and "they do not see all the evil that God brings upon his people" (2 Kgs 22:20).

20. And in fact it contradicts the nature of deceased saints that they should be present in and care for diverse and widely scattered places at one and the same time, as when the [papal teachers] want to put one and the same saint in charge of diverse and widely scattered places. Think of Saint James for the Spanish, who dwell in Europe, India, and America. Or Saints Dominic and Francis, etc., for all their monasteries spread across the whole globe. Or even the blessed Virgin, whom they call Queen of Heaven, Mistress of the Earth, and Star of the Sea (*Stella Maris*)—even though this is a wrong rendering of Drop of the Sea (*Stilla maris*)—since it is fitting only for God to "look down from the heavens and behold all the sons of men, and from his dwelling-place to look forth upon all the inhabitants of the earth" (Ps 33:13–14).

21. And therefore what Matt 24:47 says about the faithful servant's command over all his master's goods should be understood as being about spiritual goods, as in Rom 8:17: "We are called heirs of God and fellow-heirs with Christ." And also, what Rev 2 and 3 say about ruling over the nations with an iron rod, and being seated on God's throne should necessarily be understood allegorically, about the complete glory and dominion over Satan, the world, and the flesh, as Paul explains in 1 Cor 15:56 and John in Rev 5:10 and 21:7.

22. Having explained briefly the things concerning that part of the Church that is triumphant in heaven, let us go down to that part of the Church which is still fighting or battling against the flesh, the world and Satan, as Paul says in Gal 5:17; 1 John 5:4, and Eph 6:12.

23. The very many promises found in Jer 31:36, Matt 16:18, Matt 28:20, etc., about the preservation of the Church, show clearly that there always has been a Church on earth, and that there shall be one until the end of the world. The office of Christ clearly shows this, as he is the eternal King, Bridegroom, Shepherd, and Head of this Church, which he cannot be if there is no kingdom, bride, flock, and body that he makes alive here on earth. And finally, it is shown clearly by the office of all those who will be saved, because no-one can have God for a Father who does not have the Church for a mother, as Paul testifies (Gal 4:26).

24. But what the Libertines claim is not enough, that individual members of the Church of Christ say that they separately foster spiritual communion with the unknown church, even if they do not foster any outward communion at all with any meeting, or even if they pretend to foster a communion with

idolatrous and apostate meetings. But we assert that in order to establish the true Church it is necessary for believers to have communion with each other, and to be joined together by the bond of Word and Sacraments according to their institution by Christ, unless it happens because of extreme persecution that they are compelled to break off their communion for a short time.

25. The promise of particular grace that is made for those who have been gathered in the name of the Lord demonstrates this (Matt 18:20), and so too the goal of the institution of the Word and sacraments and of the use of discipline. "For faith comes by hearing, and hearing comes through the word of God" (Rom 10:17); and, "how are they to believe unless someone preaches to them, and how are they to preach unless they are sent?" For thus through baptism we have put on Christ (Rom 6; Gal 3). The supper of the Lord is the communion of the body and blood of the Lord (1 Cor 10). Indeed, Christ in Eph 4:11 "has not only given some apostles, prophets and evangelists, but also pastors and teachers, in order to equip the saints, for the works of ministry, for the building up of the body of Christ, until we shall all attain to the unity of the faith and of the knowledge of the Son of God." And for this reason, we are commanded in the celebration of the holy supper "to commemorate the Lord's death until he comes," (1 Cor 11:26) and in case a brother does not listen to us, "to tell it to the church" (Matt 18:17).

26. This militant Church is divided in different ways: first, into the Church of the Old and the New Testament. Some also call [the latter] the catholic Church because nowadays it is not bound to any particular region, city, or temple-building, as it had been formerly, "but the sound of their voice has gone into all the world, and their words even to the ends of the world" (Rom 10:18). And although formerly the gentiles apart from Christ and alienated from the nation of Israel were strangers to the covenants of promises, "yet now in Christ Jesus those who once were afar off have been brought near through Christ's blood, for he is our peace who has made us both one, and has broken down the middle wall of partition" (Eph 2:12 ff.).

27. Second, we divide the Church into visible and invisible; and although some confuse visible with particular and invisible with universal, we—unless there is a better judgment—think that we should not confuse those elements.

28. The invisible Church is called the multitude of elect believers who, whether they are in specific individual meetings or in all the churches and places throughout the world, are conspicuous to the eyes of God. And so, it

is called 'invisible' because its inner, essential form, namely its true faith and holiness, are not seen by mortal people. For whereas we do not deny that through confession and good works the very faith and inner sanctity also make themselves evident, yet because hypocrites are able to imitate all these for a period of time, it follows that on the basis of only those things one cannot make an infallible judgment about other people. Therefore, also the wise man in 1 Kgs 8:39 testifies that "only God knows the hearts of all the sons of men." Similarly, Christ says in John 10:14: "I know my sheep and my sheep know me." And the apostle Paul says against the scandal-mongers in 2 Tim 2:19: "God's firm foundation stands, and has this seal: 'the Lord knows those who are his.'"

29. Along with Scripture we give to this multitude of believers the name *ecclesia* ['the called'] because by God's Word and Spirit they have been called out of the world to faith and holiness, and because they have a genuine and inner communion and fellowship with Christ and all true believers. And therefore, throughout the Scriptures it is called by names of the sort that effectively denote this inner fellowship and communion with Christ and all the saints.

30. Hence this Church is called the "betrothed and love of Christ" (Song 4:7; Eph 5:27), "holy Zion" and "heavenly Jerusalem" and "the Israel of God" (Isa 52:1; Gal 4:26, and 6:16). And similarly: "The Church which Christ has cleansed for himself, that he should make her glorious for himself, not having any spot or wrinkle" (Eph 5:27). "The body of Christ, fitly joined and held together by what every joint supplies, according to the inner working in the measure of each part" (Eph 4:16). It is called "the people of Christ" whom he saves from its sins (Matt 1:21). "One fold and one shepherd" (John 10:16); the "house of God and holy priesthood" (1 Pet 2:5); the "temple of God" in which the Holy Spirit dwells (1 Cor 3:16), etc. "The wife of the Lamb" (Rev 21:9), etc. Since all these and similar things can in no way at all apply to the hypocrites and unregenerates (whatever mask they hide behind), it necessarily follows that the Church whereof these things are said is only that one which we have described earlier.

31. And to this Church, too, properly belong all the salutary and spiritual promises that are made to the Church of God everywhere in Scripture; both the hypocrites and the unrighteous are excluded from these promises. And among the other promises there occurs also this one: that the Church will

never be lacking in this world, as Jer 31:[35 and]36 says: "'If the ordinances for the sun and the moon cease from before me,' says the Lord, 'then also will the offspring of Israel cease from being a nation, for all days.'" And so Matt 16:18: "The gates of hell will not prevail against her;" and hence Christ testifies in Matt 24:24: "It will not be possible for the elect to be led astray." And Rev 13:8, and elsewhere, testifies that "those whose names are written in the book of life of the Lamb" will be spared from being led astray by the Antichrist and from the whole world's apostasy.

32. The visible Church is the gathering of those who through the outward Word, the use of the sacraments, and church discipline, are formed together into one outward body and fellowship, which is called the visible Church, not so much because the people themselves are visible, but because their organization, public profession and communion are displayed to the outward senses.

33. There are two modes wherein this visible Church is considered: either as some particular meeting of a single district, city, or province, i.e., of those people who are bound to each other not just in the community of faith and sacraments, but also in the form of their outward governance and rites of the Church. Or as some ecumenical and universal meeting scattered in diverse places across the entire globe, even though in the very form of outward governance and circumstantial rites they often differ very much from each other, yet they are harmonious in the essential community of faith and sacraments, and for this reason it says repeatedly in Cyprian that "there is one bishopric, and a part of it is held as a whole by each [bishop]."

34. This visible Church is strictly speaking not different from the invisible Church, but it is only considered in a different way: the former as 'coming about,' the latter as 'having come about'—like a house that is being built and a house that has been built. For that invisible Church which we described beforehand is gathered and formed within the visible Church. The invisible Church is inherent in and contained by the visible one.

35. And hence it happens that the visible Church (particular as well as universal) is never so pure and sincere that not any hypocrites and godless people are mixed in with it, just as Christ therefore compares it to a "net" [Matt 13:47–50] that catches good as well as bad fish, and to a "field" [Matt 13:24–30] and "threshing floor" [Matt 3:12, Luke 3:17] wherein the wholesome grain is grown and gathered together with the weeds, and to a

"wedding banquet" where even those people sometimes appear who are not clothed in a wedding garment [Matt 22:1–14]. And so also the apostle Paul compares it to "a house, in which there are not only articles of gold and silver, but also of wood and clay; some are for honorable use, some for dishonorable" (2 Tim 2:20).

36. But even though this Church is never entirely free of hypocrites and godless people, still it is bound, as much as possible, to expose the hypocrites and by the keys Christ has granted it to exclude the godless from its meeting, in accordance with the command of Christ (Matt 18:17; Rev 2:2 and 14). But as for the believers themselves who have fallen into sin in their conduct of life or faith, she is bound to call them back powerfully by the same discipline to genuine repentance, as Paul advises in 1 Cor 5:5.

37. With respect to doctrine and moral conduct this visible Church is either pure or impure; then again, the impure is either simply erring, or heretical, or schismatic.

38. We call a church simply erring when it does indeed harbor and foster some false teachings, but only those that do not ruin the foundation of the faith, i.e., Christ and his office (1 Cor 3:11), and yet it does so in a way that it is prepared daily to improve and to correct the false teachings of which it was convicted, as God has commanded. Such a church was the one in Galatia, Corinth, Colossae, etc., wherein the apostle reproved errors that were indeed serious, but which did not concern the foundation of the faith nor were the people themselves obstinate in their errors. Therefore, the apostle certainly reproves them seriously, but he does not remove either himself or the believers from having communion with them.

39. We give the name heretical to a church that errs in articles of grave importance—fundamental articles—to such a degree that it spurns all reproof and obstinately persists in error. "For obstinacy is a formal quality of heresy." For we ought to treat someone as a heathen and publican only at the time when he will not listen to the Church when it is rightly admonishing him, as Christ advises in Matt 18:17 and Paul in Gal 5:12.

40. There are two kinds of heresy: the kind that directly ruins the foundation, that is, Christ or his office; or the kind that ruins them indirectly and as a consequence (as they say). Scripture calls people of the first kind antichrists

and apostates, and it calls the latter by the general name of false prophets or false teachers.

41. Strictly speaking a schismatic church is one that agrees with the orthodox Church in the fundamental elements of the faith; yet because of some outward rites that are indifferent in nature, or because of some particular failings in moral conduct, it makes a break with the Christian communion and starts up separate meetings. "For in the same way as heretics violate faith itself by having false notions about God, so too do schismatics break away from the love of the brotherhood by their unjust deeds of separation, even though they believe what we believe," as Augustine rightly says (*On Faith and the Creed*). Yet we should add also this point from Thomas [Aquinas]: "Strictly speaking people are called schismatics who purposefully remove themselves without a suitable cause from the unity of the Church" ([*Summa theologiae*] book 2, part 2).

42. Here the question arises whether it is permitted for a Christian to foster communion with a church that is heretical and schismatic. And our answer is that we should foster communion with a church that is erring in the faith and moral conduct, and we should make the effort in every way so that it may be called back from its error and schism, just as we see was done everywhere by Christ and the apostles. But with a church that properly speaking is heretical and schismatic, since its works belong to the flesh, we say that we must not maintain Christian communion, according to the command of Christ (Matt 7:15) and the apostle (Rom 16:17; Titus 3:10; 2 John 9, etc.).

43. We call a church pure when it keeps the preaching of the Word and the confession of faith pure and intact. For although there is no church on earth which is so pure and intact that nothing more could be required of it in faith or moral conduct, nevertheless we deem that we here should call it thus on the basis of the dominant part of the doctrine, along with the apostle in Phil 3:15: "Let us, as many as are perfect, be thus minded, that if in anything you are otherwise minded, God will reveal this also to you. But in what we have already reached, let us walk by the same rule, and let us be of the same mind."

44. From the things that have been explained earlier there appears a satisfactory answer to the question debated between the papal teachers and us whether the Church can err and defect. For we believe that the Church of the elect, the invisible Church, although it can err in matters that are

circumstantial, can never fall away from the faith because if it should fall away, it would cease to be the Church of Christ. But as far as the visible Church is concerned, the papal teachers themselves acknowledge with us that individual churches can fall away, even though they try to make an exception—without reason—for the Roman church; both experience and Scripture bear witness that certainly very many churches have fallen away. But as for the universal, visible Church, even though it can be driven to suffer the greatest hardships and for a period of time be forced to flee from the eyes of the world and those who persecute it (as was foretold would happen during the time of the Antichrist: 2 Thess 2, and Rev 11,12 and 17, etc.), we believe that God not only will always preserve some godly and believing people in the midst of persecutions and desertion by the world, but he will even raise up faithful shepherds in all ages and times. And these shepherds will feed the same godly people with the Word and the sacraments, and shall gather others through the same Word, despite the opposition of the gates of hell, to that same invisible Church of Christ, and shall do so according to Christ's promise in Matt 28:20: "I shall be with you all the days, even to the end of the age."

45. And from this it is also sufficiently clear that the true, essential marks of this pure and visible Church are the pure preaching, and reception, of the Word, sealed by the lawful use of the sacraments, and upheld by the true use of the keys (or church discipline), according to the institution by Christ. And however great the falling-away from that institution and purity of the Word is, so great also is the falling-away from the true, saving purity of the Church.

46. For if the impure and false church is known by the impurity and falsehood of doctrine, as we have shown earlier and as Christ (Matt 7:16) and John (2 John 10) testify, then it must be the case that the Church which is pure and true is to be known by the purity and truth of its doctrine. Therefore Christ also depicts "those who belong to God" by the fact that "they listen to the word of God" (John 8:47) and "his sheep" by the fact that "they hear the voice of the Shepherd and recognize it; but they do not follow a stranger but flee from him, because they do not know the voice of strangers" (John 10:4–5).

47. This is evident also from the fact that the communication and reception of the tables of the covenant are a sure sign of a people that has entered into a covenant; for God does not enter into a covenant with anyone with whom

He does not also communicate the tables of that covenant. Therefore, the apostle says (in a place earlier cited, Eph 2:12) that the heathens as strangers to the church of Israel were without covenants. And on the other hand, the apostle shows clearly that the people of Israel right up to the coming of Christ were the Church of God by the fact that the covenants pertained to them (Rom 9:4). Moreover, no-one doubts that the tables of the covenant are the Word of God, and even the very word 'testament' proves it; and among Christians it is a matter beyond debate that the signs and seals of that covenant are sacraments.

48. And hence it even happens that when God erects his Church among some people, or restores one that had already lapsed, He brings it about in no other way than through Word and sacrament. We see in this way that God erected the Church among the Israelites through the ministry of Moses, when He gave them his Word and the seals of his Word; and through his apostles Christ extended the churches throughout the whole world with this command: "Go and teach all nations, baptizing them into the name of the Father, the Son, and the Holy Spirit, and teach them to observe all the things that I have commanded you" (Matt 28:19–20).

49. Therefore the papal teachers, when they realize that they are bereft of this truth, erroneously invent different marks of the Church, even though in identifying these they differ greatly, since some assign fifteen, others eight, and others only four marks. However, they are chiefly these: its old age, the succession of bishops, the great number of those who profess it, and miracles. Bellarmine adds to these the name 'Catholic,' the unity in the profession of doctrine, the efficacy of the doctrine, and the saintly status of some of the Doctors—especially of those who have established the orders of monks—and lastly, the great victories that have been won over those whom he calls heretics.

50. But let us pass over the fact that some of these marks are not certain, that some are not continuous, and that heathens had always claimed all of them for themselves (and the Mohammedans still do). And let me disregard the fact that the Greek and Ethiopian churches, which the papal teachers consider to be heterodox, ascribe the same marks to themselves with no less right than the papal teachers do. We state that by the truly secret judgment of God they obviously ascribe to themselves those marks that Scripture itself clearly assigns to the church of the Antichrist.

51. The first mark [of the church of the Antichrist] is its old age, for it was already in the time of the apostles that the mystery of iniquity was at work; the succession and name 'Catholic,' for he [i.e. the Antichrist] takes his seat in the temple of God; the great number and unity of those who profess it, for the entire world is worshiping the beast and follows after it; the miracles, for it is accompanied by signs and portents of the lie; the efficacy of the doctrine, for God sends the efficacy of error so that they believe the lie; the saintly status of the founders of monastic orders, for it comes in sheep's clothing and has two horns, like a lamb; and finally, the victories over the believers, whom they themselves call heretics, for the beast will rise out of the abyss and wage war against the saints and conquer them, and it will cause the Church of Christ to flee into the desert. All of these are made manifest in 2 Thess 2, Rev 11, 12, 15, and 17, etc.

ON CHRIST THE HEAD OF THE CHURCH, AND THE ANTICHRIST

President: Antonius Thysius
Respondent: Guilielmus Surendonck

In this disputation it is demonstrated that Christ is Lord over the Church, and that the Roman bishop has no authority over it. Christ is the Head, and the Church is his body (4, 15). The relation of Christ to his Church in Scripture is compared not only to that of a head to a body (3–4), but also to that of a bridegroom and husband to his bride and wife (5), a head of the family to its members (6), a father to his sons (7), a Master and Lord to his servants (8), a shepherd to his sheep or flock (9), a most elevated position in politics to his people (10), a foundation to a building (11). All comparisons explain the mystic union and communion of Christ with the Church (12) and show that the highest sovereignty over the Church belongs to the triune God only, and to Christ in particular (13), in a unique way (16). This sovereignty 'also exists in his governance and control over it by the Spirit through his Word, and that not only by internal administration but also by the external one, which is in the calling and sending forth of ministers, and in their instruction through his Word' (15), anticipating the following disputation. Not a single office in the Church called with one of the names that portray Christ's absolute sovereignty signifies that it has some preeminence over the Church of God or should exercise power over it; they all are at work as God's administrators (16). So we must reject the attribution of any superiority to the apostle Peter and his assumed successors, the Roman popes, over the other apostles or the (entire) Church (17–29). The pope, because he opposes the sovereignty of Christ, shows by that very act that he is the Antichrist (30–40).

1. Since in the previous disputation we treated the Church of God—which is the body of Christ—and its marks, it follows that we briefly consider Christ

its Head, and, on the other hand, the Antichrist, who is the head of the church that does evil.

2. With "head of the Church" we mean Christ the God-and-man, the Mediator, who both possesses and also exercises the supreme and absolute dignity, majesty, authority, sovereignty and right. Thereby he himself (as the one who has the fullness of everything that is required for salvation, and the harmony [1 Cor 12:4–6] that is appropriate to the Church, and, together with that harmony, its bond and unity) flows into the universal Church effectively by his Spirit through the Word, and imparts to it every spiritual good thing, causes it to come alive, and governs and defends it, and he does so both inwardly and outwardly for its salvation, and for the glory of God.

3. And Holy Scripture indicates this sovereignty and effective power of Christ, the Son of God and man, over the Church by means of different comparisons. Firstly, there is the comparison drawn from the realm of nature, that is, of a head and the rest of the body. For since the Church is like a body, it cannot be headless, nor can it be a single body with many heads. And that one head of the Church is Christ. The "many are one body in Christ" (Rom 12:4–5), that is, their head. "And He," that is God, "has made him to be the head over all things for the Church" (Eph 1:22). And "he is the head, from whom the whole body, fitly joined and held together through all the supporting ligaments by the power that is at work within, according to the measure of each part, takes the increase suitable to the body for building itself up in love" (Eph 4:15[–16]; also chapter 5:23). So too Col 1:18, 2:10 and 19.

4. And this comparison to a head expresses highest preeminence, a most close and proportionate harmony with this supernatural body of Christ, as well as unity, communion, and concord. For just as a person's head is the pre-eminent and superior part of the body, where the very principle of life resides, as well as that of the senses and movement, and from where these flow down and into the body, and which steers away from evil and aims at the good, and where the control over the whole body resides, so too does Christ conduct himself spiritually over, in, and around the Church. And this name of 'head' is extended in order to apply also to the other comparisons. Hence, he is called the head of the bride (1 Cor 11[:3], Eph 5[:23]), the head of his people, the chief corner-stone, etc.

5. The second comparison is taken from domestic affairs, in particular from the parties that are primarily involved in it, namely that of bridegroom, and

husband (that is, of the Church his bride and wife). The comparison to a bridegroom is in Matt 9:15, John 3:29, Rev 18:23 and 21:9, while that to a husband is in 2 Cor 11:2. There the consideration is of two coming together into one flesh or body, of whole conjugal union, and of sharing in all good things together. It is of the authority and marital rights over the woman, and, in return, of the woman's subservience to the man (Eph 5:24). Likewise, the comparison is of the feelings, or love and care towards the wife (verse 25). And this is how it is also of Christ's relation with, over, in and towards his own Church.

6. And then there is the general comparison to the head of the family and its members, or to those who belong to him and who are in his household, on whom the whole family depends and by whom it is ruled (as that is his right). Hence Christ is called the Head of the family and believers are called members of the household of God and Christ (Matt 10:25, 36; Luke 13:25; Eph 2:19).

7. In particular the comparison is to a father of sons or brothers: "And you will not be called fathers, for there is one father of you all: God" (i.e., the spiritual father; Matt 23:9), "for you are all brothers." In Isa 8:18, Heb 2:13, Isa 9:6, and 53:10 the focus is on fatherly sovereignty. Nevertheless, in other places that name is sometimes granted to the servants of God, not in the strict sense, but by metonymy, i.e., in an instrumental sense, with respect to the feelings (1 Cor 4:15).

8. And there is a comparison also to Master and Lord (i.e., of servants and slaves), in the way that he simply is called Lord, that is, the Lord of every member's heart and conscience, and of the whole Church (John 13:13–14; 1 Cor 8:5–6). Hereby his ownership, use, and his perfect and highest right of laying claim over the Church and arranging it is indicated.

9. And finally, in terms of the arrangement of possessions, the comparison is to a shepherd of sheep. For as there is one flock, so too is there one shepherd (Ezek 34[:23] and 37[:24]); John 10[:16]: "So that there is one shepherd and one sheepfold." And for this reason, Christ is called "the shepherd" in an absolute sense, that outstanding shepherd to whom the sheep belong (John 10:11–12), the "chief shepherd" (1 Pet 5:4), the "great shepherd of the sheep" (Heb 13:20). Everyone, or the whole Church, is subject to his guidance and pasturage, and it listens to his voice and his alone ([John 10:] 4–5). And to

the extent that the term "shepherd" can be communicated [to others than Christ] it means service and not rule.

10. Thirdly is the comparison drawn from political affairs, namely from that position in politics that is the most elevated: of "monarch," "king," "ruler," "over-lord," "governor," and "deputy." For kings are everywhere called heads, fathers, and lords of the people. And so also Christ is called the King of the Church (Ps 2:6; Isa 2[:2–3]; Zech 9:9; Matt 21:5; Luke 1:32; Rev 1:5, 15:3 and 19:16). And he is called "God's deputy" whereby he, having his position from the father and subject to the father, takes his place and rules on his behalf (1 Cor 15:27). By this Christ's exalted sovereignty and rule over the Church is designated.

11. In the fourth and final place is the comparison drawn from the realm of construction, that is, by the words "foundation," "rock," "corner-stone," i.e., of a building, house, temple, spiritual city, namely, of the Church of God. These words are given to Christ in the proper sense (Isa 28:16; Dan 2:35, 45; Matt 16:18 and 21:42; Acts 4:11; Rom 9:33; 1 Pet 2:4; 1 Cor 3:11; Eph 2:19): "Foundation" because he stands firm by his own strength, he is supported by himself, and it is from him that the remainder of the spiritual dwelling's structure rises up, "Rock," which shows the solidity and strength of the foundation, so much so that the focus is on the basis, on what lies underneath, on what supports it and what gives it stability, and "Corner-stone," as in him the corners—namely, the Jews and Gentiles—come together and are joined to each other. And the relationship to the building is the same as the one of the head to the body.

12. And the first of all these comparisons comes from the natural world, and, like the last one, from art that imitates the natural world; but the third comparison comes from the relational agreement, while the second comes from nature as well as relational agreement. And when the comparisons are all taken together, they explain this mystic union and communion of Christ (which in its truth and efficacy embraces and surpasses them all) with the Church with greater clarity.

13. Therefore, since these comparisons signify the very beginning, the highest sovereignty, right, power, and absolute control over the Church, they show convincingly that they belong only to "the Father, the Son, and the Holy Spirit." Christ would not have been capable of this authority and sovereignty if he were not true God (Heb 3:4–6). Nevertheless, by the order that exists

among the divine persons, and by the specific economy and arrangement suited for redemption, Christ, being God and man, has received this privilege from the Father and holds on to it in subservience to the Father, and exercises it as a deputy, even though he has been endowed with a knowledge and power that is divine (1 Cor 3:22 and 11:3, and 15:24, 27, 28; Matt 28[:18]). And likewise, the same adequate sovereignty would not be appropriate to the Holy Spirit if He were not true God, for He acts as it were as the Son's deputy (John 14:16 and 26; and John 15:26). And so this sovereignty belongs especially to Christ, indeed as the God-and-man, in keeping with his exceptional office and its efficacy.

14. This sovereignty of Christ, which in other respects extends itself very widely—as far as the angels and even to the devils and thus to every sovereignty by whatever name it is named (Col 2:10; Heb 2:7–8)—refers especially to "the Church of God" and is tied to it (Col 1:18), not only insofar as it is internal and invisible, but also insofar as it is external and visible, and universal and particular.

15. [Christ's sovereignty] exists in his primacy over the Church, in the principle of his union and communion with it, in the downward and inward flowing of his grace into it (or in his making it come alive and causing it to grow). And it also exists in his governance and control over it by the Spirit through his Word, and that not only by internal administration but also by the external one, which is in the calling and sending forth of ministers, and in their instruction through his Word, etc. All of these things belong to the greatest sovereignty, and should be conducted as prescribed and established. And so this highest sovereignty over the Church cannot be communicated but resides in Christ as the appropriate subject, and on this point every execution of sovereignty by men of whatever sort is only ministerial.

16. Therefore Christ is the unique, one-and-only, immediate and eternal Head, Bridegroom and Husband, household-Father, Father, Master and Lord, Shepherd, King, Monarch and Foundation of the Church of God, and the Deputy of God. And neither the names nor the actual substance of this highest sovereignty can be communicated to anyone except in this manner and only insofar as the instrument and ministry of this sovereignty can be included in them. For all these names are so arranged that they correspond to their counterparts, as things that are immediately and relatively opposites (Heb 3:5–6). The result is that those who are named that way are also

considered to be included in the body, the wife, the members of the household, the sons and brothers, the servants and slaves, the flock, the kingdom and the building, in whatever degree and manner they are considered, also with respect to the proper office that applies to each of them—such as when they are called ministers and dispensers of the mysteries of God, apostles and builders, prefects, presidents, leaders, overseers, presbyters, shepherds, etc., of God and the Church. Not because they have preeminence over the Church of God or look down upon it and have or should exercise power over it (1 Cor 3:21–23; 1 Pet 5:2–4), but only because they are at work around it as God's administrators.

17. Therefore it is clearly wrong of the papal teachers to ascribe to Peter among the apostles those titles that convey the supreme, highest sovereignty—titles that belong to Christ—and from that point on they attribute them (as they would have it) to Peter's successor, the Roman pope, in each and every respect whatsoever (whether of internal communication or external government). But in the Church of Christ Peter himself is his minister, in a ministry that is shared equally with the other apostles and that is on par with their ministry. For this reason, Christ called and appointed him alongside the other apostles with the same title and task (John 1:39–40; Matt 4:18, 21). He is sent and sent forth on equal terms (Matt 10:18), and with equal power (John 20:21), and the Holy Spirit is promised equally to him, and He is equally received by him. Nor does any one of the apostles present himself to the others by means of any superior title (1 Pet 1[:1], and 5:1). The highest degree, the apostolic one, is held equally (1 Cor 12:28; Eph 4:11). They carried out their office with equal power (Acts 15:28). Christ causes them equally to share the throne (Matt 19:28), and it says that the Church is founded equally on the foundation of the apostles and the prophets. The names of the twelve apostles are inscribed as equals on the foundation-walls of the new Jerusalem, and none is superior to the others (Rev 21:14). And in particular James, Cephas, and John are equally called "those of repute," and pillars of equal stature (Gal 2:6 and 9).

18. And Paul in particular states that he had not obtained his apostleship from men or through a man, and it was not from a man that he had received the Gospel, nor was it following the lead of any apostle that he preached. He states that he did in fact confer with the others, but they added nothing to him, and they actually gave each other the right hand of fellowship and went their separate ways, so that Peter would go to the circumcised and Paul

as he himself bears witness in Ezek 16 and 23. There he calls the children of the godless Israelites his own sons, whom they had begotten for God, although they were sacrificing them to Molech. And it is from these children that God also normally gathers his church through the ordinary preaching of the Word. And for this reason he also commanded the children of such Israelites (of whom many had died in their ungodliness) to be circumcised, no less than those of the godly ones (Josh 5:4 and 6)—which necessary deed also the Israelite and the early Christian church always have considered beyond debate.

51. The adjuncts of baptism are firstly its unity; for just as we are born once, so is it once that we are born again, and consequently it is once that we receive the sign of regeneration. And hence, just as circumcision once conferred was not repeated, so too Scripture teaches neither by command nor by example that a baptism once lawfully conferred must be repeated. In fact, on the contrary, wherever mention is made of baptism in the New Testament, mention is made of only one baptism, and of a baptism that is conferred only once. Hence it is also called explicitly 'one baptism' (Eph 4:5).

52. No specific time is prescribed for baptism, which was the case for circumcision. Meanwhile, however, it is our view that baptism should be sought as soon as it can be held according to the church-order and by the good health of the one to be baptized. For it is impossible for us to neglect the ordinary signs and instruments of divine grace without committing sin, and in fact we cannot despise them without grave sin and peril.

53. The place that has been appointed for all the sacred gatherings is also sacred for baptism. Accordingly we see in all the instances provided by the apostolic practice that baptism was linked to the preaching of the Word, whether it was in a public place or a private house, so long as there was a gathering of the church. But apart from times of persecution, public rather than private places should be appointed for this event, as is shown from the fact that baptism is a supplement to public ministry and not to private exhortation.

54. Even though it is not absolutely necessary that there be special witnesses to the baptism, particularly in churches that enjoy public peace, nevertheless not only does the matter itself show that the presence of such people is useful (provided they are godly and faithful), but also the practice of the whole early church, which by a very plausible argument, along with the granting of names,

was derived from the actual ritual of circumcision, as instances of it occur in Isa 8:2 and Luke 1:59.

55. But if anyone either on the testimony of the church, or parents, or witnesses, or of others cannot be sure about the baptism that he had received in infancy, or if it happened that he was moistened by no other baptism than that of the midwives or private individuals, we are of the opinion that such a man may be baptized without any scruple. For the baptism applied by the last-mentioned people is not a baptism at all, and the baptism of the first-mentioned people is worthless, as the Council of Carthage has rightly decided (5.3): "Concerning infants it has been decided that whenever no very certain witnesses are found who testify without a doubt that they were baptized, and whenever they themselves are not, on account of their age, in a position to give an answer about the sacraments that were given to them, they should be baptized without any scruple, lest that doubt should cause them to be bereft of the cleansing of the sacraments." For as [pope] Leo [I] rightly added, "what is not known to have been done cannot be said to have been repeated."

56. And consequently we should not approve of a conditional baptism that the papal teachers are used to observing in such cases, according to this formula: "If you have not been baptized, then I baptize you." For a baptism of this kind lacks any precedent in Scripture and changes the form for baptism that Christ had taught, and it also leaves the one who has been baptized in doubt as to which baptism is the real one—which goes against the purpose of baptism that does not make the promises of God ambiguous but establishes and seals them.

DISPUTATION 45

ON THE LORD'S SUPPER

President: Antonius Thysius
Respondent: Volcker Oosterwijck

This disputation forms a long and complex argument on the doctrine of the Lord's Supper, and it seeks to clarify the Reformed position within the setting of various confessional perspectives. In it Thysius brings forward many and diverse points that address Roman Catholic, Lutheran, and Zwinglian understandings of the Lord's Supper. These points are based in the text of Scripture, in the history of the Church, in philosophy, rhetoric, and grammar. Especially the doctrines of transubstantiation (Romanist) and consubstantiation (Lutheran) are refuted, but also the Zwinglian perspective that the Lord's Supper is merely commemorative in scope. The definition (6) addresses the essential elements of the sacrament: that it is spiritual food for Christ's believers, that this spiritual food is offered through bread and wine, for remembering Christ and declaring his death, for practicing communion with Christ unto his mystical body, resulting in a greater assurance of eternal life and to the glory of God's grace. After some remarks on Jesus Christ as the efficient cause of the institution of the Lord's Supper and the meaning of the temporal circumstances under which this took place (7–16), the disputation is arranged according to the New Testament account of the institution of the Supper by Jesus Christ himself (17–86). The institution narrative is divided into three parts: 1. Four actions of Christ (17–31); 2. Christ's commands (32–40); 3. Christ's explanation of his actions and commands (41–86). A considerable portion of this disputation is taken up by careful interpretations of the words of institution, most notably the phrases 'this is my body' and 'this is my blood,' which are taken figuratively (43–77). It is due to the sacramental union of the Lord's Supper that Christ's body and blood are present, not as substances but in their relation to the signs of the bread and the wine (73). So Christ himself and his benefits, as obtained for us by his death on the cross, are present in the sacrament (58). The last thesis (87) refers to God's Word as the source for the truth concerning the Lord's Supper, and expresses the expectation that what is commanded will serve as consolation for believers, and will be able to put a limit to quarreling among brothers.

1. Up to this point [we have treated] Baptism, the sacrament of regeneration, repentance, and faith, and so of "putting on Christ" and of our initiation. What comes next is a treatment of the Supper of the Lord, the sacrament that nourishes and the mystery of our perfection (as the fathers call it).

2. This sacrament goes by various names in Scripture and the fathers. In Scripture it is called: 1. "The Supper of the Lord" (1 Cor 11:20), a term that comes from its circumstance in time, in that it was a meal at evening. And it comes from the one who founded it, and also from its goal, for it was instituted by the Lord in order to be celebrated in remembrance of him (a term that the Jesuits wrongly restrict to the love-feasts). 2. "The table of the Lord" (1 Cor 10:21), and, simply, "the table" (Acts 6:2), as a metonym for this sacred banquet consisting of bread and wine (although there Paul seems to relate it to the bread, since he puts the cup of the Lord over against it). 3. "The bread that is broken and the cup of blessing" (1 Cor 10:16). 4. "This bread and this cup" (or, "of the Lord"), and simply "bread and cup" (1 Cor 11:26, 27), which by its parts expresses the whole. 5. "The bread" (1 Cor 10:17) and likewise "the drink" (1 Cor 10) through association with the word ["wine"], by synecdoche. 6. "The spiritual food and drink" (1 Cor 10:3, 4). 7. The "breaking of the bread" (Acts 2:42 and 20:7)—whereby otherwise the Jews indicated any domestic meal whatsoever—and so it is the breaking of bread *par excellence*. 8. The "body of the Lord" (1 Cor 11:29), as a metonym. 9. And lastly *Agapē* or "Love-feast" (2 Pet 2:13, Jude 12), that is, the sacred banquet that was instituted for the sake of testifying to and preserving the love, and that included this sacrament as its most powerful element.

3. Furthermore, among the church fathers, however, especially the Greek ones, it is called 1) *Sunaxis* [a gathering together]; in the Latin fathers *collecta* (what is gathered), *collectio* (gathering) and *conventus* (gathering) because it was customary to perform this public action along with the Lord's Supper in the assemblies of the church (from the passage in Acts 20:7 and 1 Cor 11:18, 33). 2) The *Eucharistia* or the *Eulogia*, that is, the giving of thanks and the benediction—i.e., derived from Christ's foregoing actions and from the purpose he stated, because it is done and should be done in a solemn act of thanksgiving for the death of Christ and his benefits, according to 1 Cor 10:16 and Matt 26:26–27. 3) *Koinonia*, that is, fellowship or communion, from Paul,

who applies to this bread and wine the name of communion and participation in Christ's body and blood (1 Cor 10:16–17, 21). 4) *Prosphora*, offering, or the offer, i.e., from the offering of bread and wine given by the believers for celebrating the Love Feast and Eucharist. This offering used to be made to the overseer and in turn was given back to the people who partook of communion (the former used to be called *doron*, the gift, and the latter *antidoron*, the gift-in-return). And it comes from the offering of praise and thanks that the entire church offered to God. But the term is not meant of the offering by Christ in a passive sense like the offering that the priests made to God the Father—except in a figurative way. 5) *Thusia*, that is, sacrificial offering or victim, in a very non-literal sense, for the prayers and thanksgiving, as well as for the remembrance of that one and only expiatory sacrifice on the cross once performed for us. The word is not to be taken in its strict sense, as the Romans would like to take it, who not only take it as a eucharistic [or thank] offering, but also as an expiatory offering for sin itself (although they call that offering "unbloody"). Furthermore, the ancients denote that sacred rite with other names, like 'symbol' and 'mystery,' i.e., the "sign and sacrament of the body and blood of the Lord, etc."—but these are almost descriptions or commendations and epithets of so great a mystery.

4. Next, the word *leitourgia*, from *leitos* (public), generally means a public function or office, and in the church it means a sacred function that denotes the whole sacred ministry of the divine Word (in the same way that *leitourgountes* means not those who bring sacrifices, as Erasmus had translated it in Acts 14 [= 13:2], but rather those who perform the sacred service, as also he himself explains it), and it specifically means the administration of the Lord's Supper. There are some who give it the specific name *hierourgia*, "performing the sacred tasks," which refers also to the preaching of the Gospel in a metaphorical sense (Rom 15).

5. About four hundred years after Christ Latin-speaking people began to call it *missa*, "the mass." And that was not, as some following Reuchlin and Genebrard, wrongly argue, [taken] from the Hebrew *mas*, "tribute," from which *missah* in Deut 16:11 [= 16:10] is derived, i.e., "offering" (as the Vulgate has it) or "sufficiency" (as the Septuagint translators have it). Rather, "mass" would have received its name from *massah*, that is, from "the testing" of God. Nor does it come from the adjective in its feminine form *missa*, "sent," as in offering sent to God, as the papal teachers commonly take it. But it comes from the noun *missa* that is put in place of *missio* (sending), like the words

collecta (what is collected), *oblata* (what is offered), *remissa* (what is forgiven) and similar ones in the time of Tertullian that were used for *collectio* (collection), *oblatio* (offering) and *remissio* (forgiveness). And so it is said that the word comes either from the offerings sent by the faithful or from the start of the celebration of the mysteries, which took place when the *missa*, or the "sending away," was pronounced upon the catechumens and the penitents. Or it comes from the end of the celebration, when after the sacred matters were concluded, the *missa*, or the "sending away," of the faithful who are about to depart, happens by means of this solemn formula, *Ite missa est*, that is "go, the dismissal is made." In worse times, it is also called "the sacrament of the altar," which even Luther, for some unknown reason, thought should be preserved by him.

6. Now the Lord's Supper is the second sacrament of the new covenant or testament, namely the one of spiritual nourishment that Christ our Lord instituted for believers, a sacrament that by means of the broken bread and poured-out wine signifies Christ as the one who suffered and died, or his body and blood that was broken and shed for the forgiveness of sins. And by participating and communing in the bread and wine the spiritual food and drink are offered to those who use them, and bestowed upon those who believe. And it should be given to believers to remember Christ while also declaring his death; and furthermore, for the union and fellowship with Christ their head unto the true, mystical body, resulting in a greater assurance of eternal life for believers, and to the glory of God's grace.

7. The efficient cause of the institution of the Lord's Supper is the Lord Jesus, the founder of the new covenant of grace, and the mediator and testator of the New Testament; consequently he is the one and only institutor of the symbols for it. For it is an act of supreme power, and the one who bestows the grace has the right to add to it the signs of grace, and to present and bring about what the signs display and promise. But it is the duty of Christ's minister to pass on to the church and to keep intact what the Lord has given to him, faithfully and without removing, adding, or altering anything (Matt 28:20; 1 Cor 11:23).

8. As for the exhibition of the sacrament, there again Christ is the proper author, who by his own authority exhibited the symbols outwardly first by himself and then by the ministers of his Word, whom he commissioned in

his own name, and to whom he is present. But he bestows the actual thing on believers inwardly through the Holy Spirit.

9. And as the host of this sacred banquet, the Lord Jesus instituted and exhibited the sacrament "on the night in which he was betrayed," that is, the evening of the sixth day of the week, or the first day of the week of the Unleavened Bread of the Passover according to the custom of the Jews, who start the day in the evening. He did this so that by this temporal circumstance he might commend this meal more effectively to those who belong to him, and indeed by this last meal might establish a monument to the covenant and testament that would be validated by his death shortly thereafter. And he did so by means of the place, that is, in the city of Jerusalem, in an inn, in the large dining room that was set out and made ready, where the Passover had been prepared as well.

10. And in fact [he established and exhibited] it "after he had eaten" (Luke 22:20), that is, after he had eaten the meal of the Passover lamb as required by the Law, together with his disciples, and he did so not according to Jewish tradition, but according to the prescript of the Law for it (Mark 14:12, Luke 22:7). The Passover meal was a type of Christ (1 Cor 5:7) and an antitype of this Supper of the Lord, as it signified both Christ the Lamb of God, and, through commemoration of the delivery from Egypt, spiritual delivery (1 Cor 5:7). Indeed, so that in this way it might show that by the succession of the new sacrament the old sacrament has been fulfilled. Regarding this fulfillment Christ said, "I have eagerly desired to eat this Passover with you before I suffer" [Luke 22:15].

11. And to be precise, [Christ instituted the sacrament] "after washing their feet," as many [sources] say. For when the meal was begun (John 13:2), he rose from the table (verse 4) and washed the feet of his disciples, as was the customary practice of eastern peoples (Luke 7:44). He did so in order that by this exemplary action he might show them the way to humility and love, and testify of his favor towards those who are his—that he is certainly the one who cleanses his people from their uncleanness (John 13:8–10, 14). And he did so in order to teach them by means of a comparison (and not a sacrament) with what frame of mind they ought to approach these sacred things. Even so the western church has, elsewhere and sometimes not without abuse, adopted the practice as a sacrament.

12. And they partook of the meal when Christ "was lying at table again" or "reclining" (John 13:23, 28) in the way that the people of God then had adopted, as they were not seated upright but reclined on couch, with their heads facing inwards and their feet outwards so that those who were second were nearly leaning upon the bosoms of those who were first (John 13:23, 25). He did so in order to show that this was a banquet and not a sacrifice, as the papal teachers would have it, who in poor imitation of Jewish and pagan customs introduced altars; if that were the case he would have performed the sacrifice while standing by an altar.

13. And [Christ ate the meal] together with his twelve disciples, or Apostles, while they were eating a commonplace everyday meal, or supping, as the Vulgate has it. He did so in order to show that this meal is a public one and not a private dinner. But the meal was connected to the rite of breaking bread and blessing wine in remembrance of the delivery from Egypt (Luke 22:17), as the Jewish books of rituals show—a rite that appears to have been replaced by the love-feast and this Lord's Supper, just as their habitual washings were replaced by baptism.

14. And so it was that Christ prepared the Supper for his dinner-guests the apostles, and for all believers whom they represent, as the apostle assures us. For the apostle [Paul] afterward applied what then happened concerning the apostles not just to the shepherds but also to the rest of the church (1 Cor 11), and the apostles did not function then as those who administer but as recipients. And Paul applied it to those who are living in a state of piety (insofar as that can be humanly known, leaving the hidden things over to God) and not to unbaptized catechumens, or those who have fallen, or to people who are among those who are repenting. Hence the apostle states: "Let everyone test himself," etc. But the fact that each person should test himself does not do away with the testing of others by the church and the shepherds. And at this point it is usual and possible to raise the question that arises from a comparison of Matthew and Mark with Luke and John: whether the betrayer Judas was present at the supper.

15. And these temporal circumstances, whether of evening- or night-time, or of the sixth day of the week or that particular day of the year (i.e., of the third day before Christ's resurrection), and also of the place (i.e., a private place), do not have any force of prescribed necessity or of observance. Nor do the following facts have any force of being required or observed: that the supper

was given to them after they had eaten a meal, after their feet had been washed, when they were lying at table, and even that there were twelve in number (some of which were observed for some time in the early church).

16. These were the prefatory remarks about the Lord's Supper. But as a whole the Supper consists of the mystical actions and words of Christ, and of the obedience of the disciples and believers that answers to them, and also in the subsequent giving of thanks. In these the causes of this mystery are summed up.

17. And of the sacramental actions by Christ that depend on their institution by Christ and on all that he did, and that were performed in such a manner that they were presented to the senses and happened through sensible things and might evoke something spiritual to the mind, the first one displayed to the apostles' eyes was the "taking," that is, "the bread that was taken" or "when he had taken the bread;" and thereupon taking "the cup," i.e., taking the cup into his hands, as he was the head of the household. Herein lies the starting point of the institution and action, and in particular of the very act of designating these things for a special purpose. And indeed, in taking them up into his hands there is an indication of his voluntary death. Similarly, the expressions "to take," "to put," "to hold," "to bear," "to carry" himself or his soul in his hands mean, by a common Hebraism: to run or undergo the greatest risk to one's life (Judg 12:3, 1 Sam 19:5 and 28:21, Job 13:14, Ps 119:109).

18. Moreover, the outward matter of this mystery resides in the two appearances that were taken, and while they are indeed two different appearances they are not really two proper sacraments (as some of the ancients say), since they come together for a single goal, namely the whole sacred meal and refreshment. For [Christ] took them up separately in order to show to them his own, bloodless body and the blood then as it were shed from his veins, and also to testify that he in his entirety is for us the complete food and refreshment (John 6:53, etc.).

19. Therefore, the papists clearly commit very serious violence against the integrity of the sacrament, and so they are sacrilegious when they withhold the chalice from believing laics, that is, withhold the second part of the sacrament—under whatever pretext of human wisdom or I know not what [eucharistic] concomitance, or out of respect for Christ's glorious body—utter folly over against the Lord! And they do so contrary to Christ's action

and commandment (Luke 22:19; 1 Cor 11:25) and contrary to the apostolic practice (1 Cor 11:26–27, 29) and, in sum, contrary to all of antiquity and God's universal church everywhere—except the Romanist church of late.

20. [Christ] used bread, real bread for eating that was thin in shape and not thick, so that it was suitable for breaking into pieces (as was the custom of those people), and it was one whole. And moreover, the bread was unleavened or unfermented; of course, that was by accident and due to the circumstance of the law about the first day of unleavened bread; otherwise Christ would have used everyday bread. That is why Christ makes a comparison with everyday bread in John 6, and the apostle when speaking about the Supper mentions simply the bread as it was used in Corinth, because unleavened bread had been abolished along with the Passover Lamb and the other ceremonies. Otherwise, this would be a matter of indifference, provided there is no belief of necessity. And therefore, the debate between the Greeks and Latins over this matter is an idle one.

21. In the same way he used the drink of the produce or fruit of the vine, i.e., wine (Matt 26:29). But it is not known whether the wine was red as it nearly always is in that region (Prov 21:31) and wherefore it is also called the "blood of grapes" (Gen 49:11), or whether it was diluted (which is called mixed wine), in keeping with the custom of blending the wine in those warmer climates (Prov 9:2, 5 and 23:30). Justin states that a cup of wine diluted with water was used. But that adds nothing to the religious character and mystery; nor does the material and shape of the cup (i.e., the chalice), whether it is wooden, silver, or gilded.

22. And the fact that for the mysteries he chose bread and wine, common things taken from everyday life, is because of the very close similarity and analogy in the properties and effects of both (i.e., as basic and very necessary nourishment) to the things they signify: the body and blood of the Lord.

23. Hence the papal teachers and others who follow them do not sin lightly when they use bread that is not bread but little slices of the smallest size and thin as a shadow, quite unlike the looks of real bread (and not worthy of that name) and not having the energy to nourish; they are wafers, or offerings as they call them. And they also use unleavened bread, as if it is necessary for the sacrament because of the precedent of Christ. And what is more, for the sake of mystery they use diluted wine, over which some ancients like Cyprian and others have philosophized in too much detail and dilutedly.

24. But if [the sacrament is held] where bread and wine are not used, or where they cannot be obtained in abundance, it is possible to use whatever takes the place of bread and wine, or whatever is the equivalent for those peoples.

25. The second action by Christ that the apostles' ears perceived is his speaking to God, expressed by the word *eulogēsas* [Matt 26:26] (with the assumption of the word "and" that Mark and Luke state explicitly [Mark 14:22, Luke 22:19]), that is, "and when he had blessed," as Matthew and Mark have it in the first part of the sentence. But in the second part of the phrase, concerning the cup, [it says] "and when he had given thanks," which appears to both phrases in Luke and Paul, so that the expressions are used interchangeably. And in fact, that interpretation is required in this place if we do not wish that only the bread was blessed and not this cup. And that is how elsewhere the expressions are used to mean the same thing in everyday meals (Matt 14:19, 15:36; Mark 6:41 and 8:6; Luke 9:16; John 6:11 and 23; Acts 27:35). In the same way one uses interchangeably the Hebrew words *berech*, that is, "he blessed, he prayed for blessing," and *yahdah*, "he confessed, praised, glorified, thanked." And with that [prayer] you must understand the words "looking up into heaven," the gesture of one praying that Christ used also elsewhere (Matt 14:19); and he did so "in the presence of all" (Acts 27:35). He "gave thanks" or "blessed," that is, he blessed God the Father, there as well as in Rom 14:6; and in fact, he gave thanks in particular for the bread and the wine as gifts of God's kindness, and especially for the gracious gift of redemption.

26. And so it is that under the name of giving thanks and blessing, that is, of invocation and prayer, this entire sacred action is understood synecdochally, and so too the consecration itself, of which that thanksgiving is only a portion. This is expressed more accurately by the word "blessing," with the fourth case of a thing, applied jointly to the bread and the cup (as the phrase appears in Luke 9:16). And those everyday things that were common aids for nourishing the body, and that God's Word and the prayer for believers sanctify for sacred use (which occurs when those things are received from God's bountiful hand and put to holy, sober use and related to God's glory; 1 Tim 4:3–5; 1 Cor 10:31), the Son of God additionally prepared, ordained, dedicated or sanctified and consecrated unto a sacred goal and spiritual function: the nourishment of the soul, so that they might be mystical symbols of his own body and blood. This is done by a change not in nature but quality (by the divine institution and ordination of doing things) and with solemn

prayer and right use. The word "blessing," when it relates to physical things, is nearly always understood in this way (Gen 2:3, etc.). It is in this sense that the apostle speaks of "the cup of blessing which we bless" (1 Cor 10:16).

27. And it is not explained to us which form of blessing and thanksgiving Christ used here, but here he did adapt that solemn formula of the old synagogue in the eating of the Passover, and the ancient liturgies show that the early church had its own prayers in the consecration [of the sacrament]. Therefore, it is out of superstition that the Romans established the consecration in crosses formed in mid-air, and in specifically adopted accompanying words, that is to say, in those four quietly mumbled words, or five (as the old translator has with the added word "for"): "for this is my body." And to those words they even attribute some operational power, a secret and even magical power, one that miraculously changes the very substance. But the consecration then was made by the words of Christ uttered in the first person; the consecration is not shown by the words of a minister that are to be uttered afterwards in the third person. Nor are they words of any kind of alteration in the strict sense, but rather of declaring what happened. Preceding the consecration, the offer and acceptance of what has happened clearly demonstrate this, as they are the offer and acceptance of what has already taken place and not of what ought to be done. For the use of something comes after the thing itself.

28. Christ's third action (which likewise is seen) is that after he had taken the bread and given thanks, he "broke it," as this is the order of Christ's words that is required by the aorist tenses. Moreover, he broke the bread in the manner of eastern peoples; he did not slice it in the manner of westerners, for the bread was so shaped that it was not compact but flat and rather broad like a pancake, so that it could be broken up easily. Likewise also the wine that was poured into the cup, and both [actions] were done in the usual and necessary ritual. For that was the duty of the father of the household, who tasted them beforehand and distributed them. And Christ broke the bread into pieces not only in order to distribute them, and he poured out the wine into the cup not only so that it could be drunk, but he did so for the mystery and the sacramental ceremony: so that it might signify his body, not as cut into pieces (John 19:33, 36) but metaphorically as completely broken up by the torments of soul and body. Indeed, as shattered by the scourgings, as punctured by the thorny crown, and as pierced in his hands and feet, and as torn by the opening of his side; and in the end, his body as broken up by the

draining of its blood and by the separation of soul from body, divided into two parts, and dead. And so breaking applies to the body and shedding to the blood, through the change into a metonym in both words.

29. And obviously for this reason in the distribution of the Eucharist the Romanists and their followers in handing out their circular crackers as unbroken have removed, in violation of the sacrament, the ritual of the breaking that from the time of Jesus Christ and the apostles (1 Cor 10:16) had been carried on in the early church, and maintained in the eastern churches, too. For they keep the ritual of breaking only for the priests when they offer the mass. Even those who are keen to be called Lutherans err by interpreting the word "to break" here only as "to distribute," because there follows "and he gave to them."

30. And Christ's fourth action (which concerns the sense of touch) is: "And he gave to his disciples." For he had taken and had broken in order to give; that is, he exhibited and gave the bread and the cup into the disciples' hands, and not into their mouths. For food is not ingested directly into the mouth except for those who are handicapped. And the receiving is in response to the giving, and in 1 Cor 11 the apostle implies the omitted giving with the receiving. And at this point the apostles do not function as shepherds but as representatives of the church as a whole, since it says that Christ gave it to them individually. Otherwise, if this is stated only concerning the apostles, what rule made the Lord's Supper common for everyone? And so this giving declares that like every sacrament so also this one exists not just in signifying but also in its application and use, and it declares that with these sacred signs God presents and gives Christ, so that he might be received and bestowed in faith. Therefore, when it says that he "gave to them," he did not sacrifice, for that is to give to God.

31. From this it is plainly obvious that the papal teachers commit a great sacrilege in the mass, in that the believers are fed only by looking upon the bread and the wine that the priests celebrating the mass give only to themselves, and so they make private that which was ordained for the whole church. Indeed, it is also idolatrous to take these elements and to raise them up to be worshiped.

32. To these actions of his, Christ also added statements for the apostles; some of them are "instructional," some are "declarative," and some "have

legal force" and fix a law for all Christianity throughout the ages, and declare the use and goal of this sacrament.

33. First, it says in a general way "and he said" (something that occurs to the ears); i.e., he said to his disciples. And he said the following things, and from that one can learn his institution of the actions. For since sacraments and sacramental actions arise "by institution," they would be bare spectacles devoid of substance if no words accompanied them. But Christ spoke intelligibly, openly, and clearly; he employed language that was not foreign but native and customary, so that everyone could understand and perceive his words. Otherwise, it would be secretly mumbling in vain. To be precise, the word "he said" refers to the subsequent command, and in keeping with Hebrew idiom it has the same force as "he ordered," "he declared."

34. Therefore, the papists would rather do anything else than perform this sacred mystery when like magicians and sorcerers they address the bread and cup, created objects which have no senses and are incapable of being spoken to, and they mumble these words, "this is my body," and say them in a strange language and with hushed tones, contrary to what the apostle says in 1 Cor 14:6, etc.

35. And then Christ orders something that concerns also the sense of touch: "Take." That means: all of you [take] this bread and this cup that I hold in my hand and place into your hands (and thus not directly into someone's mouth). The proper meaning of the word "to take" requires that it must refer to the taking that is done by the hand, just as "eat, drink" must refer to what is consumed by the mouth. The way that is unbecoming to adults, of putting food directly into someone's mouth, also requires this; so too the arrangement of lying at table that makes it impossible neatly to reach the mouths of all who are lying in a circle. The practice of the old church and also of the church of today (except the Romanist one) requires this as well. And it certainly is not a sacrifice, since these elements are offered in order to be received by the apostles and not by God. And in the command that is made to believers to take is, so to speak, the handing over of Christ into our hands and into our power, as well as our taking through faith, which is the "hand" of the soul (John 1:11–12).

36. Therefore, the papists are acting superstitiously, contrary to Christ and antiquity, because they bring in private masses when the sacrificer stands by the altar and eats and drinks by himself. So too are those who act like papists

with them when they refuse to put into the believers' hands what they offer to their mouths, as if their hands are less pure than their mouths (which have been equally sanctified: Matt 15:18, 20; Jas 3:10), and as if the hands of those who administer them are more pure than those of the other members of the church. Moreover, in so doing they very much render obscure the working of faith. Indeed, while they are making a sacrifice what else are they doing than making no distinction between giving and receiving?

37. And then Christ says something that affects the senses of smell and taste: "Eat and drink from it, all of you." That is to say, he bade them to take in order to eat (i.e., the bread) and to drink the wine. The sense is: insert the bread into your mouths, eat, chew, and crush to pieces with your teeth. And: raise the cup to your mouth, drink the wine, and let it go down into your stomach for digestion and feeding. This shows that their use is an inward one, and it signifies that for believing souls and those who take Christ by faith, so to speak as by hand, and who eat and drink him, so to speak, by mouth (a metaphor that the Holy Spirit uses everywhere throughout the Scriptures, John 4:14 and 6:51, 53), Christ becomes a spiritual, heavenly food and drink as truly as what we eat becomes food, nourishment, strength and growth for our bodies.

38. All of these commands "take," "eat," and "drink" are in the plural form, and expressly about the cup, "drink from it all of you," which by analogy we should take also for the bread, unless it is because what is said about the bread piecemeal is expressed as one whole about the cup that does not permit being portioned except by each person's drinking. These plural commands signify by their universal order a communion that is shared equally, and also that the necessity of consuming both elements (and the cup in particular) does not apply privately but publicly.

39. Therefore, we should not do with this bread what the papists do, contrary to the divinely ordained usage and the early church: lift it up for worship or like some deity; superstitiously hide it in a drinking-cup; preserve it in a safe or some alcove for idol-worship, or in monstrances (as they are called) made of gold and silver; put it on display or parade it publicly and pompously in a Persian fashion, or carry it around fields in a wagon. Indeed, equally abusive desecrations of the Lord's Supper are the private masses, wherein one person hungrily eats by himself; and the cup is withheld from laics; and they carry

the fruits of the mass even to those who have died, despite the fact that they cannot eat or drink.

40. Responding to and following this command of Christ is the compliance of the disciples, both in taking the bread and wine and also in consuming, that is, in eating and drinking. And this compliance is implied in the command, and regarding the cup Mark [14:23] explains it by saying "they drank from it, all of them"—which we should understand similarly for the bread, as the taking there includes the command to drink. And Mark reports these words as they were spoken prior to the drinking: "This is the blood of the New Testament, etc." Nor is it unusual to perform mystical actions before it is explained what they mean, as we see happen in the washing of feet (John 13:5, 12). Whatever it may be, it is of very little relevance to the topic whether the order of words is right here or whether this is an instance of *hysterologia* [a figure of speech in which the natural or conventional order of words is reversed].

41. Added to Christ's commands are declarative words, or words that explain and describe the thing that is being signified and the promise that is added to the outward symbols that contain the inward subject-matter of the Lord's Supper, when he says, "this is my body," to which Luke adds "which is given for you," and to which Paul adds "which is broken for you." And to the word "this" for which Luke and Paul have "this cup," Matthew adds "for," which is assumed also for the previous phrase, "[for this is] my blood of the New Testament" (or as in Luke and Paul, "the New Testament in my blood"). Matthew and Mark add "which is poured out for many," Luke "which is poured out for you," and Matthew has furthermore "unto the remission of sins."

42. With these words Christ reveals what he meant by those actions and commands of his, that is, when he took the bread and that cup (in fact, that broken bread and this poured-out wine) and gave them to his disciples equally to be received and eaten. By means of the outward elements and actions he meant the mystery, i.e., that with their minds and in faith they should consider, receive, and eat something else, namely, his broken body and his shed blood, for a spiritual food and drink. Thus, the meaning, or what is declared, is: this bread that I have broken is my broken body, and this cup (or what is in the cup) is my shed blood, and so what I have given you and

have ordered you to take, eat and drink is to give you my body and blood and to take, eat and drink them.

43. And next we should consider those words more closely in order to assert the plain truth, because they were obscured by differing explanations, as some have built on them the teaching of *sunousia* (consubstantiation) and others *metousia* (transubstantiation). First there is the subject of this sentence, namely, "this." And there is the predicate, i.e., "the body and blood," as well as the explanation of each. Third there is the copulative or linking verb "is." Fourth is the sentence as a whole. And finally, there is the causal particle "for" and the connection of all these words with what precedes.

44. The subject therefore is "this," a demonstrative adjective whose gender is neuter (a demonstrative which as it were points with extended finger to something that truly exists and is present). It demands that there be a noun to which it refers and which often accompanies it, like "this Passover," "this fruit of the vine" (Matt 26). And here, since in the first clause it does not say "this" in the masculine, meaning "this bread," but "this" in the neuter, the word may be taken with both phrases, "this is flesh, or body" and "this is blood." For just as they do with neuter nouns (like Hebrews do with the feminine) the Greeks and Latins use also the demonstrative in an absolute sense as "this thing." And this is especially useful when the demonstrative functions also as a relative for an earlier noun or deed. This happens in Exod 8:18, "this is the finger of God;" 1 Pet 2:19, "this is the grace of God;" Luke 22:17 and 19, "take this" and "do this." Or when they [the Greeks and the Latins] relate the supposit to a verbal phrase (as the grammarians say) with the same gender, which the Hebrews do, too. And Virgil [has]: "But to retrace one's steps, etc. ... this is the trouble, this is the toil." John 17[:3]: "To know God, this is eternal life." And therefore, one can also say, "this is my body, this is my blood." But instead of a demonstrative pronoun the Hebrews here often use the demonstrative adverb *hen* and *hinne*, that is, "look" and "behold." Thus, Paul in Heb 9:20 translates that saying of Moses "behold the blood of the covenant" (in Exod 24:8) as "this [neuter]" or "this [masculine] is the blood of the testament." And John 19[:26–27]: "Behold your mother, behold your son," that is, "this" [feminine], namely Mary, is your mother, and "this" [masculine], namely John, is your son.

45. Therefore, "this" means the same as "this thing" that has been mentioned previously, i.e., this bread and this wine, as if those things are pointed to by

an extended finger and are related to these words, to indicate the subject of the sentence. For first Luke and the apostle clearly say "this cup," albeit in such a way that the container stands for its contents, in the common and well-used custom of speaking in all languages. For it says, "drink from it, all of you" and "I shall not drink from the fruit of the vine."

46. And so it ["this"] means that which Jesus took into his hands, blessed (with the accusative case, as in Hebrew), broke, and gave to his disciples and what he ordered them to take and to drink, but this was bread and wine, as the grammatical construction demands. For since all those words are transitive in meaning, they require the fourth [accusative] case and take it, and in that passage there is no other [case]. Added to that is unshakeable logical reasoning. The statement is: you should eat and drink this (in the fourth case), i.e., the bread and the wine, because this is my body and my blood. Otherwise, if it refers to something else there could be no cause that the particle "for" indicates; nor would there be any connection between the clauses. And finally, in 1 Cor 10[:16] Paul removes any grounds for debate when he says: "The bread which we break and the cup of blessing which we bless, is it not the communion of the body and blood of Christ? Because we, who are many, are one bread, one body, for we all partake of the one bread." And, in 1 Cor 11[:26]: "Whenever you eat this bread and drink this cup." From these it is clear that "this" point to the bread and wine, and both are real bread and wine.

47. Therefore, it is foolish (as Karlstadt has falsely devised) that, because it is not "this" [masculine] but "this" [neuter], it relates to "body" [neuter], namely the body that was reclining at the table and that the apostles noted with their own eyes; for it says later: "This cup is the New Testament, etc." That is nothing other than inverting the relation between subject and sacrament. It is a similar inversion of terms, on the basis of the [definite] article "the" that is added to "body"—which indicates the subject (as it does in John 1:1, "God is the Word," and 4:24, "the Spirit is God")—to arrange the words thus with Schwenckfeld, "my body is this," i.e. what is the broken and eaten bread, or what is the spiritual and heavenly food, so that it does not point at the outward bread, nor indicate what is the bread, but what the body of Christ is, which is supported [according to Schwenckfeld] also by what it says in John 6[:51, 55]: "The bread which I will give is my flesh, and my flesh is food indeed, etc." For the [demonstrative pronoun] "this" includes the [definite] article, and it occurs in the next clause, "this cup," with the [definite] article.

But in John the word "bread" is taken metaphorically. (Yet we do not deny that also here the word "bread" includes a metaphor, albeit not an immediate metaphor; and these sentences are surely reciprocal.)

48. And the word "this" cannot mean, as it does for the papal promoters of transubstantiation, some vague individual thing, as Thomas would have it. For "this" denotes something specific and present. Either ["some vague individual thing" means] some single or individual thing of a more general substance that with the predicate refers to the same thing or supposits for the same thing—as Scotus says—in such a way that what is indicated by the subject and what is indicated by the attribute do not differ from each other (except by a different way of conceiving them), so that the sense is: "What is contained under the appearances of bread and wine" is my body and blood. For in that way the expression would be identical to the actual substance, and the sign would be destroyed. Or, alternatively, what previously was bread and wine. For according to the common understanding of the papal teachers it is only after the words have been uttered that the bread and wine becomes and so is the body and blood of the Lord. Lastly, nor is it the appearances of bread and wine, or their accidents (their color, smell, taste, shape) suspended in mid-air apart from their proper subjects, for that would really be taking away the truth of the signs and replacing them with things fantastical and delusory.

49. And though the word does so for the promoters of consubstantiation or impanation (to which view very many Schoolmen, like Scotus and D' Ailly are inclined, and which they would embrace if not the authority of the Lateran Synod held in 1215 had checked them; and which view Luther thence took over) "this" will not mean "in, with, or under this [neuter], or this [masculine]"—that is, the bread and the body, the blood and the wine. For bread is incapable of taking on a body, and a body cannot submit to bread, as both are compact, and unequal; nor is wine something under which some other liquid can hide, since both flow across their boundaries and mix with each other. Even more so the fact that this is not about one thing being contained under another thing, but about signification and exhibition, i.e., it is not about where or under what are the body and blood of the Lord—which is to turn the predicate into the subject and vice versa—but about what that bread and wine is.

50. The attribute is "the body and blood of Christ," i.e., his flesh and gore—which are dead—as in John 6. In both places the Syrian renders them as *pagra*, i.e., corpse. And then it says here, [the blood] "of the testament" or "covenant," with testament being put in place of covenant in keeping with the Septuagint, as the compound word *diatithesthai* is used for "to establish" (Luke 22:29–30), although here it means the testamental covenant. And for both testaments death occurs in order to confirm each one of them. In the old [it is] the death of a victim (hence it is called "to smite or to strike a covenant"), and in the new the death of the testator, to which the apostle alludes in Heb 9:16. And "of the new [covenant]," which is placed over against the old. The new consists in the reconciliation of an angered God to wretched men, and in the promise of salvation through the blood of the exhibited Christ himself and not that of another, as it was in the Old Testament. Therefore, it is the blood of the New Testament whereby this covenant was made and ratified. Or [it says] "the New Testament in the blood of Christ" as Luke and Paul put it, in a customary manner of speaking that is similar to the Hebrews. For them, the little word "in" indicates the instrument and the mode, that is, the New Testament is established by means of blood. The evangelists use these words interchangeably, because the blood and the New Testament are very closely linked.

51. This is connected more to the blood than to the body (for it doesn't say "the body of the New Testament," or "the New Testament in the body"), but not because both of them do not converge in the notion of "the New Testament." For a covenant was ratified by sacrificing a body, too; but it is because in the shedding of blood Christ's last suffering and death is more evident. And there is certainly an allusion made to Moses's words in Exod 24[:8] that Paul repeats in Heb 9:20: "Behold, the blood of the covenant that God has made with you."

52. And an exegesis or explanation is added to both attributes. About Christ's own body: "Which is given for you"—i.e., which will be given (as John 6:51 has it)—using the present tense for the immediate future, for the time imminent, and also to indicate the certainty of the matter and of the faith, in the customary way of speaking (John 10:17; Luke 22:22). It means to be handed over unto death, and, as Paul has it, "it is broken," metaphorically, that is, it will be fixed [to the cross], sacrificed, and destroyed by the separation of the soul from the body. Herein is an allusion to the breaking of the bread. And concerning the blood, "which is poured out for you," with

the same change in time, i.e., on the cross and not in the cup. Yet if one looks at the grammatical construction, Luke's words relate to the cup, while they relate to the blood if one considers the subject-matter, so that it appears to be a solecism, a not uncommon Hebraism in Scripture, like in Luke 5:9 etc. It also says [that it was given] "for you and for many" (i.e., believers) "unto the remission of sins," for without the shedding of blood there is no forgiveness (Heb 9:22). And in the same way we must relate it from this clause to the other one.

53. Therefore, it means the true, natural body that was lying at the table with the disciples, the body that soon would be seized, crucified, handed over to death; and it means the blood that surely then was in his veins but that soon would be poured out. Therefore, it was not a metaphorical body, a non-defined body, an imaginary, spiritual, and invisible body, and one that could not be touched and was not fixed in any place—indeed, a body that the promoters of consubstantiation think of, a ubiquitous body and one that was within the bread, nor, as the promoters of transubstantiation teach, a body that was transubstantiated from bread, i.e., a body that is not a body.

54. But although in Holy Scripture the body and blood (taking "blood" for the soul that resides in the blood, Gen 9:4) sometimes is used for a human being as a whole (Heb 2:14) and by synecdoche it is used at time for the incarnate Son of God or the person of God's Son (John 6:53; which will signify that to us Christ exhibited himself in his entirety, and that we entirely have communion with him), nevertheless that is not the only and most proper purpose for which he said it. And in fact, then the body and blood are considered as parts of a whole conjointly, and not separately, as occurs in this passage.

55. Therefore, on this point we do not consider Christ simply and absolutely as man (and even as God-and-man) but in light of a particular aspect and quality; namely, as a humbled man, a man in the final act of his humiliation, i.e., a crucified man and a dead man. And [we do not consider him here] as a living man nor a glorious one, i.e., a man who is not subject to any more afflictions and everyday conditions and death, and so no longer to be brought down to those lowly elements of the world (Rom 10:6).

56. And this is shown by the following obvious arguments: 1. Because Christ made use of appearances that are different in nature, situation and place, that is, bread and wine. And the bread was not dipped in, but dry, in order to

show the separation of body and blood. 2. Because both the body and the blood are presented thus separated, the body and blood that in a state of living and glory are joined together. 3. Because it is said about that body "which is given or broken for you," and so also the blood, "which is poured out," in order to show that in this way the body is bloodless, and the blood is not in the veins; the Latins call this flesh and gore. 4. Because it is called "the blood of the testament or covenant," or "the testament or covenant in blood," and consequently established by the shedding of blood, and death. 5. Because it is viewed as a sacrificial offering, an offering of a living creature that has been slain and that has died. 6. Because flesh and blood are here being offered for a complete meal, i.e., the spiritual food and drink. For about the bread which he called his body it is said "eat," and about the wine which he called his blood, "drink." But in fact no-one eats a whole animal, or one that is alive, but dead, nor does anyone drink blood that is in the veins, but only blood that has been poured out. 7. And finally, because Christ orders it to be done in remembrance of him, which the apostle interprets as being about his death, in 1 Cor 11:26: "You shall proclaim the Lord's death until he comes."

57. Therefore, it is beyond and contrary to the mind of Christ here that the papal teachers and others hold a mixed view of Christ: now as lowly, and then as glorious. For it doesn't suit the glorious state to drag Christ down to earth and back to the weak elements of the world. In fact by their actions they contradict themselves, when they stamp images of the crucified Christ on their wafers or offerings.

58. And finally, Christ himself is understood in this way, and indeed as humiliated and dead, so that the merits of his death are included together with himself, and the benefits and gifts, the power, the efficacy, namely the forgiveness of sins, righteousness, and life eternal (John 6:51–54). Therefore, it is added: "[The body] which is given and broken" and "[the blood] poured out for the forgiveness of sins" (thus also Matt 26:29; Luke 22:29–30). For we must join these three together inseparably: Christ and his death to the benefits that arise from it, and also to the outworking of these benefits. As a result, those who interpret the body and blood as only the merit or outworking are not passing on the truth fully enough.

59. The copula or link that ties the predicate to the subject is the substantive verb *esti*, "is." Since the Hebrews with the word *hayah* ("to be") miss the

present participle that for them takes the place of the present verb (except that they sometimes do use *yesh*) they assume that verb or they use pronouns in its place, and for the third person *hu*, "itself," that is, "this itself my body," which is equivalent to "is." Luke, too, in the second clause, the one about the cup, leaves out the same verb, a practice the Latins follow also when it is preceded by the demonstrative word. But Paul does supply it. And since its use is to join the subject to the predicate in a statement in the way that they affect one another [in reality], it should be taken in this way and not as tropological. But in the present tense it means what the thing is, and its existence at this time, and not what it is becoming or any action the thing does, or anything that it undergoes. For that is indicated by "become," "be," or "was made" (Matt 4:3; John 2:9) so that it is "the bread is," i.e., exists truly as my body, etc.

60. For this reason the papal teachers certainly behave foolishly when they ascribe to the word "is" an efficacious or an operational power, and really interpret "is" as "is changed in substance." And others explain it as "becomes consubstantial with," or is joined or united with in a sacramental manner, which they want to be not only in a real sense but also substantially. [They err] since the wording is about being, not becoming.

61. So much for the individual words whereby these statements are made. Insofar as the outward speech is concerned, they are figurative or tropological, as is clear from the link between the predicate and the subject. Not because there is a trope in the sentence as a whole (for trope belongs to a word) but there is a trope of the whole sentence. For words themselves are not tropological, but they converge into a sentence that results in a trope. For the cause of a trope is something different than the seat of the trope. On this point we should consider three things: first whether there is a trope in the words of the Lord; second, where the trope is found or what the seat of it is; and lastly, which trope it is and what sort it is.

62. The fact that it is a trope is confirmed by the cause for the trope, and firstly in view of the subject. For the subject is the bread and the wine, not the body or blood of the Lord under those appearances, as the papists would have it. Nor is it the Lord's body or blood under, with, or in the bread and the wine, as Luther would have it (referring to Pierre d'Ailly), as was shown previously. About the bread and the wine, it cannot properly be said that they are Christ's body and blood, for that would entail a contradiction. For they

are two unrelated things of which the one cannot be the other—not even, as Scotus says, by the almighty power of God nor can they be predicated mutually of one another in the proper sense.

63. Secondly, [it is confirmed as a trope] from the predicate, for the body and blood here are the broken body and the shed blood, that is, Christ in his state of humility and death, and in fact in such a condition as he had not been previously, and now no longer is, nor is able to be. For he is no longer dying. But in fact, nothing can be changed into something or joined to something substantially (nor can it properly be said so) that was not yet, and no longer is or is able to be in such a condition. Otherwise, it would entail a contradiction. For then one and the same thing would be such and not such, namely humiliated and glorious, dead and alive. Therefore, it is an improper manner of speaking, and then indeed a true manner of speaking for those [disciples] by the foresight of a thing that was going to happen and for us by the recollection of a thing that has taken place.

64. And furthermore the cup, that is, what is in the cup, is called "testament" or "covenant," or "the testamental covenant" in the blood—something that cannot be said about the cup or the wine, and not even can it be said about the blood that it properly speaking is the testament or covenant. For these things belong to different categories. In a similar way the apostle in 1 Cor 10[:16] calls the bread and wine "the communion in the body and blood of Christ," and in a similar manner of speaking he says that "because we, who are many, are one bread and one body." Therefore, the trope is obvious.

65. And then there is the added fact that Christ orders that it be done "for the remembrance and recollection of him," and the apostle commands: "Proclaim the Lord's death until he comes." And surely that would not be said if bread and wine (or something under the appearances of bread and wine) were the body and the blood of the Lord in the proper sense and in substance, because there is no recollection of a thing that is present; nor is it said that he who is present in substance is going to come.

66. And finally this tropological manner of speaking is very common in the use of sacraments. And so, it says that "circumcision is God's covenant," and soon thereafter, "the sign of the covenant" (Gen 17[:10–11]); and the apostle calls it "the seal of the righteousness of faith" (Rom 4). In Exod 12 it says, "the lamb that was slain is the Pascha or Passover;" in 1 Cor 10[:4] it says

that the "rock from which the Israelites drank was Christ," where a comparison is made with the Lord's Supper.

67. And on this point we are supported also by the consensus of the church fathers. For they say that the bread and the wine are the body and blood of the Lord "in their own way" (Prosper, *Sentences*), "somehow" (Augustine, on Psalm 33), "by a certain mode" (Augustine, *Epistle 23* to Boniface). They are "like" and "as" the body and blood (Chrysostom, *On the Eucharist in Encaenia*, and *Sermon 84* on John); a "mystery or sacrament" (Chrysostom, *Incomplete Work* [*on Matthew*], sermon 11). Augustine, in his *Epistle 23* to Boniface, says that "they are not the true body, but a mystery of the body." It is called "a type or figure" (Tertullian, *Against Marcion*, book 4; Augustine on Psalm 3; Ambrose, *On the Sacraments*, book 4 chapter 5); "an antitype or model" (Nazianzus in his *Apology to Basil*, Anaphora Syra, Macarius Sermon 27); "a symbol" (Dionysius, Clement of Alexandria, Origen, Theodoret Dialogues 1); "a sign" (Augustine, *Against Adimantus*, chapter 12); "an image and likeness" (Gelasius, *Against Eutychus*); "a pledge" of the body and blood of the Lord (Jerome on 1 Cor 11). Indeed, it says that it "is the body and blood in the mystery" (Prosper, *Sentences*); "it is not in the true reality of the thing, but in what the mystery signifies;" "in the sign, or through the sign" (Augustine, *Against Adimantus*, chapter 12); "by means of, or through, its signification" (Augustine on Leviticus *Question* 57); "in likeness" (Ambrose, *on the Sacraments*, book 4, chapter 5); "by its appellation" (Chrysostom, *To Caesarius the Monk*). And moreover, [the bread and wine] are said to "be a sign" or "to signify" (Ambrose on 1 Cor 11), "to represent" the body and the blood (Tertullian, *Against Marcion*, book 4), etc.; and Augustine (*On Christian Doctrine*, book 3, chapter 16) and also the other fathers like Clement of Alexandria state expressly that it is a "figurative" and "allegorical" manner of speaking.

68. Among the Orthodox there is a difference of opinion about the seat of the trope, although they almost entirely agree on the main point of it. Some are of the opinion that the trope does not exist in any part at all: not in the subject, nor the predicate, nor in the copula. [They mean] that individually these things are to be taken in their proper sense, but that the predication is figurative. (Thus Beza, following Zanchius.) Crellius in fact puts a figurative, logical statement over against a rhetorical one, and he defines the former by the statement as a whole, and the latter by the [individual] words. Yet because logic is a matter of thought and inner reasoning, and not of speech, and so

does not belong to speech, there is no figurative predication in it, but figure of speech belongs only to rhetorical utterance. And although it [i.e., the trope] is caused by attribution, even so the seat is in some specific part.

69. And so there are others who locate the trope in the subject, or in the demonstrative word "this," as Bucer does, so that thereby it signifies the bread with the body, and the wine with the blood, by virtue of the sacramental union. Through that union it is not necessary for each thing to be present in a substantial sense, but only in a real sense, in such a way that to our senses the bread and wine are presented, and to our minds the body and blood of the Lord. And they say that this is what happens for all utterances wherein things that the senses cannot perceive or things that are absent are promised and exhibited by means of signs. Therefore, the meaning would be: "this" which I give to you by this sign "is my body," etc. However, there was no prior mention made of the body so that the word "this" could point to it, and the pronouncement of that union occurs for the first time through those words.

70. Others locate the trope in the word "is," taking it in the sense of "signifies," thus Zwingli following Honius Batavus. And rightly so, for among its other meanings "is" often is used to mean "signify"—as when we translate a word from one language into another we say "that is," which has the force of "it signifies" (Matt 1:23). And so also about things: "The seven heads of grain" and "the seven cows" "are seven years" (Gen 40:13, 19; 41:26). "The seed is the word of God, the field is the world" (Matt 17:37–38). "The seven stars are the seven angels, etc.," and "the many waters are the many people" (Rev 1:20, and 17:15). And similarly, the word is used for "to be like," as in: I am the bread, the true vine, the door; John is Elijah; Herod is a fox. In these places the metaphor is in the predicate. To this interpretation people also relate those sacramental expressions, "circumcision is the covenant" [Gen 17:9–14], "the Lamb is the Passover" [Deut 16:2–6, 1 Cor 5:7], "the rock was Christ" [1 Cor 10:4], "the cup is the New Testament" [Luke 22:20]. Even so, these expressions convey not only a signification and comparison, but also the sealing and an exhibiting of something. However, the word "is" then functions partly as a predicate and partly as a copula, as is clear from the explanation of the word.

71. And finally there are others who with Oecolampadius locate the trope in the words "body and blood," and then "is" would be only a copula, and the

sense would be that the bread and the wine are a symbol, a sign, a seal, a promise, a pledge, and an exhibition of the body and blood. This meaning is corroborated by the following very strong argument: whatever the proper location is where the analysis or explanation of the tropical expression falls, that is where the trope is. Well now, that actually falls in the words "body and blood," the nominative case having changed into an oblique one. For just as the expression "circumcision is the covenant" is analyzed into "is a sign of the covenant," so also "the bread and the wine are the body and the blood" is analyzed into "are a communion of the body and the blood of the Lord," not insofar as the bread has communion with the body of Christ, but insofar as the believers do. Therefore, the trope correctly is placed in the predicate.

72. It does not therefore follow, however, that the Supper is deprived of the truth of the body and blood of Christ, and that instead of it a figurative or symbolic body and blood is introduced, contrary to that statement: "This is my body which is broken for you; this is my blood which is shed for you." In fact, that is the argument which the papal teachers, following Scotus, and also those who follow Luther insist upon as their chief tenet. But there is a difference between "a trope in the word body" and "a figurative body." There is a difference between "a symbol of the body" and "a symbolic body." The former leaves the verity of the body intact, while the latter removes it altogether. And surely by this sort of trope there is no denying that it is a body, but something else is signified in addition to it, and both are involved in it. Therefore, Cajetan in his commentary on Thomas, rightly responds to the argument by Scotus that the true body is not removed, even if it is determined that there is a trope, as when it says that the rock was Christ (i.e., a symbol of the true Christ who would be born of the virgin Mary, and would be crucified, slain, etc.). So also here, for it is one thing to ask what kind of predicate it is, and another to ask in what mode it is present in the subject.

73. Hence it is also clear what sort of trope it is, namely a metonym, as was recognized also by Augustine, in which the thing signified has been put in place of the sign (by analogy, in fact, that is, by bearing a proportionate likeness to the thing signified). As Augustine says: "For sacraments are not even sacraments unless they bear a likeness to those things of which they are the sacraments." And not only that, but they are signs of such a sort that the things signified—the body and blood of the Lord—being present, are joined and united with them in their own way (namely in a sacramental way, that is, in a real way, to wit, relatively, and not in substance). Indeed they [the bread

and wine] are changed, as the fathers say, although not in the substance and nature itself, but in their condition, use, and function. And moreover, they are like carriers or instruments whereby the very body and blood of Christ are exhibited or offered to everyone, but bestowed upon and given to believers, and consumed by those who have faith—for that is the innate property of the sacrament. It is with such wording that the apostle says: "the Gospel is the power of God unto salvation for all who believe" [Rom 1:17], and "the bread which we break"—that is, the breaking and eating of the bread—"is the communion of the body of Christ" [1 Cor 10:16].

74. Therefore, Christ preferred to say, "this is my body" and "this is my blood," thereby ascribing the words "body" and "blood" to the bread and wine in an improper sense and in what they are, as if it were an essential statement, rather than wanting to use the proper kind of expression. He did so for the sake of making the signification clear, of making the likeness and analogy of these signs as close as possible to the thing signified, and so also for the sealing, confirmation, certainty and ensurance, the exhibition and comparison of the thing signified through these signs. For these words possess the promise of the thing made by God included in them, and the promise added to the outward signs, the promise that from the side of God is offered to everyone and that from our side is received by faith. And the emphasis and force of that meaning is hardly achieved by any other sort of statement in a proper sense. And it is in this sacramental relation and respect that the essential form of the Lord's Supper consists.

75. Therefore, the papal promoters of transubstantiation and the others who promote consubstantiation commit a serious error when they assert that these statements have a strict, proper meaning. And as their explanation shows, they are not even saying exactly what Scripture says. For the question is not what becomes of the bread, or where is the body and blood of Christ, or where is it hidden (whether under the bare appearances, or under the bread and wine—which is, in fact, to turn the predicates into the subjects). And second, since they understand by "this" either the external appearances of bread and wine, as the former do, or the bread and wine, as the latter and [since] they include under these the body and blood of the Lord as their contents, they necessarily introduce a trope of synecdoche in the subject. And lastly, because they moreover attribute to those things [viz. the appearances of the bread and wine, or the bread and wine themselves] the notion of signs (without which there can be no sacrament), which cannot happen without

specific words of institution that declare the signifying act (for they are signs by virtue of their institution) and because those words of institution, as even they themselves think, are nothing other than "this is my body, this is my blood," therefore, in order that the proportion of the predicate to the subject be right, they have to acknowledge—whether they like it or not—that there is a metonym in the predicate, unless they do away with the entire notion of sacrament and sign.

76. And finally, in these words of Christ there is an aitiology, a connection between these sentences and the preceding command, which is made explicit by the causal particle "for." To be sure, in the prior sentence about the bread it is omitted, but in the second one about the cup it is stated expressly, and therefore it should be supplied there, too (as the translator does). Christ had said: "Eat this bread, and drink this cup," or "this [thing]," in the accusative case, because "this" in the nominative case is my body and blood. Here "this" denotes the same thing both times, so that it is the connection between the terms in the syllogism. And accordingly [he said] "eat and drink this" because to eat and drink this is to eat and drink my body. And so it declares the sublime nature and necessity of this mystery.

77. But what they infer from this does not at all follow, namely, that therefore the mouth is eating the body and drinking the blood of the Lord on the grounds that the oral eating and drinking is commanded of that which is the Lord's body and blood (which is their chief argument in support of oral eating and drinking). But it only follows that what is eaten and drunk are bread and wine (since that is what the syntax demands, as there is no other accusative case with which "eat" can be construed), which in their own way are the body and blood of the Lord. But for all those actions that Christ performed and taught to his disciples, one thing was intended for and commanded to the senses, the other for and to the mind, namely in a metaphorical and synecdochical way. For just as the bread and the wine are called the body and blood of Christ, so "take," "eat this bread" and "drink this wine" must be taken in a corporal way in such a way that they are also understood in a spiritual way.

78. There still remains the legislation, that was given to the universal church for posterity, and that was sanctioned for an everlasting law by means of these words: "Do this in remembrance of me." Luke has this for the first statement, but Paul for both, who also adds to the second one, "and whenever you

drink," from which we should supply it in similar fashion to the first statement, "and whenever you eat."

79. And moreover, in that sacred action Christ addresses the apostles as shepherds and dispensers of his mysteries and as those who stand in his stead, as well as representatives of the universal gathering of believers, because he commands them to "do this." When he had said "this," it does not refer to his body and blood and to what he was going to suffer, but it refers to all the things that the Lord had done concerning the bread and the cup, I mean to all the things that preceded, i.e., what you have seen me do as the host, that I command you also to do as the guests.

80. Therefore, "all of you," as my ministers, "do this;" that is, as a perpetual ritual take the bread, bless the bread (or give thanks for the bread), then break it and give it, and say in my name: "This is my body" or "Christ's body." And so similarly also for the cup, etc.: "Do [this] you all," by taking part in "this;" that is, take, eat, drink. This is clear from the fact that Paul applies it not only to the shepherds but especially to the whole church of the Corinthians, when he interprets "do" as "eat" and "drink," since he repeats Christ's words in this way: "Do this, whenever you drink," etc. (and by analogy, whenever you eat), which is more obvious from the appended explanatory statement: "For whenever you eat and drink," etc. And also from the conclusion: "Therefore, whoever eats and drinks," etc. This commands the necessity of obedience for all who believe, and it also reveals that the church is free in determining the frequency of the Lord's Supper.

81. From this it is clear how foolish the reasoning of the papists is, when they base the foundation of the sacrifice of the mass on these words by taking "do" to mean "sacrifice," on the grounds that in both Greek "to do a sacrifice" and in Latin "to do" or "perform" is used in this way, as in "when I do a young cow, etc." (Virgil). But in that case, it is connected to an ablative of the thing, while in Hebrew it is connected to the accusative case of the thing that is presented for the sacrifice (Num 28:3), with the addition of the goal: for a sacrifice. But never does this wording, "do this," have that meaning, but it always shows some prior action, i.e., what you have seen me doing. And surely Christ did not at that time offer himself under the appearances of bread and wine, but he said that he was going to offer himself. Otherwise, he would have offered himself two times, once in the bread and the wine, and a second time on the altar of the cross, and that is absurd.

82. And added to this commandment is the universal goal for the Lord's Supper, that it be administered and used "in *anamnēsis* of me," i.e., in remembrance or recollection of me, which Paul explains as "in remembrance of my death." He says: "For whenever you eat this bread and drink this cup, you will proclaim the Lord's death," i.e., you will celebrate with your profession of faith and with thanksgiving, "until he comes"—that is, until he appears again to judge the living and the dead. And with that last coming he describes the duration of the age, and he declares that the Lord's Supper be perpetually practiced. And we should attach a second, most excellent goal to that end, namely the union and fellowship with Christ, and the partaking in all his benefits, which Paul in 1 Cor 10:16–17 explains by saying: "Because we, who are many, are one bread," and, in chapter 12:13: "and we have all been made to drink into one Spirit."

83. Moreover, as this remembrance and declaration of Christ's death is the goal of the sacrament, so the apostle Paul defines its worthy use by each and every person's prior self-examination, namely whether he has faith (2 Cor 13:5) and whether he is moved by serious repentance, according to that statement by Paul: "Let a man examine himself and so eat of that bread and drink of that cup." This self-examination does not take away the public examination by others, but confirms it. On the other hand, it is an abuse, and he eats and drinks in an unworthy manner "who does not discern the body" (and so too the blood) of the Lord, [1 Cor 11] verse 29. That is, he does not distinguish between the two symbols (this bread and this cup, which by a sacramental relation are the body of the Lord and his blood) and the common bread and wine; and he does not make a distinction in using them, namely, between the sacred and the profane use of them, according to what it says in verse 34: "But if someone is hungry, let him eat at home, lest you come together for condemnation." And so he actually despises and treats with dishonor the very body that is offered to him; and therefore, on account of the serious injustice that is done thus against Christ "he becomes guilty of the body and blood of the Lord" (verse 27), and "he eats and drinks judgment unto himself." That is, he brings upon himself the punishment of judgment, and he brings upon himself the scourgings of God and death itself (verse 29–30).

84. And Matthew and Mark add also Christ's reminders about his own departure, and about the new life in heaven, in which they will be his fellow-partakers, when he says: "I say to you that I shall not henceforth drink from

the fruit of the wine until that day when I shall drink the wine new with you in the kingdom of my Father." These words are applied in Luke to the Passover meal. It is not certain whether Matthew and Mark recite these words in their order and place, or whether Christ repeated them twice. At any rate, we should take them as applying to both in common, and as analogous to both the Passover and the sacramental meal.

85. And as for what in Matt [26:29] and Mark [14:25?] is "but" in Luke [22:16, 18] is "for," in order to give the reason why Christ exhibited to them that cup for the last time. The wine is understood by the periphrastic "fruit of the vine," as it is called here also after the consecration and the eating. In fact, the same is understood also about the bread, by analogy, as is evident from Luke [22:16 and 22:18]. Moreover, when Christ says that he will "no longer eat and drink of (specifically) this," he means "together [with them]," based on repeating the next words, "together with you." Therefore, he himself had drunk with them, and had tasted before he exhibited them [i.e. bread and wine] to his disciples. For thus he himself willed to consecrate and commence this sacrament in himself, just like baptism before. In his case that also had a particular meaning, namely of death (Matt 20:22, 26:39; John 18:11). And then he puts forth a term to his abstaining, when he says: "From this time," or "anymore." Of course, after his resurrection he does drink with the apostles (Acts 1:4 and 10:41), but then in light of the dispensation and not in the usual manner of our current life, but to produce faith in the resurrection. But he does indicate that it will be repeated, when he says: "Until I shall drink it new," that is, an other wine. In this way the "new tongues" of Mark 16:17 are called "other tongues" by Luke [Acts 2:4], or tongues that are different from the usual. But it does mean one that is similar to it, and he moves from the proper sense to the metaphorical one, so that it both is and is not the same one, as Christ often does (John 3:14, 6:27, 32, etc.). And he adds "with you," when they will have been taken up into the same condition and fruition of blessedness, which the drinking signifies. And that will be "in the kingdom of my Father," taking them from the kingdom of grace to the kingdom of glory, thus explaining the final goal of this sacrament (Luke 22:29–30).

86. And lastly, there is added the expression of thanksgiving: "And when he had sung a hymn, they departed to Mount Olivet." This means: Christ led in the singing, and the apostles sang in harmony with him. It is not related which hymn it was. Burgos notes that it was Ps 113 and the five ones that follow it, the ones that even today the Hebrews call "the great Hallelujah," i.e., the

great hymn that they used to sing in their solemn festivals, especially the Passover, in order to remember the liberation from Egypt. And what if we relate it to that very beautiful prayer in John 17? And certainly when Christ began and completed this sacred act by means of giving thanks, he set a precedent for the church in its practice or use of this sacrament.

87. Well then, this is our clear and complete view on the Word of God about the Lord's Supper. By this view we have explained and asserted the integrity and truth of the signs and of the things they signify, as well as the connection and the relative union of them, and also their use and their efficacy. And these will be able to suffice for minds that are sober, to serve as consolation for believers, and to put a limit to quarreling among brothers, provided that there is no prejudice or desire to fight—attitudes that the church of God does not possess (1 Cor 11:16) and that do not befit those who are devout (Phil 2:3).

SOURCES

Clement of Alexandria, *The Paedagogue,* book 2 chapter 2
He himself also partook of wine, for he, too, was a human being. And he blessed the wine when he said: "Take, drink, this is my blood." The blood of the vine, the Word, which is poured out for many for the remission of sins, figuratively signifies a holy stream of gladness. (And shortly thereafter) And he showed again that it was the wine that he blessed when he said to his disciples: "I shall not drink from the fruit of this vine until I drink it with you in the kingdom of my father."

Cyprian, in *Sermon on Christ's Anointing*
At the table where he shared his last meal with the apostles the Lord gave the bread and the wine with his own hands; but on the cross he gave his body into the hands of the soldiers to be wounded, so that the sincere truth and the true sincerity that was impressed more privately on the apostles might reveal to the nations how the wine and the bread are the body and blood, and in what ways the causes match the effects; and also how the various names or appearances are reduced to a single essence, and how the things that signify and the things that are signified should be called by the same names.

Chrysostom, *To Caesarius the Monk*

Before it is sanctified we call the bread "bread"; but when divine grace sanctifies it by means of the priest, it is freed from the name "bread" and it is considered worthy of the name "body of the Lord," even though the nature of bread remained in it.

Rabanus Maurus, *On the Institution of Clerics*, book 1 chapter 31

The Lord preferred the sacraments of his body and blood to be eaten with the mouth by the faithful, and to be rendered as food for them, so that the visible work might illustrate an invisible effect. For as the material food nourishes and refreshes the body outwardly, so too does the Word of God nourish and strengthen the soul inwardly. (And soon thereafter) The sacrament is eaten with the mouth, but by the power of the sacrament the inner man is satisfied. The sacrament is turned into nourishment for the body, but by the power of the sacrament the excellence of eternal life is obtained, etc. And so in the same way that [the food and drink] changes in us when we eat and drink it, so also are we changed into the body of Christ so long as we live obedient and holy lives, etc. And because bread fortifies the heart of the body, it is therefore called the body of Christ. And because the wine affects the blood in the body it is related to the blood of Christ.

Christian Druthmar, *Commentary on Matthew*

The Lord gave the sacrament of his body to the disciples for the remission of their sins and the preservation of love, so that mindful of his deed they would always do figuratively what he was about to give on their behalf, and not forget his love. "This is my body," that is, "in the sacrament, etc."

ON THE SACRIFICE OF
THE MASS AND ITS ABUSES

President: Johannes Polyander
Respondent: Joshua van Sonnevelt

The tone of this disputation is polemical, as it criticizes the Roman Catholic Mass. It addresses the meaning and origin of the term 'mass' (3–12), denies the sacrificial character of it (13–47), and criticizes many of its features (48–61). With references to the letter to the Hebrews, the unique, one-time, unrepeatable character of Christ's sacrifice on the cross, then and there, is emphasized again and again. Only that sacrifice is propitiatory in the real sense of the word.

1. In place of the Supper that Christ himself has ordained, the papal teachers foist upon us the mass. And while Augustine rightly calls the Supper the sacrament of piety, the sign of harmony, and the bond of love (*Treatise on John*, 26), this mass can be called its opposite: the sacrament of impiety, the sign of apostasy, and the bond of dissension. For in the mass, this sort of idolaters worships a fictitious body of Christ and they deviate very far from the sacrament as Christ initially instituted it (as was shown above [disputation 45.9–77]), and with a hatred befitting Vatinius, they hate those who have reformed their faithless idolatry.

2. Before we examine the shameful abuses of the idolatrous mass, we shall take a close look at its meaning and definition.

3. Some of the papal teachers consider the word *missa* ('mass') a Hebrew word, and others a Latin one.

---

4. Of these teachers, the former try to prove that the word *missa* occurs in Deut 16:10, and that it means a voluntary offering. Bellarmine refutes their view with two arguments that are not unconvincing. The first is that "if the apostles had used that Hebrew word then surely also the Greek, Syrian and other nations would have kept it, just as they kept other similar words like amen, hallelujah, Sabaoth, hosanna, Satan, Sabbath, and Pascha. And that is because Hebrew words have come down to us via the Greeks, since the apostles themselves and the foremost teachers of the church wrote in Greek. But among the Greek writers, no mention is made of this word *missa*." The second argument is that "if it were a Hebrew word, then we should say *missah* and not *missa*; but no-one writes or says it in this way" (Bellarmine, *On the Eucharist*, book 5, chapter 1).

5. We should add to these arguments that the Hebrew word, sometimes used in the feminine and sometimes in the masculine gender, is taken to mean either a political tribute (as in Exod 1:11) or an ecclesiastical one, especially that of the first fruits, which would be kept in the early church in the worship to God. This tribute was formerly not offered by the Levitical priests (as nowadays the Roman sacrificers perform the mass) but by the other tribes of the Jewish people, as in Deut 16:10.

6. And we should not overlook the fact that when considered by itself the word *missah* does not mean an offering that is voluntary, as the unlettered papal teachers think, but simply an offering (Deut 16:10); and also, that it is not an offering of the expiatory sort, as they claim their mass to be, but a eucharistic one. It is in that sense that also the fathers call the Supper of the Lord, the Eucharist, insofar as it is a commemoration of Christ's sacrifice once offered on the cross, or the remembrance of it together with thanksgiving, just as Augustine describes it (*Against Faustus*, book 20, *On Faith to the Deacon Peter, Book against the Adversaries of the Law*, and *On the City of God*, book 10, chapter 5).

7. We grant that in Deut 16:10 God demands a voluntary offering from the people of Israel, or, as some translate it, a spontaneous offering. However, this offering is not expressed by means of one word, but by two, namely *missah nidbat*, which Arias Montanus and Pagninus render as the sufficient offering by a willing person, or a spontaneous gift, in keeping with the Chaldean meaning, since in the Targum the word *missah* is often written for the Hebrew *daw* or *daj*.

8. And the latter [of these papal teachers], those who think that *missa* is a Latin word, do not all explain it in the same way. For some, as Bellarmine in the same treatise shows, want it to be called *missa* ['sent'], because the offering and prayers are sent up to God (thus Hugh of St. Victor, *On the Sacraments*, book 2, part 8, final chapter). Bellarmine considers their explanation to be probable, but we regard it as wrong and fictitious.

9. Therefore, others think that it is called *missa*, because God sends an angel to attend the sacrifice and to present it to God, as the Master [Peter Lombard] thinks in [book] 4, distinction 13, and Thomas [Aquinas] in [part 3] question 83, article 4. Bellarmine judges this etymology to be less probable, but we deem it to be entirely incredible.

10. There are others who think that among the ancients, it was called *missa* from the sending and collecting of gifts (as symbolic things) into the midst of the community, gifts from which the holy Supper was made and given to the poor for a meal. This explanation seems probable also to some of our theologians on account of the fact that in former times, the Christian people sent its gifts, namely bread and wine, for an offering (as Evagrius reports). And from these offerings placed in a large vessel in the area of the temple-entrance, things would be taken that suited the administration of the Eucharist, while the rest was given to the poor to use.

11. Bellarmine thinks that the most probable view is of those who want *missa* to be said from the sending away or dismissal of the people so that *missa* would be the same thing as *missio*, just like the words *collecta* and *collectio* among the ancients, and in Greek *sullogē*, *sullexis*, or *remissa* and *remissio* [forgiveness] of sin. For Cyprian uses the word *remissa* instead of *remissio* everywhere (book 3, epistle 8; the book *On the Good of Suffering*, in the *Letter to Jubaianus*, and elsewhere). And that word comes from this ancient formula that the deacon used to declare before the preaching: "Let the catechumens and whoever is not a communicant go outside." And the second formula: "Go, the dismissal is made."

12. To this meaning of *missa*, Bellarmine adds four other ones, which he has taken from the orthodox fathers, the first of which is that it stands for the divine office of lessons and prayers (Council of Valencia, canon 1); 2. For that part of the liturgy that takes place from the offertory until the very end (from Alcuin); 3. For the celebration of the divine office in which the Eucharist is consecrated (from Leo, Gregory, Felix IV, the Council at Agde,

and also the Council at Orléans). 4. For the actual collects or the prayers that are spoken in the liturgy (from Milevitan Council, canon 12). But here we should point out that none of those meanings of his are proved by Holy Scripture. And also, that Bellarmine has not demonstrated from the writings of the fathers (from where he cites those meanings) what he ought to have demonstrated, namely that the orthodox fathers have recognized the mass as meaning the kind of sacrifice as he and the other Roman teachers have defined it.

13. For they define the mass as an outward sacrifice that in the real and proper sense of the word is also propitiatory, whereby the priest sacrifices and offers Christ's body and blood under the appearances of bread and wine for the sins of the living and the dead (Council of Trent, session 22, chapter 1; Faber, *On the Evangelical Mass*, book 2, chapter 1; Eck, in three books *On the Sacrifice of the Mass*; Cajetan, treatise 10, tome 3, on the same argument; Bellarmine, *On the Eucharist*, book 1, chapter 5, etc.).

14. The claims that are sprinkled throughout this definition contain nothing of the truth. For the first claim, that the mass is an outward sacrifice, does not accord with the truth, not even in the judgment of Bellarmine himself. For every outward sacrifice, and one that is properly so-called (to use the wording of Bellarmine in *On the Eucharist*, book 1, chapter 2) requires that the thing which is to be offered must be perceived by the senses. But the thing that the sacrificers in the mass are said to offer, namely the flesh of Christ, in no way can be perceived by the senses since it neither is in their presence, nor can it be seen or touched because now it is in heaven, and it will remain there until the time when everything will be restored, as the apostle Peter testifies in Acts 3:21.

15. The second claim, that the mass is a propitiatory sacrifice in the real and proper sense of the word, flies in the face of the statement by the apostle who shows by means of a three-fold contrast between Christ's priesthood and that of the Levitical priests that Christ's sacrifice accomplished on the cross is a unique expiatory sacrifice. The first of these contrasts is the fact that under the Old Testament there were many priests, but under the New only one. Of the former (as the apostle says in Heb 7:23–24) "there were many who became priests, because death would not let them live forever; but he, because he does live forever, possesses a perpetual priesthood." The second contrast is that it was necessary for the priests of the Old Testament

to offer sacrificial victims every day, first for their own sins and then for the sins of the people [Heb 5:3]; but Christ had to make an offering once only for the people, and that was all that he did (Heb 7:27). The third is the fact that the Old Testament priests offered various sacrificial victims, goats, calves, lambs, and similar animals that others had given them; but Christ through the eternal Spirit offered only himself unblemished to God (Heb 9:14). Peter also indicates this with the words: "Who himself in his own body lifted up our sins on that cross" (1 Pet 2:24). Therefore, since these statements contradict each other—"Christ's offering for the sins of the people should happen only once and did happen only once," and "Christ's offering should happen again and again, and does happen every time the sacrificers celebrate the mass"—we must consider the former statement, made by an apostle whom God had inspired, to be true, but the latter statement by the papal teachers who contradict the apostle to be false.

16. Our reply to the papal teachers' first objection (Council of Trent, session 6) that the offering made in the mass is the same as the offering that was made on the cross and differs from it only in mode and manner is: 1) that William Allen, although he understood that mode, contradicts them when he says that "Christ accomplished two sacrifices, one in the Supper and another on the cross, and that both sacrifices are different from the sacrifice of the mass" (in *On the Sacrifice of the Eucharist*, book 2, chapter 2 [10]). 2) that the mode wherein they admit that the mass differs from Christ's offering made on the cross is properly one of passive suffering and an adjunct, and that with respect to the one is actually so opposed to the other that they cannot both exist at the same time. Therefore, if we posit the following, that Christ's offering could have been made only once by Christ himself, then the second position is overturned, i.e., that the same offering still can be made each and every day by the priest vicariously for Christ. The fact that the first axiom is true may be grasped from the second necessary condition of Christ's offering, which is the death of Christ, who offered his own self to the Father, along with the shedding of his blood. For in the books of the Holy Bible, it always says that it is by means of his own bloody death that Christ offered himself to the Father. Therefore, if it is impossible for him again to die for our sins, then it is also impossible for him to be offered for them a second time in the mass.

17. If they should say (as they are accustomed to say) that the sacrifice of Christ once accomplished on the cross continues day by day in the mass, then

it necessarily follows that the earlier sacrifice of Christ was incomplete. For that which continues has not yet been completed, and that which is repeated every day must be considered to be incomplete—or else the reasoning that the apostle puts forward as proof does not hold, that the Old Testament sacrifices were incomplete on account of the fact that they were repeated very often (Heb 9 and 10).

18. We conclude from these observations that there is no consistency in the distinction the papal teachers make between the bloody sacrifice on the cross and the bloodless sacrifice of the mass. For if every expiatory offering necessarily must happen with the shedding of blood—as is clear from the following axiomatic statement by the apostle in Heb 9:22, "without the shedding of blood there is no forgiveness"—then under no pretext at all can the mass be called an expiatory offering. And moreover, we can refute this distinction by means of that admission by Bellarmine: "In the church, there is but one true and proper sacrifice" (On the Eucharist, book 1, chapter 2). And that true sacrifice, as Bellarmine admits in the same passage, is the sacrifice of Christ that was offered on the cross; and using the words of Augustine, he calls that sacrifice the most true and perfect sacrifice. Therefore, the mass cannot be that true and perfect sacrifice, since two sacrifices that are in reality different cannot simultaneously be the most true, the most perfect sacrifices coequally. But if two such sacrifices were arranged unequally and subordinately, then we should call the sacrifice that Christ accomplished on the cross, not the one sacrifice but the first sacrifice, and then the apostle's assertion that Christ offered himself only once would be wrong.

19. And Bellarmine also cannot escape this criticism of his own ignorance and that of his predecessors by taking refuge in the claim that the sacrifice of the mass is a commemorative and representative one (William Allen, On the Sacrifice of the Eucharist, book 2, chapter 11; Bellarmine, On the Eucharist, book 1, chapter 2). For whatever is commemorative and representative of something is no more the thing itself than the time past is the time present, and no more than the sign is the thing signified. And certainly, a sacrifice is that of a thing present and still to be accomplished, while a commemoration is of a thing that has been done and is past.

20. The papal teachers' third claim, that in the mass the body and blood of Christ are being immolated, is no less false than their two earlier claims. For in every sacrifice that which is truly and properly immolated must be not only

present but also mortal. But Christ has taken his own body away from earth into the third heaven, and he has shielded it from all mortality forever. For this reason, it can hardly be more foolish to say that even now, people are immolating Christ's body on this earth. We should pass the same judgment on the immolation of Christ's blood, which cannot truly and properly happen in the mass without shedding it. Also, in the sacrament of the Eucharist, Christ represents to us not his glorified body as it is today but the body that once was bound to the cross.

21. Here the papal teachers retort in vain that the sacrifices of the Law were commemorative and representative of the future sacrifice on the cross, and yet they were sacrifices in the proper sense of the word. But in fact, it was not the actual body of Jesus Christ that was sacrificed in those sacrifices (as the papal teachers claim happens in the mass) but the bodies of goats, calves, and other animals that in former times foreshadowed the sacrifice of Christ as types, and once this body was revealed, they were withdrawn like shadows before the sun, no more to be recalled to their former uses. Moreover, in those sacrifices of the Law, the bodies of the animals that were offered were ordained for a real and outward change and even destruction; and as Bellarmine himself has put it (*On the Eucharist*, book 1, chapter 2), this sort of change and destruction in the things offered is required for every sacrifice that is truly and properly so called. But in the meantime, not one of the papal teachers who call the mass a true and proper sacrifice has up till now been so silly as to affirm expressly that the mass is ordained for the true, real change and destruction of the body and blood of Christ, who is now seated at the right hand of his Father.

22. We know that Bellarmine makes the claim that it can be said very rightly that Christ's blood is shed in the sacrifice of the mass (*On the Eucharist*, book 1, chapter 11[12]). But from this claim of his, it is clear that he forgets his own position and contradicts himself. For if, as Bellarmine teaches elsewhere, the mass is a bloodless sacrifice, then it cannot at all be rightly said that Christ's blood is being shed in the sacrifice. And also, in that same chapter 11[12], he is not right to state that the representation of the sacrifice on the cross exists in the consecration of the mass. For the blood is poured out not by a figurative representation of the sacrifice but by its real offering.

23. And also wrong is the fourth claim, that in the mass, Christ's body and blood are being immolated under the appearances of bread and wine. For no

sacrifice that is properly and truly called 'outward,' ever was immolated under the appearance of something else; but whatever was offered to God was done so under its own appearance and outward form, whether by the Levitical priests under the Old Testament or by Christ under the New. An instance of something different cannot be produced from Sacred Scripture. And Bellarmine, considering this fact, admits that the bread and wine in some way are being offered in the mass, and that they pertain to the thing that is being offered. And from this position these absurd consequences follow: 1. That two sacrifices are being offered in the mass, one of bread and wine, and the other of the body and blood of Jesus Christ. For the appearances and the accidental qualities of bread and wine are not the same as the body and blood of Jesus Christ; and no-one who is endowed with reason would deny that these are different things. 2. The sacrifice of the mass consists of bread and wine rather than of the body and blood of Jesus Christ, because the appearances of bread and wine are subject to the senses; but not so Christ's body and blood (as we have shown in thesis 14). And this is also because in the mass no change or destruction at all happens to the body and blood of Christ, who is seated at the Father's right hand; but it does happen to the bread and the wine, and a change and destruction of this sort is an essential part of the sacrament which is performed by one who performs the sacrifice, as Bellarmine says (*On the Eucharist*, book 1, chapter 2).

24. The error in the fifth assertion, that in the mass the priest is offering Christ's body and blood, can be shown from Bellarmine himself. And to be sure, in the sacrifice (as Bellarmine states, *On the Eucharist*, book 1, chapter 2) "the sacrifice and the priesthood are related in such a way that the priesthood in the proper sense of the word corresponds to the sacrifice in the proper sense of the word, and that the priesthood in the improper sense of the word corresponds to the sacrifice in the improper sense of the word." But the mass is not a sacrifice in the proper sense of the word, as we have shown abundantly in the preceding theses. And therefore, the administration by the ones performing the mass is not a priesthood in the proper sense of the word.

25. Added to these things, as Bellarmine points out in the same passage, is the fact that "in the sacrifice properly speaking it is required that a lawful minister should perform the offering of the sacrifice. For it is not the duty of anyone whosoever to offer the sacrifice, but only of a certain person who has been equipped with godly authority, a person who performs it on behalf of the community." For in Heb 5[:4] the apostle, speaking about the priesthood,

says: "No-one takes this office upon himself, except him who has been called by God, like Aaron." And this is true to such a degree that Paul says in the same passage that even Christ himself did not take the priesthood upon himself but received it from the Father. But nevertheless, in those very passages in which Holy Scripture explicitly treats the ranks of the ministers of the Gospel, and their calling and authority, there is not any mention of the fact that they have received a priesthood from God. On the contrary, in the places where it speaks about the priesthood of the New Testament, there, it states clearly that it is attributed only to Christ himself (like Ps 110:1, Heb 7, and following).

26. From this it is clear that the distinction between Christ as the primary Priest and the performers of the mass as secondary priests of the New Testament is a fabricated one. For as the primary priest Christ is nowhere contrasted with other priests in excellence—as though they were secondary priests. But he is everywhere contrasted with other priests either in relation (as the foreshadowed priest to the foreshadowing priests in the Old Testament) or in exclusion (as the priest unique to many priests in the New Testament).

27. Indeed, not any one of the conditions that are required of the Priest of the New Testament is found in the Roman sacrificers. The first of these is that after the Levitical priesthood was repealed, the priest of the New Testament must be after the order of Melchizedek, and moreover, he should be without father, without mother, without lineage, having neither beginning of days nor an end of life, living forever by the power of his imperishable life [Heb 7:3]. The apostle ascribes that only to Christ (Heb 7:15 and following).

28. The second condition is that according to the definition of the New Testament priest, the one who is the priest must at the same time be the sacrifice, that is, he is both the priest through whom and the sacrifice by which people are reconciled to God. And this is proper to Christ alone by the fourth mode of predication. For strictly, by reason of formal principle, he is a priest by his divine nature, but by reason of the material principle, he is the sacrifice according to his human nature.

29. The third condition is that, as under the Old so also under the New Testament, the priest must be greater and more worthy than the outward sacrifice that he brings. But the merely human sacrificers who bring the sacrifice, since they are defiled by sin, are in no way greater or more worthy

than the body and blood of Jesus Christ, the lamb that is without blemish. And so, there is not any reasoning that allows those men to offer Jesus Christ's body and blood to God in the mass.

30. The fourth condition is that the New Testament priest be holy, innocent, undefiled, and set apart from all sin. Since Christ is the only one who is adorned with this perfect holiness, human beings who are prone to all kinds of vices—and such are the sacrificers—intrude upon the priesthood with obvious sacrilege.

31. The fifth condition is that the priest, as the New Testament defines him, should also be its Mediator. For the goal of the priesthood is the reconciliation of sinful human beings with God, and that effect is proper to the Mediator, as the apostle teaches in Heb 9:15: "He is, therefore, the Mediator of the New Testament for this very reason that, as his death intercedes for the forgiveness of those sins that were committed under the Old Testament, those who are called may receive the promise of the eternal inheritance." Therefore, just as there is only one unique Mediator between God and human beings, Jesus Christ, so he is also the one and only Priest for the people before God.

32. The sixth condition is that the priest of the New Testament also must be its testator who validates that testament by his death. For where there is a testament, the death of the testator must intervene (Heb 9:16). But, except by committing blasphemy, one cannot ascribe this characteristic to anyone except Christ; and, therefore, neither the other one.

33. The seventh condition is that the New Testament priest must offer his own sacrificial offering to God by the Spirit, who of himself has been endowed by the power of the imperishable life. For the sacrifice brought by a man who has not been endowed in this way cannot be satisfactory for the sins of other people. And to the papal teachers who raise the objection that in the mass the priest is only the instrument of the offering and not from his own person but from the person of Christ, we reply that only the priest makes the entire offering on behalf of the whole church, and in that offering, Christ is considered not as the one who is offering but as the one whom the priest has offered—and indeed has created—and accordingly, the sacrificer is more than the instrumental cause.

34. And to those same papal teachers who object that the priests offer Christ not for the satisfaction [itself] but for the application of the satisfaction that was accomplished on the cross for the people's sins we should reply that: 1) the application of the sacrifice cannot possibly be made by a mortal man but only by the immortal God. 2) that it is God who applies to us the fruit of the sacrifice of the cross in the most appropriate manner through faith. For this reason, it says in Rom 3:24 that God presented Christ as the propitiation for us through faith in his blood, and not through repeatedly sacrificing him. Otherwise, it would be necessary to apply also the fruits of Christ's incarnation, resurrection, and ascension for us by repeating them. And by equal rights as in the mass Christ would have to be sacrificed again in baptism, which is the first sacrament of the sacrifice of that same Christ. But the papal teachers frankly admit that this is not a requirement. And surely, for that reason, it also should not be necessary to repeat the sacrifice of Christ in the mass. But if that point is granted, it does not follow that the sacrifice of Christ itself is the means of applying Christ's sacrifice. For Christ's sacrifice itself and the application of that sacrifice are placed in an opposing relationship to each other, and the Word of God—being received in faith—is an instrument that applies the sacrifice of Christ to us no less than the sacrament of the Eucharist. But surely no-one is so foolish as for that reason to call the Word of God that is received in faith the actual sacrifice of Christ. 3) Although the holy Supper can be called the means that applies the sacrifice of the cross, the same thing cannot be stated about the mass, since the mass does not present God, who gives believers Christ offered on the cross, but a priest who is immolating Christ to God.

35. And these words of Christ, "It is finished" (John 19:30), prove that this final claim also is false, namely that in the mass Christ's body and blood are offered for the sins of the living and the dead. So also, the word of the apostle: "For by one offering Christ has made perfect forever those who are being made holy" (Heb 10:14). Similarly, "Christ was once offered to bear the sins of many, and to those who look for him, he shall appear a second time without sin unto salvation" (Heb 9:28). And with this axiomatic statement the apostle shows that between Christ's sacrifice once made on the cross for the sins of the people and his final coming there is no intervening time in which he offers himself a second time on this earth for the sins of those same people. And for that reason, Bellarmine is compelled to grant to us that there is no forgiveness except by virtue of the sacrifice of the cross

(*On the Eucharist*, book 1 [5], chapter 11 [25]). And from that one may gather that the forgiveness does not happen by virtue of the mass. For if forgiveness would also come by virtue of the mass, then Christ's sacrifice on the cross would be incomplete. Nor can that forgiveness happen in the mass by some ordering to the sacrifice of the cross, because the ordering of the sacrament to Christ's sacrifice does not impart to the sacrament the power to forgive sins, but only the power to signify the forgiveness of sins that Christ's death has acquired, and to seal this in the believers.

36. Besides the fact that the six claims above that are sprinkled throughout the definition of the mass directly oppose the testimonies of Holy Scripture and the conditions required in a properly called expiatory sacrifice, their falsity can be proved from the very institution of the holy Supper and from the writings of the orthodox fathers. For, to start with the institution of the Supper, in it Christ offered the bread and the cup consecrated by his blessing, not to God the Father but to his disciples. And he did not say to his Father, "Take this sacrifice of my body and blood," but he said to his disciples, "Take, eat and drink; this is my body, and the New Testament in my blood" (Matt 26:26; Luke 22:19, and following). Yet the sacrificer, on the other hand, does not offer Christ's body and blood under the appearances of bread and wine to each and every member of the church whom the disciples of Christ represented when the Supper was instituted, but he offers them to God, saying: "Accept, O holy Father, almighty and eternal God, this spotless sacrificial victim which I, unworthy servant, offer to you, my God, etc."

37. The following statements are at odds with one another: that which Christ once gave immediately to his disciples was bread and wine (or the cup in which the wine had been poured); but that which he offers nowadays mediately via the sacrificer is no longer bread or wine, but his own body and blood, contained under the appearances or accidental properties of bread and wine. Similarly, the cup that Christ once extended to his disciples was the New Testament in his blood; but now the cup that the sacrificer takes only for himself and does not extend to the lay people is part of the bloodless sacrificial victim. For by a testament, the favorable will of the testator towards his own inheritors is designated, but by a sacrificial victim, the thing that is offered to placate God is designated. We have proved by the testimony of the apostle that the bloodless sacrificial victim of the mass cannot be stated as a thing of this sort, as [the apostle] takes it for certain that there is only one

sacrificial victim, i.e., a bloody victim, whereby God can be appeased (Heb 9:32).

38. And moreover, to his disciples, after they had received the bread from him, Christ foretold the future absence of his body with these words: "Do this in remembrance of me" (Luke 22:19). It is these words that the apostle explains in 1 Cor 11[:26] when he says: "Whenever you eat this bread and drink this cup, you will proclaim the Lord's death until he comes." But with the following prayer, the sacrificer signals that Christ's body is present: "Holy Father, accept this spotless sacrificial victim that I offer to you." And with that "sacrificial victim" he means the body of Christ that he is holding in his hands under the accidents of bread and wine, and which he thereupon tears apart with his teeth. One can imagine nothing that is more foolish and farther removed from the goal of the Supper than that. For if the goal of the Supper is the remembrance of Christ who is absent until he comes to us from heaven (as one correctly gathers from the preceding words of Christ and the apostle Paul), then the sacrificer is not able to offer and handle the real body and blood of Christ here [on earth] in whatever mass you will.

39. While the papal teachers employ the authority of the orthodox fathers who occasionally called the Lord's Supper a sacrifice, the fathers never did use that term in the strict sense that the papal teachers do, but they called it a sacrifice in an improper sense. For it is by *metalepsis* that they called the sacrament of the Eucharist a sacrifice, because it is a sacrament that commemorates the sacrifice that God offered on the cross, along with the giving of thanks—and therefore, they called it "eucharistic." "What about us then?" says Chrysostom, "do we not bring offerings each and every day? Yes, we do make offerings, but by making remembrance of his death. And there is but one sacrificial victim, not many. In what way is there one sacrifice and not many? Because the sacrifice was offered once and for all in the Holy of Holies. But this sacrifice is the exemplar of that one. And this thing that we are doing is done in commemoration of that which has happened" (Chrysostom, *On the Epistle to the Hebrews*, sermon 17). And Augustine says, "Christians celebrate the commemoration of the same completed sacrifice by means of the most holy participation in Christ's body and blood" (*Against Faustus*, book 20, chapter 18).

40. And thus, it is metaphorically that they called that sacrament a sacrifice, having in view each and every believer who by participating in it, presents

SYNOPSIS OF A PURER THEOLOGY

himself to God in a special way as a living and holy sacrifice. Chrysostom's exhortation has this in view: "It is in heaven that we have our sanctuary, our high priest and our sacrificial victim. Let us also offer such sacrifices as can be offered in that sanctuary. No longer [sacrifices of] sheep, or oxen, no longer blood and incense. All of these things have become obsolete, and in their place has been brought in our reasonable service" (*On the Epistle to the Hebrews*, sermon 11) and "What is your altar? It is your spiritual heart. What is your spiritual sacrifice? Every good work" (*Sermons on the Holy Spirit*, tome 3).

41. Thirdly, the fathers in days of old called this same sacrament a sacrifice in a metonymous sense, regarding [the offering of] the prayers and the offering of bread and wine, which were connected to participating in the Supper partly for the celebration of the Supper itself, partly to support the poor with whatever was left over when the supper was finished. With regard to this Alexander of Hales grants that in the sacrament of the Eucharist we should, in the tradition of the ancients, offer three things. The first is the offer of the persons themselves; the second those things that are necessary for the actual sacrament—namely the bread and the wine. Third are the offerings that our hands bring, that is, the alms (Alexander of Hales, in the treatise *On the Office of the Mass*, part 4, question 10, page 1, folio 10). And the papal teachers do not deny that the mass can be called a eucharistic sacrifice. If it is eucharistic, as they grant us, it, therefore, is not propitiatory. For these two things are diametrically opposed to each other.

42. And what is more, the majority of the fathers (with whom Lombard agrees) understood that Melchizedek had offered Abraham bread and wine, and consequently, that the order of the priesthood whereby the apostle compares Christ to Melchizedek (Heb 7) does not consist in the offering of bread and wine but in these accompanying qualities of the two persons: the fact that we should see each as king and as priest, without father and mother, without lineage, having neither beginning of days nor end of life. That is, Melchizedek as the type for the comparison, which we should elicit from the account in Gen 14 by Moses (who silently passes over his genealogy), and Christ as the true reality that Melchizedek is foreshadowing (Chrysostom, *Sermon 36 on Genesis* and [*Sermon* on] Ps 109; Tertullian, *Against the Jews*; Augustine, *Questions on the Old and New Testament*, Question 109; Damascene, *On Faith*, book 4, chapter 14; Lombard, *Sentences* 4, distinction 8).

43. And although Bellarmine sees the point, he does not perceive it, and instead, he builds the teaching of the bloodless sacrifice of the mass on the type of Melchizedek, who in times past produced bread and wine for Abraham from his own provisions. For although he could not have been unaware that the word *howsi* which Moses uses in Gen 14:18 should be translated as "produced" or "brought forth," nevertheless contrary to the verb's meaning he feigns that Melchizedek had, for the purpose of some sacrifice or other, offered bread and wine—not to mention the fact that this is contrary to the order of the entire sacred context. For Moses ascribes to Melchizedek two different actions regarding his two-fold office, in this order: 1. Royal, because he gave Abraham bread and wine to refresh him and his army; 2. Priestly, because he blessed Abraham.

44. And although the same Bellarmine was not ignorant of the fact that the apostle Paul, led by the Holy Spirit and well-versed in all truth, did not silently pass over any of the things that would contribute to the knowledge of the [addressees of the Letter to the] Hebrews of Christ's priesthood in the order of Melchizedek, he nevertheless foists on him the notion that Paul intentionally omitted the offering of bread and wine so that he would not be forced to explain the mystery of the Eucharist, because it was too profound for them to be able to grasp at that time, and that it was a subject-matter that could not be explained (which he treats in chapter 5:11). One could attribute to the apostle nothing further from the truth than that. For nothing is more profound than the mystery of Christ, whom God ordained as High Priest according to the order of Melchizedek. And before the apostle recounts that teaching in greater detail, he does not say that these things cannot be explained (as Bellarmine wrongly translates it); they are difficult to explain, not because they are such in themselves but in light of the carelessness of the Hebrews so that with this forewarning, he might arouse them to greater diligence and attentiveness. Therefore, it is so far from the truth that the apostle wanted to pass over those more profound teachings in silence that he covered them very comprehensively and carefully. He did not wish to place the teaching of the Supper in the sense of those more profound things, because it is not more difficult to explain to simple people than the teaching about baptism, which he counts among the fundamental articles of the faith (Heb 6:2). For like baptism, so too the Lord's Supper represents his bloody sacrifice, and the papal teachers as much as our own theologians put the

teaching of both sacraments among the rudiments of the Christian faith in the catechetical instruction.

45. Neither does the following argument of Bellarmine support his own erroneous [translation] or that of the other papal teachers, "For granted that Scripture does not explicitly explain of what Melchizedek's order and the figure of Christ's priesthood consists, it does give such hints and indications that with the greatest consensus all the fathers come to the same explanation." For in thesis 42, we showed by the testimony of Lombard that some fathers reached a different explanation that can overturn the sacrifice of the mass. For they assert that Melchizedek's bread and wine do not foreshadow Christ the sacrificial victim as displayed in the mass (as the papal teachers contend), nor the accidents of bread and wine without their subject—or rather the outward aspects of bread and wine (i.e., their appearances)—but the real substance of bread and wine that the mystical table of Christ sets forth. This interpretation can be seen in Eusebius, *Proof of the Gospel*, book 5, chapter 3; John Damascene, *On Faith*, book 4, chapter 14, and the other fathers whom we named above in thesis 42.

46. It is to no avail also that Bellarmine bases the sacrifice of Christ in the sacrament of the Eucharist on the slaying of the Paschal lamb in 1 Cor 5:7, and also on the prophecy of Mal 1:11 about the *minhah*, or pure offering, that is to be offered to God throughout the world under the new covenant. Malachi could not have meant hereby that the expiatory offering of the mass corresponds to that of the Jews, since by the hypothesis of Bellarmine and the other Romanists, the mass is a bloodless offering. But all the expiatory offerings under the Old Testament were bloody ones, not to mention the fact that the Jewish offerings were expiatory only in a typical and denotative sense, while in the blasphemous meaning of the papal teachers the mass is truly, properly expiatory. Therefore, it remains that if by the teaching of holy Scripture there is but one unique sacrifice of the cross (in the proper sense of the word) that was prefigured by the Jewish expiatory sacrifices, it must be that what Malachi foretold about the spiritual and eucharistic worship of God that would be established among the nations by the preaching of the Gospel should be taken in a metaphorical sense.

47. And the very words of Christ himself, "which is given, is poured out for you" (Luke 22:19–20), do not provide any more evidence for the real immolation of Christ in the mass than his death is evidenced by those words

of his, "I lay down my life for the sheep" (John 10:15). For even those who look at sacred Scripture from a distance know well that Christ spoke both of these sayings before the sacrifice of the cross by interchanging the present tense for the future.

48. But although there is nothing good in the mass's fabricated sacrifice, nevertheless, because it does have some semblance of good in the eyes of people whose minds are corrupt, the Roman sacrificers take advantage of its deceptive mask in strange, bad ways within the pope's realm, and not without effecting error. And the first abuse in the mass is the fact that the sacrificer who is to administer it makes this opening statement: "I shall go into the altar of God." For in the New Testament the believers no longer have an altar of the sort they once had under the Old Testament, but their altar is now in heaven, namely Jesus Christ, as Thomas Aquinas correctly noted on Heb 13 verse 10, where the apostle asserts that we have an altar of the sort from which those who today are serving at the tabernacle have no right to eat; but they are bringing back into Christ's church the shadowy sacrificial victims of the Jews which Christ had done away with when he came.

49. The second abuse is in the public confession of the priest's own sins, which he directs not only to God but also to all the saints who have departed this life, and to his brothers, when he says: "I who am a guilty and unworthy priest confess to almighty God and to the blessed virgin Mary, and to all his saints, and to you, my brothers, because I, a miserable sinner, have sinned greatly against the Law of God in thought, word, deed, and omission, through my fault, through my fault, through my most grievous fault." For a confession that a sacrificer should make only to God in a devout manner becomes superstitious and useless when made to the deceased, for they are incapable of hearing it; and when the prayer is offered to the living, it is contrary to his own conscience, since he considers himself convinced that he had not given them any offense for which he deserves punishment.

50. The third abuse is seen in the idolatrous demand for intercession by deceased saints that begins with these words: "Therefore I pray the most blessed mother of God, and all the saints, and you brothers: pray to our almighty Lord God for me a sinner, that he take pity on me." When he passes by our Savior Jesus Christ, he calls upon those mortals, who cannot save him, and whom Holy Scripture excludes completely from the office of

intercession, while at the same time ascribing it to Christ alone (John 14:6; Rom 8:33; 1 Tim 2:5–6; and 1 John 2:1–2).

51. The fourth abuse occurs in this prayer of absolution to other confessors of sins: "Amen, brothers and sisters, by the mercy of our Lord Jesus Christ, by the aid and the sign of the holy cross, by the intercession of the blessed, glorious and always virgin Mary, and by the merits of the blessed apostles and all the saintly men and women, may God almighty have mercy upon you, etc." With this blasphemous prayer the sacrificer attaches to the wood of the cross and its sign the power to bring redemption from sins that belongs to the Christ who was crucified and which cannot be shared with anything else, and attaches to the blessed virgin handmaiden of God the aid that we should expect from God alone, and he attaches merits to the holy apostles, who in their own writings once refuted the Pharisees' teaching about meritorious works.

52. The fifth abuse is made by the recollection of the merits that the sacrificer attributes to the saints, who in no way at all could have entered heaven without Christ's merits, and of the relics that for a large part are made up, as if God by looking at them might be swayed to forgive him his sins, when the sacrificer says: "We pray you, O Lord, by the merits of the saints whose relics are here present, and by the merits of all the saints, that you deign to forgive all my sins."

53. The sixth abuse is the fact that the sacrificer calls the bread (which in the Supper is the sacrament of Christ, the sacrificial victim) the actual sacrificial victim of Christ itself, and he shows with the following prayer that the earthly element benefits his own salvation and that of others, both those who have died and those who are alive: "Accept, O holy Father, almighty and eternal God, this spotless sacrificial victim which I, unworthy servant, offer to you my true and living God, for my countless sins and offenses, and my shortcomings, and for all here present, and likewise for all faithful Christians living and dead, that it may be for me and them a means to eternal salvation, Amen." Here, he ascribes to corruptible bread the power to bestow salvation unto life eternal which Christ ascribes only to his own flesh when it is eaten through faith (John 6) and even for those for whom Christ did not institute his Supper, namely the deceased who are neither in heaven nor on earth, but rather in a third place that holy Scripture does not mention, i.e., in purgatory.

54. The seventh abuse happens in the mingling of the water with the wine, which is based neither on a command by Christ nor by his example. For to his disciples he served wine (or the fruit of the vine) without water, and he ordered others to distribute it in imitation of him; for this reason a decree of the Council of Orléans (canon 4.4) condemned that mingling that the sacrificer worships as something mystical, saying: "O God, you who established the nature of man in wondrous dignity, and still more admirably restored it, grant us by the mystery of this wine and water we may come to share in his divinity, who deigned to share in our humanity, Jesus Christ, your Son, our Lord."

55. The eighth abuse is in the superstitious offering of the cup filled with wine. For before the wine—to speak in the words of the Romanists—is transubstantiated or changed into Christ's blood, the sacrificer ascribes to that earthly and corruptible drink the power to bestow salvation, and a pleasing fragrance acceptable to God, of which the first good is ascribed only to Christ by Simeon in his song (Luke 2:29) and by Peter (Acts 4:12), and the latter good is ascribed only to Christ's sacrifice accomplished on the cross by Paul (Eph 1:2). For the sacrificer addresses God as follows: "We offer to you, O Lord, the cup of salvation, humbly begging your mercy, that it may arise before your divine majesty, with a pleasing fragrance for our salvation and for that of the whole world."

56. The ninth abuse is in the wicked imitation of the Jews, who in former times appeased God with incense until the time of correction when it was God's will to put an end to that figure and shadow no differently than to the other things that represent the body which we possess in Christ, as the apostle testifies in Heb 9. And also in the imitation of the Persian magicians, who with their addresses very often spoke to lifeless objects, which they manipulated for witchcraft, as is clear from these words of the sacrificer when he speaks to his incense: "Be blessed by him to whose glory you will be burned, in the name of the Father, the Son, and the Holy Spirit." And to these words he adds the following address of God: "We beseech you, almighty and eternal God, deign to bless and sanctify with the right hand of your boundless majesty this created incense so that by the power of your holy name it be wondrously empowered to put to flight all the onslaughts of the unclean spirits, and to drive out every disease with the return of health wherever its smoke may be blown, and that it may emit a most pleasing fragrance unto you, almighty God, forever." And likewise: "May the incense

that you have blessed rise up to you, O Lord, and may your mercy descend unto me." With this prayer the sacrificer, as it were, binds God to imbue the smoke of the incense with such power to put the devils to flight and to heal the sick, as neither the prophets nor the apostles, who were endowed with an exceptional gift of performing miracles ever besought God, since they rightly understood that neither by them nor by any other human creature—still less the lifeless created thing of incense—but only by the Creator invoked by prayers of faith, to be able to drive demons and diseases out of people (Matt 17:21; Jas 1:15).

57. The tenth abuse is that the sacrificer confuses things that are different in kind. For firstly, he takes the bread and wine—before they are converted into Christ's body and blood, and so are merely outward signs of Christ's body and blood—to be the very body and blood itself of Christ, when he calls those outward signs Christ's offering. Second, he calls the offering of the mass the remembrance of the offering of Christ. Third, he confuses the remembrance of Christ's suffering with the remembrance of the incarnation, birth, circumcision, resurrection and ascension of Jesus Christ, contrary to the commandment of Christ himself, who, as the apostle advises in 1 Cor 11:26, instituted his supper only for this purpose, that hereby, we declare his death, and that we put him as crucified before the eyes of our soul. Fourth, he stitches onto the remembrance of Christ the remembrance of the virgin Mary and of all the others, who have not presented God with any expiatory sacrifice of the cross on our behalf. For the proof of this matter, we shall quote the very words of the sacrificer: "Holy Trinity, accept this offering which we are making to you for the remembrance of the incarnation, birth, circumcision, suffering, resurrection and ascension of our Lord Jesus Christ, and in honor of the blessed Mary, ever virgin, and of all the saints, since the world began with whom you have been pleased, that it may redound to their honor and for us to the salvation of our soul and body."

58. The eleventh abuse is in the depiction of that which is being offered, which the sacrificer calls "the spotless sacrifices" (in the plural) when he says "Therefore, most merciful Father, we humbly beg of you and entreat you through Jesus Christ your Son, our Lord, that you hold as acceptable and bless these gifts, these offerings, these holy, spotless sacrifices." If with these marvelous epithets he designates the bread and wine that he has not yet transubstantiated, as is clear from the mass's Canon, then because the bread and wine are two different things so too are they two sacrifices—in fact, two

spotless and perfect sacrifices. But, as the papal teachers themselves admit, because of the priest's carelessness, they sometimes become moldy after the consecration. But if he is designating Christ's actual body and blood by means of those epithets, then by the hypothesis of the papal teachers they cannot possibly be called "spotless sacrifices," because Christ's body and blood make up only one sacrificial victim (as they themselves acknowledge), a sacrificial victim that, to use the words of certain Schoolmen, sometimes turns out as nothing because mice or spiders have eaten it, or that many times is found to be gnawed to pieces by worms.

59. The twelfth abuse is in the idolatrous adoration of the very light, round sacrificial victim that the sacrificer raises aloft. In this many ritual practices come together that neither Christ has instituted, nor the apostles have observed. For Paul, who asserts that he passed on to the Corinthians what he had received from the institution of the Supper by the Lord (1 Cor 11:23), does not recount that Christ, before he gave it to his disciples, had raised round-shaped bread above his head without breaking it, or that in his administering of the Supper he employed the services of some deacon or cleric who with his left hand would lift his toga from behind and with his right hand would provide him light with a burning torch. Nor [does Paul recount] that Christ himself on bended knee worshiped the accidents of bread and wine that were changed into his body and blood—or at least that he had enjoined his disciples to worship them. On the contrary, the apostle recounts that "Christ, on the night when he was betrayed, took bread, and when he had given thanks, he broke it." And although Christ said to his disciples: "Take, eat, this is my body," still the apostle calls the bread that Christ had consecrated not "the body" but "the bread," in order to teach that with the statement, "this is my body," Christ did not command the bread to turn into his body, or that it would be changed into that with the magical declaration of five words. But he showed what the bread would be for disciples who received it with faith extended to Christ, namely, his body in a sacramental sense. For although it is with different words that the same apostle repeats Christ's mandate, "do this in remembrance of me," yet he does not take the word "remembrance" to mean the worshiping of the body that Christ had immolated in the Supper (as the papal teachers do), but for the eucharistic declaration of Christ's death that the breaking of the bread designates, as we have shown abundantly above.

60. The thirteenth abuse is in the private celebration of the mass, without the participation of the people who are standing by. For in the first institution of the holy Supper it was not Christ by himself, nor later was it ever the disciples by themselves who ate the sacramental bread or drank the wine; but they did so together with the others who had been called to participate in the holy Supper. And the sacrificer can do nothing more foolish than that he when reciting the words of Christ as Christ distributed the bread and wine equally to all the disciples who were dining with him, does not distribute the sacrament of the Supper to anyone of those who are standing by him. And also that he omits this part of the institution by Christ but diligently observes that other part, which consists in the taking and consecrating of the bread and the cup, as if that part is a more important essence of the holy Supper than this part, as Bellarmine wrongly claims. For the holy Supper is called "the communion of the body and blood of Christ" for the very fact that we all, who are many in his one mystical body, partake of that one bread, as the apostle says in 1 Cor 10:17. Therefore the Greek church fathers sometimes call the holy Supper the "gathering and fellowship," and sometimes "the mystery of the gathering and fellowship" (Dionysius, *Ecclesiastical Hierarchy*, chapter 4; Clement, *Constitutions*, book 8, chapter 10).

61. The other abuses are seen in the futile storing in a pyx of the bread that has to be eaten by the believers; in the ridiculous placement of it on the chests of the deceased, who are incapable of eating, drinking, or declaring Christ's death; in the pointless parading of the drinking cup through the streets; in the processions and other ceremonies that completely disagree with the institution by Christ. It is in his name that we should pray God to expose those shameful abuses hiding in the mass to as many people as possible, people who are struggling in utmost darkness in the realm of the pope, for God's glory and for the increase of his church. Amen.

ON THE FIVE FALSE
SACRAMENTS OF THE PAPISTS

President: Andreas Rivetus
Respondent: Peter l'Agnello

This disputation is a polemical treatise against the five 'false' sacraments of the Roman Catholic church: confirmation, penitence, extreme unction, orders, and marriage. The principle underlying argument against each sacrament is that it has no basis in Scripture; it also was not administered or practiced in the early church. The disputation notes moreover that there is considerable disagreement among Roman Catholic theologians on these issues. One of the five sacraments is put between Baptism and the Eucharist, namely the Confirmation of those who have been baptized (3–13). Following the treatment of the Eucharist are Penitence by those who make confession (14–27), the Extreme Unction of those who are ill (28–37), the Orders of ministers (38–45), and Matrimony of those who take vows of marriage (46–51).

1. Since what is right is the rule both for itself and for what is wrong, anyone who considers the matter somewhat more carefully is able with very little effort to discern and reject any sacrament that has been fabricated. [He may do so] by means of the right doctrine about the sacraments in general, and from their nature, and also by means of the description of the two sacraments which meet all the conditions required for true sacraments. However, because contrary things reveal themselves more clearly when they are placed opposite each other, we deem it fitting to add to the preceding disputations about the true sacraments one about the five falsely-called sacraments that in the papacy are granted equal (and in some cases, even greater) status and that are held in no less reverence.

2. Well then, those five sacraments are as follows. One is put between baptism and the Eucharist, namely 1) the confirmation of those who have been baptized. And those that were added after the Eucharist are: 2) penitence by those who make confession; 3) the extreme unction of those who are ill; 4) the orders of ministers; 5) and matrimony of those who take vows of marriage. And we should treat them all in such fashion that we make a clear distinction between what is approved in each sacrament (as having been ordained by God, or as being observed profitably in the church) and what is not approved because mankind is using them contrary to divine ordinance.

Confirmation

3. In that series of pseudo-sacraments, they call the first one confirmation, and they define it as "a sacrament that the bishop confers upon the forehead of those who have been baptized by means of sacred oil that the bishop must consecrate. This is accompanied by these solemn words: 'I seal you with the seal of the cross, and I confirm you with the oil of salvation, in the name of the Father, the Son, and the Holy Spirit.' And he confers it with a slap of his hand—and it reinforces one's faith and grants the Christian believer the courage to boldly confess the name of the Lord whenever he must do so" (Catechism of the Council of Trent, part 2, chapter 3; Augustinus Hunaeus, *Axioms on the Sacraments*, axiom 13). And they say that this sacrament of theirs "is not only comparable to baptism but even preferable to it in two respects, namely in the worthiness of the one who administers it (since that is only the bishop) and also in the perfection of its effect" (Costerus, *Enchiridion*, chapter 11).

4. If at this point we should require what they admit is needed in every sacrament, namely 1) a direct institution by Christ; 2) a visible or tangible sign that has been given and that does not occur naturally, which bears an analogy with the thing that it signifies and which does not have its signification in the institution of it, as words do; 3) a word that accompanies the element and that contains the promise of saving grace (which they call justifying grace), then, they will certainly get bogged down. For they would have it "that the remote matter of this sacrament is oil mingled with balsam which the bishop has consecrated, but that the proximate matter is the anointing of that oil applied to the forehead in the shape or sign of the cross," and that its form is the words that we quoted in the definition above, etc.—in all of these

things they certainly are not able to point to a command and divine ordination. In fact, some of those papal teachers, like Alexander of Hales and Bonaventure, have honestly admitted that "this sacrament was instituted neither by Christ nor by the apostles, but by the church at the Council of Méaux" which was held under Lotharius (as Gabriel Biel testifies in [*Commentary on the Sentences*] book 4, distinction 7). And Scotus does not disagree that Christ and the apostles did not use that matter and form, and he thinks Christ confirmed his apostles without it. He also thinks that Christ could have made this exemption for the apostles, who did not employ this matter and form, because the miraculous conferral of the Holy Spirit and the gift of tongues [of fire] had taken place instead. "And, although one does not read about their time and manner in Scripture, that yet both the matter and the form are supposed to be instituted by God" (in the same place in *On the Sentences*, book 4, distinction 7).

5. And therefore, this entire sacrament is based purely upon assumptions, and so too is what Holcot adds (*On the Sentences*, book 4, question 2), namely that "both the form and the matter of some sacraments that are not necessary for salvation had to be kept secret in the time of the early church because of the mockery by the gentiles." And moreover, there is no agreement among even the Jesuits of our current time. For on the one hand Bellarmine makes the assertion that the matter of confirmation is the anointing oil, and he tries to prove it from two places in Scripture, namely 2 Cor 1:21–22, where it says that "it is God who established, anointed, and sealed us," etc., and 1 John 2:27, "which deals with the anointing we receive from him" (*On the Sacrament of Confirmation*, book 2, chapter 8). Also, although Gregory of Valencia is of the view (*On the Number of Sacraments*, chapter 3) "that the opinion of Waldensis and others is a very probable one, that the apostles had never bestowed the Holy Spirit without applying the physical matter of oil and the form, namely the words" (which even the Catechism of the Council of Trent, chapter 3, section 5 tries to prove with the authority of Pope Fabian). Nevertheless, the same Gregory did not dare to disprove the view of Thomas (part 3, article 2 ad 1), Paludanus ([*Commentary on the Sentences*] book 4, distinction 7, question 1) and of Scotus cited above, namely that "the apostles because of some divine exemption had bestowed the proper effect of this sacrament without its form and matter," which is something they certainly would not have done (as pseudo-Fabian would have it) if at the last Supper Christ had instructed them in preparing the anointing oil.

6. And there is no reason why anyone should be affected by those two passages adduced by Bellarmine in which the apostles made mention of sealing and anointing and even of confirmation; for those passages provide nothing relevant at all, unless he shows that the apostles were thinking of that ceremonial confirmation and that visible oil which is applied together with the prescribed form; and that they were not thinking of the confirmation by the Spirit that is proper only to the elect, and a spiritual and immaterial anointing with which Christians are made to conform to Christ their head. Certainly, the Jesuit Lorinus takes "anointing" in [1] John [2:27] to mean the doctrine or even Christ himself, as when an abstract term is used in place of a concrete one. But how could they prove that these things should be understood as being about that oil of theirs, since there is still a disagreement among them whether it is necessary to add balsam to the oil as a requirement of the sacrament? For although there is a common opinion among them that affirms it, yet Cajetan, whom de Soto follows, along with others, holds an opposing view in his commentary on the Part 3 [of the *Summa Theologiae*]. Emanuel Sa rejects neither point of view in his *Aphorisms*. But they do point out that for the physical substance "Indian balsam suffices, and that it need not necessarily be Palestinian oil, just as it is of no relevance to the consecration whether the wine be from the Rhine region or from Greece" (Aegidius de Coninck, question 72, article 3, dubium 1).

7. And for their proof that the anointing should come in the form of a cross there is no reason or authority whatsoever, but they assign some arguments of fittingness, such as the fact "that this sacrament is given so that we do not blush with shame, and that for this reason the sign should be marked upon one's forehead." But from where do they get such a goal for the sacrament that would be appropriate for it? But it is completely foreign to Scripture and to reason to conflate that anointing with the laying-on of hands that the apostles practiced at that time when the miraculous outpouring of the gifts of the Holy Spirit flourished in the church. And yet Bellarmine, following Waldensis and Hugh of St. Victor, makes the claim (book 2, chapter 9) "that the anointing (i.e., the anointing with chrism) is the same as the laying-on of hands, and that it stands for both of them, even though it is the second one that appears to be mentioned explicitly." Gregory of Valencia refutes him when he says that "in the church at one time or another the rite of the laying-on of hands was like some ceremony of the same sacrament, although it is not at all necessary to retain it since it did not belong to the substance" (*On*

the Number of the Sacraments, chapter 3). There is not any way whereby these contradictions of the Cadmaean brothers can be reconciled.

8. If it were not wrong to make fun of a serious matter, it would be ridiculous what the Catechism of Trent goes on about in detail concerning the slap "whereby the bishop lightly smites the cheek of the one being confirmed with the hand" (chapter 3, section 20), "so that he will remember that he, like a strong athlete, should bear every adversity with indomitable spirit for the sake of Christ's name." And that ludicrous action (if it means anything at all) could not be more fitting for symbolizing the exact opposite, unless they actually wish their bishop to take on the role of Caiaphas and the other persecutors of Christ [cf. Matt 26:62–68 and John 18:19–24,27] who harm Christians on account of Christ's name—something not entirely foreign to the truth.

9. Since what does not exist does not have any affections or operations, there is no reason for us to ascribe certain sacramental effects to this institution. And the ones that the papal teachers themselves ascribe are entirely imaginary; we have already rejected what they teach about 'character' when we dealt with the sacraments in general. The second effect, and it is the chief effect which they attribute, is the "grace that makes gracious, and it is greater than the one that is bestowed in baptism regarding the strengthening of the soul against the devil's attacks, but regarding the remission of sins it is lesser," as Bellarmine says (*On the Sacrament of Confirmation*, book 2, chapter 11). Someone else confirms this "by comparing the two sacraments to the birth and growth of the human body, because the human being acquires much more substance by the latter than by the former. And since we are born again by baptism and we grow through confirmation towards the perfect state of grace, we appear to acquire more grace through this latter one than the former" (Giles de Coninck, question 72, article 7, dubium 1).

10. And what is more, because the grace which is sealed by baptism grows and is confirmed in believers throughout their entire life-time without the supporting aid of a sacrament specifically ordained for that purpose, the comparison that is drawn by the Jesuit does violence to the sacrament of the Lord's Supper, to which that [growth and confirmation of grace] belong in the highest degree so that we acquire more substance, or at least maintain what substance has been acquired. And that happens also by the ministry of the Word, which we use "until we reach perfect manhood, to the measure of the stature of the fullness of Christ" (Eph 4:13); and having been reborn in

him through the one baptism, and like the sons and heirs of a father who partake of his table, we enter into a spiritual relationship and affinity, yet one that among believers does not prevent them from entering into a contract of holy matrimony, and one that does not annul a marriage that has [already] been entered upon. Much less should we believe this about the affinity contracted "between the confirmation sponsor and the one who has been confirmed"—which the oily papal wrestling-masters dream up as "the third effect" that arises from their sacrament (Francisco de Toledo, *Instructions Regarding the Priesthood*, book 2, chapter 24).

11. From what has been stated it is sufficiently clear that those histrionics have nothing in common with the laying-on of hands (as Acts 8[:17] and 19[:6] speak about it) which the people who were baptized in Samaria and Ephesus received from the apostles. By that laying-on of hands those gifts of the Holy Spirit were imparted which the Scholastics call "[gifts] that are freely given;" and concerning these gifts those same people teach that "nothing prevents them from existing even in sinners" (Lorinus, *On the Acts of the Apostles*, chapter 19, verse 6). [They teach] that Cornelius received those same gifts even before he was baptized—proof that not merely as far as the ceremony is concerned but also its effects, the apostolic laying-on of hands is of an entirely different kind than the papist confirmation. What the apostles at that time had employed with results would now be done in vain, since this effect was temporary and does not pertain to justifying grace. And what of the fact that the ones guilty of that teaching admit the very same thing? For Suárez (Tome 3, disputation 33, section 4) freely admits that "the laying-on of hands which the apostles used in Acts 8 and 19 was actually not the sacrament of confirmation, because it was much different in the sensible aspects of the ritual. In fact, [he admits that] it was not simply a sacrament, because it was not a ceremony constituted by a firm and established law." And by this admission, he removes all of book 2, chapter 2 of Bellarmine's *On the Sacrament of Confirmation*.

12. But when in their writings the ancients mention the anointing of chrism, they take it to mean mainly the anointing that was added to baptism—and not a special sacrament—whereby they immediately anointed those who were baptized "like athletes about to enter the contest," as Chrysostom states in *Homily* 6 on the Epistle to the Colossians. Indeed, not even the papal teachers themselves say that this anointing is part of the sacrament's very essence, and although the custom is an ancient one, it should be placed

among those traditions [of the church] "that have come down to us as neither the Lord's truth nor the truth of the Gospel; nor have they come down to us by apostolic commands and epistles," as Cyprian says in Letter 74 to Pompey. And the fact that, in later times, "the bishops went out to those people whom the presbyters and deacons had baptized in the smaller towns, in order to place their hands upon them to invoke the Holy Spirit," Jerome ascribes to "the custom of the churches," and not to the truth that comes from the Lord. And he contends over against the Luciferians that this practice came about "more for the prestige of the priest than for the requirement of the law." He certainly never would have said this about a rite that unequivocally was called a sacrament. Therefore, if at some time or another the church fathers gave the name of sacrament to such ceremonies, we should understand it in the broad sense whereby "signs are called sacraments insofar as they pertain to matters divine" (Augustine, Epistle 5 to Marcellinus)—despite the fact that they are not based on any divine authority.

13. It is likely, however, that the "doctrine of the laying-on of hands," which Heb 6:2 links to the doctrine of baptisms, refers to that care of the early church whereby youths who had been instructed in catechetical doctrine were presented to the church before they were permitted to partake of the Supper, in order to give answers about their faith, and were commended to God in prayer, along with the ritual of the laying-on of hands, which in the time of the patriarchs (and thereafter) was a gesture of people as they pray and give praise. In book 5, chapter 23 of *On Baptism*, Augustine had this in view when he said that "the laying-on of hands, unlike baptism, can be done a second time, because it is nothing other than praying over a person." It is clear there that Augustine did not share the view of the papal teachers in this matter, as they argue that "those who administer confirmation (or who are being confirmed) for a second time, commit a serious sacrilege," namely, because of the impression of a character. If they would be content with this prayer and commendation of the believing adult to God following a lawful examination, then even we would readily agree—if—I say, they would seek nothing else than that rite which Calvin wishes to be restored (*Institutes*, book 4, chapter 19, section 4) and the substance of which is maintained scrupulously in our churches.

Penitence

14. So much for the pseudo-mystery of confirmation. What follows is penitence, which we are not treating in this disputation insofar as it means the conversion from a vain walk of life to the true God, the conversion whereby someone initially changes his whole former walk of life for the better. For this sort of penitence is required before baptism, a time when penitence cannot have the force of a sacrament, as the papal teachers agree. They hold that "penitence is a sacrament of the new law that Christ instituted after his resurrection," that is, for those who have fallen away after their baptism. And also, that penitence is "not inward (insofar as it is a virtue of the mind), but only external." [And they say] "that the most proximate matter is the act of the repentant person; that the remote matter is the sins themselves; and that the form is 'I absolve you in the name of the Father, etc.'" (Catechism of Trent, part 2, chapter 5, section 9, 10, 12, 13).

15. Therefore, they hold the view that the notion of sacrament consists in "outward penance, insofar as it possesses some outward things that are subject to the senses," whereby they would have those things disclose "what occurs inwardly in the soul." And so, the controversy is not whether the conversion of the mind to God and an inward sorrowful abhorrence of the sins committed are a requirement for the forgiveness of sins. For we know that Christ exhorted all sinners to have such penance and that this condition for the forgiveness of sin was a perpetual requirement in both testaments. By means of this penance, the sinner does not earn forgiveness, as though (to use their words) he effectively obtains the forgiveness of sins; but through penance, the condition is met whereby he becomes disposed to obtain divine mercy, as though removing the hindrance, as it is called. It is, therefore, a slander against our people when the allegation is made against them that they reject all penance, and when they are accused of holding out to sinners' reconciliation without contrition or without detesting their former life.

16. And we affirm that only this inward penitence is sufficient in the case of hidden sins of which the sinner's own conscience is aware, and which sins are known only to God. But we deem it a matter of freedom, and one that is often a very useful one for troubled souls to take refuge in the counsel of those who by virtue of their office know the nature and circumstances of the sins more closely, and to seek comfort from their own pastor through some declaration of those sins that are torturing their troubled soul. But we reject as tyrannical the necessity of confessing before men each and every sin; and

within the Roman church there were those who also believed that Christ neither instituted it nor commanded it: The author of the *Glossa* at the beginning of distinction 5 about Penitence; Abbas Panormitanus in the extra section, *On Penitence and Forgiveness*, in the [decretal] chapter "Everyone of both Sexes;" Peter of Oxford; and Gratian himself (in the Decree on Penitence, distinction 1 when the question is proposed "whether it is necessary that this confession be made to the priest") who after having gathered the authorities supporting either side leaves it to the reader's free judgment to choose whichever view he wishes—and it is for that reason that Gregory of Valencia lashes out at him undeservedly in the book, *On the Necessity of Confession*, chapter 3.

17. We do require the outward repentance in cases of more serious sins that have been committed with scandal to the church and that have come to be known by a greater number of people. We do not deny that over against sinners of this sort the church can and should use its power of the keys to bind them with its censures and to release them after they have shown the fruits of repentance, by the ministry that God has granted to it for that matter. Especially relevant to this ministry are Christ's promises in Matt 16:19 and 18:18, as well as the commission he gave to the apostles in John 20:23, which deals with the keys and the forgiveness of sins, that is, with the outward judgment whereby sins that were committed outwardly, publicly, and conspicuously are bound by the church in keeping with the power that it has received to cleanse itself and to put away serious offenders, like sickly sheep from the sheepfold. If some in the early church wanted to make use of that service because they were stained with serious sins which they themselves wanted to be made known publicly so that as penitents they might be reconciled publicly, that ought not to be a reason to make what was a matter of freedom into a necessity, and also not a reason to turn what previously had been public into a private matter.

18. To be sure, we do not bar any remorseful sinner from hoping for the forgiveness of sin, and we also do not reject any such person who has committed public and well-known sins from public repentance or deny peace and communion to the one who makes satisfaction to the church. The papal teachers are guilty of the most shameful slander when they link us to the Novatians and reproach us for being taken in by the same wrong. Gregory of Valencia is somewhat ashamed of this accusation in chapter 4 of *On the Number of the Sacraments*, where he admits that we "do have the actual deed of

repentance (after baptism) and that we do so each and every time that a fall into sin occurs." [He admits] that the Novatians deny this altogether and consequently they have rejected that sacrament, even though at that time the controversy was not being waged about the sacrament but only about the act of repentance.

19. Having made these points, we now come to the proper question of this topic, and we state that not any outward repentance whether private or public (and whether we consider the actions of the penitent person or actions of the minister, either separately or jointly) is a true and proper sacrament of the New Testament. First, because in that entire action, insofar as even the papal teachers perform it, there is not any outward and visible element, which is a requirement for every sacrament as we have shown in the theses on the sacraments in general. Secondly, because in whatever way it is used (whether visible or, to say it this way, audible) there is not any sign in that sacrament that is by divine institution an efficacious sign of a spiritual effect, which is the second requirement that the papal teachers themselves make for every sacrament. Nor is there any validity to what our opponents say: "That it is irrelevant to the common notion of a sacrament of the new law that an external thing is applied by a minister, but [it is relevant] that along with the words of the form there is something that can be sensed and which has the aspect of matter, whether that be a substantial thing or a sensible action, such as in this case the actions of the repentant person."

20. For they say this contrary to the notion of all of the sacraments of the Old as well as the New Testament, and they are not able to show for any one of them that it has been ordained apart from some visible sign. Otherwise, to turn it into a sacrament it would have been enough to add a word to a word. And moreover, those outward actions are not efficacious signs of inward repentance, since inward repentance is more likely the cause of outward repentance. Thirdly, Augustine extends generally to all the sacraments what he requires in baptism (*Against Faustus*, book 19, chapter 16), namely the fact that they are "visible signs of invisible grace." And it is pure sophistry to take the sense of sight to mean in general any sense whatsoever; otherwise, Augustine would have made in vain a distinction between words that are invisible and words that are visible, i.e., the sacraments. And in order that no doubt should arise about what he means, [Augustine] states that "what is seen in the sacraments has bodily appearance, but what is understood has a spiritual benefit." Therefore, it is clear that the

sacramental symbol is always something substantial, and that substance can be seen.

21. I leave to one side the quarrel that exists among the papists about the material substance of that sacrament: The followers of Scotus locate it solely in absolution, while for all the others the absolution is both part of the matter and the form at the same time—which is absurd. But what should be noted especially is that the form of absolution is a human invention which is found neither in Scripture nor anywhere in all antiquity. For where there is no word of God there is no sacrament, nor is there any validity to their empty notion that those words of Christ, "the sins of those whom you forgive are forgiven, etc." contain that form virtually (to use their words). For if those words do include the form of some sacrament, then it follows also that the accompanying words, "those whose sins you retain, they are retained" include the form of some opposite sacrament, since the reasoning is the same for both. Therefore, just as the sins of the unrepentant are retained not by some sacramental efficacy but by the ministry of the divine Word so too is there no need for sacramental efficacy to forgive the sins of those who are repentant, but the ministry of the Word only, applied to those who are repentant.

22. In the church of ancient times, penance was practiced by those who relapsed into sin after their first conversion, and many examples of this can be found of those who upon repenting were granted true forgiveness without any administration of a special sacrament for that purpose. In 2 Sam 12:13 Nathan absolves David with these words: "The Lord has forgiven your sins." Nor is there anything to Bellarmine's recourse in special revelation, as this was not needed since all believers knew that the sins of those who are repentant are forgiven. And there also is no reason why Bellarmine refers to God's extraordinary providence, because it belonged to the ordinary providence of the church. And although the patriarchs were not ignorant of the Gospel, nevertheless they would not have been able to enjoy its full consolation unless the benefits of the sufferings of the Christ who was to come had been imparted to them by his own word. "For it is through the grace of our Lord Jesus Christ that we are preserved 'in the same manner' as our forefathers" (Acts 15:11).

23. Not even our opponents deny that Christ conferred the same forgiveness of sins which John the Baptist had preached. And there is no doubt that John,

who declared the wrath of God on the scribes and Pharisees, announced the mercy of God for those who were repentant. And concerning Christ it is certain that he forgave many people their sins, also that woman who, in Luke 7, confessed her sins with tears and outward gestures. Yet he did so "not by administering any sacramental word, but by his own, unique power," as Bellarmine says. And we grant that this power is in fact proper to Christ, but through the ministry of his servants he so extends it that, when they bring his word, he effectively grants his assent and accomplishes what he has promised. And for this reason he says: "Just as the Father has sent me, so too do I send you" [John 20:21–23]; and by means of that declaration he secures beforehand that ministry concerning the forgiveness of sins. From this, it follows that just as Christ, who was sent by the Father, forgave sins by means of his word without any special sacrament, so too with that same word do genuine ministers forgive sins in the name of Christ without a sacrament.

24. In the actions of the repentant person, and in the minister's absolution one cannot point to any sacramental analogy between the sign and the thing signified in such a way that what happens in the outward sign corresponds to what happens inwardly. For even though the word of the one who absolves both declares forgiveness of sins, and signifies that it has been granted—in that sense it can be placed among the signs—still there is no such analogy as exists in the other sacraments between the elementary and the heavenly thing. Add to this the fact that every sacrament is a seal that is appended to the word, and this cannot be said about absolution, which itself is the word that should be sealed with a seal. Nor is there validity to the fact that Bellarmine (*On Penitence*, book 1, chapter 10) wants to forge a sacrament from Christ's words "and those whose sins you forgive, etc." because (as he puts it) "the word is a corporeal and so sensible sign, and it is the promise of justifying grace that is attached to the word." For if all the outward actions whereby the effect of grace is promised were sacraments, then there would be a countless number of sacraments in that sense: To gather in Christ's name has the promised effect of Christ's presence (Matt 18:20); to confess Christ before men has the promise of Christ's confession before the Father (Matt 10:32); to leave one's father and mother promises a one hundred-fold reward and eternal life (Matt 19:20).

25. But the power to forgive sins, whereupon the whole idea of this sacrament rests, is a matter of such controversy among the papal teachers themselves that many of them confine it with limits which others admit ruin

the very nature of the sacrament. For Lombard (*Sentences*, book 4, distinction 18, 1, part C), Bonaventure (in the same place, article 2), Gabriel Biel, Marsilius, Major, Occam, William of Auxerre, Alexander, Thomas of Argentina, Alonso Tostado—all of them (and I do mean all) are agreed, as Vasquez admits in *Question* 84, article 3, "to the extent that it is not by virtue of the keys that the forgiveness of guilt takes place, and so too the vivification of the soul and the dismissal of the liability of eternal punishment"—in these things justifying grace certainly consists—"and [they agree] that the keys do not extend to this effect; but when the priest says 'I absolve you' he merely shows that through his contrition the person has already been absolved from his guilt." From this, it follows that justifying grace is not an effect of this absolution; and so, according to the papal teachers, strictly speaking it is not a sacrament.

26. And so Vasquez rightly concludes that it follows that "the forgiveness of guilt does not come about through the sacrament, since it does not happen by virtue of its form, and in particular of its words whereby it happens in the case of a sacrament, nor of the work that has been performed (as they put it)." That is because those authors have been persuaded rightly that the priest's power does not reach to the point where he has the power to give release from the actual guilt and stain of sin, but only to the point where he shows by his absolution that the people who have confessed their sins already have been forgiven by God; and they assert that the task belongs to God to grant release not only from the stain of sin but also from the liability of eternal damnation. To this end the Master of Sentences quotes from Ambrose that "the priest certainly is carrying out his own office, but he does not exercise any rights of power; only he, who only has died for sins, dismisses sins" (The words of Ambrose are found in *On the Holy Spirit*, book 3, chapter 18).

27. Therefore, if we consider sins from the perspective of guilt and eternal liability, according to the Master [Lombard] the power to bind and to loosen is nothing other than the power to declare or "to show publicly that the sinners have been bound and loosened," just as in former times under the old law the priests were not accustomed to cleanse lepers but to determine who were clean or unclean [Lev 13 and 14]. Hence, it is clear that at the time of the Master and those who followed his line of thinking penance was not considered a sacrament of the New Testament in the strict sense of the word; and as Scotus rightly deduces from the teaching of the same Lombard, "penance did not have any causality or causal tendency towards first grace,

since it is never received worthily except by those who already are in grace, because not anyone is shown to be set free whom God has not previously forgiven" (*On the Sentences*, book 4, distinction 18, question 1).

Extreme Unction

28. The papal teachers call the third fictitious sacrament "extreme unction," and they define it as "the sacrament of extreme unction for the person who is sick and on the point of dying, who is making penance for his sins. It is administered by the priest on some parts of the body with oil which the bishop has consecrated and which effectively bestows the forgiveness of the remnants of sin, in order to lift the spirits and to restore health to the body." They hold that the remote material substance of this sacrament is olive oil, and that it belongs to the essence of the sacrament; many think that it also belongs to this essence that the oil has been consecrated not by a simple presbyter but by a bishop (although some think this is necessary only by the necessity of command); it is oil that is refreshed every single year, although it is possible to add non-consecrated oil to it a little at a time (Francis de Toledo, book 7, chapter 1). And they hold that the proximate matter is the ointment itself, which as belonging to the essence of the sacrament ought to be put on the eyes, ears, nostrils, mouth and hands. And for the sake of its completeness, but not necessarily, for the men it is put on their loins and feet and for the women on the navel (Jose Angles, in *Flowers on the fourth book of the Sentences*, Questions on extreme unction). It is applied at all unctions with new flax that is later burned.

29. Most of the papal teachers think that the form of this sacrament of theirs is not indicative but optative and deprecative to such a degree that if it were not deprecative the sacrament would have no force. And they reject the formula used by those churches that state, "I anoint your eyes, etc.," unless they add, "so that God may be gracious to you." However, the common formula is "through this holy anointing, and through his most sacred mercy, may God be gracious to you for whatever misdeed you have committed in your sense of sight, hearing, taste, smell and touch, amen." However, it is not certain whether the words "through his most sacred mercy" are essential, even though it would be a very serious sin to leave them out (De Coninck, dubium 4).

30. The one who administers them ought to be a priest whom the bishop has duly ordained, or (even much better) the bishop himself, who must have "the

intention of doing what the church [does], etc." But the priest should be a parish priest, or one to whom this duty has been delegated by the parish priest. And even without the license from the parish priest, it would still be a sacrament, although the unqualified administrant would incur excommunication by this very deed. And as for the one who receives the sacrament, he ought to be someone who is on the point of death (or at least someone who is believed to be at risk of dying) from a disease, a wound, from childbirth, or from old age. But he should not be an infant, which cannot sin, nor should he be insane (unless for a brief time he is lucid), nor should he be someone who is about to be hanged or beheaded (since people of this sort are surrendered to unmitigated judgment), nor someone who is known to be living in mortal sin.

31. For this sacrament of theirs, they make up four effects: 1) The expulsion of the remaining remnants of sins; 2) the health of the soul that is quick to do evil and slow to do good; 3) the health of the body when this is profitable for the wellbeing of the soul; and 4) support over against temptations and the devil's attacks that a man is undergoing at the time (Toledo, *Instructions for the Priests*, book 7, chapter 4). Not all the papal teachers are in agreement on these effects, however, and it is disputed whether or not health of body is certain and infallible by the power of this sacrament, or whether this is only promised conditionally. Bellarmine (chapter 6, on *Extreme Unction*) debates this matter with Domingo de Soto. And about the sort of sins whereof remnants are forgiven they dispute whether such sins are only venial (as some would have it) or also mortal, which is what the majority (including Bellarmine) think because to remove venial sins there is not any need for a new infusion of grace, and therefore not even by means of a sacrament.

32. Whereas it suffices for refutation to have put forward such points, we shall nevertheless add the following few observations: 1) Absent from this ritual are the conditions which the papal teachers themselves required for a true sacrament, namely its divine institution, its divine promise, and its effect of divine and spiritual grace (particularly as it is intended), as well as the analogy to that spiritual effect; 2) moreover, there does not exist an established and ongoing ceremony that has been given to the universal church, which is necessary in every sacrament in the strict sense of the word. For the fact that some people make up the divine institution from Mark 6:16 (where it says that the apostles anointed many sick people with oil and restored them to health) some sharp individuals among the papal teachers

have noticed that it cannot pertain to the unction which they consider to be sacramental, such as Domingo de Soto ([*Commentary on the Sentences*] book 4, distinction 23, question 1) whom Bellarmine follows (*On the Extreme Unction*, chapter 2). They have noticed that it concerns the gift and grace of miracles, and especially those involving the body. And their statement that that unction in Mark was a prefiguration of their sacramental unction is rejected with the same ease with which they put it forward, unless they want all miracles that the apostles performed to be figures of some sacrament of the New Testament, which would be very absurd.

33. What they adduce from Jas 5:14–15 does indeed show that while the extraordinary gift of physical healings was still in force in the early church, the apostle offered the following advice: Believers who were suffering from some illness or other (but not experiencing the final struggles of life) could call to them the church's elders who in the name of the Lord would anoint the sick with oil (no mention is made that it is consecrated) and with a prayer of faith, hoping to receive healing and to obtain the forgiveness of sins, if indeed the sick person was living in sin when he was overtaken by the disease. But Cardinal Cajetan, writing on the same passage, rightly recognized that these words do not pertain to the institution of some sacrament. And so also that neither on the basis of the words nor of their effect do these words speak about a sacramental unction, but about the anointing which the disciples of the Lord carried out on those who were ill. For the text does not speak about "whoever is sick unto death," but in an absolute sense about "whoever is sick," and it says that the effect is the recovery of the sick person, and it speaks about the forgiveness of sins only in a conditional sense. Add to this the fact that the text attributes that effect to the prayer of faith and not to a sacrament (which is what the papal teachers hold) and consequently— according to them—to the performing work and the faith of both the minister and the recipient, and not to the work performed.

34. Moreover, neither James nor any other apostle had the authority to establish a new sacrament. But our opponents have falsely come up with the idea that it was instituted by Christ and promulgated by the apostle. And it is unbelievable that the evangelists, who in their writings recorded things that were much more petty, could have overlooked the institution of any sacrament if it had been made by the Lord. And Hugh of St. Victor (*On the Sacraments*, book 2, part 15) and Lombard (*Sentences*, book 4, distinction 23) behave more honestly when they assert that it was the apostles who instituted

this unction. And so it follows that this is not a sacrament. What is more, with a wrong circular argument Thomas [Aquinas] and his followers do not so much prove the matter as reveal its folly, when they presuppose that it is a sacrament, and infer that therefore Christ had instituted it. Now if they were asked, "from where is it certain that Christ has instituted it?" what else could they reply but "because it is a sacrament"?

35. Their proof for the other conditions is not from James. For although James does give the hope of some temporal and spiritual good, this is not a promise made by Christ, the one who institutes a sacrament. Next, the effect of spiritual grace is not promised directly and properly with the unction, but rather the grace of health of body—and that is not the effect of a sacrament. What is more, that effect never happens in our time, and for that reason the papal teachers add the condition "if it is profitable" (where James does not have any condition) and they turn the spiritual effect, which in James is conditional, into an absolute one. And on top of that they have the nearly unanswerable question (as we have said): What are the sins that are forgiven in unction? And as for the analogy between the anointing of the body and the remission of sins in the heart they will have no better explanation than for the other points. And lastly, in James there is nothing whatsoever about the chief and primary effect which they attribute to their sacrament, namely that the sick person is fortified with spiritual help against the temptations that come over him at the moment of death.

36. And so in James there are two prescriptions, of which one is ordinary and ongoing: After the elders of the church have been called, they commend the sick person by praying for him in faith, and when he has been comforted by the Word of God, he may look to God to restore his body to health, if that is so profitable, and to lift his spirit by the forgiveness of sins. And he becomes certain of this by his own faith, which receives the promise of grace that is given to the repentant person. The extraordinary prescription was the fact that they worked healing by means of the anointing of oil. But in the several ages after the apostles this healing still was sought from God by means of prayers, as is evident from the old rituals published by Cassander, when he quotes this formula: "I anoint you with holy oil in the name of the Father, etc., so that when all the pains and discomforts of your body have fled your strength and wellbeing may recover to the extent that through the working of this mystery and through this holy anointing of oil along with our prayer, you may be healed by the power of the holy Trinity and be worthy to receive

your former, and stronger, health." He quotes similar formulas in the *Scholia on the Ecclesiastical Hymns*, p. 288 (in the Paris edition).

37. It is clear from the change to the formula that the wording now prevalent in the Roman church is so different from the anointing of old because the church has altered not only the wording but even the sense of it, so as to create a sacrament, when it saw that the anointing was altogether ineffective as far as bodily healing was concerned, even though that is what all the old formulas were concerned about. And on this point we certainly should draw attention to what Matthew Galenus, primarius professor and chancellor of the academy at Douai, admits in *Catechism* 181: "Why is it surprising," he says, "that physical healing happens so rarely, since nowadays there is hardly any attention given to the parts of the body that have suffered harm, which our ancestors used to anoint for seven whole days? They made use of valid prayers, the merits were sufficient, and there was no lack of faith or trust in God—through which they could obtain anything at all. But nowadays since we either neglect or despise those things, it should not be surprising if there is no result when the needed prayers rarely are understood or read with care." But the power of the sacraments does not depend on the merits, trust, lack of understanding or contempt of those who administer them. Therefore, it follows that the extreme unction is not a Christian sacrament.

Order
38. Along with the apostle in 1 Cor 14:40, we hold that everything in the church should be established "in good order and decently," and that unless he has been called legitimately no one can have the authority to carry out a ministry in the church. We also do acknowledge that between some ministers who God has appointed, there are gradations of office, age, and gifts. The disputation about the ecclesiastical ministry has given a more than sufficient treatment of all of these. Therefore, at this point it remains that we should answer this one question about the *raison d' être* for a sacrament that the papal teachers apply to their orders in such a way that though every order is a sacrament, they nevertheless do not make up more than one sacrament— even though all those orders differ in material substance and form, and even in each of their effects, because (as they say) they are "one sacrament in genus," or "because they are all related to a single goal." If that reasoning has a place, then not only the orders but even all the sacraments would be one sacrament, because the sacraments are similar in genus and are related to one

and the same goal, that is, the general goal of God's glory and the particular goal—as far as we are concerned—of sealing justifying grace.

39. Among our opponents, however, there is no consensus about the number of the orders, nor about the sacramental worth of all the ones they count as belonging to their orders. For some—like the Canonists, as Navarrus relates (*Manual*, chapter 22, number 18)—make up nine orders. And he adds a tenth to these, namely the order of cantors (Titelmans, *On the Sacraments*, book 1, chapter 3). But others recognize only eight orders strictly speaking, that is, four lesser ones (porters, lectors, exorcists, acolytes) and three major ones (subdiaconate, diaconate, and priesthood). And they add an eighth, the episcopate—although there are others who disagree and deny that the episcopate is a different order than the priesthood (Jose Angles, [*Commentary on the Sentences*] book 4, and others). And again, many claim that only the priesthood is a sacrament. The vanguard of these people was led by Durand, and de Soto does not judge that his followers deserve much criticism. This position is considered a probable one by [Franciscus] Victoria (in *On the Sacraments*, question 226), while Angles deems it not erroneous. In fact, [William] Estius grants that the church has not yet dealt with the question, not even concerning the deacons ([*Commentary on the Sentences*] book 4, distinction 24, section 8).

40. There are people (Domingo de Soto, Medina, Angles, etc.) who assert that the three major orders form a sacrament, while it can be said (without the risk of making an error) that the four lesser ones are not proper sacraments that bestow grace and impress a character [upon the soul]. With some hesitation, Bellarmine himself says that "there is not so much certainty about the subdiaconate," and "there is a lower probability of the lesser orders being sacraments than of the subdeacons, since [in this case] the opinion is not that common, and it is certain that they have lesser duties" (*On the Sacrament of Order*, chapter 8). About the lesser orders, Peter de Soto (*Lectures [on the Institution of Priesthood]*, *On the Sacrament of Order*, lesson 1) admits that even concerning the subdiaconate "there is no basis in Holy Scripture, and that no mention is made about them or their names in all of the ancients." Moreover, there are those who deny that the office of bishop is a sacrament in the true and strict sense of the word, and that it impresses a new character, such as Domingo de Soto (*On Justice and Right*, question 1 article 2), and others, as Bellarmine (in the passage mentioned above) admits, who, on the contrary, contends that it is a true sacrament and impresses a new character.

These differences surely show sufficiently that they themselves have no certainty from the Word of God about the institution of this supposed sacrament.

41. This also is very powerful proof that there is no unanimity among them about the material substance and about the sacramental signs. For since in what they call the major orders, they make use of two-fold signs, namely the laying-on of hands and also the handing-over of instruments—like the chalice and the paten for the priesthood, and of the book of the Gospels for the sub-diaconate—both signs are deemed essential by some (like Bellarmine, *On the Sacrament of Order*, book 1, chapter 9) and only the handing-over of the instruments by others (like Domingo de Soto, [*Commentary on the Sentences*] book 4, distinction 24, question 1, article 4). But in the case of the other, lesser orders, they all indeed deem that extending only the instruments is enough. But if one were to ask them from where they get these signs, and when and by whom they had been instituted, they would of necessity fall silent; and if they do not, let them produce the documents of their divine institution where Christ handed a paten and chalice to the apostles and by this bestowal established them as priests to offer the sacrifice of the mass. And so too for the other orders.

42. And no better is the basis that supports the form which they ascribe to this sacrament of theirs, or to many of their sacraments. For the words which the bishop uses in ordination are clearly of human institution, like: "Receive the power to sacrifice to God and to consecrate the masses for both the living and the dead, in the name of the Lord," when a priest is ordained. Or, in the ordination of a deacon: "Receive the power to read the Gospel in the church of God, both for the living and the dead, in the name of the Lord, etc." (Roman Pontifical, *On the Orders of Deacon and Priest*, folio 16 and 20). In the ordination of an acolyte: "Receive the candle-holder and the wax taper, and know that you are entitled to light the lamps of the church" (Ibid. p. 9); and so too for the other orders. In the case of all of these they note that calling on the holy Trinity does not belong to the essence of the form. If Christ had instituted anything of this sort, who would believe that it was done so covertly and secretly that after sixteen hundred years it remains so unclear what the proper material substance of this sacrament is and what its form is? For even in the ordination of the priest, they come up with a different form: "Receive the power to forgive sins, etc." And so, they have made up a sacrament which Christ has instituted, the entire substance of which they are still unsure

about—and that not only is not found in Scripture but of which not even a trace appears in all antiquity. For that our opponents seek recourse in the fact that "they were very careful lest such holy mysteries of our religion should come to be known by the common crowd and especially by unbelievers, and thus come to be despised" (Estius, [*Commentary on the Sentences*] book 4, distinction 24.2). And that is a laughable falsehood. For how could that which should be shared with such a large number of ministers be able to remain hidden by people among whom (it is fair to think) there were many unwise, and also many who at one time apostatized, through whom such things could have been made public? And added to this is the fact that if the rites of baptism and of holy Eucharist which Christ himself has instituted had been divulged from the first times of the church, there is no reason why the material substance and the form of the lesser sacraments should be shrouded in such silence.

43. As far as the effect is concerned, they actually devise two of them; one which bestows grace and another which impresses a character into the soul of the ordained. The folly of character was rejected in the treatment of the sacraments in general. And, as we see, many deny that, in the five lesser orders, either grace is conferred, or character impressed. And regarding what they call the higher orders, we require that a divine promise be clearly and manifestly expressed in Scripture, for otherwise no-one would be able to convince us that by a certain pact God is bound to be present with some supernatural operation whenever men attach spiritual *charismata* to words that they have fabricated, and to ludicrous ceremonies (of whatever sort) that are purely human. Nor is there any reason why anyone should be moved by Bellarmine's objection from 1 Tim 4[:14] and 2 Tim 1[:6], wherein mention is made of the grace that Timothy received from the laying-on of hands. The first passage does not deal with justifying grace which is sealed by the sacraments and which Timothy obtained elsewhere, but it deals with the grace which they call freely given, which someone who is not justified is able to have.

44. Bellarmine himself admits (*On the Sacraments in General*, chapter 26) that "the authority to confer the sacraments is not a grace that makes gracious but a grace that has been given freely, and that it does not clash with a shameless lifestyle to the point that it cannot co-exist with it"—a statement whereby he confutes his own argument. Then, add the fact that among the papal teachers it still is not yet agreed whether the laying-on of hands is essential to the

order, since some of them deny it, as we have shown just now. Moreover, since the apostles did make use of the laying-on of hands not only in ordination but also in the conferral of the special gifts of the Holy Spirit, it cannot be denied that the statement in 2 Tim 1:6 can fittingly be taken to mean both layings-on of hands, and consequently does not pertain to the institution of some sacrament, since by the admission of the papal teachers the extraordinary gifts of the Spirit do not pertain to the grace of the sacraments.

45. From these statements it is sufficiently clear that not any order is a sacrament in the strict sense of the word. But we would not put up a fight if someone, taking the word 'sacrament' in a broad sense, would bestow that term also upon the genuine ordination of ministers, provided that everyone is in agreement that it cannot be counted among the sacraments in an unambiguous sense. In this sense, Calvin (*Institutes*, book 4, chapter 14, section 20) "willingly allows the laying-on of hands whereby the ministers of the church were installed into their office to be called a sacrament; but he does not number it among the ordinary sacraments." Also in this way should we understand Melanchthon (*Loci communes* and the *Apology of the Augsburg Confession*, article 13) where he holds that the order is not a sacrament in the strict sense of the word—which Bellarmine ascribes to him—but rather in an improper and general sense, in which also the ancients once gave the name of sacrament to the washing of feet, the giving of blessed bread to Catechumens, etc. (Augustine, *On the merits and forgiveness of sins*, book 2, chapter 26; Ambrose, *On the Sacraments*, book 3, chapter 1; Bernard, *Sermon on the Lord's Supper*). Even the dedication of the altar is called a sacrament (Glossa [on Gratian's Decree], case 1, question 3, chapter 15).

Marriage

46. The same thing should be said about marriage, if by chance some people have given the name of sacrament to what is otherwise a holy and even divine institution. That was observed even among the Schoolmen by Durand in his [*Commentary on the Sentences*] book 4, distinction 26, question 3, where he teaches that "marriage is not a sacrament like one of the others, and that it does not bestow grace by the work performed." The same is said in the *Glossa* [on Gratian's Decree] (case 31, question 1, chapter 9; case 32, question 2, chapter 13) and likewise by Godfried, Hostiensis and Bernard, cited by Durand. Even Lombard himself says this in *Sentences*, book 4, distinction 2,

where he holds that marriage was only a remedy against sin—which existed before the coming of Christ, and that it does not bestow grace. From this it follows that it is not a sacrament in the unambiguous sense of the word. Nowadays, the new papal teachers consider that view as heretical, since they determine that marriage is truly and properly a sacrament; but they disagree in this regard, that some like Peter de Soto (*Lectures* [*on the Institution of Priesthood*], *On Marriage* 2) and Alfonso de Castro (*Against Heresies*, on the word 'nuptials,' heresy 3) would have it that "marriage started to become a sacrament not only in the New Testament, but had been such already for a long time since it was first instituted." They took that view from Lombard (*Sentences*, book 4, distinction 26), and he from Pope Leo I (Epistle 92, to Rusticus). But others, and among them Bellarmine, say that before Christ it did not have the nature of a sacrament.

47. We deny that it was a sacrament in the strict sense of the word, whether it was exhibited from the time of its first institution or after Christ, since we are moved by the same reasons with which we took away that right from the other falsely-named sacraments, i.e., the fact that God had not instituted it as a sacramental sign or seal of justifying grace, and that it is not supported by the promise that by using it grace will be exhibited. And also that God himself has not prescribed a specific form of words (which the papal teachers require for sacraments) nor that anything can be observed in the marriage of Christians that was lacking in the marriage of believers before Christ. And that is the reason why also in this matter the papal teachers disagree amongst themselves with 'divorcing' opinions, and they have differing opinions not only about the time of its institution, but also about its material substance. Some think it exists in the "words" that express the consent "insofar as these words are being determined," and others in the persons themselves who are joining together, or in the bodies of the two spouses. Others, like Cano, think that it exists in those visible rites which are used in the church's blessing, and that is the reason why he takes a beating from Bellarmine who holds that the persons who join together are not only the material substance but even the instrumental cause of this sacrament. Others posit that the material substance is the consent of the ones who join together. And others have other views.

48. And about the form they compete in similar fashion with differing opinions. Some are of the view that the form is the words which express the consent, and since it is the married couple which declares them, they are the administers of the sacrament; and if they do not express their consent in

words, their carnal union can be considered to stand for the form and the sign (thus Bellarmine, *On Marriage*, book 1, chapter 6, 'Ex his,' and chapter 5, 'Sed quicquid'). But it sure is a strange teaching that a sacrament can be performed in the marriage bed, and in such an act, without speaking a word. Others are of the opinion that the words uttered by the priest are the form (like Cano, *Loci theologici*, book 8, chapter 5, and William of Paris, [*On the Sacraments*] chapter 9, question 1, "On Marriage"). Others reject this opinion because it would follow that the secret marriages that were entered upon before the Council of Trent were not endowed with sacramental worth, which they deem absurd. And others hold that the material substance is the words first spoken by the one spouse, for instance, "I accept you as my wife," and that the form is the words spoken in the second place by the other spouse, for instance, "I accept you as my husband." Vasquez (*Disputatio* 3, chapter 1 and following) relates nine points of view on this, of which he refutes eight and picks the one that the others reject. But in every sacrament, because it belongs to the genus of a sign and there is no sign when it is not acknowledged as such, it is clear how important—in fact, how obviously necessary—it is that it possess something of a sign in keeping with the will of the one who institutes it, the fighting among our opponents makes it sufficiently clear that marriage is not a sacrament in the true sense of the word.

49. And the fact that it represents the spiritual and very close union of our Lord Jesus Christ with the church does not add the characteristics of a sacrament to this sacred institution; for since this representation exists primarily and especially in the unbreakable bond of marriage, as our opponents acknowledge, they also admit that when understood as a bond "marriage neither is now nor ever was properly speaking a sacrament." Thus Coninck (*On Marriage*, disputation 24, dubium 2), where he also admits that "the church fathers understood 'sacrament' in the broad sense for any sign whatsoever which God has instituted for a sacred thing because they say that marriage is a sacrament not because it signifies some sanctity that it bestows by the use of it, but because it signifies the union of Christ with the church. Hence, they even say that marriage in the law of nature is a sacrament in a similar way." This is what he says.

50. From this, it is clear what our response should be to that crowning argument which very many of our opponents attach to the Epistle to the Ephesians, chapter 5 verse 32. For, leaving aside the fact that the word

'sacrament' occurs only in the Vulgate edition, it is clear that 'sacrament' is a general term and that from the word (which Bellarmine even admits) no proof can be given that it is a true sacrament—and much less, in fact, from the circumstances of the text. And although Bellarmine makes this argument with all his might, he could not persuade all his own people. For Gabriel Vasquez, who wrote after Bellarmine, says the following about the passage in Eph 5 ("This sacrament is great, etc."): "But I have always held the view that with this testimony it not only is not possible to prove what our people contend, but also that in the explanation of it they declare some things which in no way at all can co-exist with true doctrine." And following a lengthy rebuttal he adds: "It would have been better for our theologians over against heretics to avoid this passage of Paul than to be seen as foisting this testimony of Scripture upon them, and to end up in such tight spots and with a less sound explanation" (*On the Sacrament of Marriage*, disputation 2, chapter 6). Moreover, in the same place: "We grant that neither from that passage in Eph 5 nor from that in 1 Tim 2 can it be proven effectively that marriage is a sacrament."

51. And since this is the case, and since they, convinced by the strength of the truth, finally admit that they have no basis at all in Scripture for this sacrament of theirs, they return their viewpoint on that matter "to their own church's definition, which has been handed down in perpetual tradition" (a tradition which is more uncertain than the matter with which we are concerned). However, we are content with the two genuine sacraments, of which it was ascertained and manifested from the Scriptures that they were instituted by God's Son with certain signs and words, and we hold these same sacraments, "few for many, easy to observe, most useful in their efficacy, and very clear in what they signify." And we shall strengthen our faith by using them, while not hesitating in our faith. And since we have learned that whatever comes about without faith is sin [Rom 14:23], and since we know that there is not any faith that has not been preceded by God's Word, we shall have no part in the sins of those who disagree amongst themselves with foolish opinions and with human inventions bind the grace of God which we should expect from the unique author of grace, we shall always sing thanks and praise to Him in the unity of the Trinity.

Corollaries

1. We deny that the degrees of consanguinity and affinity wherein Leviticus 18 prohibits the entry into marriage, relates to the Israelite polity in such a way that they do not belong to the divine right that must be kept for all time in keeping with the law of decency.

2. We affirm that in the case of adultery or the wrongful desertion of an unbeliever the marriage is dissolved, even as far as the bond is concerned, in such a way that once the divorce has lawfully taken place, the innocent party should not be prevented from marrying.

3. And we deny that a marriage insofar as the bond, or the bed or cohabitation is concerned, can be dissolved by a vow or by entry upon a religious order (as they call it).

4. We affirm that in order to enter into a lawful marriage the explicit or tacit approval of the parents is required.

ON CHURCH DISCIPLINE

President: Antonius Walaeus
Respondent: Johannes Livensius

An important feature of the Church are the two 'keys of the kingdom' that have been given to it by Christ (Matt 16:19; see thesis 2). The first key is the administration of the Gospel and the forgiveness of sins (Disputation 42, treated in Disputation 48 in theses 5–7). From thesis 8 onward, the disputation deals with the key of discipline, which concerns excommunication—'a matter of greater controversy in the church of Christ' (8). Church discipline is a 'spiritual authority' whereby individuals are 'barred from the signs of divine grace, on account of impurity in doctrine or life and after they have neglected and despised the private and public warnings of the church.' If they 'continue in the same stubbornness then at last in the presence of the entire church they, in the name of God, are declared through the public sentence on earth and consequently also in heaven as excluded from the communion of the church until such time as they are reconciled to God and the church through true and genuine repentance' (9). It is shown from the Old and New Testament that this authority is given to the Church (10–17). The civil authority has no jurisdiction over spiritual discipline, which is exclusively ecclesiastical (19). From thesis 20 onward it is explained through whom (21–24), to whom (25–32) and in what way (33–59) this authority should be exercised. Discipline concerns not merely individual people but also entire groups that promote or practice teachings that are unbiblical. The Synopsis describes the process whereby those who wander may be brought back; failure to do so results finally in withholding the sacrament of the Lord's Supper and exclusion from the communion of saints. Nevertheless, those who are under discipline should not 'be excluded from either the public or private hearing of the Word, since it contains the warnings and encouragements unto faith and repentance, and because prayers for their conversion are offered by the church in it' (47). The goal of discipline and excommunication, 'the last and fiercest remedy for subduing a man's flesh and for bringing his soul to life' (59), is not the man's perdition, but his salvation (56).

1. Just as a family, or a state, or any other society of human beings cannot exist without the restraint of laws and discipline, so also the integrity of Christ's church in this world cannot endure unless it is bound to a fixed government and suitable laws whereby its order and arrangement are kept unharmed against the deceits and devisings of the flesh, the world and Satan.

2. This government of the church commonly is called church discipline; Christ designates it with the word "keys" in Matt 16:19, and in 2 Cor 10:8 the apostle calls it the authority given by the Lord, not for tearing down but for building up.

3. Yet this is an entirely ministering authority, in all things subject to Christ and his Word. For Christ alone is like the son who is put in charge of his house (Heb 3:6). "And he holds the key of David, he opens and no-one shuts, and shuts and no-one opens" (Rev 3:7). And, indeed, his ministers are put over his house like servants, like stewards and managers of the mysteries of God in whom the foremost requirement is that each one of them be found faithful (1 Cor 4:[1–]2).

4. And this key or authority to bind and to loosen, in keeping with Christ's explanation in Matt 18:18, is rightly divided by our Catechism into two parts: one is the authority of the Word and the other is the authority of excommunication. The former of these, based on Luke 11:52, is usually called the key of knowledge, and the latter the key of discipline (so called when taken in the stricter sense).

5. It is the key or authority of the Word whereby forgiveness of sins and reconciliation with God through Christ are not only generally declared to believers and those who repent (as is seen throughout the Scriptures), but also whereby that general word is applied individually to each person's conscience for their consolation and upbuilding, in proportion to the fruits of faith and repentance, or the signs of unrepentance and unbelief, that become manifest in them—as can be seen in the example of Nathan and David (2 Sam 12:13) and, contrariwise, of Peter and Simon the magician (Acts 8:21).

6. In a certain respect the use of this declaration belongs to the entire church as a community, because the individual members of the church, according to the command of love, in proportion to the measure of the gift they have

received from Christ, and by reason of their calling, are able and required to comfort, exhort, and admonish one another privately from the Word of God, and to do so according to Christ's command in Matt 18:15: "If your brother sins against you, go and tell him his fault between you and him alone, etc." And likewise the apostle in Heb 3:13: "But encourage one another daily, as long as it is called 'today,' so that none of you may be hardened by sin's deceitfulness."

7. However, Christ has appointed in particular the pastors of the church and the public ministers of the Word to exercise this authority publicly and, by virtue of their public authority, also privately. Hence Christ also promised to the apostle Peter individually in Matt 16:19: "I shall give to you the keys to the kingdom of heaven, and whatever you bind on earth will be bound in heaven, and whatever you loose on earth will be loosed in heaven;" and to all the disciples together [he promised] in John 20:22: "If you forgive the sins of any, they are forgiven them, and if you retain the sins of any, they are retained." And therefore, it says also that the preachers of the Word fulfill their commission in the name of Christ (2 Cor 5:20).

8. The second key, which is called the key of discipline, is a matter of greater controversy in the church of Christ, and so we must protect the nature, mode and use of it a little more carefully from Holy Scripture against all abuses.

9. Therefore, we state that the key of discipline properly exists in that spiritual authority whereby, through the agency of the pastors of the Word, in accordance with the counsel of the church's senate and with the consent of the whole church, those who are called brothers [cf. 1 Cor 5:10–11] are barred from the signs of divine grace, on account of impurity in doctrine or life and after they have neglected and despised the private and public warnings of the church; and, if they continue in the same stubbornness then at last in the presence of the entire church they, in the name of God, are declared through the public sentence on earth and consequently also in heaven as excluded from the communion of the church until such time as they are reconciled to God and the church through true and genuine repentance.

10. But before we consider more thoughtfully the individual parts of this definition, we ought from Holy Scripture to demonstrate over against some who present themselves as members of the reformed church that this

authority has been granted to the church; and then we should explain its mode and nature according to the definition that we have proposed.

11. Very many instances and examples of the Old as well as the New Testament give proof that this authority has been given to the church.

12. In the Old Testament God commanded that not only should those unclean according to the law voluntarily abstain from the communion of the sacred things (in Lev 5 and 6, and subsequent chapters) and likewise from eating the Passover lamb (Num 9), but also that the care of this matter should in preference to others belong to the priests and the Levites, namely that according to God's Word they should distinguish and judge between the clean and unclean, between the holy and the profane, as can be seen regarding every impurity (Lev 10:9, Ezek 44:23), and concerning those unclean from leprosy (Lev 13), in order to bar from the communion of the temple and the sacred things those whom they had judged to be impure, until they were made clean once again through special sacrifices, as is demonstrated besides the particular example of king Uzziah (2 Chron 26) in a general way in 2 Chron 23:18[–19]: "Jehoiada divided the duties in the house of God between the priests and the Levites, and he stationed door-keepers at the entrances to God's house, so that the person unclean in any matter should not enter."

13. And because this is obvious concerning ceremonial impurity, we should state it all the more concerning moral impurity, since that ceremonial impurity indicated a moral impurity, just as the prophet Haggai explains in chapter 2:12. And so too God, when in the exclusion from the sanctuary He also links those who are uncircumcised in the flesh with those who are uncircumcised of heart (Ezek 44:9): "No foreigner who is uncircumcised of flesh or uncircumcised of heart shall enter into my sanctuary." And although we admit that this passage must be understood in a mystical sense about the sanctuary of the New Testament, even so it clearly shows at the same time what ought to have been done in that outward sanctuary of the Old Testament.

14. But in addition to these arguments drawn from the analogy of ceremonial impurity it is also possible to borrow from the Old Testament certain proofs taken from moral impurity, such as Lev 6:2, which provides a law for different kinds of fraud and theft; and added to the law is the mode whereby men of that sort can be reconciled once again with the church and make atonement for that sin, i.e., the restoration of the stolen item along with an

additional one-fifth and the burnt-offering of a suckling ram by a priest. From this it necessarily follows that a man of this sort, before he was reconciled with the defrauded person by returning the stolen object—and with God by means of the special offering—did not have access to the communal sacrifices and sacraments of the Israelite church. For wherever there was a special atonement, there was impurity; and where there was impurity there was the exclusion from the communal sacred rites (Num 19:20).

15. And the same point is demonstrated incontrovertibly by the scolding of the Old Testament priests that is found in Ezek 44:6[–7]: "Let this be enough for you, O house of Israel, depart from all your detestable practices, you who have brought foreigners of uncircumcised hearts and flesh to be present in my sanctuary, to profane my house." Philo the Jew provides the same evidence in his book *On Those Who Offer Sacrifice*, that this practice [of excommunication] persisted also among the Jewish people of his own time: murderers were not admitted into the temple. And Josephus, in the Jewish War, book 4, chapter 10, inveighs very fiercely against the Zealots because they were found to be in the temple with hands that were still warm from slaying fellow country-men; and in his *Antiquities*, book 19, chapter 7 he testifies that there was a certain Pharisee by the name of Simon who claimed that king Agrippa was unholy and ought to be barred from the entrance to the temple. Hence also in the Gospel history of John 9:22 and elsewhere we read that those who were considered unholy were declared, 'expelled from the synagogue.' And among the other hardships which Christ predicts for his apostles is also this one, that they would be cast out from the synagogues on account of his name (John 16:2).

16. And from the New Testament there are also very many places of Scripture that are clearly of this sentiment, as they cannot in any way be referring to the office of the [civil] magistrate. There is the passage in Matt 16:19, "I shall give to you the keys of the kingdom of heaven, and whatever you bind on earth will be bound in heaven." And similarly John 20:23, "If you forgive anyone's sins, their sins are forgiven; if you retain anyone's sins, they are retained," cannot be understood, nor were they ever understood, as about the office of the magistrate, but only about the office of the apostles and the pastors of the church. Nor does the passage in Matt 18[:17] ("Tell it to the church, and if he will not listen to the church, let him be to you as a foreigner and a tax-collector") and 1 Cor 5:3–5, where the apostle commands that the man who has committed incest must by the church be handed over to Satan;

and he prescribes laws whereby this discipline should then be exercised, besides the various instances that one meets everywhere in the practice and the letters of the apostles, which we shall mention in the following theses.

17. From all these passages it is obvious that a very serious error is committed by those who dare to deny that the church has been granted this authority— an authority which rests upon the universal, fixed practice of the Old and New Testament, and of the whole Christian church.

18. Also those people make a serious mistake who grant that Christ indeed had bestowed this authority upon the church, but extraordinarily and only for a period of time, as long as the church was under the cross and lacked Christian magistrates. For the proofs that we earlier provided from the Old Testament deal with the church that was established under believing magistrates. In the New Testament Christ gave this authority to the church in an absolute way and for perpetuity, while not any mention or even suspicion of an exception of that sort was ever suggested. Hence also the early church exercised the same authority regarding every controversy, not only under the cross and before there were Christian emperors, but also under those rulers when they already had been converted to the faith and under their political government which always had been distinguished and kept separate from this ecclesiastical and spiritual government.

19. But even if we do not withdraw this spiritual authority from the purview of the Christian magistrate as the keeper of both tables of the Law, nevertheless we state that the authority or the exercise of it does not depend upon the supremacy of the civil magistrate (as more recently some people claim), because it depends on Christ alone and he himself directly bestowed it upon the church, as the previously adduced passages show. And accordingly, neither by an appeal, nor by a citation before a higher tribunal (in the strict sense), can this authority be deferred to the tribunal of the magistrate or rulers, since the execution of it is not their responsibility. Meanwhile, however, we do not deny the truth in what Beza admits to Erastus: "Because even a rightly ordained consistory could do an injustice to alleged wrongdoers [...], in smaller territories the Christian civil magistrate (without any violation of ecclesiastical government), as keeper and avenger of the two tables of the Law and of the church's good order, has the power to look out for those who submit complaints."

20. Therefore, as this first question is settled beyond controversy, it now remains for us to explain next through whom, to whom and in what way this authority should be exercised.

21. And so we hold that this authority rests in the entire church, but because God is a God of order and not of confusion, and because in the church there is an order of those who teach and those who learn, as well as of those who are in authority and those who are subject to it, it is necessary that its own distinct roles are assigned to each of the orders so that in such a difficult matter as this one everything may be directed towards building up.

22. We assert that the execution of this authority rests with the ministers of the Word, not only because this public administration of this discipline is an appendix to the preaching of the Word and to the administration of the sacraments, but also because all of the examples which we already have produced from the Old and New Testaments refer the public execution of this authority to the priests, apostles, evangelists and heralds or pastors of the churches.

23. And yet we do not therefore grant that this authority may be claimed by some single bishop, whether Roman or Eugubine, by his own initiative or plenary authority (as they call it), but we assert that the counsel of the church's rulers or presbyters must be applied, and also the agreement of the entire church (whether openly or at least quietly) according to the command of Christ and the practice of the purer church.

24. For the word "church" which Christ uses in Matt 18[:17] cannot be taken to stand for any single bishop; and in 1 Cor 5:4 the apostle Paul applies the word to the solemn assembly of the Corinthians, and since he states in the same chapter that the final excommunication is common to the entire church, it is fitting that this entire affair should be carried out also by common consent (whereby it can be achieved so much better), in the same way that in the Old Testament it happened that what preceded was not merely the authority of the ecclesiastical Sanhedrin but also the consensus of the people from whose midst that sort of man was said to be uprooted or cut off.

25. The object concerning which this discipline is exercised are those who are called brothers, as defined by the apostle in 1 Cor 5:11, "for God will judge those who are outside the church." [1 Cor 5:13] And the cause [for discipline] is either a wicked manner of life (as can be seen from Matt 18:15;

1 Cor 5:11; 2 Thess 3:11), or crooked doctrine (as is evidenced in Rom 10:17; 1 Tim 1:20; Titus 3:20; and 2 John 10). And the reason for this matter is clear, because not only the manner of life but also the doctrine that is depraved separates a man from Christ (Gal 1:8) and both of them are like yeast that can affect the whole lump, as Christ testifies in Matt 15:6 and 12, and Paul in 1 Cor 5:6.

26. But when someone who is called brother should fall into a scandal of this sort, that is not a reason immediately to be excluded from the body of the church or from the signs of grace, as is the custom of some Anabaptists; but only after he has despised and rejected both the private and the public admonitions of the church, as Christ's words clearly indicate: "If he will not listen to the church, let him be to you as a heathen and a tax-collector," and the apostle in Titus 3:10: "Shun the man who is a heretic after the first and the second admonition."

27. And at this point the question arises whether it is permitted, if the number of those who sin in doctrine or in manner of life is a large one, to make use of excluding them from the sacraments, or of excommunicating them. The cause of the doubt here is that, although this authority was given to build up, and not to break down, from this sort of separation one should expect the breaking down rather than the upbuilding of the church. And therefore, Augustine maintained that this spiritual sword should not be drawn against the drunkards in Africa because of the large number of those who sinned.

28. We, however, answer this question by posing a distinction: if a large part of the church is led astray into a fundamental error or heresy and cannot be recalled to the way despite every attempt at remedy, the following remedy still remains for the pious pastors who preside over the sounder part, namely that they may, together with those who are right-minded, separate themselves from the community of those who are heterodox. And although they do not have the power to use this discipline against them by condemning them openly because of the strength of those who mislead, yet at least by acting openly they can secede from them and condemn the heresy. In this manner Christ gives the warning in Matt 7:15, "Beware the false prophets," and in John 10:5, "Christ's sheep do not know the voice of a stranger and therefore they flee from him." Similarly, Rom 16:17: "I warn you, brothers, that you watch carefully those who cause discord or scandals contrary to the doctrine which you have learned, and stay away from them." And in the same manner

in the old church the orthodox seceded from the Arians, and our ancestors and forefathers in previous ages seceded from the superstition and synagogue of the Antichrist.

29. But if a wicked lifestyle infects a large part of the flock, in the way that the prophets everywhere lament over the Israelite church, then here again a distinction must be made. For either this great number defends its wicked manner of life by means of doctrine, or if it does not make a defense by means of doctrine, then at least it pursues that doctrine by its evil actions. And if it does defend its wicked manner of life by means of doctrine, as formerly the Nicolaitans and that Jezebel did, who by means of prophecy seduced Christ's servants to prostitution, then concerning them we should decide in the same way whereby we previously taught that heretics ought to be treated, i.e., either by means of a public sentencing of excommunication, or, if because of their great number and strength this cannot be done, to secede from them. [That is what] Christ commanded the angel of the church at Thyatira and Ephesus concerning the Nicolaitans and that Jezebel (Rev 2:6 and 20), on the basis of Christ's declaration in Matt 5:19: "Whoever breaks one of the least of these commandments, and teaches other men so, will be called least in the kingdom of heaven."

30. But if only a wicked manner of life should befall a large part of the flock—a manner of life that does not arise from wicked doctrine, but one that is contrary to sound doctrine—then according to Augustine's opinion (in book 3 of *Against the Letter of Parmenian*, and elsewhere against the Donatists) we should not make use of secession from them, nor of excommunication, but only prayers, sighings, exhortations, rebukes, threats, good examples and similar remedies. We see that in the same way only these weapons were used by the prophets and the pious priests in the Israelite church. And [Augustine] demonstrates from the passage of 2 Cor 10 that this authority is given not for breaking down but for building up, and from the parable of the weeds which Christ wishes not to be pulled up, out of fear that while doing so the wheat might be pulled up and so perish (Matt 13:29).

31. In our judgment these reasons of Augustine are solid with respect to the private persons living piously in that sort of gathering, persons who for that reason should not separate themselves from such a gathering; and so too with respect to individual pastors who in tolerating the wicked ones cannot depend upon the consent and support of a greater number of people. This is

rightly shown by the example of the pious priests within a large number of wicked ones, and by the examples of the prophets who are working among them. But if the majority of the church's rulers are of one mind for the good, then I think that for people of this sort who are clearly and stubbornly corrupt those same pastors neither have the power to (nor should) share the sacraments of divine grace with them, how great their multitude might be; but instead with unanimous consent they ought to deny them these sacraments—and entrust the outcome to God. For pious pastors are not empowered to share the signs of grace with those to whom Christ manifestly denies them, and with whom he forbids them to be shared. And it is also because in churches of our own time instances can be found where that sort of public refusal in cases of the public corruption of morals was a means and instrument whereby the church returned to a better state, and the morals were restored with greater integrity.

32. At the same time, however, it is absurd that the papal teachers prohibit even innocent subjects from using sacred things because of the vices of those who rule over them, or family members because of the sins of the father of the household, for herein the son does not bear his father's iniquity, nor the subject that of his ruler, if in his own life he does not follow or approve his example.

33. Having thus explained the object of this discipline, we proceed to its form and mode.

34. The form of excommunication, or rather its stages, are twofold: the first consists of abstaining from the Table of the Lord, and the second in being excluded from the outward communion of the entire church and in being cast out of the church. Some people call the former of these stages the "minor excommunication" and the latter one the "major excommunication."

35. Abstention from the Lord's Table happens lawfully in two ways: either when someone called brother has caused some serious scandal in manner of life or in doctrine, and having been warned does in fact make a verbal profession of repentance from it, but does not yet display the fruits that befit the repentance so that the scandal can be removed from the church, or when he does not indeed promise repentance in words but nevertheless does not yet cut off every hope for repentance through his stubbornness, so that in the interim through this first stage of spiritual discipline the church may, by

means of warnings and Christian forbearance, call that man back and lead him to genuine repentance.

36. The foundation for this first step of discipline is sought partly from the actual goal that we have explained already, partly from the abstention of those people of the Old Testament who on account of impurity according to the law were compelled to abstain from the use of the sacrifices and the Passover lamb for a period of time in order to cleanse themselves in the interim, as can be seen from Num 9 and 19, and 2 Chron 30. Finally [it is sought] partly from the apostle's command in 1 Cor 11:28: "Let a man first examine himself and so eat of this bread and drink of this cup." And whereas this examination should be done by everyone privately, yet in the case of offenses that are public the examination should be done also publicly by the church's overseers. For throughout the Scripture they are commanded to give heed to the entire flock, to separate the clean from the unclean, to judge those who are within, and as much as is possible to remove scandals from the church.

37. Also the practice derived from the times of the apostles in the early church clearly accords with this religious usage, although we acknowledge that in several canons of the ancient synods some strictness is seen in determining the length of time for abstaining, a strictness which somewhat surpasses the measure of forbearance of Christ and the apostles.

38. The major excommunication encompasses three stages, of which the first is called the "simple excommunication," the second the "anathema" of Gal 1:8 and the third the "anathema Maranatha" of 1 Cor 16:22. The use of this last one is for those who have sinned against the Holy Spirit and for whom there is therefore no hope of forgiveness and for whom it remains only that the Lord should come and take up his case against them. And so the church of the latter time which can hardly discern this sin with certainty is not accustomed to use this stage. It is customary for the second, middle stage to be used only generally for wicked doctrines and for those who stubbornly defend them. And the use of the first stage therefore properly exists for individual persons in that manner and order which we determined in thesis 9.

39. This excommunication is explained by the words of Christ in Matt 18:17: "If he will not listen to the church let him be to you as a heathen and a tax-collector." So too the words of the apostle in Gal 5:12 "If only they would be cut off who trouble you." But under the Old Testament this used to be

called "rooting out from the midst of the people," and "being cast out from the synagogue."

40. Many of the ancients have rightly determined that the same is meant by that manner of speaking the apostle uses in 1 Cor 5:5 and 1 Tim 1:20, namely "to hand [them] over to Satan for the destruction of the flesh," because it is outside the church that Satan rules. And yet what Augustine and Chrysostom observe is not improbable, that people of that sort are said to be handed over to Satan because a certain overpowering and harassment from Satan accompanies it until they repent.

41. But what Erastus has invented on this point is absurd and foreign to the apostle's intention, i.e., that they are said to be handed over to Satan so that he might deliver them to death; for the apostle is putting forward a far different goal for this handing over, namely "so that by the destruction of the flesh the soul may be saved on the Day of the Lord" (1 Cor 5[:5]). And also that they learn not to blaspheme (1 Tim 1[:20]). And the apostle himself later explains it by other ways of speaking that have the same force, namely "cleanse out the old leaven" [1 Cor 5:7], and "remove the evil man from your midst" [1 Cor 5:13], and "do not associate with them and do not eat with them" [1 Cor 5:11]—it can only be foolish to say such things about those who are deceased. Not to mention the fact that it is foreign to all the mercy and custom of the apostolic church to propose that it through Satan deprived the greedy, the drunkards, the idolaters and similar people of their lives.

42. But in order to grasp this reason for excommunication fully, we should explain a little more carefully the point to which this rejection from the church extends, and what that communion is from which that sort of men are deprived.

43. From the words of Christ in chapter 16 and 18 of Matthew one clearly gathers that a man who has been excommunicated is so bound or loosed on earth that he also is bound or loosed in heaven; i.e., that a lawfully and justly provided sentencing of the church on earth has been approved also by God in heaven. For an unjust excommunication, such as Christ, the apostle, and many pious people suffered from the slaves of the Antichrist is to be feared no more than an undeserved curse. Concerning this the Wise testifies in Prov 26:2: "Like a sparrow in its wanderings and a swallow in its flying, a curse that is undeserved does not alight."

44. But just as the communion of the church's members is twofold (one outward and regulative, the other internal and spiritual) so also in some manner and with some condition does a true and just excommunication concern the twofold removal of this communion.

45. Scripture makes the outward communion among the members of the church twofold: one is purely ecclesiastical, and the other is of the Christian social interaction in civic life.

46. The excommunicated man is excluded from ecclesiastical communion because by his excommunication he is deprived of all the signs of divine grace which it was God's will to belong to his church and through which He displays his singular favor to the church. The signs are of the following kind: 1) all the offices in the church, the use of which the excommunicated man necessarily forfeits; 2) participation in the sacraments; 3) the communion of the Word and of prayers, insofar as it entails the tables of the mutual covenant established between God and his church, or the promises and comfortings of the Gospel made for those who believe and repent. Hence also in the Old Testament the excommunicated man was barred from the use and communion of the entire tabernacle and temple.

47. But although in the first church it was customary to exclude even from the buildings those who were excommunicated, we nevertheless hold the view that this is not necessary under the New Testament, since our temples in and of themselves possess nothing sacramental (such as the tabernacle and temple of the Old Testament possessed) nor hold any special promises of grace above other places, as the papal teachers superstitiously believe contrary to Christ's assertion in John 4:21,23. Secondly, because those who have been excommunicated are not to be excluded from either the public or private hearing of the Word, since it contains the warnings and encouragements unto faith and repentance, and because prayers for their conversion are offered by the church in it. In the same way we see in 1 Cor 14:23 that even unbelievers were admitted to the gatherings of Christians for that purpose, and that Christ himself associated with sinners and tax collectors for that purpose; and the apostle expressly warns in 2 Thess 3:15: "That we not treat that sort of man as an enemy, but that we admonish him as a brother."

48. Through the use of excommunication also the communion of Christian social interaction in civic life is broken off, in accordance with the apostolic

SYNOPSIS OF A PURER THEOLOGY

command, in order that surely in this way a man may become ashamed and be called to a better frame of mind. The apostle's words in 1 Cor 5:11 are clear: "But now I have written to you that you must not associate with them, and that you not even eat with that sort of people." And 2 John 10: "If anyone comes to you and does not bring this doctrine, do not receive him into your home nor say 'welcome' to him."

49. It is not permitted under this pretext, however, for spouses to separate from each other, or to deny each other their conjugal responsibilities, as the Anabaptists are accustomed to doing without any precedent from Scripture. Nor are children hereby absolved from the obedience that is owed to their parents; and no other natural or moral bonds are severed by excommunication. For it is a fixed rule that the ceremonial and the positive [precepts] always yield to the moral and the natural [precepts]. For God desires mercy and not sacrifice [Hos 6:6]. But in the passages quoted earlier the apostle Paul and John are treating that familiarity of social interaction whereby Christians out of *philadelphia* and Christian brotherly love customarily fulfill responsibilities of that sort to one another. Those who have been excommunicated forfeit the singular debt of those offices, but not the common right of nature, which always remains untouched.

50. And the same reason also shows convincingly that the popes unjustly remove kings and rulers from their kingdoms and dominions through excommunication (not to speak here about other abuses), or remove subjects from the oath of fidelity which they had lawfully bestowed on them. For these bonds are natural and moral, ones that bind peoples' consciences by virtue of the third and fifth commandments, just as the apostle also explains it in Rom 13 and 1 Pet 3; and consequently, those bonds cannot be broken off or severed through excommunication.

51. However, there does not exist any example for actions of that sort in the ancient Jewish church, or in early Christianity, but there are very many examples of the opposite: in Philip the Arabian, Julian, Theodosius, the tyrant Maximus, and others whom the church had excommunicated yet who did not forfeit their kingdoms on grounds of excommunication. Nor is it fair that in possessing kingdoms the condition of Christian kings is worse than that of unbelieving rulers who cannot be excommunicated, or worse than that of other Christians who do not forfeit their own functions, or privately owned and inherited goods by ecclesiastical excommunication. For as Domingo de

Soto rightly has observed, "excommunication is not the deprivation of some proper good which the transgressor of the law had owned previously, but it is the deprivation of common goods which he would have received from the church, for instance (the deprivation) of spiritual communion and of receiving the sacraments."

52. Thus far the outward communion and the extent to which the excommunicated man is deprived of it; it follows that we also add a few observations about the inward communion.

53. And so we posit that he who is separated from the outward communion of the church in a certain way also is deemed a foreigner to the internal fellowship which the church has with Christ, and, as the apostle says, is handed over to Satan. For it is outside the church that Satan reigns, and God cannot be perceived other than an angry and just avenger of sins.

54. And this deprivation of the inward communion with Christ is twofold: one with respect to the present grace, and the other with respect to future grace.

55. The inward deprivation with respect to the present grace is whereby the man who remains obstinate towards the church's warnings and who is denied the outward signs of God's favor and the pledges of his grace, is also deprived by God from the inward testimonies of divine favor; and consequently, he cannot perceive God other than angry and alienated from him, as long as he persists in that particular state.

56. However, it does not therefore follow what some people think, that the man of that sort for that duration of time entirely has been cast away from God or necessarily stripped of every habitual grace. For the goal of the church that so judges (which judgment also God in heaven confirms) is not the man's perdition, but his salvation. Nor is it an indication that God has rejected that man entirely, but that the flesh dominates the spirit to the degree that he cannot be restored to his rightful position except by this extreme remedy, as the apostle's words in 1 Cor 5:5 make clear: this is taking place "for the ruin," that is, the destruction, "of the flesh" in order that "the soul may be saved," that is, gains the upper hand, on the Day of the Lord. From this it necessarily follows that in the judgment of the excommunicating church some seed of the Spirit, albeit latent and suppressed, remains alive in

that man, a seed which must be preserved from ultimate ruin by means of this most bitter remedy against the flesh.

57. And from that it also does not follow that in God's design a man of that sort is rejected entirely. For through this ultimate remedy God still is calling him to repentance, and it is his will that he be admonished like a brother even though he has been cast out from the family (2 Thess 3:15). It is the same as when a father has cast out a stubborn son from his home and removes him from his presence or from the familiar interaction with the household. And even though he takes away from him every sign and feeling of paternal love and affection in order to bring him back to repentance by means of this remedy, even so he does not therefore utterly deprive him of his inheritance nor necessarily cast off all his fatherly feelings towards him, feelings which he displays by even doing this to him, although the latter does not acknowledge it at the time but will come to realize it in earnest finally when he through serious conversion returns into favor with his father.

58. And with respect to the future grace the deprivation of the inward communion with Christ is not definite or absolute, but only conditional. For when the church by its judgment (which God in heaven confirms) excommunicates a man, it threatens him that just as he is deprived or excluded from the outward communion of the church and from the sense of God's grace, so too is he going to be excluded from the kingdom of heaven on the last day—unless he forestalls that future judgment through true faith and repentance. And this is also what Christ has in mind when he says: "Whatever you bind on earth will be bound in heaven" [Matt 16:19 and 18:18], and "if you retain the sins of any, they are retained in heaven" [John 20:23]. And since in this life these things can only be conditional, it follows that we should expect the absolute fulfillment of them only in the life that is to come.

59. It is obvious from the things that we have explained thus far that there are very many and remarkable fruits of Christian discipline and excommunication among God's people. For [excommunication] is indeed the last and fiercest remedy for subduing a man's flesh and for bringing his soul to life; and it is a very effective proof against dragging the healthy part being drawn down. But over against those who persist in their stubbornness and unrepentance it is the only remedy for ridding God's house of corruption and Christ's church of scandals, and thus for guarding the Word and the

sacraments from being profaned, and God's name from being blasphemed by those outside. For whatever outcome may follow at last, God will nevertheless be sanctified in the lives of those who are near to him, and He will be glorified in the presence of all his people, as He himself testifies following the punishment that afflicted Nadab and Abihu when they had violated the altar of the Lord (Lev 10:3).

DISPUTATION 49

ON ECCLESIASTICAL
COUNCILS OR MEETINGS

President: Antonius Thysius
Respondent: Johannes Wilmerdonck

Having subjected the hierarchical order of the Roman Catholic Church to critical assessment in Disputation 41, and having discussed the structure of the local church, ministers, and council of elders in Disputation 42, this disputation treats the broader organization of the church, ranging from a meeting of several local churches to world-wide ecumenical councils. As the Reformed Churches had to find ways to structure their internal relations in non-episcopalian ways, the Disputation dedicates careful attention to the topic of regional and national meetings. Especially the authority of the broader assemblies is addressed, as is the relationship between the State and the Church. No doubt the deliberations and decisions made at the Synod of Dort inform this disputation, which also addressed the Romanist teachings on the nature and authority of its councils. A synod is a larger assembly of the church, ordained by Christ, in which the church is represented by persons delegated by a lesser assembly for a specific place and time. The goal is to assess, judge, and determine from God's Word those matters common to the churches and which could not be achieved in the lower, classical sessions. A synod is held especially to treat the purity of doctrine, or morals and good order, for the upbuilding of the church and its integrity and peace (see the definitions in theses 3 and 7). The synod of the New Testament Church that is described in Acts 15 is the 'archetype...by whose shape all the other, subsequent synods ought to be ordained' (12). From thesis 15 onward the disputation considers those who have the authority to call assemblies (17–27), the delegates called to attend them (28–34), and the place, time, and costs of holding such assemblies (35–38). Matters and actions appropriate to synods (39–41), the importance of holding them in an orderly fashion and lawfully (42–66), and the form (67–68), goal (69), and authority (70–74) of assemblies are delineated.

674

1. Up until this point, we have treated the church, and its authority and power in declaring the Word of God, its administration of the sacraments, and its exercise of discipline (which certainly is proper to the church)—although it is not the church as a whole which must exercise discipline, but rather the authorized persons whom God through the church has delegated, that is to say, the ministers of the church. By this act of God, they become servants, not of the church strictly speaking but, in a relative sense, of God and of Christ the Lord, and they do so by their own rank and mode, that is, as prefects of the church, as superiors, overseers, shepherds, etc. Nevertheless, they do so, not as lords over the church, for it belongs to Christ alone; but they are ministers and dispensers of the mysteries of God in the church [1 Cor 4:1], that is, they are ministers of the church in an objective sense.

2. Well then, since the church in its assembly is either of the people (1 Cor 11:17–18, 22; Heb 10:25) or of the church officials (Acts 20:17 and 21:10)—which in a certain respect is placed over against the one of the people because it has been ordained for the government of the church and for public judgment within the church—we have determined in the present disputation to give a treatment of this ecclesiastical assembly. And as for the government of the church, from the perspective of Christ, it is entirely monarchical; if you consider the church insofar as it is outward and the administration of it is outward, then it is not democratic, as a certain Morély has claimed. Nor is it simply aristocratic, as many have claimed; nor, lastly, is it monarchical, as the papal teachers claimed. And it certainly is not ochlocratic, nor oligarchic or tyrannical. Instead, it corresponds to an aristocratic government, i.e., one in which lordship has been removed and replaced by ministerial rule.

3. The ecclesiastical assembly, then, is a session Christ has ordained of the whole church, and in proportion to its size, represented by the foremost members of the church and gathered together in one place in the name of Christ, for the purpose of conducting the church's affairs there, namely the soundness of the faith, the holiness of life, and the integrity of the sacraments, the good order, etc., and its practice or exercise and observance, for the right government and upbuilding of it [i.e., the church], and for the glory of God.

4. And the assembly is one of individual or several churches. And of the individual churches, it is a lawful and for the most part ongoing and regular session, which consists of the bishop or bishops of one place (Phil 1:1; Acts 20:28 and 21:18; Titus 1:5,7) and the presbyters (that is, elders) or the deputies

of the people (as integral parts of the church), in order to handle the affairs which are (and to the extent that they are) proper to that particular church. And it is called assembly or consistory (Matt 26:59; John 11:5, 47). By Paul it is called the presbytery, that is the senate or college of elders (1 Tim 4:14). And whereas this session is primary in its origin, it is, however, least in its rank and authority.

5. But the assembly of a larger number of churches is a meeting at a certain place and time of more churchmen (i.e., of ministers and ruling men) whom a lower session has delegated in order to deal with those matters which pertain to the larger number of churches and which could not be achieved at the individual lower session. And it is generally called, in Greek, a synod, and in Latin, a council (from *conciendo*, "to call together").

6. And it is either an assembly of a single diocese or domain, or of more. And the assembly of a single one is commonly called a classis, or diocesan synod, or a *topikē* ('local') one. But the assembly of more dioceses or of an entire province is called specifically a synod or council.

7. Now, to summarize all of the preceding, a synod or a council is a public and lawful assembly of the church, and a more venerable and larger one, ordained by Christ; and the church is represented by persons whom a lesser assembly has delegated for a specific place and time, especially overseers and elders, and which gathers together in the name of God and Christ in order to treat, judge, and determine from God's Word those matters which concern the circumstances common to the churches and which could not be achieved in the lower, classical sessions, and especially when there the purity of the faith and truth is treated over against those who err, and against heretics, or when there is a treatment of the morals and good order over against those who are schismatic, for the upbuilding of the church and its integrity and peace.

8. Moreover, a synod is either provincial, national, general (or plenary, as they call it), or ecumenical or world-wide, and it is gathered of people and deals with matters of the churches of an entire province, of one or more nations, or of the world-wide church. It deals with such matters of the faith and morals that are common to all the churches.

9. And ecclesiastical authority and power reaches its highest point at the synod, according to the rank and level of each meeting; and it conveys the

unity of God's entire church insofar as it is outward, and it is also the basis and binding element for its position and good order, and the wholesome remedy for troublesome evils.

10. But as for the institution of the ecclesiastical assemblies, and so also of the synod, it does not arise by human right but by divine right, for it has its basis in the words of Christ: "Tell it to the church, and if he will not listen to the church, etc." [Matt 18:17]; "And whatever you bind on earth, etc." [Matt 18:18]; "Where two or three have been gathered in my name, there am I in their midst" [Matt 18:20]. "And I am with you even until the end of the age" [Matt 28:20]. To be sure, these statements should be taken in the first place as concerning the lower sessions, but because all the churches have union and mutual participation, they pertain all the more to the higher sessions.

11. It appears that at least in the Old Testament there was one fixed and ongoing ecclesiastical session or assembly of this sort, a synagogue that was restricted to one nation; and that it was mixed together with the civic session but not also mixed as far as the cases are concerned; although this can be doubted, because the divine law embraced also political affairs, and as a whole was entrusted to the Levites and the priests as the experts in the law and judges, which session Moses had established (Deut 17:9) and Jehoshaphat had reestablished (2 Chron 19). Nevertheless, for cases of God and the king, the presiding officers at that time were clearly distinguished [cf. 2 Chron 19:11]. And so it continued up until the time of Christ, and it was made up of the chief priests, the scribes and the elders of the people (Matt 16:21, 26:3, and 27:59). This general assembly examined the most serious cases (Numb 11:16). Nevertheless, there were times when particular gatherings of the synod took place (1 Chron 13:1–2, and 23:2; Matt 2:4, 5, and 6).

12. But in the New Testament, since the church of Christ does not consist of a single nation but extends into every direction and is spread across all nations, and since the Jewish form of government, being Jewish, is not binding on the nations, and since a separation has been made between the rulers of the republic and the ministers of the church (i.e., a separation of people, session, and cases), Christ ordained not such a general, single, fixed, and ongoing ecclesiastical session, but rather one with respect to incidental matters that should be gathered together in different places. This is seen in the first synod at Jerusalem in the election of Matthias (Acts 1:15), and also at the second one, in the ordination of deacons (Acts 6). And also in the third,

in settling the controversy about observing the Jewish law (Acts 15). That is where the full basis was made for a synod, even a world-wide one, insofar as besides the Jews there were present also delegates of the gentiles; and it is the archetype, the precise precedent by whose shape all the other, subsequent synods ought to be ordained and to which they ought to conform. Lastly, the fourth one is assigned in the case of Paul (Acts 21) who had been charged with desertion from the law.

13. And from that time on this form of session was observed and used frequently in the church of Christ under the cross and under the protection of pious emperors; although under the Frankish, Gothic, and other kings, right up to the time when, while the papal tyranny seized hold of everything, it had regressed to that mixed session, to such a degree that their councils were not only ecclesiastical meetings but also assemblies of the empire.

14. Consequently, the consistory of the pope with his cardinals, which possesses an absolute power of judgment (just as also this entire order of the pope and cardinals), is a human—no indeed—an antichristian invention and institution, which actually overturns the entire notion of councils.

15. In order to give a more precise summary of the entire notion of synods, we should consider in order the persons, the place and time, the synodical matters and actions, and its mode, form, goal, and authority.

16. The persons are the ones who summon the convocation and appoint delegates, or the ones who are called together and have been sent, or the ones who come together at a synod.

17. The right and authority to announce and convoke rests with the church and the members of the church (for whoever does not belong to the church has no right in the church's government) that is to say the ecclesiastical session to which the government of the church is entrusted.

18. And so from the beginning, when some difficult matter arose in the church, especially concerning religion and the violation of it through some false thinking or heresy, the neighboring overseers and elders used to gather together spontaneously under someone's leadership or by mutual exhortation, as the Apostolic Synods at Jerusalem (Acts 15:2, 6 and Acts 21:18) and at Ephesus (Acts 20:17) teach us. And so also during the time of emperor Aurelian the Synod at Antioch, in which Paul of Samosata, the bishop of Antioch, claimed that Christ was entirely human, while the elders

of his church supported him, the neighboring bishops came together in synod, condemned him as an unyielding heretic and removed him from the church (Eusebius, *Ecclesiastical History*, book 7). And so many other synods, especially provincial ones, were convened under Christian rulers. And so it was the responsibility especially of the bishops to announce the synods, but no one possessed this as a private right.

19. Hence, it is in a presumptuous manner and unfairly that the pope of Rome, like some emperor of the church, claims for himself only the privilege and tasks of calling a synod, especially a world-wide one, even though not any special prerogative in this matter was consigned to Peter, whose successor he boasts that he is, but Acts 15:2–6 states that the apostles and the elders gathered together with Paul and Barnabas who had been delegated by the church, and who reported the controversy and deferred it to them so that they might reflect upon this matter.

20. Moreover, it is possible in this matter that the magistrate has his own special duties, if he supports the church and allows it to be public (or by decree appoints it to be such) along with its own whole order and form of government, and that his agreement and sanction are required. For since the magistrate is the keeper and defender of the state and of the good order that has been established in public, and of actions that are public, then he should be deemed also thus as far as the church is concerned. In fact, if such is the practice, then the magistrate can be the one who not only approves the time, place and other circumstances [of the synod], but also the one who appoints it.

21. And this applies so much the more if he is a Christian, orthodox magistrate, that is to say, a leading member of Christ's church and one placed in a high position, to whom (by the calling of this world) falls the jurisdiction, command, and power of outward restraint (which often is needed here); indeed the power to set things in motion for public meetings—a power which he by the law of piety and as the nurturer and guardian of the church (Isa 60:16) is bound to apply in the defense of both tables of the Law, and to the end that Christ may reign spiritually in his subjects (Ps 2:10). Therefore, his agreement, authority, support, and provision of safety ought to be sought here. Moreover, he himself is bound by the duty of piety not to deny those things, but to bestow and furnish them readily and willingly to the church.

22. In fact, the outstanding examples of pious kings in the Old Testament teach us that the higher magistrates (as kings and rulers are) sometimes were the initiators of holding synods, and that these [synods] took place at their command: David (1 Chron 13:1–3), Solomon (2 Chron 5:2), Asa (2 Chron 15:9), Hezekiah (2 Chron 29:4 ff.), Josiah (2 Chron 34:29). And so also Ahab and Jehoshaphat, who called together about four hundred prophets (1 Kgs 22:6–8), and Herod (Matt 2:5). The Christian emperors and kings followed their lead, as they of themselves very often assembled and attended to not only the *oikoumenikai* or world-wide synods (for which there is a special reason), but also, if the public need so demanded it, the *merikai* or particular synods—especially the extraordinary ones. In this way the world-wide Council of Nicaea was announced and convened by Constantine the Great (as referenced by Eusebius, *The Life of Constantine*, book 3), the Council of Constantinople by Theodosius the Elder (Theodoret, book 2, chapter 1.16), the Council at Ephesus by Theodosius the Younger and Valentinian (Cyril, Epistle 17), the Council at Chalcedon by Marcian (Leo, in the Epistle to the Emperor and to Pulcheria Augusta), and so other, even particular councils.

23. And especially if herein it was the ecclesiastical order which failed or acted contrary to its calling; for then the magistrate, as a prominent member of Christ's church, has the authority and the obligation rightly to interpose and seriously to insist on having synods, and to announce them by his own command. And this happened rather frequently, such as when king Joash accused the high priest Jehoiada and the priests of not repairing the breaches in the temple (2 Kgs 12:8).

24. If on the other hand, however, the magistrate is an enemy and persecutor of the church and the true religion, or if he ceases to fulfill his calling, namely when the church clearly is in danger, then the church must nonetheless not fail itself but must exercise the right and power of convocation—a power which in the first place resides among the leaders of the church (as is seen in Acts 15), so that thereby as quickly as possible it may address the evils that are present and pressing, if (and in the manner in which) it can be done.

25. Therefore, it is with the utmost brazenness and despotism that the pope of Rome not only arrogates to himself ahead of the other bishops the right of announcing and convoking a synod, but also he deprives the entire church of it in every way (and in her the emperor, kings, rulers and magistrates). [This is so] especially if the authority, approval, decision and agreement of the

emperor does not precede or accompany it: and accordingly, he takes away any authority whatsoever from the synod.

26. Moreover, just as the convocation rests in the hands of the church, so too does the matter of sending to the synod; and this is in keeping with the order that had been established by and in the church. In this way Paul and Barnabas and the others were delegated and sent by the church at Antioch to the Synod at Jerusalem (Acts 15:2–3).

27. And therefore the private summons, such as is the one of the pope, prejudices the church's liberty most severely.

28. And as for the people who are called, sent, and assembled by public authority, the people who should deal with the things that must be performed here, and who have the right to vote, or the final and—as they say—decisive voice, are first and foremost the people who have been ordained to the offices of the church. In the Old Testament, such people were the priests, scribes and elders of the people (Matt 2:4; 26:3, 59; and 27:1; Acts 4:5); in the New Testament, the overseers, elders, or delegates of the churches (Acts 15:6; 16:4; 20:17; 21:18). For since the church consists of shepherds along with the rest of the body (or sheep), it follows that not only should the shepherds but also the elders and the people's deputies take an interest in it and vote in it—and do that not on their own behalf but on behalf of the church which sent them. And the best subsequent synods maintained that practice (including also the deacons, especially in the lesser synods). The acts of the Synod of Carthage under Cyprian provide proof for that.

29. We should not, however, take this matter so precisely that all lay people are excluded [from attending a synod]. For if from among the laity of whatever status or circumstance there are men distinguished for their piety, their knowledge of sacred things, their wisdom and prudence, modesty, pursuit of peace, and gentleness, they can be invited and come to attend. But this can be done only after the church has called or chosen and sent them, and after they have been asked to state their opinion in the appropriate order and manner, especially in matters of the faith, which belongs to all the people. For in the church God did not ordain gifts and members that are useless. But in this public action what is requested of them is their counsel and opinion rather than their vote. Acts 15:12, 22, and 23 show indeed that the common folk attended the council, and they lent support to the apostles and elders by being listeners and witnesses, and at least with their silence (if not with their

speech) they approved and offered their consent. And it is demonstrated also by the practice and use of the first and proven synods, as is clear in the Carthaginian Council under Cyprian. At the same time, however, also for the people of Christ there remains their own judgment (albeit a private one), based on the Word of God, so that they do not accept as divine what are human opinions (Matt 7:12).

30. Moreover, if he is Christian and orthodox, the magistrate—especially the highest ranking one—has a very special function in this matter. And the council is a matter of concern to him, not only as one who listens, witnesses, and approves like any other Christian, but also as a Christian magistrate, that is, as a defender and protector of the council, and as someone who by his authority guards good order and who holds the common rabble and troublemakers in check, and who sees to it that everything is done honestly and lawfully (1 Tim 2:2). Indeed, he should be consulted, asked to give his opinion, and—if the need should arise—cast his vote. For it is his duty as the defender of the first and second tables of the Law to prohibit utterances of blasphemy, to ensure the church's peace and safety—which cannot be achieved unless first the troubles about the Word of faith are acknowledged and thereupon investigated. And it is his duty to ratify and sanction those things which are decided upon in the synod, by means of laws, and if needed, by means of adding also certain political penalties against those who are stubborn, for the health of the public observance. In this respect, he must also be an expert and judge of the relevant matters, in his own way, and to be able to cast a vote. Or at any rate, he ought to be convinced from the Word of God that the decisions are based on what is true, just, and good, i.e., that he should not be a blind protector and administrator of someone else's opinion and fancy.

31. And so it is a vain fabrication of the papal teachers that ordinarily only the bishops have the right of coming together and the power to vote, but that in extraordinary circumstances (as they call them) the presbyters, abbots, and superiors general of the orders have the right. And moreover that for the academies is reserved only the power of arbitration; that the magistrate can be present only as protector; and that the people and knowledgeable members of the public can be present and appear there—but then only as listeners and spectators.

32. It is necessary that the people who have been called and sent must come in their own person, be present at the synod and remain there until the very end; and also that no-one may easily stay away or depart from it unless old age, an illness, or some other urgency provides him with sufficient excuse, and he has submitted his reasons in writing or in personal statement. And if not, a very severe censure must be carried out on those who stay away and who refuse to come or remain, just as ecclesiastical or synodical censure is carried out on those who despise the church and the synod. Nevertheless, there was a time in the ancient church when also the bishops themselves were represented by others (and that for specific, serious reasons), for example by the elders and deacons. And all of these representatives are bound to present letters noting their dispatch and appointment.

33. And hence, it is contrary to the long-standing canons that since a few centuries—namely, from the time of the Synod of Constance when John XXIV, who was present and fled from the synod, moreover, along with two absent anti-popes, were deposed from the papacy—the pope of Rome continuously withdraws himself from the presence of a world-wide synod, partly because of the fact that he considers himself superior to the synod, and partly out of fear of being forced to submit to the synod's judgment.

34. It is possible, in fact it is very useful for the magistrate (especially if he is of the highest rank) to be present at the synod, whether in his own person (like Constantine the Great at the Nicene, and Theodosius at the Constantinopolitan Synod), or through delegates: Men who are illustrious, noble, serious, desirous of piety, well-versed in the Holy Scripture, men who by their wisdom, prudence, and authority support and assist the council, as was done by the emperors Theodosius and Valentinian at the Ephesian Synod, and by Marcian at the Chalcedonian one.

35. Closely related to the announcement, convocation, and appearance at the synod is the place and the time of assembly. The place should be a suitable one, namely a city that by its location is ideal for those who are coming together, and particularly well-suited for the session, i.e., capacious, holy—although Acts 15 does not give any specifications about this, and the Nicene Synod was held in the palace (witness Eusebius and Theodoret). But Ambrosius correctly asks: "What does the church have in common with the palace?" For this reason long ago the synods very often were held in a church (as Cyril testifies about the Synod of Ephesus), in the center of which the

Holy Gospel was placed on a high throne, to show that Christ was both present and presiding over the synod.

36. In like manner, the time of the gathering should be certain and well-suited. Thus, for the local and particular synods, that is to say, the annual ones, the decree of the Antiochene and Nicene councils determined the spring-time, that is to say, two weeks after Easter, and the fall season, namely the first week in October—although there has been some variation in this, in both the number [of meetings] and the time. Also, the emperors have established this practice through their laws and edicts, like Justinian (*Constitutions* 123). But for an extraordinary particular synod, or for a more general or the world-wide one, the time must be determined specifically, as these are announced in keeping with the urgency of a more important matter that has arisen.

37. And the commencement of the synod, and also during the synod certain times of its gatherings must be observed piously with fasting and abstinence (Lev 10:9–10; Acts 13:1; Tertullian, *On Fasting*).

38. There are costs associated with these synods. The churches should pay the expenses which those who travel to the synod incur, both on their journey and in the place where the synod is being held (Matt 10:10; 1 Cor 9, etc.). Nevertheless, on this point the exceptional generosity of Christian rulers happens frequently, as they willingly have contributed what was needed for accomplishing the synod, as is found in Theodoret, *On Constantine*, in the first book of the *Ecclesiastical Histories*, chapter 7.

39. The matter or object, i.e., the business which is to be conducted in this assembly and which provides the occasion and reason for the synod, is a purely ecclesiastical one. Matters of a political nature is entirely foreign to it (Luke 12:14; 2 Tim 2:4). Political matters obviously, belong to the civic assemblies and not to synods. In fact, [ecclesiastical] matters are of common concern to that entire church, and advance the well-being and safety of the church, for God's glory (Acts 15:1, 5).

40. Well then, the synodical business concerns doctrine, whether true or false (Matt 2:4), its supplements, [namely] the sacraments and the divine rites, the lifestyle and the discipline of the morals of the people as well as their leaders, or lastly the good order of ecclesiastical government. In sum, here must be handled any questions concerning the faith and love, the two things that comprise all the matter of a synod, or whatever pertains to the faith and deeds

of the church, and whatever could not be thoroughly discussed or duly finished in the lower session (Acts 15:24, 29). Hence in former times, besides the exposition and the formulas of the faith, also the canons were subject to the synod, as these are nothing other than the rules which encompass the discipline of morals and good order.

41. The official conduct of the synod, then, consists in treating the issues that have been proposed, and in observing or carrying out the matters that have been decided.

42. In order that the mode of doing business might be orderly and lawful, just as the apostle wills everything in the church to be done decently and in good order (1 Cor 14:40) it is necessary that in councils of this sort someone should preside as the moderator who is mindful of good order, lest the discussion and actions become muddled (1 Cor 14:29, 31). Therefore, conduct that is well-ordered rests in the president and the others seated with him. It is the president's duty in fact to preside over the place, to be in charge of the actions, and to direct the entire business.

43. The task of presiding belongs properly to a man of the church who is established in a position of some eminence. In the Old Testament, in fact, it belonged to the high priest, while in the New it belonged to an overseer or pastor well-suited for presiding, and chosen by a general election. It appears that in this manner James presided over the Jerusalem Synod; the first to speak and state his thinking, however, was Peter, and Barnabas and Paul followed him. But it was James's task to announce the decision (Acts 15:19), and everyone gave him their assent (Acts 15:22 so also Acts 21). At the Nicene Synod, the presider was Eustathius the Antiochene bishop, or rather—as appears from the subscriptions—Hosius, the bishop of Cordoba, in Spain. At the Synod of Constantinople, it was Nectarius, the local bishop; at Ephesus, it was Cyril of Alexandria; at Chalcedon, Leo, bishop of Rome, was president via his vice-bishops (insofar as it may be ascertained from the acts).

44. The same [task of presiding] belongs to the civil magistrate in his own manner, namely insofar as the presidency of the council concerns external government and good order and is understood as its oversight and protection, so that not anything should happen unlawfully and contrary to good public order, or shamefully and insolently, or through force—and if anything should happen, to intervene and check it. And in this manner,

insofar as it guides and protects good order by means of his own authority and removes whatever is contrary, the magistrate can be said to preside over the synod.

45. Therefore, in this matter we do not grant to any bishop the duty of ecclesiastical president by reason of his seat of office, or on account of a privilege that comes with some other distinction—something which the papal teachers nevertheless do claim for their Pontiff. And indeed, a president (which is a term denoting rank) is no greater than the others in power, but he is in rank and authority.

46. The duties of the president, then, are to lead in piously offering prayers, to announce the sessions in a timely manner, honestly to propose the things that must be done and discussed, to moderate the debates wisely, to request the opinions of everyone, to gather the votes attentively, to speak his own mind with a right equal to that of the others, to declare the common decision without prejudice, and to execute it carefully and reliably, or to see to it that it will be carried out.

47. Assessors can be added to the president, and they can appoint scribes or secretaries whose labors may be employed in reliably receiving and recording the acts. This is evidenced in the letter of the Jerusalem Synod, where the general acts are summarized in a concise written record and then sent to the brothers wherever they are (Acts 15:23; 21:25).

48. As for the remaining participants, their sitting ought to be in keeping with the worthiness, merits, and size of the churches which they represent, or in keeping with the high calibre of their talents or the long experience especially that gained in the sacred ministry. And on this point, God's general fifth commandment—"Honor your father"—is in force, which, just as in every other situation so too in this one does have its place. And laying aside selfish ambition and false pretense, one should hold the other in greater esteem and honor (Rom 12:10–11; Phil 2:3–4).

49. For these men, the duties are for each in his turn to speak his mind (Acts 15:7; 12:13; 1 Cor 14:29, 31), not as reflecting his mood (for personal ambition, anger, hatred, favoritism, levity, ill-will, and whatever else is carnal should be absent, Jas 3:12) or his own prejudice and personal taste, but reverently according to God's Word (Acts 15:15). Hence, the votes should not always be counted, but rather weighed in the balance, as the Nicene

Synod consented to Paphnutius when he protested against the law about clerics abstaining from their own wives. And it is also their duty to place their signatures, immediately next to the president's, to the decision that has been carried and the judgment that has been passed, and to approve the acts.

50. Further, with respect to the handling of the business matters, the synod is either deliberative or judicial, or a mixture of the two. It is a deliberative synod when it deals with those things that pertain to the good status of the church, and it deliberates about the means for it or remedies against evil (thus Acts 20:17 and 21:18). And herein, it is the synod's duty to derive from the Word of God the formulation of its decision and agreement, and of the unity of the church in doctrine and discipline, and to establish the arrangement and good order insofar as it is of benefit for the church. And concerning all these matters, it is the synod's duty to publish some public written documents (and they should be brief and clear), and also to alert the people and the pastors to keeping them while subjecting stubborn violators to the church's discipline.

51. A judicial synod takes place when the facts or case of this or that person, especially of a pastor who is causing great offense, trouble or division in the church (i.e., by means of schism, error, heresy, apostasy, and other things) are investigated, and sufficiently and fully known, and when lawful judgment is passed on the basis of the known facts.

52. And on this point, the men whose business and controversies the synod must discuss, whether they are members of clergy or laity, especially men who are the authors of a weightier error or defenders of someone else's (like the brothers who gave occasion to the dispute in the Antiochene church, and those who were noted at the Synod of Jerusalem, as being from the party of the Pharisees, Acts 15:1,5)—these men, I say, must be invited with every honorable reason, warned, and in the end summoned to appear at the synod. And if they should not come, they must be cast out of the church, like the stubborn men by the decree of the third Carthaginian Synod, and they must not be received again until they repent.

53. And if they do appear, they must be granted a courteous hearing on the basis of their writings, their personal statement of confession, and on the basis of the testimonies of other persons. Their doctrine and its status should be determined, then conferred, and if necessary, debated about in a friendly manner; and the arguments and circumstances of the cases should be

examined duly, diligently, and attentively, in good conscience and without any prejudice, according to the rule of God's Word, in such a way that if it can be done, the men themselves would be called back to the way—or at least a correct judgment could be made. In this manner at the Synod of Jerusalem a great enquiry and much debate preceded the declaration of the decision (Acts 15:7). And later, it was not irksome to the fathers to enter into discussion with Paul of Samosata, Arius, and other heretics at synods, even though it was often in vain. But diligent care must be taken lest anyone can justly complain that he was condemned before he was heard.

54. But on this point, at least concerning the doctrines that have been adduced for controversy, we must examine carefully what they are, and how many, and whether they belong to the foundation (or the fundamental things) or in fact to matters adjunct to theology (1 Cor 3)—and if they do belong to matters that are necessary, then to what degree of necessity (Acts 15:28). And moreover [we must examine] whether it is an opinion or an error that can be tolerated (and also whether it comes from a teacher); or, on the other hand, whether it should be refuted and condemned as a doctrine that is not to be tolerated.

55. And concerning the persons who are entering into the controversy [we must examine carefully] whether their opinions are right or wrong; how they are erring (lightly or seriously); whether they have been led astray or are the ones who lead others astray; whether they are students or teachers; members of the laity or pastors. And [whether they err] out of weakness, i.e., simple ignorance, foolish innocence and ready belief, or out of a pretended ignorance and a blind zeal, or even out of malice, with or without stubbornness. And so too concerning the facts and accusations, a thorough investigation should be made into everything in a lawful and discreet manner. And in keeping with this sentiment, each and every person should speak up, and they must pass judgment together as one (Acts 15:22, 25).

56. And as for the verdict, it should be one of acquittal or conviction of the case and also of the person. For either the true and just case is approved and those who think or act rightly are released, or the false and unjust case is condemned and those who think wrongly (and that stubbornly), or who act wrongly and without repenting, on behalf of the church are sentenced as schismatics, heretics, or shameful people (Acts 15:24).

57. However, in case the decision or sentiment is divided, we should maintain a certain restraint about the finer points of religion and about things that are less necessary for salvation, and as much as it is possible, we should reduce rather than enlarge the controversies. In fact, in matters of indifference some things should be endured and tolerated according to the law of love. Thus in Acts 15, at the Apostolic Synod, even though it was against brothers from among the Pharisees who were causing the souls of pious gentiles to waver (namely, by the observation of circumcision and other ceremonies) a decision is made; still, according to the law of love a decree is established about abstaining from what is offered to idols, from blood and what is strangled, and also from fornication, from which things the gentiles are commanded to abstain as being necessary, although not with the same degree of necessity since they did not have the same causes for the necessity. For the prohibition of fornication belongs to God's perpetual will and so also belongs to the law. The other commands have acquired necessity by the prescription of love for a period of time until, with the increase and strengthening of faith, this law would cease. And thus both for faith its purity is protected and also for love its purity is observed by this precept, while help is being provided to the weakness of some others.

58. The conviction of persons, which should be carried out very slowly, consists of suspension and separation, and of excommunication and anathema. The former consist in the prohibition from the sacred rites, in particular the sacraments (Matt 18:7; John 16:2), and besides that in prohibition from the more familiar and non-necessary use of the laws of nature and of God (1 Cor 5:11). Occasionally, it was accompanied by shaking off the dust from one's feet (Matt 10:14–15). But as for the latter, it took place along with the curse which in Hebrew is called 'Schematha' (i.e. 'name'), namely that tetragrammaton of God, and it is called 'Maranatha' by the apostle, that is, "the Lord shall come"—in order to avenge, obviously (1 Cor 16:22; Jude verses 14 and 15). This was carried out only on the most deplorable persons such as apostates.

59. But there is a special censure for people who are in ecclesiastical office: the suspension and removal from office, even without the hope ever of recovering it.

60. The handling and conclusion of matters proposed in synod are followed by the execution of them, and it consists of ensuring that the things which have been decreed are carried out.

61. And at this point a question arises that is not a light one: Who are responsible for that execution? Here a distinction must be made between the powers, the ecclesiastical one and the civil one. The church or the synod does not act or restrain by means of physical force, but only spiritual force: By admonishing the churches in their duty, by removing heretics and shameful people from the communion of the church. But not, as the pope and the papists do in their antichristian manner, by casting the father of the household out of his home, the citizen from his city, and the king from his kingdom.

62. Therefore, to this extent the matter is one of the church, and consequently also of the synod which carries out the decisions either via synodical letters sent to the churches, or through delegates. In this manner the Synod of Jerusalem writes a synodical letter to the church at Antioch and to other churches; and besides Paul and Barnabas, it sends Jude and Silas as delegates to announce verbally the things which the synod had decreed and recorded in writing (Acts 15:22 and 30; 16:4. and 21:25).

63. The execution belongs also to the other power, namely the civic one, since it consists in outward coercion, such as it is and in keeping with its appointment. For because it is the guardian of both tables of the Law and so has the duty to prohibit blasphemous opinions, and since it is the defender of the church and of good public order, it ought—because it is a member of the church—to obey the synod. But it also ought to ratify the synod's just decrees in accordance with the Word of God, and to enact them by means of laws and penalties (if it is necessary), insofar as it befits the spiritual kingdom of Christ, for the well-being of public observance, and also to check shameful heretics. In this manner, Aurelian, although he was a gentile, ordered the deposed Paul of Samosata to be driven from his bishop's dwelling when he was not willing to leave it; Constantine ordered the banishment of Arius, Theodosius the Younger of Nestorius, etc., who had been condemned in synods.

64. But on this point, we should diligently remind the civic power not to exercise its authority and power too easily in matters that the church has not examined and adjudicated lawfully before. The civic power is not excluded

from both this examination and adjudication as if it is entirely foreign to it. But [the civic authority] is contained in and under the church as its leading member and part, as we have shown previously. It is so far from having to be only a blind performer of another party's decision, that the pope of Rome committed an intolerable crime when he made every effort to lead magistrates, rulers, kings, and emperor to that point.

65. But on this point, we must guard against the use of a means or remedy that is not sufficiently suitable for eradicating the diseases of soul and mind which have been caught by wrong opinions (as these are cured only by putting the truth over against them)—that is to say, with an overly-strict outward severity that is entirely unbefitting to the kingdom of Christ, as that does not heal people but turns them into hypocrites. Nevertheless, we must absolutely keep in check the offense, sedition, and disturbance of the peace that are public, and we also must prevent, insofar as that can be done, private individuals from being led astray and overthrown.

66. But this entire involvement of the civil power in the affairs of the church at the synods which we have recounted thus far does not disturb the good order in the church, as though in this way it intrudes upon the office of someone else and not one's own. For indeed, good order demands that these functions are distinct; but distinction does not conflict with collaboration, and nothing blocks those who are in charge of different offices from together taking care of many tasks in a common endeavour and rolling one boulder— in fact occasionally entering into the other's domain when the need is present and urgent.

67. But with respect to the judge and norm of every act and the decision for it, the judge here indeed is Christ, but through his servants whom he has brought together at the synod in a spirit of unity. It is their task to consider ecclesiastical business, and after the debate has been held to speak their opinion in an orderly fashion (Acts 15:6–7), thus, also finally to make a conclusion and to pass judgment. Acts 15:22: "The apostles, together with the elders of the church, decided." And verse 25: "And so we, having come together in harmony, made a decision." And verse 28: "It seemed good to the Holy Spirit and to us"—not jointly, of course, but subordinately under the leadership of the Holy Spirit. And obviously just as the individual judgment belongs to each and every believer and member of the church (Matt 7:15; 1 Cor 2:15; 1 John 2:20, 27 and 4:1), so too does the communal

judgment belong to the shepherds who are gathered at synod. And that is the judgment of God, of Christ, and of the Holy Spirit, if and insofar as it is ordained and brought about by the norm of God's Word. Ordained and done in such a manner, the judgment is ratified by God.

68. The norm and rule for this synodical act and decision should be entirely, uniquely and irrevocably the Word of God, contained in Scripture (Matt 2:5; Acts 15:14), which by its own evidence can also be called the judge (John 5:45). And it grants form to a lawful and holy synod, so that it is of God. But apart from this Word, the writings and sayings of whatever sort, whether private or public, are not the norm or form of truth, but only the formula of the sentiment and consensus of the church.

69. The mode of this judgment ought to be such that everywhere faith and the pursuit of truth shine forth, and that love prevails and rules supreme. And its end is in the removal of scandal and the upbuilding of the church, to the glory of God.

70. And from this it is clear what and how great the authority of the synods is, namely, one of ministry (in fact, that is the authority of the church); that is, in a certain respect, in its own way and small measure, the authority is divine. But we should not place such confidence in any and all synods indiscriminately and loosely. For also shepherds can be misleading shepherds (Isa 56:10; Jer 16:14 [12:10 or 23:2]; Ezek 22:25), and at a synod the church can be a gathering not of God but of malicious people (even when it holds forth God's name) and can misuse its own power against the truth (Matt 26:3–4, 57 and 27:1; Acts 5:5 etc.). And it can be a gathering precisely of the true church, which (and to such extent that it) is gathered in the name of Christ, according to that statement in Matt 18 [20]: "Where two or three are gathered in my name, in their midst am I." And it follows the guidance of the Holy Spirit: "It seemed good to the Holy Spirit and to us" (Acts 15[:28]).

71. But there is not an equal relation between the apostolic synod and the other ones. For the authority of that one is purely divine because of the direct and continuous assistance of the Holy Spirit (Acts 2:4). But not so the authority of these other ones, at least in some respect, since these are synods of men who are certainly pious and also guided by the Holy Spirit, but only to the degree that it does not protect them against every error. For they can be ruled by the Holy Spirit in such a way that the desire of the flesh comes over them and they experience something after the manner of mortal men

and accordingly in some matters deviate from the truth. And so, we see that not only the particular synods but also the world-wide ones have gone astray.

72. Therefore, the synods are divine insofar as they are brought together in the name of Christ, and insofar as they decide something in harmony with the Word of God as Scripture expresses it (and not as they determine). And they have only as much authority as they borrow and receive from Scripture, as the moon does from the sun. Consequently, it is so far from being the case that they themselves are the norm of faith, that they should be judged according to it.

73. The pope's approval adds nothing to the authority of these councils, nor does his rejection remove anything from it. Indeed, he himself, whenever the reform of the church is treated, from its head to its members, is subject to the synod. This is stated also to Peter, whose successor the pope claims to be: "Tell it to the church" (Matt 18:17). And thus, the church at the Councils of Pisa, Constance, and Basel always unanimously has maintained and defended in face of the power over the synod which the pope has appropriated unlawfully for himself.

74. From all these observations, one can see what here we should think about the pope of Rome who does not leave any duties for others when he appropriates for himself all the tasks of a synod, namely: 1. Of the one who announces it; 2. Of its president; 3. Of its adjudicator; 4. And finally of the one who approves it. In fact, in his antichristian haughtiness and encroachment he makes himself superior to the council. And also, what we should think of the councils that were held since some centuries ago under the popes, namely that they were neither legitimately called nor rightly held.

SOURCES

Theodoret, book 1, chapter 6
At the Nicene Council Constantine, the Great addresses the fathers: the books of the evangelists and the apostles, and the oracles of the ancient prophets teach us clearly what we ought to ask of God. Therefore, laying aside dissension, which is the cause of discords and conflicts, we shall receive from the divinely inspired Word the answers to the questions which are posed.

Emperor Justinian, *New Constitutions* [1]37 c. 4

Since, moreover, what is laid down in the canons concerning the synods of the most holy bishops which are to be held in each province has until now not been observed, it is necessary to correct this first and foremost. The holy apostles and fathers, then, have decreed that in each province synods of the most holy priests should be held twice in each and every year, and that matters which arise should be examined and receive suitable correction; that is, they set the meeting of one synod on the fourth day in the holy week of Pentecost, and the second in the month of October, etc.

Augustine, *Epistle* 118 to Januarius

The authority of the plenary councils is very salutary for the church.

Gregory, book 9. *Epist. 110* to Syagrius, etc

And in this part of our care, we also should not neglect what for the sake of usefulness the fathers in their thoughtfulness prescribed for the holding of councils in the parishes. Therefore, it is necessary for the priests to convene as one, lest there be any discord among the brothers or any kindling of disharmony between the leaders and their subjects, in order to discuss cases which arise, and to have a sound comparison of ecclesiastical observances, insofar as through this practices from the past are corrected and also the practices in the future receive regulation, and the almighty Lord be praised by the harmony of the brothers. And you should know that his presence is there for you, if you observe this, because it is written: "Where two or three are gathered in my name, there I am in the midst of them." If then, God deigns to be present where there are two or three, how much more will he be not absent where more priests are convened, etc.

ON THE CIVIL MAGISTRATE

President: Johannes Polyander
Respondent: Michael van Gogh

There are several forms of political governance (e.g., monarchy, aristocracy, and democracy, 4–12). God uses them all, so none of them in itself is better or worse than another, and every form is in some way present in the others (13–14). Civil government is appointed by God 'to govern the society…by fair divine and human laws,' and is 'armed with the sword to protect those who are good, to punish the wicked, and to keep the enemy in check, for the preservation of outward discipline and public peace' (15). God is the author of every magistrate (16), so the political office is in itself good (17). Even an unbelieving and wicked magistrate should be tolerated (18). However, lower authorities may rebel against higher ones (19). Government has authority over all people, none excepted, not even clerics (20–28). There is only one exception, which is when something is commanded that is contrary to God's Word and conscience (28). God bestows the magistrate with lawful authority to exercise judgment and justice among his citizens, with legal and military skills (29–39). In the remainder of the disputation (40–65) it is stressed that civil authorities, both as members and as supporters and protectors of the church, have the duty to guard the well-being of true religion, to confront false teachers, and to reform corrupted worship. The different responsibilities of civil and ecclesiastical administration are explained in detail. Much attention is paid to the question of whether the government is authorized to put to death persistent heretics. Compelled 'conversion' is never to be considered. 'For faith wishes to be convinced, not forced, and nothing ought to be so volitional as the inward religion and worship of God, nothing ought to be so foreign to the Christian magistrate as perverse and ill-timed severity whereby he turns people into hypocrites, and forces them to profess with the mouth what they do not believe with the heart' (59).

1. The public administration of the offices ordained by the almighty God is either ecclesiastical or political. Since the former was treated above, the order we have established demands that in this place we deal also with the latter.

2. The political administration of affairs is that which the magistrate exercises in the republic over every sort of citizen whom God wills to be subject to him in some manner.

3. For God alone possesses the highest, absolute rule over human creatures, but the magistrate has a subordinate and conditional rule, namely to the extent that as God's servant he governs subjects committed to his trust and care in accordance with the prescript of God's law and of right reason inscribed upon the hearts of all people (Rom 13:4).

4. This governance by the magistrate is either uniform (or simple) or multiform (or composite).

5. Uniform governance is that which exists by the rule of one or more persons, whether they are noblemen or commoners. The former of these is called a monarchy, the latter aristocracy and democracy.

6. It is a monarchy when the greatest power to rule resides with a single person who looks to the common benefit of human society, whether in a simple republic or city, or in some duchy or kingdom made up of many cities.

7. We have an example of each type of monarchy in the Old Testament. [An example of] the former are the kings of the cities of Sodom, Gomorrah, Admah, Zeboiim, and Bela (Gen 14:2). [Examples of] the latter are Saul, David, Solomon and the other kings who in days of old held the twelve tribes of the Israelite people under their rule.

8. For both types of monarchy, and especially in the latter, the best way is to add to the highest magistrate lower and intermediate ones who under him as his officers were to govern the republic throughout the regions entrusted to them, as is evident from Jethro's advice (Exod 18:21) and from God's command (Num 11:16).

9. Both types of monarchy decline into tyranny if they are arranged for the personal benefit of a single person. For as a king or leader considers the good of his citizens, so a tyrant considers only his own advantage, and he acquires that for himself from the misfortunes of his own citizens.

10. An aristocracy is a polyarchy wherein some noblemen, i.e., the citizens who especially stand out for their worthiness and contributions to the republic, control the magistracy, and who devote it to the common good. Such was the governance of the Jewish people under the judges in days of old. But when aristocracy is twisted for the benefit and domination of a few people, and the wealthy among them, then it is called an oligarchy.

11. Democracy is a polyarchy wherein the more powerful part of the citizens (even of the commoners) administers the republic in accordance with the votes, gathered tribe by tribe, of the entire populace. In Jewish polity there was some government of this sort, when by the vote of the entire Israelite people decisions were made about war against the Benjamites, and about electing a king to replace Samuel (Judg 20 and 21, 1 Sam 10:12). If this sort of government is changed for the profit of only the common folk, then it deteriorates into anarchy and unrestrained license.

12. A multiform government is one that has been constituted not from a separation in the above-mentioned forms for governing a republic, but from a combination or mixture of them. One observes an example of this in some provinces in which there are two types of government, namely, orders of noblemen and of cities all of whom together possess the power in the republic.

13. One ought not rashly and insistently argue which of those forms of political government is more outstanding, since God in his own private reasoning first appointed Moses and Joshua as his delegates to be leaders of his people, and to these He added a few counsellors, as we have stated in thesis 8. And thereafter He introduced judges and noblemen of Israel in their place; and lastly through king Saul He reduced the Israelites to a state of monarchy.

14. There is the added fact that in his marvelous providence God so mingles in due proportion each and every form of political government that of them the one can be seen as present in the others. For even though the first form of government, monarchy, is so called for the one person who is foremost in it, and the second and third derive the name of polyarchy from the many men who rule the republic, nevertheless just as in a monarchy there is one man who predominates over all the others, so also in a properly established aristocracy and democracy there exists a good order of such a sort that some single person is foremost—at least in rank and in casting his vote—and the

singlemindedness among the majority in number is so great that they altogether are deemed to occupy the position of a single governor. And contrariwise, just as there is something aristocratic in the assemblies of a kingdom which lesser magistrates attend, so too something democratic is seen in the meetings of the noblemen, wherein the cities reserve for themselves the right to vote through men whom they also have delegated.

15. Therefore, the magistrate, whatever the state of the republic, is a person whom God has appointed to govern the society of all manner of people whatsoever by fair divine and human laws. And he is armed with the sword to protect those who are good, to punish the wicked, and to keep the enemy in check, for the preservation of outward discipline and public peace (Rom 13:1 and following).

16. It can be demonstrated from the following testimonies of holy Scripture that God is the principal efficient cause, or author, of every magistrate whatsoever. Deut 1:17: "In judging do not respect the person, for judgment belongs to God himself"—that is, God himself has set up judgment for you, to practice it according to his law. And Ps 82:1: "God takes his stand in the assembly, and He judges among the gods"—that is, among the magistrates who as his vice-regents are representatives of his divine majesty and authority in administering what is right. With a view to this God's own Wisdom, or the Son of God, says in Prov 8:15: "It is through Me that kings reign and rulers determine what is just." And king Jehoshaphat says to the judges of his people in 2 Chron 19:6: "You are not practising the justice of man, but of Jehovah." And also the apostle Paul, in Rom 13:1: "There is no authority except from God, and the authorities that exist have been established by God. Consequently, whoever opposes himself to authority is resisting what God has ordained." To these over-arching authorities God sometimes calls men in an extraordinary manner, either immediately, as Moses [Exod 3:10], Gideon [Judg 6:14–16], and Samson [Judg 13:5, 25], or mediately, as David through Samuel [1 Sam 16:13]. Sometimes He calls them in an ordinary manner, whether by order of the highest magistrate and the right of hereditary succession, as He called Solomon by David's order (1 Kgs 1:32), or by means of election, by employing the lot—as He called Saul [1 Sam 10:20–21]—or by another rite in accordance with the common consent of all the people, in keeping with the nature and custom of each and every kingdom.

17. And concerning this matter the Anabaptists err when they reckon the function of magistrate among things that are wicked and unlawful in and of themselves, and when they think that even though he is a believer he should be denied a place in the Christian church. For the political office, which the entire Scripture of both Testaments attributes to ordination by God, is in itself good for all time, and therefore our churches should approve of it no less than the apostolic church did. The following people have been admitted to this office: Nicodemus (John 3:2), the ruler (John 4:53), Joseph of Arimathea (John 19:38), the centurion Cornelius (Acts 10:34), the proconsul Sergius Paulus (Acts 13:12), and other magistrates who believed in Christ, men in whom began to be fulfilled what Isaiah once had prophesied about the magistrates of the catholic Christian church in chapter 49:23. And also in chapter 60:2–3: "Jehovah shall arise upon you, and his glory shall appear over you, so that the nations will come to your light and kings to the brightness of your rising." Hence David, moved by a spirit of prophecy, exhorts those kings to kiss the Son of God (Ps 2:12).

18. Moreover, they also err who think that God's people should not tolerate an unbelieving and wicked magistrate. For we should make a distinction between the authority of the magistrate, which derives from God himself, and the unbelief that exists in the magistrate's evil heart—like good order from disorder, or an office from the vice that fastens upon it. And in no way whatsoever should it be a cause for prejudice or offense against an ordination of God which in and of itself is good. Instead, on this point we should take repose in the providence of God, who sometimes uses wicked and criminal men to govern the republic, in order through them to set right the sins of his own people. Accordingly, the apostle Peter teaches that it is for the sake of God that we must obey the magistrates, even pagan ones (1 Pet 2:13). And Paul [that we must obey] for the sake of conscience (Rom 13:5), lest by their rebellion against the magistrates people should bring condemnation upon themselves (Rom 13:2).

19. But from rebellion of this sort the lesser magistrates are exempt, because they are rebelling against the highest magistrate (whom they, on behalf of the entire social order, have chosen in collegial fashion and endowed with only limited power) for the fact that by his own wicked perjury he is violating what God has ordained and what he has confirmed by his solemn oath, and both obstinately and cruelly is despoiling the political classes and the republic of their privileges to which he had sworn allegiance before they had set him up

as ruler. The power to ordain him resided with them by this rule: that if he should rule justly and according to their laws, then they would use the sword in support of him; but if he should rule unjustly and contrary to their laws, then they would use the sword against him. For they themselves in no way whatsoever can (nor should) neglect or expose to violent seizure this right to preserve their own freedom as well as that of the fatherland, which lawfully has been entrusted to them by their predecessors and approved by the ruler who was to be chosen.

20. The material or personal object with which the function of the magistrate concerns itself is every person (whom the apostle by synecdoche calls 'every soul,' Rom 13:1) of whatever condition he may be, whether he is a citizen of church or state. Chrysostom rightly understood this when he explained that passage of the apostle as follows: "The apostle shows that those commands are for everyone, also for the priests and monks and not only laypersons—even if he is an apostle, or evangelist, or prophet, or anyone else; nor does subjection of that sort destroy piety." So also, Bernard, when he addresses the clerics of his own age thus: "Every soul should be subject to the higher authorities; if anyone endeavors to make an exception, he is trying to deceive. If 'every' soul, then also your soul. Who has made you an exception to the whole?"

21. Therefore, the experts in canon law and the other papal teachers err who state that clerics are entirely and unconditionally exempt from the yoke of the political magistrate, and who think that their statement is based in divine right. For it is with a view to the divine right that the apostle exhorts every soul (Rom 13:1) to subject itself to civil authorities and obey them. And therefore either every Roman cleric lacks a rational soul, or, if he is endowed with one, he is included in the number of those whom the apostle in writing to the Romans designates, by way of synecdoche, 'every soul.'

22. We know, of course, that some papal teachers interpret the word 'soul' used by the apostle as the natural man, i.e., laic. But besides the fact that this interpretation does not rest on any testimony in holy Scripture, and is even completely contrary to the Hebraism used by the men of God whereby 'soul' stands for 'man,' it is clear from chapters 12 and 16 of the same letter to the Romans that with the phrase 'every soul' [Paul] means all the saints who were living at Rome, while he [calls] by name the men and women who ministered,

and in the list of names, he puts Urbanus, his co-worker in Christ, Tryphaena, Tryphosa, and Persis, who worked hard in the Lord.

23. And surely, by as much as those people who are Christian have a calling that is more holy and devout, by so much should they keep God's law about showing obedience to the magistrates, since Christ, who was set apart from every sin, did not diminish their rule (Matt 17:27; John 19:11), nor did the priests, prophets and apostles of God's early church, who were consecrated in a special manner. And to that I add the fact that the apostle Peter, whose successor the Roman pope proudly claims to be, exhorts all persons God has chosen for sanctification of the Spirit (among whom the pope's clerics wish to be counted) to subject themselves not only to the highest but also to the lower magistrates (1 Pet 2:13[–14]).

24. The fact that in the passages quoted above the two apostles Peter and Paul are discussing only civil authority, is clear from the epithet 'human institution' Peter uses to distinguish political administration from the ecclesiastical one, and from the sword whereby, Paul states, God has equipped the political magistrate as keeper and avenger of peace (Rom 13:4).

25. Therefore, clerics wrongly overturn this divinely ordained political order by exempting themselves from the authority of the magistrate; and the Roman bishops, too, make unlawful seizure when they transfer to themselves the right of secular leaders; and so also the pope, who subjects even the highest monarchs to his own rule, nor allows them to draw the temporal sword against anyone without his own permission. And yet he nonetheless calls himself the vice-regent of Christ, who put matters of temporal concern away from himself and placed them upon the civil magistrate (Luke 12:14; John 8:11), and [the pope] calls himself the successor of Peter, to whom—no less than to the other disciples—Christ said: "You know that the rulers of the gentiles lord it over them, and their great men exercise authority over them. But it shall not be so among you, but whoever wishes to be great among you must become your servant, just as the Son of man did not come in order to be served by you but in order to serve" (Matt 20:25[–28]).

26. The papal teachers impiously despise that same political institution when they call kings and civil rulers not sacred (Bellarminus, *On the Exemption of the Clergy*, chapter 2), men whom holy Scripture calls 'the Lord's anointed,' 'gods,' 'sons of God,' and 'those who foster the church' (Ps 18:51 and 82:6; Isa 49:23).

27. And they behave even like cut-throats—not like theologians—when they ascribe to God's church the power to depose unbelieving magistrates, and to remove from them not only their reign but even their life. For the law of grace which God has revealed to his church does not take away the law of nature and nations whereupon the magistrate's authority rests, but it establishes and perfects it. For this reason, just as the evangelical doctrine does not annul the marriage contract of unbelievers, which—as equally as the marriage contract of believers—belongs to the law of nations and nature, but only distinguishes the one from the other, so also with the help of the same doctrine can the unbelieving magistrate be distinguished from the believing one, but he never can be abolished by those who are subject to the unbelieving magistrate, as he has been instituted by divine ordination. And for that reason, they are bound to pour out to God even their prayers for his safety, according to the apostle's admonition in 1 Tim 2:1, and by the example of the early church which always tolerated the rule of Julian the Apostate.

28. At the same time we should distinguish the authority of the unbelieving magistrate over his subjects on the grounds of the different nature and character of the things. For if the things which he commands pertain to one's conscience and diametrically oppose God's Word, then in no way at all should we obey his unholy and unfair orders, because as Peter once replied to a magistrate of this kind: "It is necessary to obey God rather than men" (Acts 5:29). But if those things concern only matters of the bodily sort, or things beneficial for this life and to the outward state and good order of the republic and human society, then in those things we should obey him for the sake of keeping the peace and calm among the citizens.

29. The form of the magistrate finds its place in the lawful authority bestowed upon him by God, whereby he executes each and every part of his office. For it is this which—like a soul—breathes life into his function, and gives it the efficacy whereby he rightly exercises judgment and justice among his citizens.

30. For the correct administration of judgment and justice he has need of two skills, namely legal and military.

31. Legal skill is that whereby the magistrate prudently conducts what in times of peace is most fitting, and skillfully directs it for the common good, to keep peace and calm in the republic.

32. Military skill is that whereby the magistrate forcefully and exceptionally well does what is fitting in times of war, in order to restore the lost common good, to defend religion, to drive out unjust force, and to assert the right of freedom.

33. Both skills are required of the magistrate: the former, to be cherished by those who do good and to be bestowed with due honor; the latter, to be feared by those who are wicked [Rom 13:3].

34. And if the magistrate is endowed with these two skills, he shall carefully see to it that: 1) he does not accept judges, counsellors, chief officers, and generals of war whose consciences are wicked, but makes use of the advice and labors of men of proven faith and integrity. 2) he does not lend an ear to informers, flatterers, enemies, and disturbers of the public order, but drives them out. 3) if he must exact punishment from either insolent or disloyal subjects, or protect himself against wicked enemies, he does not yield to his natural desires but is led only by his zeal for his calling.

35. For the ancient magistrates under the Old Testament God has prescribed laws for both the military and the legal skills, sometimes after having been consulted and asked by them (as is seen in Judg 1:1, 20:18, 28; 1 Sam 23:2 and 30:8; and 2 Sam 5:19), and sometimes without being asked (as one reads in Num 31:1; Deut 13:12). In addition, God from heaven has blessed judges and kings who waged war according to his laws, as king David realized (Ps 18:36 and 144:1), and Solomon (Prov 12:21). In Heb 11:33 also the saints under the Old Testament are said to have defeated kingdoms by faith in God, and consequently their battles pleased God. For just as what is not done by faith is sin and displeases God [Rom 14:23], so on the other hand what is done by faith is in agreement with God's word and is accepted by him.

36. Moreover, what God in the Old Testament both prior to the law of Moses, according to the law of nations, and under the Law from the authority divinely granted to the magistrates, considered binding and pleasing to him, cannot be displeasing to him in times under the Gospel. For the Gospel does not abolish the law of nations, nor the political [laws], nor the laws of war which are needed to preserve human society.

37. And so the Anabaptists and Socinians are rambling mindlessly when they say that war is not divinely permitted even to the Christian magistrate. For they do not take into consideration the fact that neither John the Baptist, nor

Christ, nor the apostles advised the centurions and soldiers, who were seeking from them the knowledge of salvation and professing their faith in Christ, to throw away their weapons but to be content with their wages (Matt 8; Luke 3; Acts 10). We should add the example of the apostle Paul, who when a plot of some Jews against him was discovered, using the protection and defense of the tribune of the Romans against those Jews, demonstrated by this action that any magistrate whatsoever can, by divine right, make use of the sword for the protection of good people (Acts 23:21).

38. The same apostle, in appealing to Caesar and in replying to Festus that he ought to be judged at the tribunal of Caesar (Acts 25:10[–11]) meant that the judgment of magistrate over those charged with a crime belongs to the divine and also common laws, and therefore is permitted also under the Gospel. For he never would have said that something ought to be done which opposes divine law or perpetual law. The same apostle warns the Romans (Rom 13:4) that the magistrate can lawfully and deservedly strike with the sword those who are charged with a crime. With this statement the Socinians' axiom falls down completely, that the doctrine of the Gospel does not allow to Christians that a man can deprive another man of life. For their axiom can be refuted with Christ's statement in Matt 26:52: "Whoever takes up the sword shall perish by the sword." Christ calls upon an old penal clause in the divine law to show that it belongs to the ancient and perpetual law, i.e., the clause in Gen 9:6: "Whoever sheds a man's blood"—in private and non-regulated vengeance—"by man shall his blood be shed," namely, by public and regulated vengeance. The Socinians mix this up with private and non-regulated vengeance, and from the places where the former is prohibited (namely Matt 5:39 and Rom 12:17, 19) they incorrectly derive the prohibition of the latter, too.

39. The necessary skill of the magistrate in times of war as well as of peace is either universal or particular. The universal skill is the one that has the power to establish civil laws, and to adorn the civil community with good morals. The particular one is that which is busy with settling particular cases and actions. And this skill is either consultative and in the consultation of particular actions that must be taken, or it is adjudicatory, and concerns the handling of an action by those who have been consulted.

40. The two skills of the magistrate consist of the following duties. First, that the civil laws which he has established are in manifest agreement with the

universal law of nature and with the recorded moral law. Secondly, by means of ecclesiastical administration, rightly to establish the worship of God according to the norm of his law, in the region over which he presides, to keep pure and sound the worship that has been determined by ecclesiastical decision, or to reform it if it has become corrupt or wicked; and, as far as he is able, to go against all those who mislead the people, and heterodox teachers who block the way of progress of true religion.

41. In order to take heed to all of these things, the magistrate must know what is the true Christian faith whereby God's churches should be built up or reformed, so that in a matter of such great import he does not undertake or decide something on the basis of only the judgment or decision of others, but only on the basis of his own firm knowledge and solid faith.

42. All of these things were heeded by the saintly men, even in their capacity as leaders in the Israelite republic, like Moses who instituted the sacred religion in accordance with God's law (Exod 19:20), and Joshua, Moses's successor, who in his civil constitution promulgated God's law (Josh 5) and renewed God's covenant with the Israelite people (Josh 24). And after the entry into the promised land, by God's special command he restored the practice of circumcision which had been stopped and celebrated the Passover in its appointed time [Josh 5:1–12]. Upon entering further into the land of Canaan he carved the Ten Commandments upon the stone tablets [Josh 8:32], and when he was about to die he exhorted all the magistrates not to turn to the right or to the left from the prescript of God's law [Josh 23:6].

43. Those who followed the example set by these men were the judges of Israel: Gideon, who after the death of Joshua destroyed the altar of Baal (Judg 6), and Samuel, who exhorted the people to repair the corrupted religion, and who commenced the repair [1 Sam 7]. And also the kings, such as David, who like Samuel, as a man of God, together with Gad and Nathan assigned to the Levites their posts and ecclesiastical duties (1 Chron 9 and 23). And so, as king of the people, he ordered the ark of God to be brought to his own city, and he made the other preparations necessary for building the temple [2 Sam 6; 1 Chron 13, 15, 16, and 22]. Solomon, who had dedicated the house of the Lord, celebrated the feast of booths, and made sacrificial offerings to God on the altar which he had built (2 Chron 8). Asa, who removed from his kingdom all the filthy gods which his ancestors had set up (1 Kgs 15). Jehoshaphat, who destroyed also all the idols, and paid special attention to

restoring the true worship of God (1 Kgs 22; 2 Chron 23). Joash, who reminded the priests who were being negligent in their care of the temple building of their duties and punished them (2 Kgs 12; 2 Chron 24). Hezekiah, who as diligently as possible cleansed God's temple of every superstition, restored the pure worship which had fallen away under his fathers, announced the Passover to the Jews, and made provisions of food for the Levites (2 Kgs 19; 2 Chron 29). Josiah, Hezekiah's grandson, who very faithfully restored the worship of God which had been adulterated under Manasseh and Amon, and who punished the workers of idolatry. Some of the Christian rulers have followed in their footsteps, namely Constantine the Great, who was the first to make the churches available for the Christians, and Theodosius, who closed the temples of the heathens and ordered that throughout his whole empire only the Christian religion be practiced. And also other kings, rulers and magistrates who reformed their regions from the leaven of ungodliness and superstition—in our own times no less than in the times of our ancestors.

44. In order to be informed about sacred religion, the believing magistrate should employ the ministers of the divine Word as if they were his eyes; he should determine fair stipends for them; safeguard their meetings (both consistorial and synodical); preserve in these meetings the external good order and on occasion, when a serious matter demands it, he should be present, following the example set by Constantine the Great, who ordered that the case of Arius be examined first in the lawful Synod of Nicaea while he himself was in attendance, in order that he might come to understand the entire matter as it arose from the unanimous votes of the bishops who represented the church, in accordance with the norm of sacred Scripture.

45. The administration of civil affairs is connected to the ecclesiastical one by three shared elements. The first is that each, with respect to God, is a service and ministry subordinate to the highest rule of God (Ps 2:11; Rom 13:4; 1 Cor 3:5 and 4:1). Second, that by virtue of their ministries the magistrate and the shepherds are guardians of God's law (Deut 17:18; Isa 49:23; Mal 2:7; 2 Cor 5:18 and 12:20; 2 Tim 2:2). Third, because of that ministry which they carry out according to God's prescript, they should be shown the honor that is owed to them, in keeping with the accordant calling (Rom 13:6–7; 1 Tim 5:17; Heb 13:7).

46. On the other hand, the two administrations are distinguished by their difference, both insofar as it concerns the guardianship of God's Word and of discipline (which are the two parts of divine law), and insofar as it concerns a disproportionate sharing of honor that is owed to them. In the guardianship of God's Word the political authority should be distinguished from ecclesiastical ministry by six differences. The first is that in setting forth God's Word the pastors should speak, and interpret; but the magistrates should listen and be informed, for the same reason that the centurion Cornelius and Sergius the proconsul were instructed, the former of them by Peter and the latter by Paul (Matt 28:19–20; Ps 2:10; Acts 10:32; Acts 13:7). The second is that in carrying out their ministry the shepherds and elders in the name of Christ are declaring especially and specifically to the inward person the rewards and punishments that are spiritual; but the magistrates furnish the outward man with physical goods or punishments (Matt 18:17–18; John 20:22–23; 1 Tim 1:20; Rom 13:3–4). Third, that ministers of the Word are responsible for the bare proceedings of the law and the execution of only those rewards and punishments which are contained in God's expressed Word; but the civil authority has the sanction and execution by way of arbitration over the corporeal rewards and punishments, in keeping with the variety of circumstances that occur in practising it—in such a way, however, that the sanction belongs to that authority which possesses the highest execution of things, i.e., the authority of the king or ruler in a monarchy, and of noblemen in an aristocracy (Deut 4:2; 1 Cor 1:23; Gal 1:8; Rev 22:18–19; Matt 20:15; John 19:11; Rom 13:4). Fourth is that the elders of the church do not prescribe anything except by the command of another, namely, of Christ, but the magistrates prescribe some things also by their own command. For ecclesiastical governance is entirely *hyperetike*, or ministerial. But political governance, even though it is administrative with respect to God, is equipped with command and authority. The fifth is that elders by means of spiritual weapons, i.e., warnings, threats of divine wrath, and excommunication lead people to repent and win them over to Christ. But the magistrates, when necessity requires it, use punishment, imprisonment, and the sword to compel them and to keep them in check. Sixth, that shepherds have responsibility when it concerns the conscience, but magistrates when the discussion concerns the body.

47. To these things which regard the discipline of the church we should attach three other differences. The first of these is the fact that strictly speaking the

right to determine ecclesiastical discipline belongs to the shepherds together with their consistory, from the analogy of faith and sacred doctrine; but the magistrate who possesses the highest authority of command can either in person approve that discipline, or in his absence examine it, and if anything in it is rightly to be desired he can demand from the shepherds that it be either supplied or emended from the analogy of God's Word. The second is that the ministers of the Word, together with their consistory must consecrate Christ's servants who have been approved both by a civil magistrate—if he professes the same religion—and by his church. The magistrate, however, can make use of his own intervention and also his own authority in order to bestow his services upon the church, to halt corrupt practices or to set them straight if anything worthy of civil attention should arise. Third, that in the church at peace the shepherds should, with the approval of the civil authority, be present together with the consistory at ecclesiastical meetings which the magistrate has announced, and in them to consider the doctrine and moral conduct of the church. But in a church that is troubled and struggling with schisms the magistrate has the power—with the approval of the church, if that is possible—to call the most devout and wise theologians to the synod and also to attend their meetings. And if there is an urgent need, [he has the power] to preside over them as far as the outward handling and direction is concerned, according to the precedent set by Constantine the Great, mentioned above.

48. The honor that is owed to both functions is not of equal weight. For just as the ministers of the Word do not have their authority by any command of their own, so also they ought not to lord it over the consciences of people to whom they administer God's Word (1 Pet 5:2). But it is to the civil authority that God has granted the command over the bodies and goods of their subjects (Rom 13:4). Moreover, since ecclesiastical dignity is more like the authority of a father than that of a king, so it should be honored only by reverence, a willingness to learn, and financial contributions. But the civil authority, which is bound up with its command and majesty, ought to be honored by its subjects not only with obedience and submission, but also with the payment of taxes, according to the example of Christ in Matt 17:27, and his command: "Give to Caesar what is Caesar's" (Matt 22:21).

49. The greatest possible harmony should be fostered between the two administrations, i.e., the political and the ecclesiastical one, so that each may be supported by the assistance of the other, and so that the foundations of

the sacred religion, and of the divine law in the church may be supported no less by the authority of the magistrate than in civil society the principles of justice, and of common right may be supported by the ministry of the elders of the church.

50. It is true that the glory of God first of all, and also the wellbeing of the people, should be the supreme law for the Christian magistrate as guardian and avenger of both tables of the Law, and this man should not only as private individual but also as ruler be bound to keep himself busy with God's Word both day and night, so that by his leadership he may be able to preserve the lawfully established religion and to restore it if it has fallen. Nevertheless, he should not for that reason appropriate for himself the ecclesiastical function, but by virtue of the duty he shares with the other members of the household of faith, like a sheep of Christ, he should listen to his Word and take part in the sacraments. And like God's servant he should 'kiss the Son' [Ps 2:12] who is presented to him in the Word of God by the preachers of the Gospel, and he should take upon himself the yoke of his discipleship.

51. Moses's administration was a mixed one, outside the common order and suited to the times; for after he had installed his brother Aaron as high priest by God's special order, he no longer acted as high priest but stayed in the order of the Levites [Lev 8]. The function of Melchizedek king of Salem and priest of God most high was figurative [Gen 14:18–20], and, together with the other figurative ceremonies, was abolished by Christ, who for that reason ordained the ministry of the Word for his apostles, and forbade them political lordship, lest they and their successors should give the charge of pastoral administration to a man of politics or the administration of his kingdom to a man of the church.

52. In the theses on the calling of the churches' ministers [42.70] we have demonstrated what kind of care the devout and believing magistrate ought to exercise in the election of shepherds, namely that in this matter he ought to conduct himself according to the ordinance which Christ himself has established. It consists in the fact that as guardian of the fourth commandment he should see to it that by means of the consistory (supported by the consent and approving vote of the magistrate himself first and foremost, and also that of the whole church) men who are suitable should lawfully be called to the office of shepherd, and be ordained before the church, according to the practice of the apostles and the evangelists (Acts

14:23; Titus 1:5), which our forefathers living under the devout magistrates observed consistently.

53. The example of Moses, which is raised in objection to this viewpoint of our theologians, is entirely outside the common order and is irrelevant to this disputation. For it was not as political leader but as God's extraordinary priest that Moses installed Aaron; and we must distinguish between the act of Aaron's installation and his election. For God first chose Aaron and mentioned his name to Moses; thereafter, by God's command, through his installation he was confirmed in his calling by Moses.

54. If the shepherd is factious and a proven violator of the public peace, then the highest magistrate, with the intervening advice of his leading subordinates, has the power to depose him with the same right with which king Solomon deposed Abiathar (1 Kgs 2:26 and 8:2).

55. Harder to explain is the question how the magistrate should treat heterodox teachers and heretics who lead the people astray, who lawfully have been convicted of deadly errors and who are persistent in their revilings? Our answer to this question is: if such times should befall him that the magistrate does not have the power to call those heretics back to peace and good results by his own gentle spirit, nor by harshness and threats to scare them off their obstinate pursuit of fostering false teachings which cause the very foundation of the faith to totter, then his tolerant attitude is worthy of excuse in the eyes of God and his church. For wisdom bids that from time to time even those things be tolerated which are not approved at least out of zeal and love for the truth, but which cannot be prevented or removed by a coercive authority in keeping with the laws of wisdom and avenging justice.

56. But if in fact he is able to compel them, and to check them with his sword, others are of the opinion that it is his duty to bestow the penalty of death on them, following the example of the devout king Josiah who slew the superstitious priests of the high places on the altar and who burned human bones upon them [2 Kgs 23:20]. And Jehu, who completely erased the entire family of Ahab and Jezebel for their idol-worship, and who to a man killed all the priests of Baal [2 Kgs 9 and 10]. And likewise Elijah, who also to the last man slew the priests of Baal [1 Kgs 18:40]. But whereas Elijah the prophet did this upon extraordinary prompting by God because at that time the ordinary magistracy had ceased to exist, yet Josiah and Jehu did so in keeping with the strict rule of the political law that had been specially suited to the

Jewish people—and that in a case of extreme necessity and out of fear that their entire kingdom would be overturned, which could be avoided in no other way. I prefer to follow the thinking of those theologians who assert that where another way is provided to keep heretics in check in a way that is fair and good, when the church has condemned the majority of them, it would be better for them to be deposed, or relegated, or restrained in some other way by the magistrate arbitrarily than for them to be struck down in death, in order that their disease not gradually creep, like gangrene, in their republic. In that matter they will follow Constantine the Great and Theodosius, of whom the former punished Arius with exile, and the latter Apollinaris and Nestorius, after they first were found guilty by the synod.

57. At this point the pious and wise magistrate can make an exception for men who are altogether atheists and revilers of the highest degree, who very irreverently deny God himself entirely or his providence in human affairs, who overturn the common religion of Christ's church with their shocking revilings and who disturb the peace and harmony of the whole republic out of pure delight in another's misfortunes and incurable malice of soul, and who can be curbed by no other beneficial and gentler means of political coercion or remedy.

58. For this reason I think that we should understand this statement of Augustine to apply only to heretics of the common sort: "It is not acceptable for anyone in the catholic church to rage unto death against anyone—not even a heretic" (*Against Cresconius, a Donatist Teacher*, book 3.50). And in the Letter to Donatus: "With regard to dreadful judges and laws it is our wish that heretics be corrected, and not slain, lest they meet with the penalty of eternal judgment; and it is our will not to neglect discipline of them, nor to neglect carrying out the punishments they deserve: therefore, curb their sins in such a way that they become people whom it grieves to have sinned."

59. Even though the magistrate should hold his subjects back with the bars of his laws lest they openly slander the religion which he approves, nevertheless he does not have the power to compel them to the faith whereby they approve the form of the accepted religion and openly profess the approval of it before men. For faith wishes to be convinced, not forced, and nothing ought to be so volitional as the inward religion and worship of God, nothing ought to be so foreign to the Christian magistrate as perverse and ill-

timed severity whereby he turns people into hypocrites, and forces them to profess with the mouth what they do not believe with the heart.

60. And yet we do not join in stipulating with those who, just as they say that people's own thoughts are free, so also think that the magistrate ought to bear the opinions of anyone whosoever about the faith. For although we do grant that we should not punish people's inward opinions, nevertheless we do not say that the magistrate should permit each and every citizen an impious confession of religion that is destructive to the republic.

61. But at least we do acknowledge that it is first by means of spiritual weapons we should drive back the spiritual darts with which the false teachers make their attacks upon the church. But if there is no longer any opportunity to use them and the heretics, even though sometimes they are convicted of their errors, nevertheless cause new troubles to arise in the republic through the cultivation of these errors, then they must be stopped by the authority of the magistrate lest the republic should meet up with some more serious hardship for having put up with their faction. For in the doctrine of the truth stubborn discord and division drag along with them trouble for the whole human society and overturn its calm state.

62. Although the magistrates in former times no less punished heretics who seditiously violated God's spiritual law than other insurgents who violated their civil laws, it was not by right but by force that the Roman leaders dragged off to their own ecclesial court their power to investigate heretics with God's Word, and according to that Word to strike them bodily.

63. For the believing magistrate, as an eminent part of God's church, both by the analogy of faith and by the judgment of the faithful theologians (whom he has called together) in agreement with God's Word, out of his own wisdom and gravity of the case, does have the power, along with his theologians, to make investigations concerning the heretic, and to compel the heretic if he no longer can enjoy the company of the other citizens without an uprising in the republic.

64. And by as much more authority Christian magistrates have received from God than private citizens, they should use as much more care and diligence lest any heterodox teaching or disagreement in the Christian faith should spread wider in their region. For besides the fact that the guardianship of God's universal church is jointly entrusted to them as members of the

church, as supporters and protectors of the church the same guardianship is demanded especially of them more fully. Therefore, they should be warned not to indulge their subjects who are strangers to the true religion the freedom to publicly profess a false religion; and with whatever means they are able to, they should halt even the private practice of it.

65. The highest goal of the magistrate is God's glory; the subordinate goal is the harmony and civil calm of his subjects. For this reason, the apostle's will is that we offer prayers and intercessions on behalf of kings and all who are placed in positions of prominence, that under their authority we live a peaceful and quiet life with all godliness and reverence (1 Tim 2:2).

ON THE RESURRECTION OF THE BODY
AND THE LAST JUDGMENT

President: Andreas Rivetus
Respondent: Henry W. Berkelius

Disputation 51 addresses the topic of general eschatology, that is, the resurrection of the body and the last judgment. To some extent this topic had been anticipated in earlier disputations; for example, Disputation 39 treats Purgatory and 41 the Christ and the Antichrist. Whereas those discussions focused on criticism of the Romanist teaching, here the author offers a positive treatment of the end of times. Belief in the resurrection distinguishes Christians from unbelievers (3–4). Resurrection is certain and has two very solid foundations (5): God's will regarding the resurrection, as revealed in the Scriptures (6–14); and God's power that makes the resurrection possible (15). Thesis 16 defines the resurrection of the body as a work performed exclusively by the Triune God (elaborated in 17–22; the role of angels is discussed in 23), that takes place at the end of times, and concerns all human beings, the living as well as the dead, the righteous as well as the wicked (31–36). Special attention is given to stillborn, miscarried fetuses and malformed babies (36), sexual differentiation (37), and physical deformities (38). Questions about the number and precise substance of the resurrected bodies are discussed (24–30). The internal form of resurrection is treated (39) as well as the outward form (40), the goals (41), and the many uses of this doctrine (42–44). The Triune God is the one who brings about the final judgment (45–58), yet the administration of it will be conducted by the Son in his human nature (47–49). Judgment befalls the wicked angels and all human beings, both good and evil (50–51). Of the latter, all deeds will be judged (52). The form of the judgment will consist in the knowledge of the case, in declaring the verdict, and in the execution thereof (53–54). After drawing attention to the goals of judgment (55), the places where the upright and the wicked will be gathered, and a warning not to calculate the years up to

Christ's return (56), the disputation ends with a definition of the last judgment (57) and the many uses of this doctrine (58).

1. Everything that is done by man or concerning man is enclosed by two terms which the ancient theologians, not deviating from the words of Scripture (Prov 2:20 and 4:26, 27; Matt 7:13–14; 2 Cor 7:7; Heb 4:14), expressed with the words 'the way' and 'the fatherland.' Equivalent to them is the distinction of the church into 'militant' and 'triumphant.' Up until now we have disputed what pertained to 'the way' and to the state of the church militant on earth. What we should discuss in detail next pertains to the 'fatherland' and the 'end-goal,' or, to the state of the church triumphant in heaven, and to the complete defeat of its enemies, and to adjudicating them and handing them over to the eternal punishments of hell. What must of necessity occur before these last, very different states of the upright and of the wicked are the resurrection of the dead and the last judgment. For "it has been appointed for men to die once, and after this the judgment" (Heb 9:27). But it is not possible for the dead to be judged as long as they are dead, because they must appear before the judgment. In order for that to take place the resurrection of the dead must happen first—and we shall have to treat it first; thereafter, we must examine the circumstances of that fearful judgment.

2. What in the active sense, from the working of its efficient cause, is called 'resuscitation,' in the passive sense is called 'resurrection.' The former is nothing other than the raising up of that which has fallen; but the latter (which is the effect of the former) is a kind of second standing-up, called *anastasis* in Greek, as though the second standing-up of one who has fallen. Since 'fall' or 'collapse' can be understood figuratively, so too can 'resurrection' be taken in the same way: either by reason of the calamities and dangers into which someone falls in this life, or by reason of the sins whereby the soul comes to ruin and falls. Leaving aside the figurative meaning and also a consideration of that resurrection which is called the 'first' resurrection (which was sufficiently treated when the disputation was held about the regeneration and renewal of man) we shall offer a treatment about resurrection in the strict sense of the word, which denotes the restoration of a body that by dying has become a corpse, and which denotes the reunification of the soul with it. For, to say this in passing, we do not avoid applying the word 'corpse' to any dead body whatsoever, including even the body of Christ in the three days of his death—although this seems

blasphemous to [Franciscus] Fevardentius (*Theomachia [Calvinistica]*, book 6, page 176) and to [Petrus] Cotonus (*Geneve Plagiare*, at Acts 2:27). But Chrysostom is not afraid to apply the word to Christ himself, in *Homily* 24 on 1 Cor, "calling the body a corpse because it has died." And Gregory of Valencia, *Commentary on Thomas*, volume 4, question 4, point 1 approves: "In the three days of the death of Christ, his flesh, no rather, his corpse (insofar as it is by nature without reason and sense) was sustained hypostatically by the Word."

3. This article [of the Creed] separates gentiles from Christians, for it is placed beyond the scope of reason, and it is a declaration peculiar to the church, as Tertullian stated rightly: "The faith of the Christians is the resurrection of the dead" (*On the Resurrection of the Body*). And what Augustine said about the head should be applied also to all its members: "The fact that Christ died is believed by pagans and his enemies; but the fact that Christ rose again is a belief specific to the Christians." And so the gentiles perceive and grant that all people are subject to death; but when it comes to the resurrection, then it seems silly talk (Acts 17:32) and childish nonsense (Pliny, *Natural History*, book 2, chapter 7, and book 7, chapter 55). Thus, Caecilius, in [M.] Minucius [Felix's] Octavius says: "The Christians make up old wives' tales as they claim that they will be born again after they die, when they are dust and ashes; and by some strange faith they believe their own lies." Simply put, "the denial of the resurrection of the body is assumed from the entire school of all philosophers" (Tertullian, *On the Prescription of Heretics*, chapter 7). And accordingly, the apostle writes about the resurrection of the dead that generally the gentiles "are without hope" (1 Thess 4:13).

4. But because "philosophers were the patriarchs of heretics" (Tertullian, *Against Hermogenes*), it is no wonder that from the very beginning also the church suffered objections from them in the doctrine of the resurrection. The Jewish church suffered objections from the Sadducees, "who said that there is no resurrection" (Matt 22:23); the Christian church suffered objections from Hymenaeus and Philetus, who taught that "the resurrection has taken place already" (2 Tim 2:18), namely, denying the actual resurrection while granting only a figurative one. [The church] at Corinth [suffered objections] from many people whom the apostle refuted (1 Cor 15:12). Afterwards, their heresy was refurbished by the Simonians (Irenaeus, book 1, chapter 19), by Saturninus, Basilides, Carpocrates, the Gnostics, Valentinus, the Ophites, Cainites, Sethians, Archontici, Cerdoniani, Marcionites, Lucian,

Apelles, Severus, followers of Origen, the Seleucians, and many others whom it would take long to number—concerning whom [see] Epiphanius (in *Panarion*), Augustine (*On Heresies ad Quotvult Deum*), Theodoret (*Compendium of Heretical Accounts*), Philastrius (*On Heresies*), and others. The Acts of the Council of Constance ascribe this heresy also to the Roman Pope John XXIII: "At the persuasion of the devil, he stubbornly believed that the soul of man dies and is extinguished with his body, like dumb animals, and that, once it has died, it will in no way whatsoever be raised even on the last day" (Session 11, page 106 in the edition of Quentel 1551, volume 1).

5. But in fact, since the apostle links hope together with the resurrection of the dead (Acts 24:14) and teaches that "we of all people are most wretched if in this life only we have hope in Christ" (1 Cor 15:19), "in order to hold fast the possession of our hope without wavering" (Heb 10:23) we must fortify our soul with the solid and unmovable foundations on which our faith and hope in the future resurrection rest securely. Therefore, we set aside arguments that are secondary and based on probability, as well as some comparisons with nature or similarities drawn from it—which illustrate rather than confirm the matter, and which are not able to sustain the careful examination of a strict disputation. We shall bolster our belief by means of those two supports which Christ has indicated to us in Matt 22:29, when he called the Sadducees, who deny the resurrection, back "to the Scriptures and the power of God," and revealed that the source of their error was their ignorance of these things. And against them, he laid two foundations about this article of faith: Knowledge of God's will from Scripture, and the power of God, arising from his nature. For since restoration to life is a divine action and there are two principles that are necessary and sufficient for this action, namely the will and the ability, in this work of resurrection we must consider them, too. For these two qualities which are combined in God—God in whom there is no lack of power—bring the thing [resurrection] into actuality because "our God is in heaven and does whatever He wills" (Ps 115:2).

6. The will of God is made known to us in his revealed Word, in which we possess also the pronouncements of divine origin about the resurrection from the dead given by the prophets and the apostles. To be sure, in the Old Testament they are rather shadowy, but yet they are clear enough to produce faith; in the New, however, they are described as clearly as daylight so that to not perceive them would be a matter of greatest blindness, and to not put faith in them once they have been seen and heard would be the mark of utter

lack of faith. From the very beginning the promise about "the seed of the woman that will crush the head of the serpent" (Gen 3:15) included the doctrine of God's will about the resurrection. For that seed which was to destroy the works of the devil would not have done so sufficiently unless it had destroyed the wages of sin—that is, death, both temporal as well as eternal [Rom 6:23]. For he who breaks the power of Satan conquers also death over which Satan holds the power (Heb 2:14). Connected to this is the fact that that promise, which was later more fully revealed to Abraham, as referring to the Messiah who would be born from Isaac's seed, carries with it the added blessing which in his seed is to be shared with all the nations of the earth. And since that blessing is placed opposite the curse to which the whole human race is subject on account of sin (of which the final point is the death of the body and of the soul), it is also entirely fitting that the resurrection of the body and life never ending of that body joined with the soul are included in that blessing.

7. As guarantee of this necessary consequence we have the Son of God himself, who gathers from the words of the covenant, "I am the God of Abraham, the God of Isaac, and the God of Jacob" (Exod 3:6)—the force of which remains in effect even after the separation of the soul from the body—that contrary to the false teaching of the Sadducees there is a resurrection of the dead, because "God is not the God of the dead but of the living" (Matt 22:32; Mark 12:26; Luke 20:38). For since God struck that covenant not with souls but with persons, and the names Abraham, Isaac and Jacob stand for whole persons, life must of necessity be related to whole persons, and not only to some of their parts. Therefore, life relates not only to the immortality of souls, but also to the resurrection of bodies. Since the resurrection was certain in God's decree, Abraham, Isaac and Jacob—though deceased—were alive in God's eyes. Accordingly, it was his will that believers receive the sign of the covenant in the flesh, to demonstrate that this body would in its own due time be revived again from the dead and become a partaker of life everlasting.

8. Jerome, in writing to Pammachus, has assessed Job's statement (chapter 19:25 and following) to be so clearly about that matter that he thought "no-one after Christ speaks so clearly about the resurrection as Job did before Christ." And to be sure, according to its reading in the Vulgate edition, hardly anything can be said about that topic more clearly: "For I know that my Redeemer lives, and that on the last day I shall be made alive from the earth.

And once again I shall be clothed in my own skin, and in my flesh shall I see my God. I myself, and not another, shall see him, and my own eyes shall behold him. This my hope is safely hidden away in my heart." And even though these words appear slightly different in the Hebrew text, and are rendered somewhat differently in the Septuagint translation also, there will be nothing that cannot be adduced more fittingly to explain and confirm the faith in that mystery, as was done by the very learned interpreters Tremellius, Junius, and others. We prefer their opinion—which was that of the entire ancient church—to the interpretations of the Jews, although the very learned Mercerus followed in their path. We are dissuaded from this opinion by that protestation of Job about having his words engraved with "an iron pen" [19:24], and by that full knowledge which he professes, which he could not have had without a doubt about temporal liberation. And by those words that "he would later be raised from the dust," which, whether they relate to the Redeemer or to the person of Job, can hardly be applied to the restoration of his possessions in this life. [We are convinced also] by his certainty "of seeing God in his own flesh" after it "would be eaten by worms" [19:26]—which is a periphrasis for the state of death and the decay of the body, etc. And yet we think that Job, too, had weighed these matters so that from it he could base his own hope for his own temporal restoration by him who by his power would call the dead back to life again.

9. If we look closely at the words in the prophecy of Isaiah the prophet in chapter 26:19, "Your dead shall live, my fallen shall rise up again, etc.," and of Ezekiel in chapter 37:1 and following, which is a treatment of the valley full of bones (very dry bones at that) to which God said: "I shall send my Spirit into you and you shall live, and I shall bestow sinews upon you, and I shall make flesh to come upon you, etc.," then it appears that it is describing the resurrection of dead bodies, even though many interpreters are not wrong to understand it as a figurative resurrection, as in the delivery from the Babylonian captivity and the restoration of the former strength. Nonetheless, it does contribute to confirming the doctrine of the resurrection in the strict sense of the word, because if these things are spoken in some comparative way, it is not customary for a comparison to be drawn either from things that are impossible or from things that either have never happened or never will happen. But [it is drawn] from things that are well-known, either from nature, or from faith through revelation, as in this passage, so that the argument would run like this: if you have unwavering faith in the resurrection of the

dead whereby God will gather together the dust of scattered corpses and join them together and again will bind together dead, arid and dried-out bones and restore them to life, then you should have no doubt about the promise of the restoration of God's people, even though their strength is completely sapped. For the one who can by his own divine power recall at one time to life bodies that had been reduced to ashes and dust, shall also be able to bring back the exiles to their fatherland, as they are not unlike the arid bones, and to restore to them their former strength of freedom.

10. But Daniel's testimony is very clear: "And many of those who are asleep in the dust of the earth will awaken, some to eternal life, others to eternal shame" (Dan 12:2). And we should not think that this prophecy is not relevant to the universal resurrection on the grounds that the promise is made about many but not about all. For 1) those many who are asleep can be taken to mean all who are asleep, even though they are called many in comparison with those who will be found living on the day of the resurrection from the dead; 2) the word 'many' can be taken to refer not to the determination of the subject but to the two members of the distribution that are joined together in the predicate, as if to say: "many to life, many unto death." And we add to it that the collective noun sometimes is taken in a universal and extensive sense for "all" in Scripture, as Rom 5:19, where "many," that is, all who are in Adam, are said to be declared sinners. It is evident, however, that this passage of Daniel, in the way that Porphyry has twisted it, cannot be applied to the state of the republic of Israel after the generals of Antiochus were slain: 1) From the goal of that resurrection: Everlasting life or shame; 2) From the fact that it speaks about the resurrection in which there will be a precise distinction between the upright and the wicked—which certainly did not happen when peace was restored to the Israelites; 3) From the fact that the teachers of the Jewish church did not begin from that time onward to shine forever like the heavenly firmament, but—as the law was corrupted and slowly declined—they rather fell little by little from their position. And add the fact that this genuine passage occurs in the words of Christ which appear to explain Daniel (John 5:28–29), as Augustine well advises (*On the City of God*, book 20, chapter 23).

11. What also contributes to this is Hosea's prophecy: "After two days the Lord will revive us, on the third day He will restore us, and we shall live before his countenance" (Hos 6:2). This is an allusion to the resurrection of Christ, and it speaks also of the church, because in Christ the head also the

members of his mystical body are said "to be raised up together with Christ" (Eph 2:6) because of the unfailing promise of the resurrection. To Hosea's testimony we should add another one from chapter 13:14: "I shall redeem them from the power of hell, I shall redeem them from death, and I shall be your death, O death, and I shall be your destruction, O hell." The apostle relates this prophecy to the resurrection from the dead: "When this perishable will be clothed with the imperishable, and this mortal shall put on immortality, then will come to pass that word which was written: 'Where is your sting, O death? Etc.'" (1 Cor 15:54).

12. In the New Testament, the matter is so clear and obvious that whoever wishes to gather all the testimonies would need a whole book. From the many testimonies we choose the following few but outstanding ones as supplement to the ones that already have been produced above, together with the testimonies of the Old Testament from which Christ obtained his own: 1) From Matt 12:40–41, where it says of the Ninevites that they shall arise, in the judgment with this generation, etc., and of the queen of the South that she will rise up, etc. From this, it follows that they will be raised from the dead, since the bodies of those people who were spoken about were reduced to dust. 2) In Luke 14:12[14] Christ makes deliberate mention of the resurrection of the just. 3) In John 6:39–40, 44, and 54, he promises that on the last day he will raise up to life all that the Father has given him, everyone who sees the Son and who believes in him, whosoever the Father draws to him, and whoever eats his body and drinks his blood.

13. The preaching and writings of the apostles very often emphasize the same mystery. And so in Acts 4:2, the Sadducees were disturbed when the apostles "in the name of Jesus proclaimed the resurrection from the dead." Paul declared Jesus and the resurrection to the Athenians in Acts 17:18, and they (as was reasonable) understood the apostle's words to be about the resurrection of the body, for "they would not have altogether mocked him," says Tertullian, "if they had heard from him only of the restoration of the soul, for then they would have heard what was assumed very frequently in their own common philosophy" (*On the Resurrection of the Body*, chapter 39). The same Paul cried out, in Acts 23:6: "It is for the hope and the resurrection of the dead that I am being put on trial." And in Acts 24:15 he confessed in the presence of Felix the governor, that he "was looking for the future resurrection of the righteous and the wicked."

14. But in the first letter to the Corinthians, chapter 15, the same apostle gave an explicit treatment of this article, and because a controversy then arose over it, he reinforced it with many arguments, in order not only to rebut those who spoke in objection, but also to lend support to those who already believed over against all the sophistic claims. The first of his arguments, he drew from the resurrection of Christ; the second from the goal of the redemption obtained by Christ; the third, as some people think, from the rite of the early church, whereby they received their baptism over gravesites as a testimony of the faith in their own resurrection—or rather, as we prefer to think, from the baptism of affliction and calamities, which the pious would undergo for the sake of the doctrine of Christ's resurrection from the dead, and of the resurrection unto salvation of others who were asleep in Christ, which is called "the baptism of blood." This interpretation seems to be confirmed by the fact that in Acts 23:6 Paul was relating his own persecutions for the sake of righteousness to the hope of the resurrection of the dead. Secondly, [it seems to be confirmed by the fact] that immediately after he treated those who are baptized on behalf of the dead he applies to himself in a literal sense what he had said figuratively about others: "And why do we risk our lives every hour?" [1 Cor 15:30]—namely, to be baptized with the baptism of blood. Why "I die daily" if there is no hope of resurrection? He adds arguments from diverse foolish consequences which come from the denial of the resurrection, arguments from putting Adam opposite Christ, and [arguments] from Christ's victory over all his enemies, among which the last one is death. From all of these arguments it follows very clearly what he himself is teaching: We must trust in God "who raises up the dead" (2 Cor 1:9).

15. Since from these words, there is enough certainty about God's will, there is no reason to call into question God's power, for with Him nothing is impossible except that which is not his will (Luke 1:37). As God has an incorruptible essence, so He also has unimpeded activity, "He who is exceeding abundantly to do more than what we ask or think" (Eph 3:20), whose power concurs with his will. Therefore, "the established law of dying does not take away the law of being raised up, because the law does not impose obligation upon the one who determines the law. Nor does God deprive himself of the right to make alive, when for us He determined the law of death," as Hilary well puts it on Ps 51. "Therefore, God will make our mortal bodies into immortal ones by reviving them: For He is better than

nature, possessing in himself the will because He is good; and the power, because He is powerful; and the perfection, because He is rich and perfect" (Irenaeus, book 2, chapter 51).

16. Having laid these two foundations of God's will and power as basis, we have sufficiently answered the question whether there will be a resurrection of the dead. We must now investigate what it is, and explain the nature of it. Therefore, we shall here define resurrection as the act of God the Father, the Son, and the Holy Spirit whereby in his own almighty power, at the archangel's trumpet at the end of the ages, He will restore the bodies of all people that have been reduced to dust, both the holy and the impious, in order to reunite them with the souls from which they had been separated in death, and to be informed by them for a time-period that will never end, so that the impious pay the penalty for their misdeeds for evermore, and the pious enjoy the received eternal blessedness forever.

17. From this definition, we understand that God the Father is the efficient cause of the resurrection, as "He who raised Jesus from the dead shall also restore to life your mortal bodies" (Rom 8:11). "Through his power, God both raised the Lord from the dead, and He will raise us also" (1 Cor 6:14 and 2 Cor 4:14). Moreover, since the outward workings of the Trinity are not divided, it follows that the Son and the Holy Spirit work together with the Father in that operation. But the active resurrection is also ascribed explicitly to the Son (John 5:28): "Those who are in the graves will hear the voice of the Son of Man, and shall come forth, those who have done good unto the resurrection of life, but those who have done evil to the resurrection of judgment" (John 6:39–40, 44). "On the last day I shall revive him" (John 11:25). "I am the resurrection and the life." But we should not understand this in such a way that the power to restore the dead is bestowed on the human nature of Christ, for the power is clearly divine; but it is attributed to the person in such a way that we must of necessity keep the principle of it distinct—contrary to what some do who start a process against us on the grounds that we, with Nestorius, split Christ into two—which is not done by those who acknowledge that Christ "in the communion of both natures performs what is his own, with the Word working what belongs to the Word, and the flesh carrying out what belongs to the flesh." Those who do not make a distinction between these things fall into the Charybdis of Eutychianism while they think that they are escaping the Scylla of Nestorius.

18. We do acknowledge, however, that as in the preliminary instances of the universal resurrection—that is, in the particular cases of Lazarus and the son of the widow from Nain, so too in the general resurrection, he [Christ] will carry out that task, as his human nature will in his person perform the task which belongs to it, namely when some obvious and clear sign is given of him coming to judge, through which like an instrument of his divine power the dead are going to be raised up. And for that effect it will have instrumental power like those words, "Lazarus come forth." and "Young man, I say to you, arise, etc.," and statements like these which had the instrumental power to raise up the dead. The Scripture calls this sign, "the voice of the Son of Man" (John 5:28), "a loud voice" (Matt 24:31), "a cry which will be rung out at midnight" (Matt 25:6), "a trumpet call" (Matt 24:31), and "the last trumpet" (1 Cor 15:52)—although this last one is attributed to Christ in only a mediate sense.

19. We do not doubt that the very same Christ, to the extent that he is our Redeemer and Mediator, through his death and suffering has merited resurrection and immortality for all his members. Moreover, that by his own resurrection he is the exemplary cause for our resurrection, for he himself is "the first-fruits of those who have fallen asleep" (1 Cor 15:20); "the first-born of the dead" (Rev 1:5; Col 1:18). Hence among the other arguments for our future resurrection (1 Cor 15:23) the apostle derives from Christ's resurrection as precedent the future resurrection of all who believe in Christ, because "Christ is the first-fruits, and then also those who belong to Christ." For members should not be separated from their head, and it would be rather inappropriate and ill-suited for the rest of the body to remain dead while the head is alive. For it would be fitting "that where the glory of the head has gone before thereunto is called the hope also for the body" (Leo, Sermon 1, *On the Ascension of the Lord*).

20. Contrary to what some others think, we reckon that these two ways of causing the resurrection in Christ—merit and precedent—do have their place in the elect only, the true members of Christ. Because even though all those who are wicked shall be raised up, as we shall prove later, nevertheless it seems that this will not be effected by the power of Christ's merit, because if Christ had not come, in keeping with the first divine ordinance, the people who through sin were subject to death would have arisen at some point in time, in order to receive the punishments for what their sins have deserved— not only in soul, but also in body. From this, it follows that also for the elect

Christ has merited not simply resurrection, but a resurrection of such kind that is blessed and glorious. For thus in the elect the effect becomes like its exemplary cause. But those who are reprobate will not become like Christ, except in some general way, which is not sufficient for this goal. Hence it follows that the apostle teaches that it applies only to those who are predestined "that they would be conformed to the image of the Son of God, and that he himself would be the first-born among many brothers" (Rom 8:29).

21. It cannot be denied that the Holy Spirit will revive the dead with the same power as that of the Father and the Son—except by the Pneumatomachi [those who oppose the Spirit] and the followers of Macedonius. For since the Spirit is of the same essence (*homoousios*) as the Father and the Son, he also has the operations in outward matters in common with them. But more so, the apostle testifies clearly in Rom 8:11: "If the Spirit of him who raised Jesus from the dead dwells in you, then He who raised Jesus from the dead will give life also to your mortal bodies for the sake of his Spirit which dwells within you." This passage, however, says something only about the glorious resurrection of those who believe, for only in them does the Spirit dwell. Nonetheless, He will manifest his power also in those in whom He does not dwell, insofar as in them He works also the renewed union of soul and body, and also the final arrangement of physical material for it.

22. This effect common to the three persons cannot be brought about by virtue of any natural cause, but only by divine power. For no natural cause is able to reproduce what is numerically identical, and there exists no natural return from dispossession to possession, such as is necessary from death to resurrection. Therefore, from the side of the starting point the resurrection will be supernatural; but if one considers its endpoint absolutely, that is to say, the being of a man, it is something natural. Not so, however, if one considers its end-point relative to the 'terminus from which,' namely, as the being of a man after death. Therefore, we ought not to listen to some Scholastics who think that sometimes (albeit not always) the same in number, once decayed, is reproduced. For since the individual receives its essence through change and through the action of a natural agent, and it is not possible for the same motion and the same action to return, it also will not happen at all that by strength of a natural agent the same in number, once decayed, can be reproduced. Therefore, it follows that no natural cause

converges with God for the resurrection of the dead, and that it happens entirely by God through a miracle.

23. And therefore, we should readily accept what is commonly said about the angels as instruments and ministers in the resurrection. For if 'resurrection' is taken in a strict, exact, and so to speak formal sense, it is an immediate work of God which does not proceed from any proper instrumental cause that truly influences the effect. In other words, if we consider the formation of bodies from the dust of the earth and the unification of them with their souls. But if the word 'resurrection' is understood to mean some of the prefatory and preceding things, or the actions immediately before or after the resurrection, and the word 'resurrection' is taken for the entire complexity of those things that happen before and after the resurrection, then we do not hesitate to acknowledge the angels as ministers of the resurrection and as instrumental causes, because they, too, will have their own roles to play on that last day, "gathering together the elect from the four winds and all the regions of the world, from one end of the heavens to the other" (Matt 24:31). But whatever the angels or any other creatures do in this matter (including even Christ's human nature), if we regard it in and of itself and by reason of its formal principle (as they call it), then it will happen as if by a cause or instrument that is moral (to use their word). However, if, as stated, we take the word 'resurrection' in its exact sense, then it is not as if by a proper cause that immediately attains its effect.

24. To this point, we have treated the efficient cause. Now, we must treat the material, which some call the "subject in which." And it, strictly speaking, is the flesh or body of the human being, because the resurrection happens according to the body, and not to the soul, strictly speaking. And moreover, the human being's soul does not perish, since it is immortal, and when the body returns to the earth "the spirit returns to God who gave it" (Eccl 12:7). Therefore, the Lord says that "those who can rage against the body cannot kill the soul" (Matt 10:28). From these and similar passages, the heresy is refuted of those people who either state openly that souls perish along with bodies, or who say that to die is to be thoroughly blotted out, and that to rise up to life means to live a second time after non-existence—such views are found nowadays in the writings of the Socinians. Therefore, the soul that has been separated remains immortal, and it does not yield to a dormant state and become deprived of all happiness nor freed entirely from all punishment; but in keeping with people's different conditions, it either is immediately after

death taken up into realms of the blessed where it awaits with joy the restoration of its own body, or it is tortured by hellish punishments until through the resurrection its body is restored to it for its share of the punishment.

25. Therefore, we state that the body shall rise up again, the same in number and substance, as is sufficiently clear from the passages of Scripture cited above. For "this perishable must put on the imperishable and this mortal must put on immortality" (1 Cor 15:53), and, Phil 3:21: Christ will transform "this very, this lowly body," etc. Therefore, the resurrection will also happen in such a way that "everyone may receive in the body"—or (as the Complutensian edition reads at 2 Cor 5:10) "things proper to the body"— "according to what he has done, whether good or evil"—which should not happen in any other body than the one by which everyone has performed good or evil deeds. Even Christ who is the example for our resurrection, arose with no other body than the one in which he was nailed to the cross, and in which even after death the traces of the nails were apparent. "But our bodies shall be made to conform to Christ's glorious body" (Phil 3:21).

26. God's justice also requires this, that in the very same body in which one has obeyed God or sinned the rewards are bestowed or the penalties are applied. Nor is it that one thing contends while another receives the crown, or that one sins while another is beaten. But rather, as Ambrose well put it in the *Sermon on Faith and the Resurrection*, chapter 19, "the order and cause of justice is that since the body and the soul share in an act which the soul conceived and the body executed, both enter into judgment, and both are either subjected to punishment or kept unto glory." And it would not be fitting if the bodies which were members of Christ along the way should be barred from the fatherland, while others took their place. The resurrection likewise would not be a true resurrection, but rather a new creation. Nor would the condition of those who had died beforehand be the same as those whom the last day will snatch while they are alive. For in that transformation these latter ones shall not be allotted other bodies as far as the substance of them is concerned. Add to this the fact that in the Scriptures death is called sleep and sleeping, and resurrection awakening, so that we understand that the resurrection will be of the same body in number. "Therefore, the flesh shall arise again, wholly in everyone, with its own identity, and with absolute integrity" (Tertullian, *On the Resurrection of the Flesh*, chapter 63).

27. Having duly weighed these matters very carefully, it follows that it is a destructive error of those who either in former times denied or who also in our own time deny that there is a resurrection of bodies that are numerically identical with the ones we are clothed with in this age. They rather have judged (or even now do judge) that the resurrection must come about in bodies made of air, or of material lighter than air, but not made up of flesh and limbs. Some people formerly ascribed this error to Origen, although others have attempted to release and exculpate him from every error concerning resurrection. Whatever the case, it is certain that in our time very many Anabaptists are engaged in this error, and also that Socinus with his adherents deny the resurrection "of this flesh," and who accordingly call into the question those words of the Creed, "I believe in the resurrection of the flesh," words which they say do not have such great authority that they should believe them contrary to the testimonies of Scripture. But we have shown that those words clearly are contained in Scripture. Moreover, we should note in passing that a mistake has crept into the edition of the Letters of Calvin in the folio of the year 1576, page 84, where a letter with the incorrect heading, *Farel to Calvin*, has misled not only Fevardentinus (who impudently attacks Calvin under that title), but also Cl. Vossius, who in his theses about the resurrection thought that letter to be from Farel in which he was instructing Calvin in this matter, although it is clearly from Calvin to Coelius Socinus, who had started that dispute, and whom Calvin under that name refutes in a most erudite fashion.

28. This statement which they make is a false one: "that these bodies which we bear will not be raised up again, but that the apostle teaches us that we shall be given other bodies." For what the apostle says in 1 Cor 15:50, "flesh and blood shall not possess the kingdom of God," should not be taken to mean that resurrected bodies shall lack flesh and blood, because as Tertullian aptly states, "'Flesh and blood' in of the sense of sin, and not in light of their substance, are barred from God's kingdom" (*On the Resurrection of the Body*). And from what follows ("Nor will corruption possess what is incorruptible"), it is clear that it is [meant] with regard to our corruption and not with regard to our nature. But it is clear that flesh and blood can exist without corruption from the fact that the Holy One of God who had flesh and bones after his resurrection nevertheless did not have a mortal and perishable body such as that of Adam after the fall, and such as our own in this life, but an immortal and imperishable one, indeed, even a spiritual one—yet not one that was

turned into a spirit, but in distinction from a natural body which must be kept alive by food. Spiritual, therefore, because it will have no need for any food; but the presence of the spirit will suffice for life, and also because of the other qualities and gifts of the glorified body.

29. And no less erroneous is the opinion of Durand of St. Pourçain, who thinks that for the resurrection of the same person the identity of form in any sort of material is sufficient, because he says that the identity of material follows from the identity of form, since in and of itself material has no actuality but receives its peculiar existence from the form. Therefore, even though Peter's soul should assume the body that had been Paul's (and vice versa), nonetheless it is the same Peter who would rise up again, and the same Paul, because he gets his body from the same soul, so that it becomes the same person (*On the Sentences* 4, distinction 44, question 3). This opinion is taken over by Alberius in his speech "On the Resurrection," where he advances the argument that "they shall be raised up composed of the four elements as new material for the human being, so that their identity will not be in the material but in the form." For it is wrong that the numerical identity of a person is contained by the identity of the soul alone and by the identity of the prime, bare matter, because for that identity the same soul must necessarily be present, the same human body and the same flesh and bones, an identity that also requires the same arrangements of the prime matter for the soul, through which it has its peculiar arrangement in respect of this soul which informs this body, and in this way the secondary material is brought about, material which is assigned to this form.

30. For if those final arrangements, and consequently also the same body, were not reproduced, it would not be the same person, because this person is substantially made up of this soul, and also from this body and from this flesh and bones, which do not exist without these final arrangements. Otherwise, a genuine resurrection of the very same people would have happened in the transmigration of souls from some bodies into other bodies (which the Pythagorean philosophers made up and which even some of the Jews believed), because in that transmigration of souls, there would remain the same soul of the person who had died before, and the same prime matter, of all sorts of bodies, would be everywhere. And to be sure, if the identity of the soul is required for the identity of the person, then the identity of the body is required for the same reason, since a person consists not of a soul only but of a soul joined together with a body.

31. These are the observations about the "subject in which," as they call it. It follows now that we speak about the "subject which," i.e., concerning the persons who will be raised up again. The last day will find all people altogether, who either are still alive or who have died. Concerning those who will be found living, one can ask whether or not they will be raised up, since they have not perished. For since Christ is called "the one whom God appointed as judge of the living and the dead" (Acts 10:42), if all people truly died then this distinction would appear pointless. The apostle certainly seems to hint at such a distinction in 1 Cor 15:51 and 1 Thess 4, because (to use the words of Tertullian in *On the Resurrection of the Body*, chapter 41), "by a way shorter than death, which will be destroyed in the change" those who then are found living shall not die but shall put off mortality and put on immortality "in a moment, in the twinkling of an eye, when they shall be caught up together with those who are being raised up" [1 Thess 4:17]. For the passage of the apostle which provides the strongest proof of this, 1 Cor 15, has various readings in the Greek and Latin codices; yet a comparison of it with the other passage in 1 Thessalonians 4 hardly permits a different reading than the one which the Greek [codices] adopted, and with which wording also the apostle's introductory statement very strongly agrees: "Behold, I tell you a mystery" [1 Cor 15:51]. And the concluding statement would not fit, *pantes men oun koimēthēsometha* ("we all therefore sleep"), when *ou* ('not') is changed to *oun* ('therefore'). In writing on this passage William Estius, professor at Douai, was right to consider this reading suspect.

32. Therefore, the customary reading of the Greek [codices] seems more likely to be true: "We shall not all sleep, but we all shall be changed," despite the vain objections by Catharinus and Stapleton, who contend that the passage is corrupt, and to which the latter even adds an irreverent interpretation. Estius says: "But the reading of the Greek codices is not at all an unlikely one, but actually in many ways the probable one; so far is it from the truth that whoever follows or recommends it should be charged with rash impudence of the same sort that is alleged in his commentary by Catharinus, who himself rather should be condemned for his inconsiderate opinion in this matter." Moreover, all the ancient Greeks whose works we possess from this reading draw the conclusion that not all people shall die, and therefore that not all shall be raised up again (strictly speaking). This opinion received favorable support from some of the Latin writers like Tertullian (*On the Resurrection of the Body*, chapters 41 and 42) and Jerome (*Letter to Marcella*).

Estius admits there is nothing risky in this interpretation. Augustine, as is his custom in matters which are not clearly certain, states discreetly: "For either they shall not die, or, in the very quick change from this life to death and then from death to eternal life, like the twinkling of an eye, in the transition they shall not feel death" (*Retractions*, book 2, chapter 33). The author of the book *On Ecclesiastical Doctrines*, chapter 7 [states]: "Because there are other, equally orthodox and learned men who believe that while the soul remains in the body those people shall be changed to incorruption and immortality who at the Lord's coming will be found alive, and for them this will be counted as a resurrection from the dead because they shall put off mortality by means of the change, and not by means of death: Whichever means one finds acceptable, he is not heretical."

33. We are of the opinion also that neither of the two views should be condemned in those people who commonly hold that "according to the law of the church it is enough to believe that there will be a resurrection of the dead." We affirm this about each and every person who has died, both good and evil, with the exception of no-one. For the resurrection will take place in order that all people will be judged, and "each person may receive the things proper to the body, whether it be good or bad" (2 Cor 5:10). Since the judgment and the retribution will be for all people, there will also be a resurrection of all people. Thus, in John 5:28 all people who are in the graves and who will be raised up are divided into those who have done good and those who have done evil. And Acts 24:15: "And we have the same hope which they also have, that there will be a resurrection of the righteous and of the wicked." This passage shows that also the Jews of Paul's time, whereas they did not believe in the Christ, nevertheless considered the doctrine of the resurrection of the righteous and the wicked as true and certain, contrary to what is thought by the Jews of today, who consider it an age-old tradition that "only the righteous will be raised up again, while the wicked will disappear entirely and will be covered over in eternal darkness, never to return to life," as is reported by Buxtorf, *The Jew's Synagogue*, chapter 1. Several indications of this error are found in the more recent writings of the Jews, although they are not in collusion to the point of speaking with one voice.

34. The adherents of Socinus speak equivocally also about the resurrection of the wicked, for they say that "it should be ascribed to the sacred writings rather than to their own opinion if anyone concludes that the wicked shall not live forever from the fact that only the pious shall live forever is drawn

from the inner recesses of Holy Scriptures, which comfort the pious with the sole promise of eternal life" (Smalcius, *Refutation of the Theses of Frantz*, page 409), and on page 415, he also says: "There is nothing anywhere in the sacred Scriptures which furnishes proof that the wicked shall become immortal, namely to their eternal disgrace, and it appears that from them nothing can be adduced from which that view can be demonstrated." He had said previously that "he and his followers had never openly promoted that view." That is to say, as they state elsewhere, it is possible for the time being to say some things which suggest this view to people, until finally the time is ripe, and people have grown accustomed to this manner of speaking. But whatever those people think or reveal in words about the matter, it is clear that the view which denies that the wicked shall be resurrected and endure forever by that same effort does away with "the eternal fire prepared for the devil and his angels" (Matt 25:41 and 45), "the unquenchable fire" (Matt 3:12), "the worm of the wicked that will not die" (Mark 9:43). For it is impossible that those who are not going to endure eternally should undergo eternal punishment.

35. And in response to the points that are made against us we should observe in general that just as the word 'life,' even though it makes no distinction between life that is good or bad, or between life that is happy or wretched, nevertheless sometimes is taken strictly in such a way that it means a suitable, happy, and desirable life, as when the poet says "it is not living but living well." In the same manner as we state in the Creed that we believe life everlasting, so also "resurrection" in the sacred writers is often understood only in a good sense, so that it denotes a life whereby one arises to a life that is blessed. What is more, "resurrection" is properly speaking said about the life that really overcomes death, obviously meaning that a life follows which is more desirable than death. Since this is not the resurrection of the sort that the wicked will have, because their souls will receive their own bodies again in order to be punished more severely, and for them it would be better to not rise up again rather than to rise up to such a state, hence it follows that Scripture speaks about the wicked in such a way as though they never shall be recalled to life, by which is understood a life that is happy and desirable. Therefore, we should consider the expression "eternal life" in such a way that it means, firstly, life according to the essence of the living creature as such; secondly, with respect to the living creature's relation to the eternal principle of life, that is, God, who accordingly in the Scriptures is called life everlasting.

With respect to that essential life, the wicked will live forever; with respect to the other mode, only those who are righteous in Christ Jesus shall live victoriously.

36. Questions about babies who have died in their mothers' womb, about miscarried fetuses, the malformed and similarly abnormal babies can be duly resolved once the hypothesis is laid concerning the infusion of the soul. For either the bodies truly were animate with a human soul, or they were not animate. If the former, then the resurrection applies to them, too. If not, then consequently excluded from the resurrection are such bodies to which the definition of human being does not apply. We do, however, agree with Augustine's opinion that bodies with defects will be raised up in such a way that their nature will be set right and made sound. And "each and every single birth which is called monstrous because it has something superfluous or lacking, or because it is horribly misshapen, will through the resurrection be restored to the form of its human nature" (*Enchiridion to Laurentius*, chapter 87).

37. And with the same Augustine we do not hesitate to assert that at the resurrection the difference between the sexes will remain. This is rightly gathered from the fact that Christ, when he was asked whose wife, she will be of the seven brothers who each had had her as spouse, did not state that there would be no women in the resurrection—which if that were true would have been a very short answer—but he stated only that there will be no marriages. In fact, he even confirmed that the female sex will exist by saying "they shall not be married," which applies to women, and "they shall not take as wives," which applies to men [Matt 22:25–30]. Therefore, both those for whom it is customary here to be married, and those for whom it is customary here to take as their wives will exist, but they will not have marriages there (*On the City of God*, book 22, chapter 17). And from this it follows that the same body in number must arise, as was demonstrated above, which would not be possible unless it had the same individual conditions, of which not the least is the determination of one's sex. To this can be added the fact that at the resurrection the individual nature will not be done away with, nor the species in their perfection or wholeness, but only the defects of the nature, among which we should not put the difference between the sexes.

38. The question also arises whether each of the following will be set straight: every body that is deformed because of a defect in a useful body part or in

the equal number [of body parts]; or because of the addition of a hindersome body part; or because of an awkward location of body parts. These questions, like that pertaining to people's physical stature, because they do not have an explicit answer in Holy Scripture, are answered only by conjectures of probability, which some give differently from others. And so, we think that nothing certain can be determined about them; but we do think only this is true that in the glorified bodies of whatever sex or stature God will remove everything that caused them some deformity. But as far as the wicked are concerned, "we should not weary our minds with uncertainties about the appearance of those whose damnation will be certain, and eternal" (Augustine, *Enchiridion*, chapter 92).

39. The form of the resurrection can be considered in two ways: As internal or external, and the former again either with a view to those who will be raised up strictly speaking, or with a view to those who will be changed. Both of these can be understood well enough from what has been said, namely that the form of the resurrection of the former consists in re-forming their bodies from the dust of the earth, and in the renewed indestructible union of their souls with their revived bodies. In this regard the final resurrection differs from that particular one of Lazarus and people like him. But regarding those people who are alive, we have stated above that towards them God's action will be engaged in their instantaneous, sudden change whereby it is not the actual substance of the body that will be abolished, but its quality will be altered. And whatever is subject to decay and death will take on an imperishable and immortal nature; that change, will for them be in lieu of their death and resurrection (1 Cor 15:51; 1 Thess 4:15 and 17).

40. The outward form of the resurrection will consist of that manner and order which Christ will follow, namely that suddenly he will appear on the clouds in the visible form wherein he ascended into heaven, and he will take his seat upon his majestic throne. And he will have his angels as his servants and attendants who will blow the trumpet, and with his powerful and effective voice he will issue a sound with which he will rouse all who are asleep in the dust, and he shall cause them to stand before his judgment seat, and he will draw into his presence also the living who have been changed, along with the others, and he will divide them both into two separate groups for sentencing (which we shall treat in the description of the judgment). All these points are derived from Matt 13:41; 24:30; 25:31; John 5:28 and 29; 1 Cor 15:1; 1 Thess 4:15, 16, 17, etc.

41. The primary and ultimate goal of the resurrection is the glory of God, who works all things for his purpose (Prov 16:4), in the same way as He established all things for his glory at the beginning. To this goal belongs also seeing the glory peculiar to Christ the Mediator in his work of resurrection. But regarding the people who are going to be revived, their common goal is that of standing before the judgment seat of Christ in order to hear the verdict of the judge. And regarding those who believe, the proper goal is their everlasting glory as a reward that will be bestowed upon them by his mercy, freely given. But with regard to unbelievers and the wicked, [the proper goal is] their eternal shame as punishment that they must bear from God's just retribution (Dan 12:2; John 5:28–29; Jude verse 15; 2 Thess 1:6–7).

42. There are many uses for this doctrine. For in the first place our minds are impressed by such an important article of the faith that they retain it forever; and we also have a possession whereby we may present ourselves over against each and every opponent more readily and steadily in asserting such an important doctrine. But besides the theoretical benefit, with a view to both ourselves and others, the practical one will be very useful if we, stimulated by the promise of the future life, defy whatever hardships there are in this current life, and so defy even death itself—whether it is an ordinary death, or even (if need be) a death inflicted for a confession of the truth—with great courage so that we are (as it were) rendered blind to the dangers and punishments of this life, that we soothe the grief that arises from the death of our friends (1 Thess 4:13), and that we present our bodies—which in due time shall be raised up to immortality—as weapons of righteousness for God, and so that in this way "he who wishes not to be condemned in the second resurrection rises in the first resurrection" (Augustine, *On the City of God*, book 20, chapter 6).

43. On the basis of this doctrine, too, we should be stimulated to treat the bodies of the deceased, which are asleep in the hope of the resurrection, with modest and decent care, as was done in former times by those who wished by means of this burial rite to testify to their faith in God's promises, choosing for themselves even a location where this would be noticed by others in their time. And when Christ and the apostle Paul, in order to strengthen the hope of the resurrection, compared the bodies of those who died righteously to seeds that are sown in the earth, they showed enough that they should be placed carefully in the earth (John 12:14; 1 Cor 15:37). In this matter, we should denounce the contempt shown by those who allow the

bodies of the deceased to lie unburied (except when it happens to some people because of a just decree of the state); in the same way we also reject every superstition of the sort frequent among the followers of the pope in their care for the dead: The extravagant, pointless luxury of the kind displayed with exceeding ostentation by many people in lavishly preparing their funerals, considering it callous, because they are actually changing mourning into magnificence, and with their ostentatious pomp as it were making sport of human misery.

44. Meanwhile if through the tyranny of the wicked it should befall the upright that their bodies are hindered from being buried, or if they are dug up after they have been buried (something which occurs often in the pope's realm, as once upon a time following some conspiracy the Donatists "did not allow the bodies of the orthodox to be buried, but in order to frighten the living, they maltreated the deceased by denying them a place for burial," in Optatus, *Against Parmenius*, book 6), then let that passage of Ps 34:21[20] provide help: "The Lord protects all the bones of the upright;" and also what it says in Rev 20:13: "The sea and death some day will give up their dead." To which should be added what Augustine says: "The bodies of many Christians were not buried in the earth, but none of them has been removed by anyone from heaven or earth—which are entirely filled by the presence of Him who knows whence He shall bring back to life whatever He has created" (*On the City of God*, book 1, chapter 12).

On the Last Judgment

45. In the fundamental principles of the Christian doctrine by the apostle in Heb 6:2, the following two are joined together: The resurrection of the dead and everlasting judgment. And among the other arguments for the resurrection one of the more important ones was taken from God's justice, which requires that everyone stand "before the judgment seat of Christ, and each shall receive in the body what is due to him for the things he has done, whether good or bad" (2 Cor 5:10). And so it follows that we should speak about that judgment, but only with a few words because we have touched on most of its circumstances in the related material on the resurrection. And as for the judgment, we understand it not as the particular judgment which God carries out in this life or at each person's death, which can be called the antecedent, partial, and hidden judgment, but the universal, final, total, eternal, and manifest judgment, which will take place on that last day after

the universal resurrection, which Jude verse 6 calls "the judgment of the great day;" 2 Pet 3:12 "the day of the God;" and Paul in Rom 2:5 (with respect to the reprobate) "the day of wrath," and Eph 4:30 "the day of redemption" (with respect to the upright), just as, in Acts 3:20, it is called the time "of refreshment" and "the restitution of all things" (verse 21).

46. We understand that among the gentiles there was a somewhat mixed perception of this day and judgment, either because they wisely understood that God's justice requires a judgment of this sort, or because they were convinced from the dictates of what is honorable and what is base divinely implanted in the human heart and from the witness borne by their own consciences that at some future time it would go well for the good and badly for the wicked. Or even because something in the teaching of the church reached their ears—a perception which they obscured and corrupted with many myths. And therefore, it can be said that this mystery is beyond natural knowledge and must be believed by faith to the extent that it is revealed to us in the Word, wherein the clearest explanations are provided about its future existence and all of its causes, circumstances, and benefits, and whatever else is worth knowing. About its existence, there are almost countless testimonies in the two Testaments, but two are especially clear— Acts 17:31: "God has appointed a day on which He will judge the lands of the earth with justice," etc., and 2 Thess 1:6[–9]: "It is right for God to recompense trouble for those who trouble you, and to you who are troubled rest with us, when the Lord Jesus will be revealed from heaven with his mighty angels in flaming fire taking vengeance on those who do not know God, and who do not obey the Gospel of our Lord Jesus Christ, who will be punished with everlasting destruction, away from the presence of the Lord and from the glory of his might."

47. The primary efficient cause of this judgment, when we consider the authority in the pronouncement of the verdict, or the power in carrying it out, is God the Father, the Son and the Holy Spirit. But that judgment will be administered in visible form through the Son in the human nature he has assumed, "through him whom God has appointed, giving proof of it to all men by raising him from the dead" (Acts 17:31). "All authority in heaven and on earth has been given to him by the Father" (Matt 28:18); "all judgment" (John 5:22). For this reason, that judgment is attributed in Scripture particularly to Christ the God-and-man, although not exclusively or in opposition [to someone else], but through some appropriation, because he

who appears to people in judgment will be none other than the Son, who will be made manifest while the Father is hidden, as Augustine says in *Treatise 21 on John*. Moreover, he will judge not only by his divine nature but also by his human nature, to which by grace autocratic power is given. Against that [power] there is no appeal, because by his death he has obtained for himself the right of dominion over all people. "For this very reason Christ died and returned to life, so that he might have dominion over the living and the dead" (Rom 14:9). And part of that dominion is the judgment.

48. On this point we should make the observation that in the judgment some elements can be considered as not going beyond the power of Christ's human nature, such as the fact that Christ, as man, is Lord of all and superior over all; and the fact that he knows everything that is necessary for carrying out that judgment justly, through a created knowledge in his soul (which is called the knowledge of the union). If one looks at these elements only as they are in the person of the judge with his outward public declaration of the verdict, then they proceed from his human nature as from the formal principle. But if one considers that infinite power whereby Christ will render everlasting rewards to the righteous and everlasting punishment to the wicked—which consist in the contemplation of his divine nature or the privation of it—then it is not as man but as God that he, along with the Father and the Holy Spirit, will judge the living and the dead, because in an absolute sense it belongs only to his divine power to make people blessed or wretched. Hence in Matt 20:23 Christ says: "It is not mine to grant you to sit at my right hand, but it is prepared for them by my Father." That is, it does not belong to my human authority, as Augustine explains in *On the Trinity*, book 1, chapter 12. In this sense he says in the same place that it is not by his human authority that the Son of Man is going to judge, but only by the authority which he has as the Son of God.

49. But, whether we have in view the supremely pre-eminent human authority granted to Christ over all created beings or his divine power (both of which he will exercise in judging), it is not in partnership with either of them that the saints and believers can be said "to rule with Christ." And so when it says that they will be seated and will judge, together with Christ (whether they are apostles or all believers, Matt 19:28, Luke 22:30), it should not be taken to mean the authority or power to judge which they have in and of themselves, but 1) about what they are going to do in Christ their head; 2) about their approval of the verdict which Christ has handed down (Rev 19:1); 3) about

the witness they bear from the point of view of their service and preservation, and in comparing their life with that of the wicked, whereby the justice of the judge will be made manifest.

50. The "matter concerning which," or the object of the final judgment are—if we are viewing the persons—all the wicked angels and all good as well as bad human beings. For although the evil spirits were subjected to punishments from the very moment they fell and were condemned to everlasting damnation, and although they always carry their own underworld with them wherever they go, nevertheless we do not doubt that they, whom "God has pushed down in hell, handed over to chains of darkness, and kept for" (2 Pet 2:4; Jude 6) will receive the full complement of their punishment on that day, when they no longer will be able to harm human beings, to extort from their slaves worship as if they were gods, because they will be so bound up in their underworld prison that no further escape will be open to them. To this point, we should refer what the apostle says in 1 Cor 6:3: "Do you not know that we shall judge the angels?"—a statement we should understand as judging in Christ the head.

51. And as far as it pertains to the human beings about whom especially, we should be concerned in this question, they all will be judged, from the greatest to the least, with no exception—but the good only by the judgment of distinction, and the wicked by the judgment of condemnation. "For we shall all stand before the judgment seat of Christ" (2 Cor 5:10). John explicitly distinguishes "great and small" (Rev 20:12) and he includes both of them among those people who are to be judged, so as to make no exception for anyone. So too for "the living and the dead" (Acts 10:42). Nor is an exception made for saints: "Set aside for me is the crown of righteousness which the Lord, the just judge, will grant to me on that day" (2 Tim 4:8). And the same time is given for the bestowing of the reward to the servants of God, and for the destruction of those who destroy the earth (Rev 11:18). Therefore, we should understand the statements that believers "will not be judged" and "shall not enter into judgment" [John 5:24] as being about the condemnation. But if the wicked "will not be raised up in judgment" [Ps 1:5], we should refer that to their remaining steadfast under judgment, because they will lose their case.

52. To the object of that judgment pertains also every act of all good as well as evil people, and every good as well as evil act, which includes their words

and thoughts; the manifestation of them all on the future day of judgment is indicated by the opening of the books (Rev 20:12). And then "concerning every idle word which they have spoken people will give an account on the day of judgment" (Matt 12:35). For the good deeds will be approved and will be given the freely bestowed reward, whereas the wicked deeds will be disapproved and judged worthy of punishment. There is no exception for the sins of the upright, for which they have received forgiveness through Christ, and at that time their sins will be revealed also, but in such a way that they will not cause them any consternation but rather immeasurable joy from the fact that just as many as are the forgiven sins which will be revealed, so much will be revealed the greatness of God's mercy towards them. And so, there will be no record of sins for punishment, or for the removal of their glory, but for the giving of thanks.

53. The form of this judgment will consist: 1) in the knowledge of the case; and for it, the judge will have "no need of anyone to bear witness about man, for he knows what is in man" (John 2:25). And moreover, he will need no examination of witnesses, or personal confession by guilty parties—"all things are naked and open to his eyes" (Heb 4:13)—but rather, so that the case might be clearly understood by others he will place every secret and hidden thing into the clearest light (1 Cor 4:5). [It will consist] [2)] in deciding the case once it is known and in declaring the verdict. The first part of this verdict, which concerns the righteous, will be most pleasant: "Come, you blessed of my Father, and inherit the kingdom prepared for you from the foundation of the world." But the second part will be by far most sorrowful and horrible: "Depart, you accursed ones, into the eternal fire prepared for the devil and his angels" (Matt 25:34 and 41). The delivery of the verdict will be preceded by a separation of the sheep from the goats, and in putting the former to the right and the latter to the left side (Matt 25:32 and 33).

54. [3)] Thirdly, the form of the judgment is considered in the execution of the verdict that has been handed down. And it will not consist of the upright beginning to enjoy blessedness for the first time, or of the wicked paying the everlasting penalty. For the upright shall be blessed already through their resurrection in the glorious body which they take on, and of the wicked, on the other hand, being accursed in the shameful body they take on. But, it will consist of the righteous in heaven (whereto they will set forth with Christ) beginning to enjoy blessedness with a certain public, solemn declaration, and thereupon at a specific, appointed place, and on the other hand, with the

wicked beginning to be punished in hell (whereto they will be banished), according to that statement: "And they shall go into the everlasting fire, but the just into everlasting life" (Matt 25:46). And in the execution of his verdict, the authority and truthfulness of the judge are manifested, just as his truthfulness and wisdom are manifested in the enquiry, and his justice in the declaration of the verdict.

55. The ultimate goal of that judgment will be "that God will be glorified in his saints, and admired in all those who believe on that day" (2 Thess 1:10). And also, that when the truthfulness in his justice towards all the wicked is revealed, "all nations shall come and worship before him, because his judgments will be revealed" (Rev 15:4). And a subordinate goal will be the salvation and blessed state of the upright, the banishment of the wicked, the liberation of Christ's church, the execution of the eternal decree, and the declaration of God's justice upon the reprobate and of his mercy upon his chosen ones.

56. It cannot be determined from Holy Scripture what the special place is where the upright and the wicked will be gathered. For what the Jews, whom the papal teachers follow, contrive about the valley of Jehoshaphat does not rest upon any solid foundation. But we should understand the citation of Joel 3:2 and 12 figuratively: "I shall gather together all nations and I shall lead them into the valley of Jehoshaphat;" unless someone prefers to take the valley of Jehoshaphat, i.e., [the valley] of God's judgment, in an appellative sense for each and every place where God will carry out his judgment. For in the same chapter, it is called the "valley of decision" [Joel 3:14]. And as far as the time is concerned, "it is in vain that we strive to calculate and fix the years which still remain to this age; since we hear from the mouth of truth that it is not ours to know," as Augustine well advises us in *The City of God*, book 18, chapter 53, pondering the fact that Christ explicitly prohibited the investigation of it (Acts 1:7). And the apostle, being instructed in paradise [2 Cor 12:4], deemed it not at all necessary to write about the "times and seasons" of the Lord's coming (1 Thess 5:1). Therefore, because the appointed place and the set time lie hidden in the storehouses of God's wisdom, an enquiry into them would be foolish. And those people who have made assumptions about the time have been proven guilty of folly by God from by so frequently contrary outcome of events which followed. It was God's will to conceal one day, so that all days might be observed and that no people might fall asleep on the pillow of complacency.

57. From the things that have been said, a definition of the last judgment can be drawn up as such, that it is an act of God through Christ the God-and-man whereby, at the end of the ages, He will summon all people, both living and dead, to his seat of judgment, and He will reveal everything that they have done, both good and evil, so that following the separation of the just and the unjust He will render a verdict and enforce it according to the norm of the Law and the Gospel, by causing the upright to be blessed forever; and by adjudging the wicked together with the devils unto everlasting punishments, for the glory of his name and for the everlasting joy of his chosen ones.

58. There are many uses for this doctrine: 1) That we fortify our belief in Christ's last coming over against the blasphemous scoffers (about whom 2 Pet 3:3 writes), and so with faith in our hearts and the profession upon our lips we separate ourselves from all who either stubbornly deny that judgment or overturn the sound doctrine of it. But we should apply it [2)] especially in our own practice over against unholy living and complacency, "that we fear the Lord because the hour of his judgment is coming" (Rev 14:7); over against carousing and drunkenness (Luke 21:34); "lest that day should come upon us suddenly," contrary to the too many cares of this life (Luke 21:34); and, in short, every injustice and sin. [We should apply it in our own practice] so that we might, on the other hand, be roused to repentance, seeing that "God has appointed a day on which He will judge the lands of the earth in equity" (Acts 17:30–31). And [3)] also to rouse us to acts of kindness towards our neighbors [Phil 4:5], especially the poor—which kindness the great Judge on that day will deem as having been done to him [Matt 25:40]. And [4)] lastly, to rouse in us comfort and patience in every adversity, being mindful that day for the upright is called the day of deliverance, so that in anticipation of it "we raise up our heads" (Luke 21:28). And that in faith we continually repeat, with John (Rev 22:19), "yes, come Lord Jesus."

ON LIFE AND DEATH
EVERLASTING AND ON
THE END OF THE WORLD

President: Antonius Walaeus
Respondent: Franciscus Boogardus

This disputation deals with the doctrine of the last things. Life everlasting requires not only faith, but also a living, personal trust (2). It is 'man's everlasting blessedness and happiness which arises from the fellowship or never-ending communion of God with us' (3). Through faith and communion with God in Christ, eternal life has already begun on earth; this life will culminate in the beatific vision of God (4–8). This perfect blessedness of the human being and inexpressible joy reaches its final state after the resurrection (8–9), and consists in beholding God in full, in conjunction with the complete sanctification and glorification of our nature (10). Various aspects of the beatific vision are discussed (11–24). The full restoration and sanctification of the whole human being is the inextricable result of the beatific vision (25–27). The same goes for the complete glorification of the human body and the entire human being (28–30). All of this together brings unspeakable joy (31–32). This blessedness will yet be perfected (33) by the everlasting quality of this blessed life (34), the loveliness of heaven (35–37), and fellowship with the saints and the angels (38–44). Next, eternal death is pictured in contrast with eternal life (45–53). The new earth and new heaven, finally, do not entail the destruction and replacement of the present earth and heaven but a qualitative change to them (54–60). The very last thesis (60) refers to the very beginning, when God created the heavens and the earth: 'And thus once again from that same vast lump, God is going to summon up new heavens and a new earth, i.e., the blessed habitation, which will be suited to the uses of the future age. And those uses were partly explained when we gave a treatment of life everlasting, but will be fully and clearly perceived by us when we really shall be the possessors and dwellers of this new heaven and new earth.'

1. Having explained everything that leads to mankind's final end, it remains for us in this final disputation to treat that last end itself for man, and also the outermost consummation of the whole world.

2. In the Apostles' Creed the final goal of man is called life everlasting, and it is placed opposite everlasting death, although this second goal is therefore not counted among the articles of the faith because the Creed draws our attention to the fruit of faith only, and not also to the fruit of unbelief. And because it draws our attention to the fruit of those objects of faith only, concerning which we must not just believe from Holy Scripture that they are true, but of which also the particular application to the human heart by a living, personal trust is required.

3. To be sure, by life everlasting is meant here not the everlasting and unbroken reunion of body and soul, for that will be shared in common with the reprobate; but man's everlasting blessedness and happiness which arises from the fellowship or never-ending communion of God with us. For in the same way as the soul is the life of the body, so too is God the life of the soul. Hence also the prophet David says in Ps 33:12: "Blessed are the people whose God is Jehovah," and the apostle in 1 John 1:3: "What we have seen and heard we declare to you, so that you may have fellowship with us, and that our fellowship might be with the Father and his Son Jesus Christ."

4. And this fellowship with God has two modes: Either through faith during this life it is inchoate, or perfect in the future life by sight (properly speaking). Accordingly, the apostle makes a distinction in 2 Cor 5:7 when he says: "We walk by faith not by sight"—although he also attributes sight to faith, albeit dimly (1 Cor 13:12).

5. The fellowship we have with God through faith is some beginning of that life everlasting, which will have its fulfillment in the future and which is approximately expressed by 'the adoption as children': "For as many as have received Christ by faith, to them He gave this right or worthiness to be children of God" (John 1:12).

6. And this beginning of life everlasting includes: 1) A living awareness of the forgiveness of our sins and our reconciliation with God; "for even when we

were dead in our sins, He made us alive together through Christ, by whose grace we have been saved, and He has raised us up together and has seated us together in heaven in Christ Jesus" (Eph 2:5–6). 2) Our being renewed according to the image of God, a renewal which the apostle therefore calls "of the newness of life" (Rom 6:4). And lastly, being sealed by the Holy Spirit, which not only confirms in us these prior gifts of the spiritual life and makes them vital, but also makes us certain of the future fulfillment, and produces in us that peaceful conscience and gladness of heart which the world does not know (John 14:17) and which surpasses every human understanding (Phil 4:7). Of this, the psalmist says: "When the poor see this they will rejoice, and your spirit will live, O you who seek God" (Ps 69:33). Indeed, because of all this Gal 2:20 says that we live by faith in the Son of God and that Christ dwells here in us.

7. But frequently these benefits are meant in the Scriptures also by the word "life everlasting," not only because it is to life everlasting that they lead, but also because they are some of its first fruits, just as Christ declares in John 6:57: "Truly, truly I say to you, whoever believes in me has life everlasting; I am that bread of life, etc.;" and chapter 11:25–26: "I am the resurrection and the life; whoever believes in me, even if he dies, shall live and whoever lives and believes in me will never die."

8. It is by sight that the fulfillment and consummation of this blessedness is obtained, and strictly speaking this pertains to the coming age, as the apostle testifies in 1 Cor 13:9; the blessedness is either (again) of the soul alone, separate from the body ("when we depart from here and go to take up our dwelling with Christ," 2 Cor 5:8) or of the entire person after the resurrection of the flesh and the last judgment, "when we shall be taken up to Christ in the air, and so we shall forever be with the Lord" (1 Thess 4:17).

9. As far as it concerns the former state (the one regarding the soul alone, separate from the body), we have given a fuller treatment of it when we dealt with the church triumphant in heaven, and so it is not necessary for us to treat it more fully here. Therefore, we next should offer a treatment of that second, final state of man after the resurrection.

10. And so this last, and perfect, blessedness of man consists in beholding God in full, in conjunction with the complete sanctification and glorification of our nature. An inexpressible joy is born from these mutually conjoined elements—a joy which goes beyond every human comprehension. In what

follows we are going to examine and explain the elements of this definition a little more closely.

11. The Scripture of the Old and New Testaments testifies in many places that beholding God is the foundation and cause of this blessedness as a whole. So, Job says in chapter 19:26: "I in my flesh shall see God;" David in Ps 16:11: "Fullness of joy in your sight," and in Ps 17:15: "In righteousness I shall behold your face; I shall be satisfied with your likeness, when I awake." And so Christ in Matt 5:8: "Blessed are the pure in heart, for they will see God." And 1 Cor 13:12: "Now we see as in a mirror, dimly, but then face to face." Likewise, 1 John 3:2: "We know that when He appears we shall be like Him because we shall see Him as He is."

12. Concerning this beholding the question arises firstly whether man will see God with his corporeal eyes, and secondly, if this beholding should be referred entirely to the soul, what the mode or manner of it will be.

13. As far as the first question is concerned, we approve the opinion of those who assert that God, when human beings are glorified, is indeed going to manifest his own majesty in a special way to their bodily eyes illumined with heavenly light—not only by certain signs (just as He sometimes revealed his presence to Moses and the prophets in an extraordinary way through signs), but especially in the human nature of Christ now made glorious; and through it, as an instrument conjoined to the divinity, He will show his divine properties and glory more fully and openly in order to be seen in some way. In the same manner He displayed some evidence of that matter in the glorification of Christ (Matt 17 and Luke 9) and also in those visions which were given to the apostle Paul, when he was taken up into Paradise (2 Cor 12), and often were given to the apostle John, when he was taken by the Spirit, in many places throughout the book of Revelation.

14. Meanwhile, however, we do assert that the beholding of God wherein the very essence of the highest good has its existence belongs, strictly speaking, not to the body but to the soul, because the spiritual essence is not visible to bodily eyes. Hence in Col 1:15 the apostle calls God, too, absolutely invisible. This is evident also from the fact that the souls of believers in heaven are already enjoying this blessedness of beholding God, and because the angels in heaven always are beholding the Father's face, even though they lack bodies. Similarly, and for the same reason, also the apostle interchanges the words "knowledge" and "beholding," and he clearly places this seeing face

to face over against knowing that is in part (1 Cor 13:12), and also over against faith (2 Cor 5:7).

15. The Scholastics hold many ingenious and elaborate disputations about the mode of this seeing, but we shall touch only on those which are based on the foundations of Holy Scripture or sound reasoning, and which relate to "edification in what is useful" [Eph 4:29], leaving the other, vain speculations to the authors of them.

16. And first, they hold disputations about whether the blessed are going to see the actual divine essence directly, or actually only some spiritual splendor and radiance of it. But our assertion is that whatever they make that splendor out to be, it must of necessity be something created and, therefore, distinct from God. But Scripture testifies that our blessedness consists in beholding God himself, as was shown above. And so, it says that "we are going to see Him face to face, and we shall know Him as He is, even as we are known" (1 Cor 13:12) and that "we are going to see Him as He is" (1 John 3[:2]). And clear reasoning also furnishes proof, because no thing that has been created can be our highest good, but only the uncreated God is able truly to fulfill and satisfy man's longing and mind.

17. From this the conclusion is rightly derived also that the blessed see God not even through some abstract or expressed image of Him, but through his essence. For knowledge that comes via an abstract image is imperfect knowledge, and it is necessarily imperfect because of the absence of the thing seen or because of its distance away from the intellect. But the essence of God is spiritual, and present to and conjoined with the minds of the blessed intimately. And therefore, that very essence, like an object with no element to intervene is able to represent itself easily to a man's mind, for which reason it says even of God himself that "God himself is going to be (i.e., directly) all in all" (1 Cor 15:28). We grant however that in man's very intellect an extraordinary light has to be imprinted whereby he is able to take hold of the divine essence as a beatific object by means of an intuitive seeing, in the same way as in this life there is need of supernatural light in man's intellect in order for us to be able to have true fellowship with God through faith, as the Scripture testifies in Matt 16:17, Acts 16:14, and 1 Cor 3:14. "For God who commanded the light to shine out of darkness has shined the light in our hearts to give the light of the knowledge of God in the face of Jesus Christ" (2 Cor 4:6). And it is customary to refer to this also the passage of the psalmist

in Ps 36:10: "With you is the fount of life, and in your light do we enjoy the light."

18. However, the Scholastics have the habit of debating rather copiously whether the blessed behold the divine essence with all its properties and workings, and this in its infinity. And also whether this vision is necessary, or instead voluntary, from the side of God. Concerning these questions, we have made the following determinations.

19. The matter itself suggests that God's infinite essence in its infinite state can be grasped adequately only by a mind that is infinite; but because God's infinite being everywhere is entire, for that reason the incarnation of God's Son shows that the entire essence can be united with a finite creature, and consequently, it does not conflict with nature that it can be perceived by a finite mind by means of a beatific vision. Indeed: The entire essence, albeit not entirely or in an infinite mode, but in a mode that is suited to the finite nature, as the passages of Scripture that were adduced in thesis 11 show. And therefore, it is said that the angels in heaven, although they always behold God's face, yet before the throne of God's majesty, they cover their faces with two wings lest they be destroyed by his majesty (Isa 6:2).

20. We assert then that the same vision (if it is regarded as active) and also its extent and mode depend only on God's will and free dispensation, not from some natural relationship or disposition of the object towards its own power. Accordingly, our Savior says in Matt 11:27: "No-one knows the Son except the Father, nor does anyone know the Father except the Son and anyone to whom the Son has chosen to reveal Him." And so, therefore, just as in this life He bestows his own spiritual gifts in different measure to people individually in accordance with his will (1 Cor 12:11), so too in the life to come every one of the blessed will perceive of it as much as it will seem good to God's gracious will and good pleasure, and it will be sufficient for their full blessedness. "For He has mercy upon whom He has mercy and He has compassion on whom He has compassion" (Exod 33:19).

21. But it is a harder question whether, in accordance with the extent to which the essence is shared, so too necessarily and naturally the extent of seeing the persons, attributes, and workings of God is shared.

22. The Scholastics are generally convinced that everything that in God is natural or that by the necessity of nature flows forth from his essence

necessarily is shared along with the essence, and so together with his essence also all of God's essential attributes are perceived intuitively, because God's essence is most simple and in reality, not different from his attributes. As the blessed see God just as He is, they therefore see also his attributes; accordingly, by beholding Him they break forth in adoration of his attributes in general, as can be seen in Isa 6 and in Rev 4 and 6. And they [the Scholastics] rightly conclude that the same reasoning goes for the persons, because although one person differs in reality from another, yet the person does not differ in reality from the essence, and just as the person of the Father by Himself and necessarily subsists in the divine essence, so also by natural necessity the person of the Son and the Holy Spirit are brought forth in that [essence]. Therefore, because the blessed see God just as He is, and in this life believers have fellowship with all three persons, it necessarily follows that in heaven the same fellowship is not stopped but brought to fulfilment. Hence in John 14:9 Christ also says: "Whoever sees me sees the Father," and "All that the Father has is mine" (chapter 16:15).

23. It follows, however, they conclude that the divine decrees are a different matter, and so too the workings thereof, which depend upon God's free decrees—like all the divine works that are called "outward works" because they are not in God by absolute necessity. As it is not by absolute necessity that He produces these outward works, but according to his own freedom, therefore it is not by absolute necessity that they are seen when God is seen, but [only] as much of them as it is in the will of God to reveal to anyone. Hence it is that the angels always see the Father's face and yet do not know the day of judgment (Mark 13:32), and only by an extraordinary revelation of God do they receive what according to his will they reveal to Christ's servants for the upbuilding of the church, as can be seen in Rev 1:1 and Rev 5:3.

24. And from these things it is also clear that the "mirror of the Trinity" which several papal teachers fabricate, as if in it the inward and outward needs and prayers of all humanity are reflected to the blessed in heaven, in no way accords with their more reasonable hypotheses, since all these workings are dependent on God's free decree. This is why God everywhere claims for himself the examination of the hearts and the certain knowledge of all the other things which depend upon contingent causes, along with his care for the world—as we have shown elsewhere when we treated the invocation of saints. And in fact, Holy Scripture expressly testifies that "just as no-one

knows the things in man except the spirit of man that is in him, so no-one knows the things in God except the Spirit of God" (1 Cor 2:11).

25. From this beatific vision of God, a beholding which surpasses all of man's comprehension, there necessarily is born the full restoration and sanctification of the whole man, so that in proportion to the blessed soul's gazing upon God face to face in his glory also man's heart must be kindled with love for him and with adoration of all his works.

26. This is shown firstly by the very nature of this beatific vision. For also here "all believers, with faces unveiled, are beholding God's glory as in a mirror, are changed into the same image from glory to glory," as the apostle states in 2 Cor 3:18. How much more will that glorious contemplation of God's essence seize man's will and all his other powers and faculties into concord with God's holiness and glory. It will be just as the sun shares its image and brilliance with the mirror which takes it in.

27. It is shown secondly by the whole tenor of Holy Scripture. For just as this beholding of God is promised only to those "who are pure of heart" (Matt 5:8), it is withheld from those "who have not been born again" (John 3:3) and also "from flesh and blood" (1 Cor 15:50). And because likewise into that heavenly Jerusalem "entry is denied to everything that is polluted or that works abomination or lies" (Rev 21:27), it follows necessarily that in that complete fruition of blessedness the whole man will be completely restored and sanctified. Hence also the apostle Peter promises in 2 Pet 3:13 that there will be "new heavens and a new earth in which righteousness will dwell;" and the souls of the blessed in heaven "are clothed in white robes and palms are placed in their hands" (Rev 7:9), as people who have conquered Satan, the world, and sin. And the bride of Christ herself when she will go into the bridegroom in order to make full celebration of the wedding feast, "is first arrayed in clean and white linen, which is the righteous acts of the saints" (Rev 19:8).

28. These two beatific benefits of God will even be followed by a third one: The complete glorification of the actual human body, and consequently of the entire human being. This glorification is indicated in the Scriptures partly by the removal of every imperfection and partly by the opposite affirmation of every sort of perfection.

29. Therefore, from the glorified man is removed not only everything that comes from sin or that has the character of punishment, but also whatever pertains to man's animate condition by virtue of the first creation in this world. And so Rev 21:4 asserts not only that "God shall wipe away every tear from their eyes and that death shall be no more, nor sorrow, nor crying, nor grief," and that "they shall hunger no longer, and thirst no longer, and the sun shall not smite them, nor any heat" (Rev 7:16), but also that "God shall do away with the stomach and with food" (1 Cor 6:13) and also that "in the resurrection, they will not lead into marriage nor be given into marriage, but they will be like the angels of God in heaven" (Matt 22:30).

30. And concerning the body, it is affirmed that "what is sown perishable will be raised imperishable; what is sown in dishonor will be raised in glory; what is sown in weakness will be raised in power; what is sown a natural body will be raised a spiritual body" (1 Cor 15:42[–44]); also that "this mortal will put on immortality" (verse 53). And it is affirmed that "as is that heavenly one, namely Christ, so also they shall be heavenly, and as we have borne the image of the earthly, we also shall bear the image of the heavenly" (verse 49). Indeed, "the righteous shall shine like the sun in the kingdom of their Father" (Matt 13:43). And "those who are wise shall shine as with the brightness of the firmament, and those who turn many to righteousness like the stars for ever and ever" (Dan 12:3). For "our citizenship is in heaven, from where we also expect our Savior, the Lord Jesus Christ, who will change our lowly body to be like unto his glorious body, according to the working whereby he is able to subject all things unto himself" (Phil 3:20[–21]).

31. And the final thing which we put in the definition of this heavenly blessedness is the inexpressible joy which here surpasses all of man's understanding.

32. For it could happen in no other way, when indeed the body of man is set free from every weakness of sin and nature and is in conformity with Christ's glorious body, and the soul is free of every struggle of the flesh and the spirit enjoys beholding the divine essence and glory, when indeed, I say, the whole man will be drenched with real comfort and his soul in inexpressible joy, just as Christ promised, "Blessed are those who mourn, for they shall receive comfort" (Matt 5:4), and David, "They shall feast on the abundance of your house, and you will make them to drink from the river of your pleasures" (Ps 36:8).

And this is the hidden manna which Christ promises to the victor (Rev 2:17); and indeed, this gladness will be so great that the apostle testifies that "no eye has seen, nor ear has heard, neither has entered into anyone's heart, what God has prepared for those who love him" (1 Cor 2:9). Even so, it is foreshadowed in some fashion in the Scriptures by the pleasures of the garden of Eden or Paradise, by the feast and merriment of the banquets and the royal weddings, by the delight and entertainment in the songs, musical instruments, and similar activities of this age whereby the heart of man is used to being filled with virtuous amusement and joy.

33. And although the very essence of blessedness exists in the things we have explained thus far, nevertheless some circumstances and accompanying things (which Holy Scripture everywhere joins to them) will in no small way cause it to be perfected in all its parts.

34. The first of these is the everlasting quality of this blessed life; for while the pagan philosophers themselves admit that full and real blessedness cannot exist alongside the fear of sometime losing it, Holy Scripture also sufficiently in this matter comes to bolster the certainty of those who are blessed: "Whoever is faithful even unto death, to him will be given the crown of life, and he who conquers will not be harmed by the second death," as Christ promises in Rev 2:10–11. And for that reason, everywhere in the sacred writings this blessedness is called everlasting life, the everlasting inheritance, and the everlasting kingdom. Boethius rightly defines that everlasting quality as "the complete and at the same time perfect possession of life that is without end," and for that reason it is called also by the apostle Peter "the inheritance which cannot perish, nor be defiled or fade away" (1 Pet 1:4) and the "unfading crown of glory" (chapter 5:4), and so it says that "they will reign with God forever and ever" (Rev 22:5).

35. Also the majesty and loveliness of the place makes no small contribution to it. The same apostle Peter testifies in the same passage (chapter 1:4) that this is heaven when he says "this inheritance is preserved for you in heaven"—by which heaven we do not mean this visible heaven in which the planets and the other stars can be seen, much less some everywhere-present and incorporeal heaven such as the Lutherans imagine, but that heaven which is called the throne of God, and which is the most glorious and resplendent heaven above all of these visible heavens, and which accordingly is called the third heaven, and Paradise (1 Cor 12), and which is placed above all the

heavens (Eph 4:10), the glory and splendor of which is very fully depicted by the figure of the heavenly Jerusalem and of the most lovely and precious things in this world in Revelation chapters 21 and 22.

36. But on this point we should not heed those who declare that heaven indeed will be the realm of the blessed souls until the time of the last judgment, but that afterwards the earth, having been set free from its slavery to corruption, and having been made glorious, will be granted as dwelling-place to blessed human beings, while heaven then will be reserved only for the angels. For Holy Scripture locates the entire and unfailing reward of the saints in heaven, as is seen in Matt 5:12, Luke 12:33, Heb 10:34. Secondly, because the actual kingdom of heaven is promised as the final reward for believers (Matt 5:10; likewise 19:14). Thirdly, because in contrast with earth heaven is called "our everlasting dwelling-place" (2 Cor 5:1) and "our citizenship" (Phil 3:20), and "our fatherland" (Heb 11:26). And so, we shall dwell there not only for a period of time and as sojourners, but in perpetuity. For otherwise believers who are going to die around the time of the ending of the world will spend only a brief time in that place, and those who are seized by the last day while they are alive shall enter that place never. All this is absurd and foreign to the truth of God's promises.

37. But in addition to what we have brought forward, Christ, too, clearly testifies the opposite in Matt 8:[11–]12 when he says: "those who believe from all peoples shall recline with Abraham, Isaac and Jacob in the kingdom of heaven; and the sons of the kingdom"—that is, the Jews—"shall be cast into the outer darkness, where there will be weeping and gnashing of teeth." And in John 14:2[–3], he declares to his disciples: "In my Father's house are many mansions; I go to prepare a place for you, and when I go and prepare a place for you I shall come again and shall take you unto myself, so that where I am you also may be." Likewise, Rev 3:21: "If anyone conquers, I shall grant him to sit with me upon my throne, even as I also overcame, and sit with my Father upon his throne." Hence it is what the apostle says in 1 Thess 4:17: "We who are alive, who remain, shall be taken up with them in the clouds to meet the Lord in the air" (that is, away from earth) "and so we always shall be with the Lord." Hence the same apostle calls the kingdom of Christ for which he himself has been kept "Christ's kingdom above the heavens" (2 Tim 4:18).

38. The third accompanying element which we should take into account in life everlasting is the company or fellowship of those who will be partakers of that same future happiness, a fellowship which Holy Scripture everywhere also promises to us as the crowning of blessedness.

39. For the blessed in heaven, although they shall fully rest in the enjoyment of God alone (Ps 73:25), they nevertheless will rejoice both in their own glory and blessedness and in that of the other believers. And in their midst Christ, as the Head of the church, even also as man, always will occupy the foremost place, as the apostle shows in 2 Cor 5:8 and Phil 1:23. Secondly there are the holy patriarchs, prophets and apostles, with whom it says we shall recline in the kingdom of heaven (Matt 8:11 and 19:28). And also the angels and their myriads are numbered among this company (Heb 12:22 and Rev 7:11). And lastly, there will be so great a multitude of believers that no-one will be able to number it (Heb 12:23 and Rev 7:9).

40. And on this point the question is asked whether there will be mutual recognition, conversation and interaction among the blessed. But while we should not make overly curious investigations beyond God's Word into the manner of these things, yet we do not doubt that on the basis of the trustworthy foundations of Holy Scripture that matter can be gathered and demonstrated sufficiently.

41. For Christ, the patriarchs, prophets and apostles, as was noted earlier, always will keep their special place, station and order in this gathering and festal assembly of the blessed. And Christ himself will always be that good shepherd who knows his own sheep and who is known by them (John 10). Moses and Elijah conversed with Christ and they were recognized by the apostles (Matt 17:7 and Luke 9:32). Abraham knew Lazarus (Luke 16). Wealthy believers will be welcomed into their everlasting dwellings by the poor believers whom they had treated well (Luke 16:9), and the believers at Thessalonica will be Paul's crown of glory on that day (1 Thess 2:19). Even the angels will know not only each other, but they will recognize also all the chosen ones on that last day and set them apart from those who are reprobate (Matt 13:41 and Mark 13:27). Paul, when he was taken up into Paradise, not only saw Christ but he also heard things which no human being can speak (2 Cor 12), and throughout the book of Revelation references are made to the specific order among the blessed angels and men, of conversation, of

doxology, and of the declaration of God's judgments and His benefits for each of them in particular.

42. And we state that the saints will employ not merely mental speech but also that of the voice; for the use of language will not be abolished, but perfected, as is clear enough from the preceding. It is not so certain as to which language the blessed will use, although it is certain that the variety of languages—which is a consequence of sin—will cease there, according to the apostle (1 Cor 13:18). Hence some also draw the not improbable conclusion that use of the Hebrew language will remain, because it is not a consequence of sin, and because Christ when he spoke to Paul from heaven even though the latter was originally Greek, used the Hebrew language, as the apostle explicitly observes in Acts 26:14.

43. There are also some who hold disputes about the clothing, because to human beings the angels always appeared in white and brilliant garments, and because Christ at his transfiguration with Moses and Elijah took on a brilliance not only in his body but also in his glorious garment, as the evangelists note in Matt 17:2 and Luke 9:29. However, a more probable sentiment is that of those who think that the blessed shall lack all clothing, and they hold that this was done only on account of the dispensation, lest naked bodies be exposed to the eyes of sinful people. But in the future age, when all the effects of sin shall cease, and nothing in the human body will be indecent or liable to shame, then the brilliance and majesty of the glorious body will far surpass all the splendor and majesty of clothes.

44. But we do hold, contrary to some people, that the difference in gender will remain entirely in the exact same way as God created human nature in the beginning, as Augustine rightly gathered from Christ's statement in Matt 22 and other places. And yet we do hold that the remaining maimings or imperfections of limbs or old age shall be removed from bodies, because Phil 3 states that our lowly bodies will be conformed to Christ's glorious body, and what is sown in weakness will be raised in power, as the apostle says in 1 Cor 15:42. And from him it is rightly concluded also that even that earthly heaviness and weight will be removed from their limbs, because the animate body will be rendered spiritual, and when Christ is coming from the highest heaven in as short a time as possible—as fast as lightning (as he himself says in Matt 24:27)—then we shall be taken to meet him in the clouds, as the apostles testifies in 1 Thess 4:17.

45. From the things that have been explained thus far about the nature and circumstances of life everlasting it can be sufficiently understood from the contrary what we should state about everlasting death, so that it is not necessary for us to be delayed with rehearsing all the little details. However, so that we might know the truth of it more precisely we are adding the following few observations.

46. First, that the opinion of the Socinians who are accustomed to defining everlasting death by the everlasting extinction of the body and the soul is blasphemous because Holy Scripture teaches in nearly countless places that everlasting death is accompanied by everlasting pains and torments, and that also the very conscience of criminal men is afraid of, and has foreboding feelings about, far different punishments and torments from an angry God.

47. Secondly, also erroneous is the opinion of the Origenists and some Anabaptists who imagined that there will at last come some ending to these torments. For in the Scriptures everlasting death and everlasting life are opposed to each other in one and the same sense, as is seen in Dan 12:2 and Matt 25:27[=41]. And so also in Luke 16:27 it is stated expressly by Abraham that it is impossible for anyone to cross over from the place of torments to the place of comfort. Similarly, in Mark 9:47, mention is made of "the worm which does not die and the fire which is not put out;" and hence in Rev 14:11 and 19:3 the Holy Spirit bears witness that "the smoke of their torment rises up for ever and ever, and they will have no rest, day or night."

48. Therefore, together with the whole orthodox church we state that everlasting death consists of those people being forever cast out from the presence of God and from the company of all the blessed ones into hell; and of a living, effective sense of the wrath of God against their impenitence (as that of a just judge), a wrath which rightly was aroused against them in keeping with the amount of their sins; hence there follows also the anguish and torment of conscience which will possess them forever.

49. In this definition the basis for this death is placed in those men being forever cast out from God's gracious presence, for Christ bears witness in Matt 8:12 that they "will be cast into the outer darkness, where there will be weeping and gnashing of teeth;" and chapter 25:41: "depart from me, you evildoers, into the everlasting fire which has been prepared for the devil and his angels." And therefore, it says in Rev 22:15: "outside will be the dogs, the

sorcerers and the sexually immoral, and murderers and whoever loves and practices falsehood."

50. And this being cast out from God's countenance will be joined to the everlasting torments of soul and body, and these not only will arise from the fact that those wretched people will see that they are deprived of all happiness—which they call the punishment of damnation—but also because they will realize in earnest God's wrath against their sins—which they call the punishment of the senses. In this manner the apostle says in Rom 2:8[–9]: "Wrath and anger, tribulation and anguish upon every soul of man who does evil." And to this may be referred also that everlasting fire which does not go out, and the worm which does not die—with which Christ threatens them in the passages cited earlier.

51. It is not necessary for us to enter into a disputation overly worrisome with the Scholastics about whether or in what way a real and corporeal fire thereafter is going to afflict them. It will suffice for us here that the force of their torments is going to be so great that "it would be better for those men if they had not been born" (Matt 26:24), and that arising merely from the fear and presentiment of their grief it says of the unrighteous that "they shall gnaw their tongues, and curse the God of heaven" (Rev 16:10[–11]), and that on that last day "they shall say in vain to the mountains and the rocks, 'fall on us, and hide us from the presence of Him who sits upon the throne, and from the wrath of the Lamb'; for that great day of his wrath is coming, and who shall be able to stand?"

52. But even though all the punishments of this second death will be everlasting, from that it does not follow that they will all be the same. Instead, just as there will be different degrees in life everlasting (according only to the different sharing of God's grace), so too the punishments in everlasting death will be different, in keeping with the different measure of men's sins and stubbornness that will be inflicted upon the unrighteous by God's just judgment. In this manner Christ himself testifies (Matt 11:[21–]22) that "it will be more bearable for Tyre and Sidon on that day of judgment than for those cities in which he displayed his powers, and they did not repent." Similarly, Luke 12:47: "Because that servant who knew the will of his master, and did not prepare himself or did not do according to his will, will be struck with many blows; but the one who did not know and did things deserving of blows will be struck with few."

53. The place destined for those people, just as it is for the devils, very often in Scripture is called Hades, that is, hell, or abyss, Gehenna, the pit of the abyss, or the lake burning with fire and sulfur, in order that from the very horror of the place the seriousness of the punishments can be grasped so much better. But we should not make an overly curious investigation into where the site of this place is, but rather into the way and manner whereby we are able to avoid it. In the meantime, however, just as we do not dare to disapprove the thinking of those who locate the place in the shadowy depths of earth and sea (because of the idea common to the previously-mentioned names; because it is everywhere placed opposite to the highest heaven; and because for the most part there is spoken of descending down to it), so also do we not wish to reject the thinking of Chrysostom, Luther, and more recently others, who think that it is situated beyond the visible world, and who accordingly judge that it is located beyond the heavenly Jerusalem (Rev 22:15) and is designated by the name of outer darkness (Matt 8:12 and 25:30).

54. And this is the future final condition of human beings, both the upright and the wicked, after the last judgment; and it will be followed immediately by the consummation and end of this visible world and so of the entire age, just as that angel "swears by him who lives for ever and ever, that time shall be no more" (Rev 10:6), and as the apostle [says]: "Then the end will come when Christ shall hand over the kingdom to [his] God and Father, when He will have put down all rule, and all authority and power" (1 Cor 15:24).

55. And although there were some philosophers—and Aristotle among them—who wrongly maintained that the universe is everlasting, nevertheless the Christian faith places it beyond controversy that just as it was established in the beginning out of nothing by God's word alone, so also will it again come to ruin in due time, just as the prophet says: "You in the beginning, Lord, have laid the foundations of the world and the heavens are the works of your hands. They shall pass away, but you remain, and all will grow old like a garment, and like clothing you will change them, and they shall be changed" (Ps 102:26). And Christ [says]: "Heaven and earth shall pass away, but my words will never pass away" (Luke 21:33).

56. And just as some ruination of the world occurred previously through the flood of waters, Holy Scripture testifies that so also the final ruination of the world will happen through the fire to come. And so Isa 66:15 says: "For behold, Jehovah is going to come with fire, and with his chariots like a

whirlwind, to render his anger with fury and his rebuke with flames of fire." And the apostle Peter states even more clearly: "The heaven and the earth which now exist and are kept in store by the same word, are preserved for fire unto the day of judgment and the destruction of the wicked" (2 Pet 3:7). But there is no agreement among theologians of what sort this future ruination of the world through fire is.

57. For very many think that by this ruination of the world is meant nothing other than a change in the qualities of this world, and liberation from slavery to corruption which in the world now is a result of sin or even from the first condition of the natural state of men. That is based on various places in Scripture which only appear to indicate such a change, like Ps 102 where Scripture uses the word "change;" and so Paul in 1 Cor 7:31 says "the outer form of this world is passing away;" and 2 Pet 3:6 compares this final change of the world to the destruction of the world through water—which would not be a comparison if this world must be completely destroyed. But a remarkable passage that they especially press forward is Rom 8:19, where the apostle asserts: "the creature (or, the created world, as Beza renders it) with eager longing looks for and expects the revelation of the sons of God," and it adds the cause: "for the creature was made subject to vanity, not willingly, but by reason of him who has subjected it to that vanity in the hope that also the creature itself will be set free from slavery to corruption into the freedom of God's children, etc." And in whatever way these words are translated, they can be understood in no other way than about the makeup of this visible world, which on account of man's sin is subject to slavery to corruption and vanity, since in the same passage the apostle explicitly distinguishes this creature from the sons of God, and it cannot be taken to mean the angels, who are not subject to slavery to corruption.

58. Others, however, judge that this visible world is going to be completely destroyed, and that another one is going to be put in its place. And [they gather] that from the passages of Scripture in which it says that this world will pass away, perish, and have a consummation and ending; and also that time will be no more, etc.; but especially from the passages of Rev 20:11, "From the presence of him who sits upon the throne the earth and heaven flee away, and no place is found for them;" and of chapter 21:1: "I saw a new heaven and a new earth, for the first heaven and the first earth had passed away and the sea now was no more."

59. But these expressions seem to be reconciled very well by others, from the passage of Peter, 2 Pet 3:10 and following, where it, indeed, says that "the heavens will pass away with a great sound, and the elements will be dissolved with intense heat, and the earth and the works that are in it will be burned up"—but verse 12[–13] follows: "The heavens will be resolved with fire, and the elements shall melt away with intense heat, but we according to the promise look for new heavens and a new earth in which righteousness will dwell."

60. Namely in such a way, that this whole visible universe is going to be dissolved by that fire, turned into liquid, and purified of corruption and other impurities or effects of natural life, in the same manner as it is customary for different types of metals to be liquefied through fire, to be mingled together, and purified of their dross. And thus, once again from that same vast lump, God is going to summon up new heavens and a new earth, i.e., the blessed habitation, which will be suited to the uses of the future age. And those uses were partly explained when we gave a treatment of life everlasting but will be fully and clearly perceived by us when we really shall be the possessors and dwellers of this new heaven and new earth.

Bibliography

The titles in the following bibliography were selected for their pertinence to the *Synopsis of a Purer Theology* and its historical, theological, and ecclesiastical context. Only English texts are included.

Primary Source:

Synopsis Purioris Theologiae / *Synopsis of a Purer Theology*, Vol. 1–3. Trans. R. A. Faber; vol. 1 ed. D. te Velde; vol. 2 ed. H. van den Belt; vol. 3 ed. H. Goris. Leiden: Brill, 2014–2020.

Secondary Sources:

Asselt, van. W. J., Dekker, E., eds. *Reformation and Scholasticism. An Ecumenical Enterprise*. Grand Rapids: Baker Academic, 2001.

Asselt, van. W. J., et al. *Introduction to Reformed Scholasticism*. Grand Rapids: Reformation Heritage Books, 2011.

Asselt, van. W. J. "Reformed Orthodoxy: A Short History of Research," 11–26 in H. J. Selderhuis, ed., *Handbook of Dutch Church History*. Göttingen: Vandenhoeck & Ruprecht, 2015.

Asselt, van. W. J., and Abels, P. "The Seventeenth Century," 259–360 in H. J. Selderhuis, *Handbook of Dutch Church History*.

Belt van den. H., and de Vries-van Uden, M. "Herman Bavinck's Preface to the *Synopsis Purioris Theologiae*," *Bavinck Review* 8 (2017): 101–114.

Belt, van den. H. "Developments in Structuring of Reformed Theology: The *Synopsis Purioris Theologiae* (1625) as Example," 289–311 in H. J. Selderhuis and E.-Waschke, eds., *Reformation und Rationalität*. Refo500 Academic Studies, vol. 17. Göttingen: Vandenhoeck & Ruprecht, 2015.

Belt, van den. H., de Jong, K-W., and van Vlastuin, W. eds. *A Landmark in Turbulent Times. The Meaning and Relevance of the Synod of Dordt (1618–1619)*. Göttingen: Vandenhoeck & Ruprecht, 2022.

Boer, den. W. *God's Twofold Love: The Theology of Jacob Arminius (1559–1609)*. Trans. A. Gootjes. Reformed Historical Theology, vol. 14. Göttingen: Vandenhoeck & Ruprecht, 2010.

Broeyer, F. G. M. "Theological Education at the Dutch Universities in the Seventeenth Century: Four Professors on Their Ideal of the Curriculum," *Dutch Review of Church History* 85 (2005): 116–121.

Faber, R. A. "Intellectual Property in the Era of Reformed Orthodoxy: Questions of Authorship in the *Synopsis of a Purer Theology*," *Westminster Theological Journal* 82.1 (2020): 61–75.

Faber, R. A. "Scholastic Continuities in the Reproduction of Classical Sources in the *Synopsis Purioris Theologiae*," *Church History and Religious Culture* 92.4 (2012): 561–579.

Faber, R. A. "The Function of the Catechism's Spirituality in the *Synopsis of Purer Theology* (1625)," 84–94 in A. Huijgen, ed., *The Spirituality of the Heidelberg Catechism: Papers of the International Conference on the Heidelberg Catechism Held in Apeldoorn 2013*. Refo500 Academic Studies, vol. 24. Göttingen: Vandenhoeck & Ruprecht, 2015.

Fesko, J. V. "Lapsarian Diversity at the Synod of Dort," 99–123 in M. Haykin and M. Jones, eds., *Drawn into Controversie: Reformed Theological Diversity and Debates Within Seventeenth-Century British Puritanism*. Reformed Historical Theology, vol. 17. Göttingen: Vandenhoeck & Ruprecht, 2011.

Goudriaan, A., and van Lieburg, F., eds. *Revisiting the Synod of Dordt (1618–1619)*. Brill's Series in Church History, vol. 49. Leiden: Brill, 2011.

Ha, P. "Discovering Orthodoxy? Rethinking the Purpose and Impact of the Synod of Dordt," 37–54 in van den Belt, de Jong, and van Vlastuin.

Haykin, M., and Jones, M., eds. *Drawn into Controversie. Reformed Theological Diversity and Debates Within Seventeenth-Century British Puritanism*. Reformed Historical Theology, vol. 17. Göttingen: Vandenhoeck & Ruprecht, 2011.

Leeuwen, van, T. M., Stanglin, K. D., and Tolsma, M., eds. *Arminius, Arminianism, and Europe Jacobus Arminius (1559/60–1609)*. Brill's Series in Church History, vol. 39. Leiden: Brill, 2009.

Lehner, U. L., Muller, R. A., and Roeber, A. G., eds. *The Oxford Handbook of Early Modern Theology, 1600–1800*. Oxford: Oxford University Press, 2016.

Moehn, W. "Debating Regeneration. From Baptismal Water to Seed of Rebirth," 211–224 in van den Belt, de Jong, and van Vlastuin.

Muller, R. A. *Dictionary of Latin and Greek Theological Terms: Drawn Principally from Protestant Scholastic Theology*. Grand Rapids: Baker, 1985.

Muller, R. A. *Post-Reformation Reformed Dogmatics: The Rise and Development of Reformed Orthodoxy, ca. 1520 to ca. 1725*. 4 vols. Grand Rapids: Baker Academic, 2003.

Muller, R. A. "Diversity in the Reformed Tradition: A Historiographical Introduction," 11–30 in Haykin and Jones.

Novikoff, A. J. *The Medieval Culture of Disputation: Pedagogy, Practice, and Performance*. Philadelphia: University of Pennsylvania Press, 2013.

Reeling Brouwer, R. *Karl Barth and Post-Reformation Orthodoxy*. Barth Studies Series. Aldershot, Surrey: Ashgate, 2015.

Schilling, H. "Confessionalization in the Empire. Religious and Societal Change in Germany between 1555 and 1620," 205–245 in H. Schilling, ed., *Religion, Political Culture and the Emergence of Early Modern Society*. Leiden: Brill, 1992.

Selderhuis, H. J., ed. *A Companion to Reformed Orthodoxy*. Brill's Companions to the Christian Tradition, vol. 40. Leiden: Brill, 2013.

Sinnema, D., and van den Belt, H. "The *Synopsis Purioris Theologiae* (1625) as a Disputation Cycle," *Church History and Religious Culture* 92.4 (2012): 505–537.

Stanglin, K. D. "How Much Purer is the *Synopsis Purioris Theologiae* (1625)?" *Church History and Religious Culture* 98.2 (2018): 195–224.

Velde, te, D. "Reformed Theology and Scholasticism," 99–214 in P. T. Nimmo, D. Fergusson, eds., *Companion to Reformed Theology*. Cambridge: Cambridge University Press, 2016.

Scripture Index

23:19 61, 66
27:16 60
28:3 602
28:9-10 228
28:11 219
28:22 334
28:25 225
30 216, 463, 465
30:13 212
31:1 701

DEUTERONOMY
1:17 696
4:2 16, 24, 34, 705
4:6 36
4:8 420
4:12 59
4:15 198
4:35 61
4:37 262
5 225
5:12 223
5:14 222
5:15 222, 224
5:26 62-63
6:4 61
6:13 206, 209
7:5 243
8:3 106
9:15 247
9:18 439, 460
10:4 20
10:14 62
10:16 376
10:17 57-58, 59
10:20 206, 209
12:32 402, 564
13:12 701
15 446
15:4 449, 450
15:8 453

16 219
16:2-6 598
16:10 577, 608
17:8 21
17:9 675
17:18 704
17:19 45
21:22-23 422
21:23 307
23 469
23:19-20 454
24:10 453
25:1 384, 391
27:26 185, 417, 477
28:13 454
28:16 203
28:22 449
28:44 454
28:56 34
29:4 128
29:21 20
29:29 46
30:6 376
30:11 46
31 29
31:9 21, 34
31:11 21
31:11-12 45
31:24 21
31:26 21, 22
32:4 34, 163
32:39 61
32:40 63

JOSHUA
1:13 19
2:12 214
4:2-9 550
5 703
5:1-12 703
5:4 573

5:6 573
8:30 440
8:32 703
9 215
10:13 120
11:15 407
23:6 703
24 703
24:24 464
24:25 211

JUDGES
1:1 701
6 703
6:14-16 696
11:31 464
12:3 581
13:5 696
13:25 696
17:3 195
17:14 195
20-21 695
20:18 701
20:28 701
21:1 215
24:23 463
24:24 464

RUTH
1:17 209

1 SAMUEL
1 465
1:11 212, 464, 465
1:13 437
1:26 209
7 703
7:6 459
10:12 695
10:20-21 696
10:24 261

3:15 16, 52
3:16 57, 84, 278, 279, 280
4:1-3 213, 458
4:3-5 583
4:4 100
4:4-5 424
4:6 6, 531
4:7-8 6
4:8 5, 458
4:14 534, 649, 674
4:16 386
5:3 450
5:8 451
5:9 539
5:16 450, 451
5:17 526, 538, 539, 704
5:18 451
5:21 118, 261, 299
5:22 532
6:3 4
6:4 6
6:8 451
6:15 65, 67
6:15-16 59, 65, 67
6:16 60, 67
6:17-18 446

2 TIMOTHY
1:6 649, 650
1:8 240
1:9 263, 267, 386
1:12 361
1:13 554
2:2 533, 704
2:4 682
2:18 714
2:19 502
2:20 504
2:23 571
3:8 272

3:15 5, 19, 34, 47, 342
3:16 4, 9, 16, 19, 20, 23, 34, 37
3:17 23, 36
4:8 410, 475, 737
4:11 27
4:13 360
4:14 443
4:18 751

TITUS
1 531, 540
1:1 3, 5, 6, 36
1:2 66
1:5 532, 673, 708
1:7 52, 532, 673
1:9 51
1:15 424
1:16 67, 68
2:2-3 346
2:6 346
2:9 346
2:11 346, 386
2:12 244
2:13 84
2:14 337, 478
3 567
3:3 175
3:4 66, 386
3:4-5 385
3:4-6 372
3:5 94, 175, 372, 387, 392, 564, 565, 568
3:7 352, 384, 392
3:8 392
3:10 505, 662
3:11 11
3:20 662

PHILEMON
14 170

HEBREWS
1 79
1:1 5, 9, 20
1:2 96, 98, 99, 324
1:3 70, 82, 85, 103, 323, 480
1:6 85, 433
1:7 88
1:10 83, 96
1:11 61
1:12 84
1:14 88, 113, 117, 120
2 324
2:2-3 245
2:4 343
2:7-8 323, 513
2:9 287
2:10 293, 312
2:11-13 346
2:13 511
2:14 280, 285, 287, 319, 593, 716
2:15 415
2:16 72, 279, 283, 287, 299
2:17 281
3 230
3:1 240
3:4 496
3:4-6 512
3:5-6 513
3:6 358, 656
3:7 434
3:13 382, 657
3:14 358
4 230
4:2 24
4:3 223
4:8 223
4:9 223
4:12 49, 355

4 36
4:1 50, 689
4:2 279
4:8 61
4:9 293
4:9-10 293
5:3 407
5:4 178, 500
5:7 70, 76
5:8 407
5:10 362
5:16 441
5:18 167
5:19 265
5:20 63, 84
5:21 203, 243

2 JOHN
3 433
9 505
10 506, 662, 668

3 JOHN
9-11 522

JUDE
1 11
4 272
6 113, 114, 261, 299, 735, 737
11 368
12 576
14-15 687
15 733
20 517

REVELATION
1:1 20, 116, 747
1:3 46
1:4 58, 62, 94, 434
1:4-5 76

1:5 337, 433, 434, 512, 565, 722
1:8 58, 65
1:10 233
1:19 9
1:20 598
2 20, 500
2:1 20
2:2 504
2:6 663
2:7 132
2:10 475
2:10-11 750
2:14 504
2:17 750
2:20 663
2:23 84
3 500
3:3 460
3:7 656
3:20 343
3:21 499, 751
4 747
4:7 66
4:8 58, 59, 62, 499
5:3 747
5:5 116, 432
5:8 435, 499
5:9 85
5:10 500
5:11 122
5:12 85
6 747
6:9 129
6:10 435, 443
7 120
7:3 117
7:9 129, 267, 499, 748, 752
7:11 752
7:16 475, 749

8:3 326
10:6 208, 756
11 506, 508
11:17 58
11:18 737
12 118, 506, 508
12:7 122
12:8 122
13:8 272, 335, 503
13:13 120
14:6 238
14:7 740
14:11 754
14:12 401
14:13 474, 497, 499
15 508
15:3 512
15:4 739
16:5 58
16:10-11 755
16:15 460
17 506, 508
17:14 84
17:15 598
18:23 510
19:1 736
19:6 84
19:8 748
19:10 117, 496
19:16 512
20:2 122
20:11 757
20:12 737, 738
20:13 734
20:15 272
21 303, 517, 751
21:4 749
21:7 500
21:8 203
21:9 502, 510
21:14 514

Author Index

Albertus Magnus 485

Alexander of Hales 620, 631

Alfonso de Castro 651

Allen, William 611, 612

Ambrose of Milan 128, 200, 289-90, 316, 339, 460, 483, 597, 641, 725

Angles, Joseph 492-93, 647

Apollinaris 289, 309, 709

Aquinas, Thomas xv, 109, 151, 199, 307, 357, 479, 492, 505, 549, 591, 609, 623, 631, 645

Aristotle 34, 55, 206, 756

Arius 203, 288, 686, 688, 704, 709

Arminius, Jacob viii

Athanasius 23, 30

Augustine of Ancona 486

Augustine of Hippo 4, 44, 98, 99, 108, 127, 134, 142, 144, 145, 146, 151, 152, 155, 158, 163, 168, 172, 174, 177, 179, 193, 194-95, 201, 202, 260-61, 262, 266, 270, 275-76, 293-94, 313, 318-19, 339-40, 352, 354, 361, 369, 377, 382, 398, 401, 404-5, 409, 411, 421, 428, 456, 461, 473, 474, 479, 481, 482, 490, 505, 522-23, 533, 548, 550-51, 555, 556, 558-59, 567-68, 572, 597, 599, 607, 608, 612, 619, 635, 638, 662, 663, 666, 692, 709, 714, 729, 731, 732, 733, 734, 736, 739, 753

Basil of Alexandria 2, 35, 57, 203

Bavinck, Herman xv

Bellarmine, Robert xv, 32, 33, 38, 39, 40, 48, 82, 109, 152, 191-92, 194, 198, 199, 200, 254, 255, 296, 353, 358, 363, 418-19, 466, 467, 468-69, 471-72, 473, 474, 476, 477, 478, 481-82, 483-84, 487, 489, 491, 507, 522, 546, 548, 549, 551, 553, 608, 609-610, 612, 613-14, 617-18, 621-22, 628, 631, 632, 633, 639, 640, 643, 644, 647, 649, 651, 653

Bernard of Clairvaux xv, 156, 344, 398, 412, 429, 483, 698

Beza, Theodore ix, 276, 597, 660, 757

About the Editors

William den Boer, PhD (2008) Theological University Apeldoorn, is postdoctoral researcher at the Theological University Kampen / Utrecht. He is author of *God's Twofold Love: The Theology of Jacob Arminius (1559–1609)* (2010), general editor of *Synopsis Purioris Theologiae / Synopsis of a Purer Theology: Latin Text and English Translation* (2014–2020), and author or editor of several books and articles on church history and (historical) theology. Dr den Boer is chairman of the Dutch branch of The Gospel Coalition and pastors a church in the city of Almere.

Riemer A. Faber, PhD (1992) University of Toronto, is Professor of Classics at the University of Waterloo. His research interests range from the reception of Greek poetry in Augustan Rome to neo-Latin literature. Recent projects include an English edition of *Erasmi Annotationes ad Galatas, ad Ephesios* (2017), an edited volume of essays, *Celebrity, Fame and Infamy in the Hellenistic World* (2020), and a forthcoming co-edited volume, *Comparing Roman Hellenisms in Italy*. He is general editor and translator of *Synopsis Purioris Theologiae / Synopsis of a Purer Theology* (2014–2020). Dr. Faber serves as chair of the editorial board of the *Collected Works of Erasmus*.

MORE FROM DAVENANT PRESS

INTRODUCTION TO PROTESTANT THEOLOGY
Reformation Theology: A Reader of Primary Sources with Introductions
Grace Worth Fighting For: Recapturing the Vision of God's Grace in the Canons of Dordt

PETER MARTYR VERMIGLI LIBRARY
Dialogue on the Two Natures in Christ
Philosophical Works: On the Relation of Philosophy to Theology
The Oxford Treatise and Disputation on the Eucharist, 1549
Predestination and Justification: Two Theological Loci

VERMIGLI'S *COMMON PLACES*
On Original Sin (Vol. 1)
On Free Will and the Law (Vol. 2)

LIBRARY OF EARLY ENGLISH PROTESTANTISM
The Laws of Ecclesiastical Polity: In Modern English, Vol. 1 (Preface–Book IV)
James Ussher and a Reformed Episcopal Church: Sermons and Treatises on Ecclesiology
An Apology of the Church of England
Jurisdiction Regal, Episcopal, Papal
Radicalism: When Reform Becomes Revolution
Divine Law and Human Nature
The Word of God and the Words of Man
In Defense of Reformed Catholic Worship
A Learned Discourse on Justification

DAVENANT GUIDES
Jesus and Pacifism: An Exegetical and Historical Investigation
The Two Kingdoms: A Guide for the Perplexed
Natural Law: A Brief Introduction and Biblical Defense
Natural Theology: A Biblical and Historical Introduction and Defense

DAVENANT RETRIEVALS
A Protestant Christendom? The World the Reformation Made
People of the Promise: A Mere Protestant Ecclesiology
Philosophy and the Christian: The Quest for Wisdom in the Light of Christ

The Lord Is One: Reclaiming Divine Simplicity

CONVIVIUM PROCEEDINGS
For the Healing of the Nations: Essays on Creation, Redemption, and Neo-Calvinism
For Law and for Liberty: Essays on the Legacy of Protestant Political Thought
Beyond Calvin: Essays on the Diversity of the Reformed Tradition
God of Our Fathers: Classical Theism for the Contemporary Church
Reforming the Catholic Tradition: The Whole Word for the Whole Church
Reforming Classical Education: Toward a New Paradigm

OTHER PUBLICATIONS
Enduring Divine Absence: The Challenge of Modern Atheism
Without Excuse: Scripture, Reason, and Presuppositional Apologetics
Being a Pastor: Pastoral Treatises of John Wycliffe
Serious Comedy: The Philosophical and Theological Significance of Tragic and Comic Writing in the Western Tradition
Protestant Social Teaching: An Introduction
Begotten or Made?

ABOUT THE DAVENANT INSTITUTE

The Davenant Institute supports the renewal of Christian wisdom for the contemporary church. It seeks to sponsor historical scholarship at the intersection of the church and academy, build networks of friendship and collaboration within the Reformed and evangelical world, and equip the saints with time-tested resources for faithful public witness.

We are a nonprofit organization supported by your tax-deductible gifts. Learn more about us, and donate, at www.davenantinstitute.org

Made in the USA
Middletown, DE
18 November 2024

64912464R00249